WISDOM, JUSTICE, AND CHARITY

Canadian Social Welfare through the Life of Jane B. Wisdom, 1884–1975

One of Canada's first social workers, Jane B. Wisdom had an active career in social welfare that spanned most of the first half of the twentieth century. Competent, thoughtful, and trusted, she had a knack for being in important places at pivotal moments. Wisdom's transnational career took her from Saint John to Montreal, New York City, Halifax, and Glace Bay, as well as into almost every field of social work. Her story offers a remarkable opportunity to uncover what life was like for front-line social workers in the profession's early years.

In *Wisdom, Justice, and Charity*, historian Suzanne Morton uses Wisdom's professional life to explore how the welfare state was built from the ground up by thousands of pragmatic and action-oriented social workers. Wisdom's career illustrates the impact of professionalization, gender, and changing notions of the state – not just on those in the emergent profession of social work but also on those in need. Her life and career stand as a potent allegory for the limits and possibilities of individual action.

(Studies in Gender and History)

SUZANNE MORTON is a professor in the Department of History and Classical Studies at McGill University.

STUDIES IN GENDER AND HISTORY

General Editors: Franca Iacovetta and Karen Dubinsky

Wisdom, Justice, and Charity

Canadian Social Welfare through the Life of Jane B. Wisdom, 1884–1975

SUZANNE MORTON

UNIVERSITY OF TORONTO PRESS
Toronto Buffalo London

MT

ISBN 978-1-4426-4675-9 (cloth)
ISBN 978-1-4426-1461-1 (paper)

Printed on acid-free paper

Library and Archives Canada Cataloguing in Publication

Morton, Suzanne, 1961–, author
Wisdom, justice, and charity : Canadian social welfare through the
life of Jane B. Wisdom, 1884–1975 / Suzanne Morton.

(Studies in gender and history)
Includes bibliographical references and index.
ISBN 978-1-4426-4675-9 (bound)   ISBN 978-1-4426-1461-1 (pbk.)

1. Wisdom, Jane B., 1884–1975.   2. Social service – Canada –
History.   3. Social workers – Canada – Biography.   I. Title.   II. Series:
Studies in gender and history

HV40.32.W575M67 2014   361.3092   C2014-901123-7

University of Toronto Press acknowledges the financial assistance to its
publishing program of the Canada Council for the Arts and the
Ontario Arts Council, an agency of the Government of Ontario.

  Canada Council   Conseil des Arts
for the Arts   du Canada

University of Toronto Press acknowledges the financial support of the
Government of Canada through the Canada Book Fund for its
publishing activities.

12/16/14

Contents

Acknowledgments

Elements of this project have surrounded me most of my life – long before I was aware of the connections. Midway through the project, I realized that I probably had travelled within a couple of hundred metres of Jane Wisdom herself. She lived until her death in 1975 in her niece's home adjacent to the TransCanada Highway, a place I passed on a childhood family vacation to Cape Breton. I first met the "historical" Jane Wisdom in my MA thesis on the Halifax labour movement, encountered her again in my PhD when using the Halifax explosion records, and yet again in a project that examined the post–First World War labour unrest. Much later in a completely different context, a study of unmarried mothers led me again to the name Jane Wisdom. Living in Montreal, I walk the streets and work on the campus where she also spent much time. Visiting Nancy Forestell and Peter McInnis in Antigonish means that I regularly drive past the family house at Sutherland's River, and I had noticed it along the highway before I had any McQueen association.

Like Jane, I am single, professional, culturally Scottish Presbyterian, and claim both Montreal and Nova Scotia as my home. Defining home and community is relational and situational for both of us. I also entered middle age with her. This project got underway about the time in my life comparable to when Wisdom entered graduate school, and I am finishing it at a time comparable to when she was struggling with the worst of the Depression in Montreal. Again, like Wisdom, who had many distractions and demands on her time, I began this book during a period of academic administration and ended shortly after a time of similar service. It would have been completely and utterly unimaginable without the administrative support of Georgii Mikula, Colleen

Parish, and Savy Marino. My empathy for Wisdom's bureaucratic life grew as I became more implicated in the life of an institution. In ways I could never imagine, I even had to face the challenge of having a school of social work located within a faculty of arts.

The McGill history department is a stimulating and congenial home where I learn daily from my students and colleagues. In particular, I want to acknowledge Catherine Braithwaite, Caroline Durand, and Elizabeth Kirkland for sharing my interest in gender and philanthropy. I am especially grateful to Amanda Ricci, Catherine Ulmer, Colin Grittner, Carolynn McNally, Lana Povitz, and Daniel Simeone for helping me understand better what makes a good book. Revisions to this manuscript were made both easier and more challenging by the echoes of their insightful critiques in my head. The 2008–09 social history seminar (Rachel Abs, Fred Burrill, Alicia Dotiwalla, Mikael Dumont, Christine Elie, Meagan Hanna, Maggie Mullrooney, Lana Povitz, Daniel Simeone, and Claudia Spina) deserves recognition for reminding me of history's bigger project. It is truly a privilege to teach, and I am daily aware that my students have taught me as much as I have taught them. I also continue to learn from present and past colleagues such as Kate Desbarats, Allan Greer, Elsbeth Heaman, Catherine Le-Grand, Brian Lewis, David Meren, Carman Miller, Jarrett Rudy, Jon Soske, Andrea Tone, and Brian Young.

Karen Dubinsky, Judith Fingard, Daryl Leeworthy, Peter Lambly, the late A. A. Mackenzie, Jean MacFagden, Joan Payzant, and Chantale Quesney all played a part in finding records that were believed to be lost. Meagan Beaton, Amélie Bourbeau, Gwendolyn Davies, Sandra den Otter, David Frank, Jarrett Rudy, Daniel Simeone, and Janis Zubalik provided useful references and connections, and I benefited from the meticulous research work of Nick Butcher, Tiffany Loiselle, and Anna Shea.

I am especially grateful to Jane Wisdom's great-nephews and -niece, Sandy Mackay, Jock Mackay, David Mackay, and Mary Kay Mackintosh, for welcoming me into the Sutherland's River house and sharing family photos. Jock Mackay was especially generous with his time. I appreciate their patience, as this project took much longer than any of us suspected. That Mary Kay Mackintosh, who was so encouraging from the first, did not live to see the book finished is a source of great sadness. Mrs. Jean MacFadgen trusted me with Wisdom's papers and I remain deeply in her debt. Her instincts were to be very protective of a woman she knew, admired, and respected, and I hope I have not betrayed her confidence.

I was able to share some of my initial findings at conferences as a result of financial support from the Montreal History Group, which was supported by SSHRC and FQRSC funds. I also appreciate all the assistance from archivists and interlibrary loan staff. Without their professionalism, this work would have been inconceivable, and there is no way I could have done this project without borrowing microfilm through the now-defunct LAC interlibrary loan program. The support staff at working agencies, the Brooklyn Bureau of Community Service, and the Batshaw Youth and Family Centres who made room for me at their busy offices merit particular and sincere gratitude.

The University of Toronto Press has been a pleasure to work with, and I am the grateful beneficiary of the professionalism and wisdom of Len Husband and the careful reading and insightful comments of its anonymous readers. Patricia Sanders lent her skills to copyediting.

Janet Guildford, Lynne Marks and John Blakeney, Tina Loo, Janet Morton, Diana Hilton and Nika and Toby Lennox, Nancy Forestell and Kieran and Peter McInnis offered hospitality at various points. Janet Guildford, Nancy Forestell, and Shirley Tillotson generously put aside their own work and carefully critiqued an earlier draft. Lana Povitz turned her good humour, meticulous eye, and sophisticated skills as a gifted historian to give the manuscript an intense reading, with the result of a much better book. At the last minute, Mike Bienstock generously lent his expertise to render images usable. I remain responsible for all shortcomings and errors, but the manuscript has benefited from their generosity, skills, and intelligence. Indeed, I am fortunate to have such talented people as friends. Cecilia Morgan, Nancy Forestell, and Tina Loo were among the good friends who regularly asked after Jane. Their encouragement in asking "how Jane was" or if I had "seen Jane lately" helped keep the project alive and is deeply appreciated.

Well into the project, I was blessed to share yet another identity with Wisdom – becoming an aunt. Just as she took great pleasure from her niece, Caleb Morton Couch and Maeve Couch Morton are a great source of joy.

Abbreviations

ANQM	Archives nationales du Québec Centre de Montréal
AR	Annual Report
BBC	Brooklyn Bureau of Charities (Brooklyn Bureau of Community Service)
BCA	Beloit College Archives
BCARS	British Columbia Archives and Records Services
BI	Beaton Institute
BYFC	Batshaw Youth and Family Centres
CASW	Canadian Association of Social Workers
CCCW	Canadian Council on Child Welfare
CCCFW	Canadian Council on Child and Family Welfare
CCSD	Canadian Council on Social Development
COM	Catherine Olding McQueen
Corr	Correspondence
COS	Charity Organization Society
CPF	Canadian Patriotic Fund
FWA	Family Welfare Association
GB	Glace Bay
GBMWD	Glace Bay Municipal Welfare Department
HLCW	Halifax Local Council of Women
HRC	Halifax Relief Commission
JBW	Jane Barnes Wisdom
JBW Papers	This is a set of personal papers currently in the author's possession. I will arrange for their deposit as this project finishes, and hope they will form part of the MLFP fond.
KFW	Katherine Forester Wisdom
LAC	Library Archives Canada

MBW	Mary Bell Wisdom
MCSA	Montreal Council of Social Agencies
MLFP	McQueen-Lowden Family Papers
MSSW	Montreal School of Social Work
MUA	McGill University Archives
NSA	Nova Scotia Archives
OP	Office of the Principal
PANB	Provincial Archives of New Brunswick
PCCA	Presbyterian Church in Canada Archives
RVC	Royal Victoria College
SCVF	Susan Cameron Vaughan Fonds
UTA	University of Toronto Archives
WDM	Women's Directory of Montreal
UMW	United Mine Workers

WISDOM, JUSTICE, AND CHARITY

Canadian Social Welfare through the Life
of Jane B. Wisdom, 1884–1975

Introduction

The story of the Canadian welfare state can – indeed, must – be told through biography. The ordinary but poignant life and career of Jane B. Wisdom, one of Canada's first professional social workers, stands as a potent allegory for the limits and possibilities of individual action. Jane Wisdom lived from 1884 to 1975. Born a year before the completion of a railway across Canada, she died during the crest of second-wave feminism. Between these years, the world changed almost beyond recognition. The field of social work, barely nascent at the start of the century, had professionalized, becoming a massive, bureaucratic entity that reached systematically into citizens' private lives. The full story of social services in Canada would not, of course, be limited to those who provided them. Ideally, it would also encompass the experiences of both the "clients" of social work and those deemed "undeserving." The prospect of reconstructing, from scant archival traces and fragments, individual life stories of the marginalized and obscured may not be possible beyond the common social-history practice of collective biography or community study.[1]

The role of a biographer is uncomfortably close to that of a social work caseworker. I have conducted a detailed investigation based on description and documentation, gathering evidence on as many aspects of my subject's background, social context, and actions as possible. Just as Jane Wisdom tried to construct coherent explanations for her clients' situations, I have put together a life story based on available sources to explore the particular themes that preoccupy me. This account is just as incomplete, partial, provisional, and subjective as the files Wisdom assembled on her clients. It is not a biography that assumes totality, interiority, or its subject's importance as a force for historical change.

It does not even always place the subject at the centre of the narrative; sometimes, the context, networks, and social identities matter more.

Crucially, this is not a neat record of twentieth-century poverty, its diagnosis and its remedy. It is a messy case file describing the emergence of an inadequate liberal welfare state, one that never quite succeeded in meeting its clients' needs, and that often produced burnt-out, frustrated social workers. Investigators should not hope to find a smooth path from voluntary charity to professional social work or a tidy trail from private to public responsibility. Instead, what Wisdom's case file shows above all is that the Canadian welfare state must be viewed at the local and even agency level. Place-based activism affected larger policy developments and ensured variability in the application of new laws, procedures, and attitudes in social welfare.

The various levels of the Canadian welfare state were not created solely by elected politicians and bureaucrats or by the organized demands of citizens, churches, and labour. They were also built from the ground up by the thousands of pragmatic and action-oriented workers in the social work field. Jane Wisdom was one of these Canadian pioneers; her active career in client-oriented social welfare spanned almost the first half of the twentieth century, a time marked by rising living and education standards and increased bureaucracy. She had a knack for being in important places at pivotal moments, not necessarily taking on leadership positions, but always competent, thoughtful, and trusted.

While Wisdom never experienced public renown, she was important as one of the many contingent factors that determined the direction of state formation. In the late 1940s in Glace Bay, Nova Scotia, her experiences came together to conduct groundbreaking social work that was later used to create legislative change. In some situations, Wisdom's influence merely bore the force of larger cultural–intellectual currents and socio-economic interests. In others, her individuality was key.

This type of significance is distinct from the way that historical importance is often measured. Wisdom's name is not attached to any piece of legislation. She never headed any national agency, nor would she have ever considered a public political career. Ottawa-based Charlotte Whitton, the only individual Canadian social worker who may meet these particular criteria, has cast a large shadow over the reputation of individual female social workers in Canada. Wisdom's very minor presence in historical literature is as a correspondent and member of Whitton's "circle." This circle was far less homogeneous than even

Whitton may have understood, and the cohort's other individuals remain largely unknown.[2]

Wisdom's remarkable career brought her into contact with three, parallel, local welfare systems, and was part of a general transition from voluntary charity to professional public-welfare work. Historians have argued that welfare reforms and local-level feminism were intertwined and that we need to link charity work to local reforms and national policy making.[3]

The story of Wisdom's career does this. She had roots in both the settlement house movement and charity organization societies. Her involvement in North American and international networks, and in the development of a Canadian profession, meant proximity to continuous debates about the professionalization of social work and appropriate training. Private organized charity worked within legal structures, and Wisdom's career highlights the changing role of the state in welfare. We see this evolution from the emergency reconstruction efforts that followed the 1917 Halifax explosion to interwar government commissions to Wisdom's front-line position as a post-war civil servant and municipal employee. As a liberal with left-of-centre tendencies, she valued both individuals and communities. Ultimately, Wisdom's life story and career tell us a great deal about the development of Canadian social work as it was connected to British and American currents, reflecting an impressive array of people, ideas, institutions, and legal frameworks.

Jane Wisdom's transnational career bridged distinct welfare regimes. In 1910, she worked with elderly female clients in Montreal who had been children during the Irish Famine; by the 1960s, she was still involved informally in social work, assisting neighbours in negotiating the complex and expanding provincial and federal welfare bureaucracy. By the time of her death in 1975, the Canadian federal welfare state was already in decline, the transition from a state focus on needs to one based on rights nearly complete. Wisdom's career also provides an important corrective to existing scholarship, which, with the exception of Nancy Christie's work and a 2011 survey on the history of the profession, has tended to claim Toronto as *the* centre of Canadian social work. This view would have made little sense to contemporaries, who claimed Montreal as Canada's metropolis and industrial centre. Indeed, in the words of a 1932 report, Montreal was "by its very nature a social laboratory and a key centre for social work training in Canada."[4] Wisdom's career was not only national, but also transnational, and, like all welfare work, simultaneously deeply rooted in particular local or municipal contexts.

In arguing for the importance of the local, I follow James Struthers's focus on provincial and municipal needs-based programs.[5] The local view also insists on the ongoing importance of private agencies; I am clearly disagreeing with both a functionalist interpretation that treats welfare development as the inevitable result of industrialization and any explanation that links the welfare system to national values. "Local" in this account ranges from the particular agency and neighbourhood, a linguistic–religious community, through to the provincial level. Wisdom's career was specifically an eastern Canadian story. The personal connections her background afforded, her proximity to professional networks in Ottawa, her experience in both Quebec and with the poor law of the Maritime Provinces, and her integration into early American welfare circles would have looked quite different had she come from the Prairie West or British Columbia.

Providing the specific details of Wisdom's career and world has a twofold purpose. The first is to richly evoke the social, cultural, religious, and institutional contexts that made Wisdom who she was.[6] In offering the "look and feel" on the ground, I hope to capture the common sense of a pre-welfare-state world, and to reveal the intellectual and cultural currents that fed the politics of change. The attention to specifics explains so much of why women were present for those changes in such large numbers and what they brought by way of skills and commitments. Finally, this reconstructed world underscores the religious content of the story and shows religion's role as recourse and inspiration. I hope to illustrate how the identities of place, family, and generation belong with those of class, race, and gender. Second, the detail is essential to make visible the extensive web of personal connections (and, therefore, the possible intellectual relationships) that linked and connected a transnational, English-speaking, social-welfare community. Although Jane Wisdom was never in any prominent leadership role, she was separated by only one or two degrees from all leading figures in Canada, as well as in the United States and Great Britain. This social world extended from England's Eleanor Rathbone to Chicago's Jane Addams. Interpersonal dimensions belong in social history, not just political history.

In my head, I think of her as Jane. If I had known her, like most people, I would have probably called her Miss Wisdom – although the length of our acquaintance by now may have made "Jane" acceptable.

She was a private person, someone who was more comfortable taking photographs than being photographed. As a twenty-two-year-old crossing the border for the first time, she recorded her thoughts of going through customs: "It did seem barbarous however to have one's grip opened by a stranger before one's eyes. But I don't believe I felt more ashamed than the gentlemanly official who had to do it. What an outrage when a gentleman has to apologize for doing his duty."[7] As a caseworker, Jane Wisdom spent most of her career going through others' most private situations and intimacies. Her own sense of privacy and respect may have made her unusually discreet and attuned to ethics when dealing with others.

In 1951, as Wisdom began making plans for her retirement, the president of the Canadian Association of Social Workers pitched a story about her career to the *Montreal Standard*. The newspaper editorial staff rejected the idea. Joy Maines, the association's president, responded, "I am not a bit concerned about the decision in regard to Miss Wisdom, because she would heartily agree with it, if she had any knowledge of the possibility of publicizing her story."[8] Even her close colleagues commented that they knew little about her career. A friend and co-worker of more than twenty years described her "royal reticence about herself and her work."[9] Other than the 1953 Coronation Medal, she received few honours in her lifetime. Her nominations for the 1935 Jubilee Medal and for an honorary degree at St. Francis Xavier University were rejected.[10] Indeed, apart from a gravestone she shares with her sister, the only enduring commemoration of her life I have come across is the Jane Wisdom Memorial Bursary at the Dalhousie School of Social Work. The fact that this is a bursary and not based on merit seems perfectly fitting. But Wisdom was not completely self-effacing. She had enough of a sense of self to keep a meticulous record of her career, carefully listing all the jobs she had been offered, not just those she accepted.

The narrative path of following a single life avoids the generalizations of approaches based on broad overviews, or a narrow focus on single-issue identity politics, while simultaneously illustrating the encompassing power of experience, personality, and circumstance. Wisdom's ability to act was an unpredictable combination of individual personality, social identity, and membership within formal and informal networks. The accidental, the contingent, and the particular come together in the traces left by an individual life.

There is no denying the current fascination with biography by historians. I conform to David Cannadine's observation about the distinction between historians and biographers. While the latter are interested in what makes their subjects unique, historians focus more on how their subjects reflect their context.[11] There has long been a tradition of "social biography" or "life and times," typified by Nick Salavatore's work on Eugene V. Debs, Brian Young's biography of George-Étienne Cartier, David Frank's biography of J.B. MacLachlan, Barbara Roberts's study of Gertrude Richardson, and Linda Gordon's work on Dorothea Lange.[12] But these individuals had at least some renown in their communities. Work focused on the life stories of ordinary people has been more likely to be classified as microhistory, and this version of Wisdom's life story falls easily into this category.[13] I have self-consciously chosen to recount a version of the past that acknowledges the limits of my sources and conforms to the story Wisdom fashioned for her public self. What follows is Wisdom's public persona, based on very limited sources. This is a biography of a professional life and a profession. It is not a totality of a life. It is not a psychological study emphasizing interiority and subjectivity. Rather, I am interested in what my subject did, her circumstances, and her context. Outward expressions of her character and personality matter a great deal, as they were essential to her ability to network and interact successfully with peers, clients, and employers. Other colleagues did not share this ability to "get along," and, as a result, had markedly different careers.[14]

Women's history itself has had a strong association with biography. Looking back at the books I read in an undergraduate North American women's history course in the early 1980s, I am struck by the number of biographies on the syllabus. One leading historian has shown that biographies comprised the primary topic for books and dissertations between 1998 and 2000 in the field of American women's history.[15] But even most of those female subjects were "important." Wisdom, on the other hand, is interesting as an ordinary person whose career saw the convergence of many significant forces and events. As many have noted, it is the interaction of the individual with society, a person moving across time and space, that generates a different perspective on issues of wider interest.

There are two additional aspects that may explain the current popularity of biography and that shape the way this project has evolved. In an *American Historical Review* roundtable, David Nasaw argues that the appeal of biography at this particular time "is that it allows, even encourages, us to move beyond the strictures of identity politics without having to abandon its ever-expanding and often useful categories."[16]

I agree. Wisdom's life shows how gender, race, and class played out in the life of a single woman who was always some combination of daughter, sister, and aunt, and sometimes a Nova Scotian, immigrant, English Montrealer, Canadian, British subject, or New Brunswicker. Her coexistence in domestic realms and public service follows the shape of feminist biography and its challenge of bringing together both realms.[17] The focus on an individual not only liberates the historian from isolating and reifying aspects of identity; it also creates space for personal agency and empathy. Lois Banner recently called our attention to Jo Burr Margadent's words, reminding us that biography encourages us to "empathetically imagine" an individual life.[18] A twenty-first-century reader may not agree or even sympathize with Jane Wisdom or her world view that places such confidence in professionalism and an organic, cohesive community based on individualism and religion, but I hope a modern reader will understand her.

When I have introduced Wisdom to any audience, one of the frequent responses has been to state that, as a single woman, she had no family. Wisdom definitely had a family, with all the obligations and comforts that come along with it. True, it was never restricted to a nuclear, two-generation, isolated unit, but much of her emotional life centred on family, and there are many ways in which she was "clannish." Although nominally a "Wisdom," she was culturally a "McQueen," her mother's family's name. The McQueens kept things, and had a sense of their own history. A remarkable number of family papers have found their way into public archives, and Jane Wisdom's aunts' correspondence form the basis of Jean Barman's wonderful book *Sojourning Sisters*.[19] While reading through the letters of her mother, aunts, and grandmother, I occasionally recognized an editorial comment for clarity in Wisdom's careful pencil script. Some of these letters had also been edited with scissors. I frequently suspected that this was her hand and wondered what had been removed.

In line with Wisdom's approach to casework, I have tried to keep ethics in mind and the limits of an historian's rights to intrude on a life. I am also aware that on at least one occasion, I, too, have altered the record. A 1971 Polaroid depicts an eighty-seven-year-old Wisdom sitting in her niece's living room at Sutherland's River, looking bright and engaged with life. In the original image, the combination of her knee-length dress and the camera angle conspires to reveal her underwear. I am certain that this public presentation of self would have been deeply embarrassing for her, and I initially cropped the image without really considering what I was doing. Upon reflection, I do not think that this expression of respect for my subject in any way undermines the story I wish to tell. At the same time, I cannot but wonder if I have mindlessly repeated this offence elsewhere. I am also reminded that those who knew and cherished her were even more likely than I to be protective in their memory and accounts.

For a very long period, I had very little of Jane Wisdom's own words. I comforted myself with the notion that I was still adhering to the scholarly culture of social history. The lack of personal papers meant that she could make claims for typicality, as most historical subjects do not end up with private papers in public archives. I also had virtually no records of Wisdom's clients; the only case files I was able to locate were from a time when Wisdom was supervising and not in regular contact with clients. But this project also met with some amazing moments of serendipity. Sometimes, lost items were found by accident. In the winter of 2005, when double-checking a reference, I came across some of the Wisdom girls' private correspondence from their time as undergraduates at McGill. The correspondence had been completely misfiled when I first consulted the file of course notes. In another instance, an existing welfare agency did not know it possessed one of its antecedents' records, nor was it able or willing to look until a colleague accidentally came across something that encouraged me to press further and harder. Chance continued to the end. Some "lost" Glace Bay Town Council minutes appeared when Darryl Leeworthy, a visiting doctoral student from England, happened to show me a document in another context, which I had been told did not exist. He had come across it at the Nova Scotia Archives, where a microfilm copy existed, somehow separated from the rest of the municipal records held in Sydney.

From the beginning, I knew that Wisdom had kept at least some papers. Peter Lambly referred to a personal letter then in the family's possession in his 1977 Dalhousie bachelor's honours thesis, and several copies of Wisdom's personal photographs were part of the McQueen collection at the Nova Scotia Archives. Near the beginning of the study, historian A.A. Mackenzie informed me that, in the late 1970s, Wisdom's family had lent papers to someone doing a thesis at an Ontario university. Unfortunately, he could not remember who it was, and, by the time I asked questions of the family, Wisdom's niece, Relief Williams Mackay, had passed away and her children had no recollection of such a story. In 1998 and 1999, I contacted anyone I could think of who might have been able to help solve the mystery of the papers or track down the thesis, but I met with no success. In 2004, A.A. Mackenzie was tragically killed in a road accident before I had the chance to interview him. I also "missed" Frances Montgomery, whose obituary I came across while reading the Saturday *Montreal Gazette* in 2005.[20] I reconciled myself to producing a different kind of history. Even without personal papers, it was still astonishing how much one could find out about an individual in the past. Before the digitalization of many newspapers, tiny nuggets of information could still be gleaned from public documents, newspapers, and institutional reports. But the evidence was highly selective. I knew exactly how many times Jane Wisdom was late for school in grade eleven and her high school and university marks, but I did not know if she had ever been in love in her entire life.

In the fall of 2005, I gave the Phyllis Blakely Memorial Lecture to the Royal Nova Scotia Historical Society on Jane Wisdom. Three months later, I received a totally unexpected call from an active society member, Joan Payzant. That previous summer, Payzant had been visited by a friend, Jean MacFadgen, now living in British Columbia. MacFadgen had asked Payzant if she had ever heard of Jane Wisdom. She had not, and thought it was a remarkable coincidence when she received the season's program with Wisdom's name on it, but the matter fell from thought. Christmas correspondence revived the memory, and Payzant tracked me down via a colleague, passing along MacFadgen's name.

Jean MacFadgen was originally from Glace Bay and had worked for Wisdom as a summer student in the 1940s. In the late 1970s, she returned to school for a Master's of Social Work and wrote a major research paper entitled "A Study of a Social Worker's Organization and Administration of a Municipal Welfare Department," borrowing Wisdom's professional papers from the family. Even if she had included "Glace Bay" or "Wisdom" in the title, I would never have come across her research because it was not a thesis. MacFadgen still had a box of Jane Wisdom's papers in her home. She generously sent them to me on the understanding that they would be given a public archival home afterwards.

How does a project change when all of a sudden you are confronted with a completely new type of evidence? I had been living with my subject in my head for years and now had to await the arrival of a box that might completely alter my very core preconceptions. Indeed, it was very strange. Overall, the papers were a source of delight, allowing me to eliminate much of the conditional tense and affording some satisfaction with my own research ability. Wisdom kept clipping files that amounted to years of my research. I was pleased to see that I had already found many of the print sources on my own. Yes, there would need to be rewriting, but the basic structure and interpretations seemed to hold.

It was strange to touch Wisdom's pass granting access to the devastated area after the Halifax explosion, to immediately understand private jokes on a few kept mementoes, and to have analytical deductions confirmed or dispelled. I had to confront the fact that she had consciously preserved and shaped her own professional biography, leaving notes and outlines that closely followed my half-written manuscript. The box of records Wisdom left contained few personal items; like my project, it was a record of her career and involvement in welfare service. There was little of her personal life other than notes of outings, death dates, and a collection of photos of primarily professional friends. Among this assortment were also three taped interviews conducted by MacFadgen in 1979 with Relief Williams Mackay, and colleagues Frances Montgomery and Esther Wilson Kerry.

A few weeks after the box arrived, I received an e-mail saying that there was a file, too large to send electronically, available to pick up at a virtual postbox. Intriguingly, the sender of the message had the surname of MacFadgen, so I decided to risk that it was not a computer virus. The file downloaded, and a voice started speaking in mid-sentence. It took several seconds before I realized that this was the interview, mentioned in one obituary, conducted by Patricia Tanabe in May 1975, days before Wisdom had her stroke, and three weeks before she died. On 21 February 2006, across thirty years and various technologies, including a disintegrating cassette tape, I encountered the voice of my subject.

Voice embodies an individual in a way that photographs do not. The voice was fragile and tired but also precise, self-deprecating, and funny. The clipped, northern Nova Scotia accent of a ninety-one-year-old woman with a slight Scottish lilt was coming from my computer, connecting me to my subject in the most intimate fashion yet. The surviving twelve minutes of tape forced me to question everything I had seen. When friends read her letters, did they also understand the dry sense of humour behind her words? We all constantly edit our own stories. We highlight certain accomplishments, certain relationships, and try to forget others. Some postcards become cherished keepsakes while others are tossed into recycling. This book, what it portrays and neglects, is the result of such processes. Jane Wisdom preserved Christmas cards sent by Charlotte Whitton in the 1960s; if Wisdom sent Christmas cards to Whitton, they were not kept.

Historian Veronica Strong-Boag has called for a "more innovative, more complex, and, above all, more inclusive and realistic" version of Canadian history.[21] This book attempts to answer this call. In the last forty years, historians have struggled to find and include voices of the marginalized and oppressed. History is richer for these efforts, but historians have inadvertently created a one-dimensional reformer, intent on regulating, condemning, and generally deprecating those people he or she intended to help. As an individual, Jane Wisdom was much more complicated. She was also surprisingly original, compassionate, and willing to contest the status quo. Rather than sympathizing with her, my aim has been to understand. Wisdom both conformed to, and deviated from, this reformer image. Despite being a product of her culture and class position, she always worked for something better. She was not famous in her time, outside her professional group, yet she made a difference in the lives of real people. Today, in a time and culture where the ability of an individual to have an impact is greatly in doubt, the social biography of a single individual may carry a valuable political and moral message.

Chapter One

Saint John: Religion, Philanthropy, and the Poor Law, 1884–1909

Jane Barnes Wisdom was born on 1 March 1884 in Saint John, New Brunswick. The city she grew up in had been devastated by an 1877 fire that destroyed sixteen kilometres of downtown streets and cost an estimated $27 million in damages.[1] In the fire's aftermath, Saint John was rebuilt as a commercial and industrial centre with impressive mercantile and domestic Victorian architecture, a large number of solid and elaborate public buildings, and magnificent new churches. While the aesthetic appeal of Saint John today may be its worn, weather-beaten patina, the city of Wisdom's childhood was largely new and modern.

A knowledge of the time, place, and family circumstances of her upbringing is crucial to understanding her formation as the sort of young woman who would move into the new, expanding employment opportunities in the field of social welfare. The period, locale, and cultural context of her childhood shaped Jane Wisdom as a social actor and sculpted her world view and values. Her family background, the attitudes she was exposed to concerning charity, and the legal context of the poor law in New Brunswick came together with individual factors such as character and networks, and social categories such as gender, class, age, and race, to create a foundation from which she developed.

The origins of Wisdom's career began in Saint John, where the post-fire reconstruction coincided with the 1879 National Policy, which encouraged the development of Canadian industry through the introduction of tariff barriers on manufactured imported goods. Local industry took off, and Saint John boasted of having among the highest rates of manufacturing growth of anywhere in Canada.[2] Yet, any sense of celebration had to be balanced with serious concern. The local population was falling in absolute terms, notwithstanding municipal amalgamation that brought the large industrial suburb of Portland into the city in 1899. At a time when progress was equated with population growth, Saint John was the only urban centre in Canada during the 1870s whose population declined in actual numbers. Although, by 1904, the value of grain shipped through Saint John was equal to that of both Halifax and Quebec City combined, in terms of population, the city had fallen from the third-largest urban centre to Canada's eighth.

Saint John was shrinking, both through out-migration and its inability to attract new immigrants. In 1901, with slightly more than 40,000 residents, the city's population was roughly divided between Irish and other Britons, with approximately a third of the city Roman Catholic. As Scottish Presbyterians, the Wisdoms were part of the British Protestant majority culture. Nearly 800 citizens claimed French origins, and there were significant and visible Black (nearly 500) and Jewish (nearly 300) communities. The city's Chinese population was so small (around fifty) and so recent that, not twenty years earlier, in 1883, the arrival of two Chinese men in the city attracted a "great crowd."[3] The vast majority of Saint John residents, like the Wisdoms, were Canadian-born. Again, the 1901 census indicated that although the city hosted 5,663 immigrants, nearly half of these "new arrivals" had actually been in Canada since before 1875. While Canadians in other cities were increasingly preoccupied with immigration, in Saint John, the issue was out-migration.

Out-migration, primarily to the United States, was one of the most important social phenomena for Maritime society from the 1880s to the First World War.[4] During the 1880s, the Maritime Provinces lost 12.5 per cent of their population, and the population of Saint John fell from 41,000 to 39,000, continuing the decline of the 1870s.[5] Within Jane Wisdom's immediate family, two of her father's brothers, her mother's only surviving brother, and her father's business partner left for the United States during this period. Immigrants from Europe were landing in Saint John but they kept on going, with local newspapers reporting the arrival of immigrants in the city and their immediate departure on trains to central Canada and the West.

The result was a remarkably stable and relatively homogeneous population. Sectarian differences remained entrenched, with important divisions between Catholics and Protestants, and local communities taking pride in their respective Irish and British Loyalist origins. The city was also divided on the basis of wealth. Saint John was an unusual nineteenth-century city in that mere blocks separated different classes in a city-wide patchwork of small neighbourhoods rather than the usual emerging pattern of class divisions dividing cities by broader spatial areas. Even after the fire, the layout of the city, crowded for the most part onto a narrow peninsula, meant that rich and poor lived in unusual proximity. Unlike in other cities, it would have been very difficult to ignore their plight.

Notwithstanding its economic and population concerns, Saint John was struggling to adapt to modern society and its social problems, which historians of this period have often encapsulated in the triad of urbanization, industrialization, and immigration. Older systems of social support and social regulation were breaking down. Understandings of these problems were refracted through the prisms of family, religion, school, and civic life; these were the primary means by which children such as Jane Wisdom gathered knowledge about their world and came to understand their place in it.

Jane Wisdom grew up in a world that placed family, education, and church at its core. Although born a Wisdom in New Brunswick, throughout her life she considered herself a Nova Scotian and strongly identified with her mother's Nova Scotian Pictou County families, the respectable McQueens and the more prominent Oldings. Her mother, Mary Bell McQueen, was born in 1851 in Sutherland's River, a small farming settlement on the eastern edge of Pictou County.[6] The population of Pictou County also was remarkably stable and uniform. According to the first Canadian census in 1871, 85 per cent of the county's residents had been born in the province, 85 per cent of the county was of Scottish descent, and 80 per cent of the population claimed allegiance to the Presbyterian Church.[7] When Mary Bell died in nearby New Glasgow in 1928, her death certificate claimed she had lived in Nova Scotia "all her life," overlooking the thirty years she had raised her family and lived in New Brunswick.[8] The McQueen family was marked by powerful women who maintained strong ties based on obligation, duty, and intense affection. Historian Jean Barman describes Mary Bell's mother, Catherine Olding McQueen, as the "guardian of the faith ... who held strong views on belief and even stronger opinions about conduct." In spirit, Mary Bell McQueen Wisdom never left Nova Scotia and maintained close relations there, where the categories of friend and family were deeply entwined, overlapping and reinforcing each other.

Mary Bell McQueen met Freeman Wright Wisdom while teaching in Halifax, through her friendship with the publishers of the *Presbyterian Witness*. The publisher's wife, Harriet Wisdom Barnes, was Free's aunt.

Freeman Wisdom was fourteen years older than Mary Bell, Presbyterian, and had lived all his life in Saint John, remaining even after the rest of his family returned to its native Dartmouth, Nova Scotia.[9]

Free was born in 1838 and was the oldest of five surviving children to John Wisdom and Sarah Anne Pitts. He began working at age seventeen with no immediate success. At age twenty-eight, he was still listed by the Saint John *Hutchison Directory* under the adolescent occupation of messenger, and it was not until he was nearly thirty years old that his designation changed to clerk. By 1874, Freeman Wisdom was employed by E.T. Kennedy, who owned a "steamfittings, mill supplies and beltry" company. Also employed as the bookkeeper was a fellow Masonic lodge member, John A. Fish. Around the time of the 1877 fire, Kennedy retired, and a new steamfitting supply company with the hapless name of Wisdom and Fish was created.[10] The 1878 Saint John directory boasted a large ad for Wisdom and Fish "Importers and Dealers in Rubber and Leather Belting, Rubber Hose, Steam Packing, Lubricating Oils, Cotton Waste, Wrought Iron Pipe and Fittings," located at the waterfront. In 1880, at the age of forty-two and in business for himself, Free Wisdom married and brought the much younger Mary Bell McQueen to Saint John. There, he established his first independent household on Elliot Row, within walking distance of the business.[11]

Wisdom and Fish were not only business partners; they also shared a common bond as members of the influential fraternal Masonic Order. As Freemasons, they adhered to a code of "Brotherly Love, Relief, and Truth," emphasizing charitable work, belief in a Supreme Being, and moral behaviour. Wisdom himself held senior local and provincial leadership positions as grand secretary of the Grand Lodge of New Brunswick, and reached the penultimate standing within the fraternal order. His place within this network was obvious when the newlyweds were welcomed to Saint John by a gathering of around a hundred Masons and the presentation of a service of silver plate. Other aspects of Wisdom's public life included his appointment in September 1881 as a Justice of the Peace. Finally, Freeman seems to have had Liberal Party connections. His name appeared among prominent Saint John Liberals on an 1893 petition presented to Parliament, protesting revisions to the shipping laws that might eliminate local shipping of oil into the port in favour of international companies.[12]

Wisdom's participation in civic life was mirrored by his presence on federal government contract lists. One of the consequences of Confederation was the flood of federal dollars into the region to fund the construction and maintenance of the Intercolonial Railway, and the physical infrastructure of the state in the form of penitentiaries, post office buildings, and customs houses and lighthouses. The company of Wisdom and Fish, later F.W. Wisdom, appeared on Public Works accounts until 1894, and, during the 1880s, was associated with important federal government contracts. Wisdom and Fish installed the steam heating system for the largest building in the region, the new federal Dorchester Prison, in 1880–81, along with various post offices and federal buildings. While we are generally aware of government spending in the twentieth century, it is perhaps easy to overlook the large role the federal government played in the Maritimes' economy in the decades following Confederation. Wisdom and Fish, hardware specialists in heating and steam equipment, relied on federal spending for the success of their business. The completion of the region's new public buildings in the late 1880s hit the company hard.[13] Except for church duties, Freeman Wisdom withdrew from his fraternal life, as business appears to have taken up increasing amounts of time and proved a constant source of worry.

Historian Judith Fingard has noted that the Maritime region was not just losing population but was also witnessing a "surge in the capital outflow of the region."[14] One of the most dramatic signs of this problem was the failure of the Saint John-based Maritime Bank in March 1887.[15] Throughout the mid-1880s, Wisdom and Fish, buoyed by large government contracts, continued to advertise regularly in local newspapers such as the *Saint John Globe*. In general, however, conditions were poor. Moreover, Freeman Wisdom was very much on his own. By October 1885, the partnership was in trouble, and John Fish had opened up a branch store in Boston, with the hope of moving there permanently and selling out his portion of the business. On 1 February 1887, a legal notice of dissolution of partnership of Wisdom and Fish was published, noting that Wisdom would continue the business. Fish, meanwhile, relocated to Boston with his capital.[16] F.W. Wisdom struggled along. In 1892, on a list of Saint John municipal taxpayers, Wisdom claimed $0 in real estate, $4,000 in personal property, and an income of $1,000. By 1894, his income had dropped below the tax threshold and was no longer listed among city taxpayers.[17]

Free Wisdom declared insolvency in August 1893. There was sufficient remaining in the business to satisfy the creditors, but the family was left with nothing. The Conservative Montreal-based *Journal of Commerce* concluded cruelly: "Too much politics, consequent neglect of business and leaving things largely to employees are said to have told against him. He was more of a success as an express messenger." Rumours reached family in Dartmouth, Nova Scotia, where the consensus was that it was "perhaps best that Free did not try to struggle along any longer."[18]

The gradual downward mobility of the Wisdom family was reflected in its housing. Free brought Mary Bell as a bride to a grand home in Saint John. Her younger sister Jessie, direct from the farm at Sutherland's River, marvelled at the urban luxuries of hot and cold running water, the marble basin and taps, the inside privy, the zinc bathtub, and the many "fires" that ran day and night.[19] The family rented five different houses before 1886, all on solidly middle-class streets, with most of their neighbours listed as merchants. The advantage of renting meant that the Wisdoms could easily move to accommodate a growing family. Katherine Forester (Katie) was born 29 July 1881, Roy Pitts 2 January 1883, Jane Barnes (Jennie) 1 March 1884, and Elizabeth (Bessie) 10 June 1885. In the spring of 1887, the Wisdoms left the urban density of the peninsula and moved to the northeast area of suburban Portland. The move was to reduce rental expenses in order to keep a hired girl, who was receiving $8 a month and was essential in the care of the young, closely spaced children.[20] The rented houses on Summer Street, and, later, nearby Goodrich Street, were described by Mary Bell as "well out of town," and, as a result, the children "almost live out of doors." The home was still close to good schools and almost adjacent to the land being acquired for Saint John's large urban park.[21] This Victoria Ward neighbourhood was mixed, sandwiched between the city's elite homes up the hill on Mount Pleasant and the poor, dense neighbourhoods of Saint John's east end. Many of their immediate neighbours were skilled artisans and lower middle class, marking a real difference from their previous homes on the peninsula.

Moving out of the city did not solve the Wisdoms' domestic financial troubles. In January 1890, Bell's mother wrote her daughter in British Columbia that "Bell and Free are having their anxious times." The tightness of family finances was clear in October 1890, as Bell wrote to her mother describing her work at "making over" clothes for the children and noting that her "own personal needs must wait a while." At this point, the family still had domestic help, although Mary Bell was fretting that she was losing her current girl to the pull of high wages in Boston. Other family members worried that the Wisdom children looked "tall and thin for their age."[22] One thing that was not compromised was education. The Wisdom children did not attend public schools until high school, but rather were educated at the private school operated by the Church of England.[23]

There is evidence that the children themselves adored their semi-rural existence. The girls occupied themselves come May with picking wildflowers, which, at least once in May 1892, they made into small bouquets for children in the hospital. In winter, they skated. In summer, they picnicked both informally and at large Sunday School gatherings. This idyll ended in 1895 when finances forced the family back to the city.[24] While Mary Bell put on a brave face, stating that the house was "comfortable" even though it had almost no yard, anyone familiar with Saint John would have understood how far the family had fallen.[25] Moore Street was dirty, loud, and cheap. The loss of the business did not only mean physical domestic disruptions. It also signalled that Freeman was failing the basic requirement of middle-class masculinity, the ability to provide for his family. In 1894, Mary Bell wrote home to Sutherland's River that "we are glad that August is behind us but though nothing definite has occurred & we are as UNCERTAIN as ever about the future, yet 'tis wonderful as I say to Free that our minds are so calm & easy. The best things hope & health & trust in God has been left us so we do not grumble I do not say that we do not sometimes WONDER what next. It was a horribly hard ordeal for Free to go through but already the burdens that pressed so sorely are gone & even his health is better." While Free had temporary work at the Customs House, the Wisdoms were preparing themselves to pack up and move to wherever Free "can get a good situation & where chances of educating the children will be good." Mary Bell reported she had given up domestic help, that the house was paid for through May, and that the children were well clothed with made-over coats and second-hand clothes from cousins, a trend that would continue for some time to come. Family in Sutherland's River also took in the children, when money was available for travel fares. As things remained unsettled in Saint John in the spring of 1894, ten-year-old Jennie spent five months in Sutherland's River, going to school and staying through the holidays.[26] Jennie returned to Saint John in August "stronger and fatter than when she went away" and with new dresses courtesy of her aunt. Material support from the family also took the form of provisions, such as a tub of butter from Sutherland's River, a gift that seems to have thrilled Jennie in particular.[27]

Work for Free after 1894 was often irregular, and the loss of the business had coincided with Free's mother's moving more or less permanently to Saint John.[28] Anticipating her mother-in-law's proposed 1898 visit (without an invitation), Mary Bell uncharacteristically complained that she had already done her duty by providing a home for Free's mother for "a number of years while I was able, and for two years when I was not."[29] Free's work as a freelance bookkeeper barely supported the family. Even with the extra income contributed by Jane's brother Roy, who began work as a clerk in 1899, things were tight for the Wisdom family, as the three daughters finished high school with aspirations to continue their educations.[30] A 1906 newspaper article mentioned F.W. Wisdom of McLean Oil Supply, but, by 1908, Freeman W. Wisdom had neither an occupation nor an employer listed beside his name in the city directory. In the 1909–10 city directory, he was almost literally back where he began, boarding and working as a clerk. This was the last time there was any entry for the Wisdoms in Saint John. The family subsequently relocated to New Glasgow, Nova Scotia, presumably to take advantage of McQueen and Olding family connections.[31]

Historians interested in the development of social work have often too quickly characterized the middle-class origins of its first professionals.[32] The Wisdom family adhered to middle-class values but, at the same time, the material context of their life was much more complicated. As noted earlier, Freeman Wisdom's inability to support his wife and children left them vulnerable and dependent on family charity and was a challenge to male breadwinning, self-sufficiency, and independence. After a workplace accident in 1898, the family also seems to have been supported by the Masons' fraternal private charity, owing to Freeman's past active involvement.[33] Roy, the only son, could not be found in the high school registry and appears to have left school early to contribute to the family income. Mary Bell may have also been regarded as unsuccessful in her role as domestic housekeeper. In another context, her granddaughter, Relief Williams Mackay, used the Biblical analogy of "homemaker" Martha and "scholar" Mary to recount that "Mary Bell was a Mary by nature as well as by name, and the duties of a Martha lay heavily on her shoulders."[34]

But the ways in which the Wisdoms did not conform to middle-class standards were much broader. Like his father before him, Mary Bell McQueen's only brother was also an economic failure, even though he had had the advantage of university education, and further transgressed middle-class respectability by divorcing his much older wife. Freeman's brother in Dartmouth embarrassed his family's reputation and drove his mother to hide in Saint John, away from local gossip, when his wife gave birth to their first child less than six months after marriage.[35] Exhibiting a different form of social transgression, Mary Bell's oldest sister, Jane, suffered from unstable and sometimes violent mental episodes and was regularly institutionalized.[36] Mary Bell herself had poor health and neuralgia, a common nervous disorder marked by aches, exhaustion, and the sharp pain of migraine-like symptoms.[37] In addition, there may have been a miscarriage between her first two pregnancies, and all four successful pregnancies were marked by Bell's ill health.[38]

With four children under five and three born within two and a half years, care for an aging mother-in-law, economic stress, Mary Bell's poor general health, and the normal challenges of operating a household, the Wisdoms were dependent on hired domestic help or the assistance of family members. Finding and keeping a "good girl" was a constant theme in family letters.[39] It is perhaps not surprising that in February 1886, Mary Bell's health collapsed. A nurse was brought in, neighbours helped in the sickroom, and two "girls" were engaged, one for the kitchen and one to look after the children. Mary Bell did not leave the house until Easter and remained ill until September.[40]

The significance in family letters placed on Mary Bell's ability to leave the house to attend church at Easter alerts us to the importance of religion. In the Wisdom family, church was an important extension of home and kin. Religious belief shaped identity and provided a way of understanding the world and all social relations. Providence and free will – the two existing in ongoing tension within late-nineteenth-century Canadian Presbyterians – provided the framework within which the Wisdoms understood their lives. Jean Barman, while exploring the importance of Presbyterian culture in shaping the lives of Jennie's aunts, draws upon Michael Gauvreau's characterization: a mixture of "original sin, human depravity, God's absolute sovereignty, and the apparent contradictions of predestination, free will and divine grace."[41] Certainly, the McQueens adhered to a notion of religiously based appropriate conduct, embraced temperance, rejected dancing, card playing, and dice games, and were strict Sabbatarians.[42] But the McQueens' Presbyterianism also emphasized service, duty, self-denial, and the negation of self. As adults, the Wisdom girls would seldom ask for anything in their own names but would express personal desire by inquiring if their wants might be of interest to someone else: Would you like some tea? Would you like to go for a walk? In her speech and personal writing, Jane Wisdom avoided "I," adopting what her contemporaries fondly called "the royal we." The expectation that others' needs should come first was foundational to Wisdom's understanding of service. She was a lifelong member of the Presbyterian Church, and her niece, Relief Williams Mackay, later recounted that Wisdom took parts of the New Testament quite literally, such as the injunction to feed the poor. When she died in 1975, there were two books by her bed: the Bible and the popular Edwardian devotional volume, Margaret Fairless Barber's *The Roadmender*.[43] Her belief in the universal brotherhood of man, her understanding of the meaning of "community" and the purpose of one's life, and her sense of obligation to others all stemmed from a particular spiritual perspective.

In Saint John, the Wisdoms attended St. Stephen's Presbyterian Church where Free was an elder and, in the late 1880s, before his financial troubles, had served as a church trustee.[44] The decision to attend St. Stephen's among the four Presbyterian churches in the city was probably linked to the minister, who, like Mary Bell, was from Pictou County. His successor, Daniel J. Fraser, was barely thirty when he arrived at St. Stephen's in 1897; Jennie was thirteen, and Fraser would have an enormous effect on her life over the next ten years. Fraser had deep regional roots, a Scottish background, and a superb educational pedigree, having degrees from Prince of Wales College, McGill, and Harvard. His youth and education made an impact on the Wisdoms, with whom he became particularly intimate. In family letters, the usual formal use of proper titles was replaced by terms such as "Rev Daniel" and "Rev D.J.," suggesting a more casual intimacy. Fraser was Presbyterian, modern, and, according to historian Keith Clifford, "not a theological conservative."[45]

The church was not only the site of religious community. It was also closely tied to social, cultural, and educational activities. St. Stephen's Church hosted special services for children, exhibitions of "dissolving views" and "lime light views," lectures, classical concerts, annual garden parties, and picnics. During at least one cultural evening, Jennie Wisdom sang as part of a quartet. Prominent Canadian preachers and visiting international missionaries who came to speak placed Canada in the context of a larger world.[46] In 1887, for example, St. Stephen's hosted a "Hindoo" missionary ordained by the Presbyterian Church who was about to leave for Jamaica. The audience was promised not a biblical sermon but a lecture in his native costume, where he would "illustrate the manners and customs of his countrymen."[47] In 1894, when Jennie was visiting Sutherland's River, her mother noted with particular regret how much her daughter would have enjoyed seeing the various artifacts displayed by missionaries from Formosa as part of the Presbyterian General Assembly meeting in Saint John.[48]

The variety of activities associated with the church forces us to think about the place of technology, internationalism, and cosmopolitanism in an institution perhaps too easily dismissed as only conservative and parochial. Saint John families like the Wisdoms literally saw the world through new photographic and projection mechanisms, and had the opportunity to hear people from outside their cultural experience. Clergymen were always proselytizing, and there was no sense of cultural relativism, yet, even as the Presbyterian Church seemed to reinforce the self-referential influences of ethnicity, family, and Pictou County, involvement with the church also afforded access to a larger world through exposure to other peoples and places.

There are plenty of examples of the closed, conservative, and parochial nature of the church in Saint John. The older minister of St. Stephen's, Dr. Macrae, was prominent in local efforts to enforce observation of the Sabbath and was especially vocal on contemporary anti-Catholic issues such as the Jesuit Estates Question, demanding that the imperial government in London intervene to save Confederation, which he believed was threatened by the actions of the Quebec legislature.[49] Fierce anti-Catholicism was a vibrant aspect of this Presbyterian culture: in 1891, Rev. Father Charles Chiniquy, the well-known former Catholic priest who now crusaded against Rome, spoke at several local churches on "Why I Left the Church of Rome with 35,000 of My Countrymen" and "What Does the Church of Rome Understand by Liberty of Conscience."[50]

But there are also examples of the denomination's openness. St. Stephen's, in particular, was a mission-oriented congregation concerned not solely with saving souls but also with offering charitable relief. St. Stephen's embodied the nascent social gospel as it sought to apply Christian ethics to social problems. There were specific instances, such as the July 1892 collection for the victims of the St. John's, Newfoundland, fire or the 1902 Thanksgiving offertory for the Protestant Orphans Asylum, but there was also the ongoing willingness of its members to allocate significant funds for mission work. Although St. Stephen's was not the largest or wealthiest Presbyterian congregation in Saint John, its annual budget allocated the most money to mission work.[51] Mary Bell was a member of the St. Stephen's Women's Foreign Missionary Society, and a second women's congregational group, the Willing Workers, raised funds for the local poor.

In 1894, when the Presbyterian national church held its annual meeting in Saint John, much of the local press coverage focused on mission work. The attendance of two missionaries from China and two from India attracted particular attention, especially when missionary Rev. George L. Mackay of Formosa was elected moderator. At this remarkable meeting, at the same time as Presbyterians were focusing on mission work among immigrants in the Canadian West, they also passed a resolution condemning discrimination against the Chinese through the head tax. In an effort to discourage Chinese immigration once Chinese labour was no longer required for the construction of the Canadian Pacific Railway, the federal government had introduced a head tax in 1885. The Presbyterian 1894 resolution stated that "Canada ought to welcome people from all countries who will aid in the developing" of its resources, and that, contrary to British practices, "the Parliament of Canada does discriminate in an unjust and odious way against the government and people of China." Rev. Mackay stated that "it was high time the people removed the scales of prejudice and national pride from their eyes and looked across the Pacific to China to see that nation, as one ... destined to exercise a mighty influence upon the countries of the world, Canada not the least."[52] This is not to argue that mission work was not fundamentally culturally imperialist, but rather that it must be understood in a nuanced manner. Foreign mission work created real, albeit hierarchical, links between people. In doing so, it introduced a language of justice and solidarity that would also be adopted by reformers – and social workers – whose concerns lay much closer to home. The first urban social workers were often referred to as 'city missionaries.'

Notions of justice and community solidarity were also current within the public school system. Notwithstanding economic restraint, the Wisdoms' was a house of books and a home that valued education. Jennie's mother and all the Nova Scotian McQueen aunts (except the oldest, who was mentally ill) taught school at some point in their lives. Jean Barman has noted that a "fundamental attribute of Pictou County, growing out of Scots descent and Presbyterianism, was a commitment to literacy."[53] Although Free did not come from a family of schoolteachers, he also valued education and read widely. When he brought his new bride to Saint John, his home boasted a collection of books that ranged from literature to the political writings of Benjamin Disraeli. The family subscribed to specialized periodicals such as *Educational Review* and mass journals such as *Ladies Home Journal*.[54] New fiction also passed through the household. In 1892, a McQueen sister in British Columbia reported that the Wisdoms had forwarded a new book by Louisa M. Alcott. Before marriage, Mary Bell had presented a paper to the Halifax Teachers' Institute, and, once the children were older, she returned to this interest in writing papers for the Women's Missionary Society and literary groups. It is perhaps not surprising, then, that all the Wisdom children did well in school. In 1892, eleven-year-old Jennie Wisdom wrote to inform her grandmother McQueen of her school prize, acknowledging that Katie and Roy had also received awards.[55] In June 1898, both Jennie and Bessie wrote the high school entrance exam along with 190 other Saint John students. Both girls had results in the top twenty-five, with Bessie placing twelfth and Jennie twenty-first. It was not unusual for girls to do so well. Of the top twenty-five places in the city and surrounding area, twenty were held by women.[56]

Education was valued not only within the family but also within the community. Enormous civic pride was invested into the public high school, and its twice-annual term-closing ceremonies received much attention in the local press and full attendance by local politicians. When the new school opened in 1896, it boasted modern classrooms and the most up-to-date ventilation and sanitary arrangements in Canada.[57]

The Wisdom girls were directly affected by the highly controversial 1895 decision to amalgamate the separate high schools for girls and boys, with the integration of the boys' Grammar School and the girls' Victoria School to form the Saint John High School.[58] In 1896, following much public debate and the resignation of the former girls' school principal, a new high school building was erected. Supporters of the girls' school mounted a futile opposition by emphasizing the achievements of its alumna, such as academic success in the McGill University matriculation examinations. The pride of female graduates was evident in their active Alumnae Association, which maintained social networks established in the school and raised funds for various supplemental school projects. In 1898, Katie Wisdom was elected to the executive of this organization.[59]

Katie Wisdom was a member of the first graduating class of the new high school in 1898. The new school was not only coeducational but also racially integrated, with a picture of the 1898 graduating class clearly including one Black female student.[60] In addition, there were several Jewish students, reflecting the presence of this growing community. While African and Jewish students were a tiny minority, and any Acadian students would have been at one of the local Catholic high schools, it was evident that the growing high school population was predominantly female. The number of students attending high school in Saint John at this time increased dramatically. In the fall of 1898, 140 new students enrolled, bringing total numbers close to 500. The number of girls not only overwhelmed the male student body, but, in a co-educational environment, the young women were also walking away with top prizes, and many continued on to post-secondary education. Debates and anxieties about education and women did not disappear with the new coeducational high school; instead, they shifted from concern for the girls to worries about the boys not keeping up.[61]

When Jennie and Bessie graduated in June 1902, they were among a class of sixty-five, the largest class ever to graduate in Saint John, boasting forty-eight girls compared to only seventeen boys. At the graduation ceremony, Jennie read her essay "Concentration," which one newspaper described as "interesting and instructive." Bessie did not participate in the ceremony, but, like her older sister Katie, she was awarded an honours certificate. Graduation at Saint John High School meant passing grade eleven. Both Jennie and Bessie were, therefore, among the number of students who returned the following September for grade twelve. The large graduating class resulted in sixteen students returning in August for an additional year, again setting a school record.[62]

Among Bessie and Jennie's contemporaries was a range of students whose careers reflected the variety of opportunities available to young men and women during this time. Classmate Solomon Hart Green became the Maritimes' first Jewish lawyer in 1906 and, the following year in Winnipeg, the first Jew to be called to the bar in western Canada. When, in 1910, he was elected to the provincial legislature for the Liberals, he became the first Canadian Jew to be elected to public office outside Quebec. While a member of that legislature, he was a spokesman for labour and campaigned for women's rights through the dower.[63]

Other male classmates followed less public careers and went into business, and the young women entered teaching and nursing. Jennie Wisdom would not be the only classmate to follow a career in social service work. Samuel Prince, who became one of Nova Scotia's most prominent social service workers, was only one class behind, graduating in 1903, while Jennie shared her year with classmate and neighbour Grace Hatheway.

Although her family lived a much more public life than did the Wisdoms, Hatheway reinforces the point that Jane's interest in social service was not exceptional. Grace was the oldest daughter of W. Frank Hatheway and Ella Marven, two of the city's most prominent social activists. Like Freeman Wisdom, Hatheway established a new business in the aftermath of the 1877 fire, but, unlike his neighbour's, Hatheway's grocery business was an unqualified success. The Hatheway family had a domestic servant and boasted an income more than three times that of the Wisdoms. In 1901, both families lived in multi-generational households and shared a close association with a church. Both men's names appeared on petitions to Parliament to protect the commercial interests of the port of Saint John. The Hatheways, however, were much more politically active. Frank Hatheway broke with the Conservatives in 1896, became chairman of the local Independent Party, and, in April 1901, established the Fabian League of Saint John. Fabian ideas in Saint John were, in fact, largely associated with the Women's Enfranchisement Association (WEA), of which he and Ella had been founding members in 1894. After running unsuccessfully as a Labour candidate, he returned to the Conservative fold and was elected to the provincial legislature in 1908, where he was responsible for important pro-labour legislation. Together, Frank and Ella Hatheway also established a free kindergarten for the benefit of working mothers, which appears to have emerged from an interest of the WEA as early as 1899.[64] Jennie Wisdom volunteered as a student assistant here during college vacations and considered visits to the homes of "poor children" as her first professional activity.[65]

Grace shared many of her parents' interests. She received her bachelor's degree from Oberlin College in 1911, specializing in economics and psychology, and, after graduation, seems to have been a social worker and settlement house worker in Philadelphia. In 1919, she began graduate work at Bryn Mawr College in labour relations and was subsequently employed as a researcher by the Wharton School of Business at the University of Pennsylvania. Thereafter, Grace Hatheway appears to have supported herself through writing and editorial work until her death in 1936.[66]

Grace Hatheway's parents were at the centre of a small but active reform community that contained virtually all the main currents of reform sweeping across the continent. In Saint John, the Protestant social gospel and a preoccupation with urban poverty, especially as explored by Charles Dickens in popular fiction, were visible aspects of everyday life. The social gospel movement sought to apply Christian principles to society, placing a concurrent emphasis on national and personal salvation. The kingdom of heaven could be realized in Canada through social reform, legislation, and activism.[67]

It is difficult to untangle religious and secular reform movements. Academics spoke on research that might improve society. For example, in March 1899, a University of New Brunswick professor's public lecture on "Housing for the Working Classes" used statistics to emphasize the importance of sanitary regulations to preserving health.[68] City newspapers reported on urban experiments such as Jane Addams's Hull House, explained by the *Globe* as "sort of a Toynbee Hall" in Chicago's "foreign quarter." It is significant that the article assumes its readers would already be familiar with the first and most famous British settlement house, Toynbee Hall. The *Globe* described the work as both "sociological and educational," without "the patronizing spirit of condescending philanthropy" that would educate "would-be benefactors out of the Pharisaisms of modern charity as in the way of encouraging the neighbors to lift themselves to a higher level of life." The ideal of individual personal service, however, remained central: Addams's original idea was intended not "so much to help the poor as to help the rich – the idle society girls who had no worthy object in life and who needed to be brought into practical sympathy with their fellow creatures."[69]

Other currents of reform were also present. The Women's Enfranchisement Association came under the influence of utopian socialist novelist Edward Bellamy, whose 1888 *Looking Backward* describes a state socialist commonwealth where private profit is replaced by a paternalist, collectivist new order. This enthusiasm spawned a local Fabian league.[70] More conservative and explicitly Christian influences were often linked to radical alternatives. When Evangeline Booth, field commissioner of the Salvation Army in Canada, addressed a large crowd at the Mechanic's Institute on the subject of slum work in London, "the richest city in the world," a newspaper report emphasized the injustice of extreme poverty rather than the work of saving souls.[71]

As is true of the Maritime Provinces more generally, Saint John is not often associated with reform during this period. But this stereotype belies the extent of local activity, much of which was focused on poverty, disease, juvenile delinquency, and moral vice. Reformers determined to transform or regenerate society addressed their concerns within the legal framework of the regional poor law system.

In Canada, care for the poor was a provincial responsibility, and New Brunswick and Nova Scotia entered Confederation with the poor law on their statutes. Basically, it made local communities responsible for the care and support of their own through a compulsory, annual public assessment. This care and support would always be parsimonious, as it was based on the principle of "least eligibility," in which the amount of support given could never exceed the benefits of someone earning the lowest wage. The legal system was adopted almost directly from England, but, as one historian of the poor law in New Brunswick has noted, it was "designed for a comparatively static, socially immobile, wealthy and well settled environment."[72] These conditions did not conform to the circumstances of the new colony, and new jurisdictions to the west roundly rejected the poor law, which had also been the basis of legislation in most of the first American colonies. The poor law differentiated between the deserving and undeserving poor. Those who were considered "idle and disorderly," despite being capable of work, could be sentenced to hard labour in prison. In contrast, those who were unable to provide for themselves through no fault of their own (orphans, widows, the sick, and the infirm) were deemed "deserving" and could receive local support. Distinct treatment for the deserving and undeserving poor and the principle of least eligibility were preserved throughout the twentieth century and extended to jurisdictions with no poor law of their own.

With local communities responsible for the care of their own paupers in New Brunswick, the incentive was to keep costs as low as possible. The relatively poor and sparsely populated Colony of New Brunswick did not have even the flexibility of the original British legislation, which assisted local communities that could not meet expenses. Instead, the local law permitted overseers to "oblige" able-bodied paupers to take employment and to contract out poor children as apprentices. "Outdoor Relief," whereby the poor were assisted in their own homes, was terribly expensive, but the diffuse and relatively sparse New Brunswick population made institutions such as poorhouses associated with "Indoor Relief" usually impractical. One solution to emerge was the contract system. Through a reverse "sale," paupers could be auctioned off by the poor district to the lowest bidder, who would gain the labour of the pauper in exchange for the money and providing room, clothing, and board. The price of a physically strong man was much lower for the community than an infirm elderly woman who might be incapable of work and require care. This system, at its best, could amount to what we might recognize as foster placement, and could permit families to stay together as extended families might board kin. However, it also held the potential for severe exploitation. The public pauper auction was, not surprisingly, compared to slavery by the press and by its critics, and there were no incentives other than decency to treat the pauper well.[73]

In the 1840s, Saint John County constructed its own poorhouse, or what was locally referred to as an "almshouse," with an adjacent farm to keep costs down and occupy able-bodied inmates. Much remains unknown about this institution, but we do know that there was internal racial segregation and that, during the 1870s, there was a daily average of about 200 people in the asylum.[74] We also know that the expense of building and maintaining these institutions meant that as late as 1900, there were only six almshouses in the province, and some counties were still billeting out paupers by auction to the lowest bidder.[75]

The province's most important philanthropic expenditure was the lunatic asylum. New Brunswick established British North America's first provincial lunatic asylum in 1835, with a new, larger building opening for patients in 1848.[76] Although the province was at the forefront of mental health care, this was not the case with other public health institutions. No public hospital existed in Saint John until 1865. Even then, it remained a municipal institution supported by modest annual grants from the provincial government.[77]

In the vacuum of the minimal provision provided by the state, churches and private associations addressed the gap by establishing residential facilities. Catholic and Protestant communities opened respective orphanages for boys and girls in the 1850s. Religious orders and private bequests also provided for the elderly and chronically ill. The Salvation Army and the Catholic Order of the Good Shepherd "rescued" what were known as "fallen women" in the late 1880s and 1890s.[78]

Although the poor law obliged some kind of public support, this support was often accompanied by private charity in the form of help from individuals or national or sectarian associations. In February 1896, the *Globe* reported that a well-known King Street merchant had assisted an impoverished mother with grocery orders and a visit to her home. There was also a tradition of "individual subscription" or donations to relieve misery after such "acts of God" as fire, flood, and shipwreck.[79] National societies dated from the eighteenth century with the creation of the St. Andrew's Society in 1798, the St. Patrick's Society in 1815, and the St. George's Society in 1819. The Catholic St. Vincent de Paul Society came to Saint John in 1857, and, by 1900, there were two branches. There were also particular denominational efforts to assist the needy. For example, the Methodist Church operated the Glad Tidings Mission on Brussels Street, which included a dining room and an employment agency. Other congregations looked after their own members and adherents. One stereotype of the "exploitive poor" was the widow who sent her children to different Sunday schools so that they might benefit from the generosity of different churches.[80]

Middle-class and elite women were especially active in charitable work. Their involvement may be explained by a combination of gendered beliefs about women's supposedly innate sympathetic qualities, the opportunities provided for meaningful work when few other options were available, and sincere religious or ethical motivations. National societies and various churches all had women's auxiliaries or organizations, such as the Church of England's Girls Friendly Society. The Women's Christian Temperance Union, for example, distributed soup tickets to the poor in 1883, and, in 1897, it assisted with a sale held by the Women's Exchange, a largely American organization that provided impoverished women with a place to sell their own handiwork. The Dominion Order of King's Daughters ran a boarding house for working women and girls, operated an employment office, and offered night classes in English, reading, and writing.[81]

It was a female-led reform association, the Saint John Local Council of Women, that ultimately brought modern scientific philanthropy to the city. Established in 1894, this umbrella organization united the city's female associations and linked them to both a national and international women's movement.[82] The Local Council of Women combined conservative and progressive female forces in a wide range of areas with interests that ranged from women's political and legal rights to philanthropy.

Local councils were associated with Canada's National Council of Women. At its first meeting in 1894, the president of the Montreal council, Julia Parker Drummond, addressed the assembly on scientific philanthropy through the charity organization movement.[83] Drummond claimed this was "largely a women's movement," in part because of the central role that the volunteer visitor would play; she would bring with her the "true and enduring helpfulness of a friend ... who in the true sense of the word become[s neighbor] to the poor." She stated:

> Its ultimate aims are nothing less than these – not only to relieve poverty, but to cure it; not only to redeem the feeble and the vicious, but to do away with the conditions that create them. We recognize that the moral

shiftlessness of the pauper has much to do with his miseries, but behind and before this with cause we see another, his dwarfed and debased social conditions, and with this recognition comes the knowledge that he can only be restored by the moral and spiritual force of personal influence, that the conditions which re-produce him must be altered by the readjustment of social relationships.

The charity organization movement, while embracing notions of the deserving and undeserving poor, promised not short-term relief but rehabilitation and, even more broadly, to mend "a society divided against itself" as "rich and poor be brought to know and respect each other." While old forms of charity were portrayed as impulsive, ad hoc, and isolated actions that addressed only the immediate needs of the recipient, organized charity, investigated fraud, rehabilitated the deserving poor, eliminated pauperism, and fostered a more connected and stable community.[84]

This trans-Atlantic movement originated in London, England, in 1869, and was influenced by principles of the German Elberfeld system. It retained some of traditional charity's focus on personal service, but it also sought to uncover structural explanations for poverty so that volunteers could help those in crisis recover their independence and self-respect. Nineteenth-century structural problems were as likely to be understood as deficiencies in individual character and moral culpability, alongside economic downturns, declining trades, inadequate housing, and poor health.[85] This moral and material understanding of poverty is evident in one 1898 report to the National Council of Women that reminded readers that "it should not be forgotten that besides the inculcation of habits of cleanliness, thrift, industry and steadiness, besides moral, intellectual and religious teaching, the poor require better food and more of it, warmer clothes, better and surer shelter, and greater security of permanent employment on decent wages." Therefore, it was incumbent on everyone to "'lend a hand' as well as a voice" to provide working people with "better dwellings, healthy recreation, public play grounds, public bathes and wash-houses, shorter hours and better wages; and by so doing help fulfil the law of love and service which shall one day rule the world."[86]

Concurrent to its use of religious language, the charity organization movement also positioned itself as modern, and adopted contemporary bureaucratic and business systems. Since the early eighteenth century, philanthropic institutions had mimicked commercial enterprises by using boards of administrative officers, member subscriptions, annual meetings, and reports. But the charity organization movement also borrowed from social science, employing methods of quantification, statistics, graphs, maps, and charts to explain objectives and document achievements. Its growth in late-nineteenth-century North America reflected its connection to two, growing social forces: the Progressive movement with its preoccupation with modernization, efficiency, and the elimination of waste; and the social regeneration promised by the social gospel movement.

In the context of growing social inequality and visible urban poverty, organizations followed. In 1877, Buffalo, New York, established the first North American Charity Organization Society. In Canada, Toronto established an Associated Charities in 1880 but it was moribund within a decade, as was the Montreal society originally organized around 1883. Scientific charity was resurrected in 1898 and 1899 by these cities' local council of women, with their national organization subsequently supporting the establishment of local associated charities.[87] During the discussion of this motion, a delegate from the Saint John council noted unsuccessful past attempts by fraternal associations, benevolent societies, churches, and officers of public charity boards to create an umbrella structure in Saint John. Now was the time of the local council to "take the matter up," she argued. Indeed, it did: in March 1899, the local council initiated the Saint John Associated Charities.

The Saint John Associated Charities was promoted foremost by Mary Caroline Babbitt Ellis, wife of the *Globe*'s publisher. This connection gave it an immediate platform for publicity and promotion. Its initial message emphasized that a coordinated body would deal better with "schemers whose fraud and persistence enable them to cheat the charitable and to deprive the deserving of what they might otherwise receive." It also underlined scientific philanthropy's core belief that "indiscriminate alms giving to ordinary beggars is found to do more evil than good." In contrast, the Associated Charities would provide work for all who needed it so that "nearly everybody" would "earn what he or she receives."[88] The pragmatic benefits were always underscored: a single organization could claim efficiency by eliminating the needless duplication of services, uncovering fraud, and directing resources only to the most deserving and needy (those admirably suffering in silence and reluctant to ask for help, rather than "professional paupers").[89] In contrast to its practical aspects, Associated Charities also loftily attempted to raise "the needy above the need of relief, [to] prevent and diminish pauperism, to encourage thrift, self-dependence and industry through friendly intercourse, advice and sympathy, and to aid the poor to help themselves, to prevent children growing up as paupers, to aid in the diffusion of knowledge on subjects connected with the relief of the poor." It was idealistically believed that these objectives would be achieved by centralizing information and investigating each applicant, not by actually distributing funds.[90]

Although the organization was theoretically against the distribution of direct aid, it was pragmatic enough to understand that immediate assistance was required for certain structural problems, such as the impact of winter on employment prospects, ill health, and economic downturns. Because it sought to rehabilitate and prevent permanent dependency or pauperism, organizational efforts focused only on those who could be saved. Those deemed undeserving had legal entitlement to assistance through recognized residency or "settlement," and could always find shelter and board at the almshouse.

At a time when single-sex organizations were the norm, Associated Charities brought men and women together in leadership positions. It was less successful in overcoming other divisions within the community. The Saint John organization was predominantly Protestant in a city where confessional differences mattered. This ultimately limited its effectiveness. There were some attempts to reach out to Jews and Catholics; during the second year of its operation, there was some coordination with the St. Vincent de Paul Society, and, in 1905, the Saint John Jewish community was specially noted as having "borne their share of labor in an admirable manner." The Associated Charities also brought together private charity and municipal government, as the city began making an annual grant to the organization in 1907.[91]

Associated Charities popularized the idea of scientific philanthropy beyond its organization. In 1908, a report of the Saint John Associated Charities commended the local Salvation Army, commenting that "all relief work is less subject to spasmodic and impulsive modes of administration than in the past."[92] Associated Charities also tied local benevolence to an international movement. Its supporters made connections with Boston, and, during the first years of the twentieth century, Saint John was one of the few Canadian cities to report to the American National Conference of Charities and Correction. In 1904, it sent a delegate to the American association's annual meeting.[93]

The precise impact of the Associated Charities on its clients remains difficult to assess, but it is hard to believe it greatly benefited the city's poor. In December 1900, forty-eight cases were investigated, of which twenty were classified as fraudulent, eight were provided with employment, and eighteen were given immediate relief. Employment took the form of placements in local establishments or day work at a woodyard operated by the Associated Charities in conjunction with the Seamen's Mission. In an effort to eliminate personal charity and fraudulent begging, it produced small cards for distribution to housekeepers, who were encouraged to request an investigation from the Associated Charities office when they were approached for help by someone they did not know.[94]

The Associated Charities of Saint John, like charity movements elsewhere, placed particular emphasis on protecting children. In keeping with the logic of efficiency, work with children was a direct investment in the future of the nation, and it was cheaper to invest in playgrounds than in reformatories. But children did not always fit into the deserving/undeserving paradigm; they were innocent, vulnerable, and even sentimentalized, but they could also be active agents in the perpetuation of pauperism by skipping school or participating in family charitable fraud. Saint John reformers proposed enterprises such as free kindergarten and supervised playgrounds. As noted earlier, Jennie Wisdom claimed volunteer work as a summer assistant in the free kindergarten as her first exposure to social service. The free kindergarten was organized by the Hatheways in 1899. In seeking to provide this service for working mothers, they gained the support of the Women's Enfranchisement Association and raised concerns about exposing children to positive influences.[95] The Saint John's Playground Association was operated by the Local Council of Women and was among the earliest to be established in Canada. The impetus for the playground movement in Saint John was entangled with the 1902 murder of fifteen-year-old William Doherty by fellow adolescents. The victim and the assailants were not much younger than Jennie, and the body was found near the Wisdoms' former neighbourhood. In the community soul-searching that followed the brutal killing, several residents turned to the idea of a wholesome, supervised playground as an antidote to, or preventive measure for, juvenile delinquency and reformatories. While the Hatheways saw kindergartens as an aid to working mothers, others saw them as "one way of improving the moral status of the youth."[96]

Through Dr. Clara Olding, a close first cousin of Mary Bell, the Wisdoms had an immediate connection to the heart of the Saint John reform community. Clara Olding arrived in Saint John after 1896 upon the completion of her medical studies at Dalhousie College. She was immediately a visible member of the reform community, due, in part, to her sheer conspicuousness as a woman practising medicine. She joined the Medical Society, which was generally progressive, and was soon a member of its executive. Olding was interested in outreach, lecturing to the public on first aid and, together with another female doctor, Margaret Parks, establishing a clinic for poor women and children. Her family remained close to the Wisdom children; her oldest son, Donald Olding Hebb, the so-called "Father of Cognitive Psychobiology," and his sister Catherine, a research scientist, retained close, lifelong relations with Jennie.[97]

Jennie Wisdom left Saint John in 1903 but she carried with her the values of her family, religion, and education. The ideals of mission and vocation were firmly established, as was an awareness of those less fortunate. She would have already strongly associated women with philanthropy, been exposed to new standards of trans-Atlantic scientific philanthropy, and linked benevolence with Christian service. But charity was not a personal or denominational response; it was organized and had generally moved from individuals to the collective. Saint John can too easily be dismissed as a stagnant backwater, but, like larger metropolitan centres of North America, it was clearly struggling with the consequences of modern urban society. The legal framework of the poor law offered a marginal role for the state, with its jurisdiction limited to indoor relief for legitimate paupers, hospitals, and asylums. Succour was the domain of individuals, extended families, religious, national, and fraternal associations, and specialized reform societies. Wisdom's family circumstances would have also led her to understand that self-support was not always possible all the time. By the time she was an adolescent, she may have become sensitive to the humiliation often associated with accepting charity.

Chapter Two

McGill: The Ethos of Female Service, 1903–1911

In September 1903, Jennie Wisdom left Saint John for Royal Victoria College and McGill University. At the Royal Victoria College (RVC), she found herself firmly in the midst of a culture that emphasized British female civic service, and, in her courses at McGill, she encountered questions of poverty and philanthropy at a philosophical rather than emotional or religious level. These two streams – intellectual and civic-minded – came together in the settlement house movement, where, for Wisdom, the experience of communal living in a women's college was replaced by residency among the city's immigrant poor. Wisdom's experience in Montreal was remarkably insular, even when she encountered some of the city's poor. Her city was not French, Catholic, or Jewish. While her background and status as a RVC undergraduate offered her many important connections to Montreal, they also isolated her within Canada's largest city.

In going to RVC, Jennie was following her sister. Familial chain migration took women out from the Maritimes to the United States and throughout Canada, where these networks assisted them in quickly integrating to new environments. In 1899, Katie had won a bursary, likely an exhibition scholarship worth $300, to attend McGill University.[1] McGill had first admitted women in 1884, the same year as Jennie's birth, but the opening of a separate women's college corresponded with Katie's arrival in Montreal. Beginning in the fall of 1899, based on the English collegiate model, RVC offered a unique educational experience for women as the only sex-segregated college in Canada. Female students normally took their first- and second-year courses at the college and then moved to McGill for senior and laboratory classes.[2] This hybrid system emerged as a pragmatic response to the financial cost of offering a completely separate course of study for women and the condition of Donald Smith's (or, after his 1897 elevation, Lord Strathcona's) endowment to support the education of women at McGill. From 1884 until 1899, women students, or "Donaldas," as they were named in honour of their benefactor, shared segregated space in the main McGill arts building.

Katie's arrival coincided with a grand new building and a largely new teaching staff. The most important member was Hilda Oakeley, first warden of RVC, a poet and philosopher, and the first woman to be appointed as a full member to the McGill Faculty of Arts. Historian Margaret Gillett described her as "raised in an upper middle-class atmosphere of learning, gentle manners and public service." English-born, she studied at Somerville College, Oxford, and was not yet thirty-two when she arrived in Montreal to assume her new position.[3] Photos show a beautiful woman, and contemporaries noted her stylish taste in dress. Her students and her generally older fellow instructors clearly adored her, and she had influence on them long after her return to England in 1905. Glamorous and intelligent, she was also idealistic. Hilda Oakeley spoke at one of the first YWCA meetings Jennie attended in Montreal, "impressing upon the students the importance of lofty ideals to spiritual growth."[4] Her close friend Eleanor Rathbone, later a leading British politician and reformer, urged Oakeley to use her position as RVC warden to support women's suffrage in Canada. In the summer of 1904, Oakeley visited Hull House in Chicago, having already visited the settlements in New York. Her subsequent educational career led her to the University of Manchester and the University of London, but it also included important social service. Between 1915 and 1921, she served as the first female warden of London's Passmore Edwards Settlement. Jane Wisdom and Hilda Oakeley sustained some kind of correspondence at least until 1939.[5]   ˙

The grand new college on Sherbrooke Street did not, in fact, have sufficient accommodation to house all its students, and, as a result, Katie boarded in a private home.[6] Before RVC opened, McGill had no residences, and male students from outside Montreal were lodged in recommended boarding or rooming houses or among the fraternities. The construction of a residential university college for women provided them with a very different experience from their male counterparts. Hilda Oakeley wrote that the RVC allowed students to "meet constantly with others who have come from very different homes, but who, bearing a kindred interest, are looking forward to the same goal."

She emphasized that the residential college created friendships among students and permitted students to "know personally" the instructors engaged in research.[7]

Katie was the brilliant, outgoing, and even athletic older sister. She played basketball, was president of the RVC literary and debating society, Delta Sigma, and emerged as the star in the senior class play. A Saint John paper announced her success with first-class honours in French and German and second-class honours in English and psychology. Around this time, Katie also was falling in love with Harry "Daisy" Williams, who had graduated in 1901 and begun to study law, was active in theatre, and boarded at the same rooming house in the winter of 1902.[8] It is difficult not to see Jane as in her sister's shadow. Katie's classmates came from similar backgrounds. They included fellow Saint John High School graduate Marion Belyea and Katie's particularly close friend Euphemia "Effie" McLeod, daughter of Nova Scotian-born McGill engineering and astronomy professor Clement Henry McLeod. Other classmates were Maude E. Parkin, daughter of prominent Canadian educator and imperialist George Parkin and mother of philosopher George Grant, and future international peace activist and scholar Grace Julia Wales. The very act of being a female undergraduate at RVC immediately offered important connections and networks.[9]

Jane's desire to attend university was stoked by Katie's frequent letters home. She described meeting various men with Nova Scotian connections, socializing with "Aunt Annie" and Ephriam Scott, editor of the *Presbyterian Record* (and seeing her real Aunt Liz and Uncle Norman Cunningham at their house), and getting to know Professor McLeod's family. Katie's friendship with the McLeod family opened doors to important academic connections. For instance, she attended a tea in honour of visiting principal Henry Smith Pritchett of the Massachusetts Institute of Technology. Whether through older Saint John connections or through the Ephriam Scotts, Katie also wrote of being spotted by Montreal's most prominent Presbyterian, Dr. James Barclay of St. Paul's Church. One encounter elicited an editorial "Ugh!" when Barclay stated that both he and his wife hoped "they would see more of me this winter than last." On at least one occasion, Katie dined at the Barclays' before attending a concert with Mrs. Barclay and a Miss Budden. No letter home exists regarding this, but it is probable that Katie was among the RVC students invited to the exquisite home of Julia and George Drummond to view their impressive collection of European paintings.[10]

Montreal both shocked and delighted Katie. She wrote of attending dances, both those where she did not dance and those where she danced with her future husband. She described the riot by McGill students during the South African War. She asked Jennie not to tell "Rev Daniel" (Fraser) that she had skipped church for a walk but also claimed to find it "perfectly dreadful the way people go snowshoeing and skiing on Sunday in Montreal – especially in the morning." She also recounted the visit of their "Royal Highnesses," the Duke and Duchess of York (later King George V and Queen Mary) in September 1901 and her evening tramway tour around Montreal with Professor McLeod and Effie to view the illuminated decorations in their honour.[11]

Katie's experience at RVC also literally made her world larger. In February 1902, she attended the YWCA conference in Toronto and returned to Montreal convinced "that the Student Volunteer Movement is a great thing."[12] The YWCA movement not only opened up another city and the student movement to Katie, but also introduced her to the local reform community when she was invited to prominent Montreal reformer H.B. Ames's home to speak to Louise Ames. The anglophone Montreal reform community was small enough that transient undergraduate students of the right cultural background had no trouble incorporating themselves into that social fabric.[13]

In the first semester of her final year, Katie wrote to Jennie at home in Saint John that "college is full of disappointment." She admitted that the "nearer I get to the fatal plunge the more people I meet who are making a success of their lives without any college training and also – this is the bitterest of all – the more graduates and college girls I see who might just as well have been asleep for years for all the difference college has made in them." Katie offered these "reflections to calm [Jane's] enthusiasm." It is difficult to know how much this reflected her state of mind and how much she was trying to console her sister, who was expected to have to wait another year before something could be managed financially.[14]

But the unexpected happened. On 14 September 1903, Hilda Oakeley wrote directly to Mary Bell Wisdom, asking if one of her daughters might like to make use of a Residential Bursary for $200, which had suddenly become available for that session. The bursary was not based on examinations results; rather, it was awarded at the discretion of the warden to "some promising student." Mary Bell had written to Hilda Oakeley the previous April, expressing how anxious she was that her two daughters at home be able to follow their older sister.[15] An amazing six days after Oakeley's letter was sent, Jennie Wisdom wrote to her parents from "ROYAL VICTORIA COLLEGE!" to let them know she had "just arrived in the abode of bliss and girls." The windfall of a bursary made university possible for Jane Wisdom, although it by no means covered all expenses. Residence at RVC cost between $290 and $440 a year (most rooms were $290) and covered room and board from 9 September to 26 June. Students who did not attend the spring session received a rebate of $50. Jennie's bursary would, therefore, have covered all but $40 of her housing expenses, leaving another $65 for tuition and spending money to be covered by family members.[16]

Like Katie, Jennie did not come to Montreal a complete stranger. She moved into a world that had pre-existing networks of family, Presbyterians, and Maritimers. She was met at the train station by two women, an unidentified "Ruth" and "F.," and had plans to see "Helen" later that day. She, too, had access to Montreal Presbyterian society via the Barclays, the Scotts, and, after 1904 when he joined the staff of Presbyterian College, her Saint John minister, Rev. Daniel Fraser. Professor McLeod and his family also welcomed Katie's sister. Her meeting with the famous Hilda Oakeley did not disappoint ("My!" she wrote), and the fact that she was given the bedroom next to the warden merited three exclamation marks; such grammatical exuberance was typical of Jennie and would characterize her writing throughout her life.[17]

She quickly settled into a routine. Breakfast was served at 8:00 a.m., luncheon at 1:00 p.m., and dinner at 6:30 p.m. All students were expected to meet in the reception room before dinner and adhere to quiet time during set working hours and after 11:00 p.m. If students left the college in the evening, they were to leave the address of their whereabouts with the warden and check in with her when they returned before 11:00 p.m. Occasional exceptions were permitted for later curfews with the warden's permission, but students were expected to consult with her before accepting invitations to public places of entertainment.

Many of Jennie's classmates shared her Maritime background. There was a cousin, Elizabeth (Bessie) McQueen, originally from New Glasgow; Muriel Massey, originally from Prince Edward Island; Edith Mowat, formerly of Fredericton; and Evelyn Coates of Amherst, Nova Scotia.[18] Other Maritimers in the college included Emma McQueen of New Glasgow; presumably another cousin, Florence Estabrooks, another graduate of Saint John High School; and, for one year, Clara Dennis, daughter of Halifax feminist Agnes Miller Dennis and William Dennis, Conservative senator and publisher of the *Halifax Herald*. Anna

MacKeen, a year behind, came from Glace Bay and would later serve as dean of women at Dalhousie University. She would also become a lifelong friend of Jane's. Scottish-born Lily Laverlock came to Montreal via Vancouver and returned there to become the first female "general reporter" before founding one of Canada's few women's newspapers, the *Chronicle*, which operated for less than a year. The rest of the class was mainly from Montreal. Many of these women would go on to professional careers. Ten of the twenty-two Donaldas of '07 never married, with teaching being their most prominent occupation.[19]

Life at RVC centred in part on single-sex social events. There is nothing to suggest that Jennie had a particular close friend at college, and she seems to have relied on her sisters and cousins for support. Life at RVC was not only female; it was also explicitly white and middle class. Preoccupations with race were perhaps most obvious in Jennie's October 1906 description of a "dress up social" held at the college. The costumes the girls put together were interesting. Jennie seems to have dressed as an elderly woman, but most of her descriptions focused on college mates and faculty who dressed as male and female "Indians," Japanese ladies, "Chinamen," and "Darkies." The inversion of age (in the case of Jennie) or sex (in the case of the Chinamen or Indian chiefs) could be magnified further by those who transgressed into inverting race. It was incongruous that an Aboriginal, Asian, or African-Canadian should attend RVC at the time.[20]

Jennie's world was not without men. She was voted "Freshman Favorite," and, as a senior, at the dance following the October 1906 McGill theatre night, she wrote: "I had my program filled & enjoyed some of the dances with *some* of my partners *extremely*."[21] As a twenty-two-year-old woman, she was both fond of, and prudish around, men. In the spring of 1906, she went without a bath for three weeks rather than "screw up my courage" to ask the man at the hotel desk for a key to the bath facilities. At the same time, she counted several men among her summer correspondents.

Jennie embraced her studies and extracurricular activities. She was vice-president of her freshman-year class, active in the McGill YWCA as treasurer in 1904, and membership convener in 1906. The YWCA reinforced her emerging interests in Protestant social activism as its goal of "keeping our good girls good," directed at young, urban women living outside family and religious supervision, by providing wholesome recreation and service opportunities. Like her older sister, Jennie also served as president of the prestigious literary and debating society,

Delta Sigma, in her final year. At her first meeting as president, she was so nervous that she claimed she shook "the chair almost to splinters."[22] She participated in debates on the organization of domestic labour or whether all higher education should be free and under state control, and read papers on nineteenth-century British politicians. In the 1904 debate on higher education, future preoccupations became evident. Perhaps not surprisingly, considering her own circumstances, she began with the financial advantages but argued that free access to university would be of great advantage to both the state and the individual. She claimed that putting university within the "reach of all" would open the doors to talent, since "Geniuses came usually from among the working classes."[23]

Jennie Barnes Wisdom was not a brilliant student. In her first year, she followed a course of English, history, Greek, Latin, math, and physics. Latin, math, and physics were an obvious challenge as she received final marks of 54, 51, and 38, respectively. Her second year was more successful, and she added botany and zoology, and logic and psychology, to her studies. Her third courses at McGill focused on English composition, Greek, philosophy, and political science, while in her final year she studied English, English composition, history of philosophy, and political science.[24] Twenty-five years later, she recalled that she yearned for more classics, philosophy, and English literature than her first two years offered. She claimed never to regret taking, in her third and fourth years, Greek and philosophy courses, even though it meant working harder to make up economics courses, which she felt were important but lacking in her field of professional work. She graduated in 1907 with a BA, Second Class.[25] Political science courses had an enormous impact on her life. Her third-year instructor was probably Stephen Leacock, best remembered today as a humorist but then known as a leading political economist and prominent public speaker. Jennie Wisdom, like other young RVC women, may have had a crush on her handsome professor, even though he opposed women in the classroom. For the rest of Leacock's life, Jane Wisdom clipped newspaper accounts of his speeches, and she saved a personal note from him agreeing to speak at an RVC function. On the back of his note, in Jane's handwriting, is "Stevie Leacock."[26]

In her final year at McGill, the university hired Joseph Clarence Hemmeon as a sessional lecturer in economics and political science. Hemmeon was a fellow Nova Scotian and a recent graduate from Harvard, where he had completed a history degree. Hemmeon was also far to the left of his conservative colleague Leacock in his theoretical orientation, and he has been described as both a "declared socialist" and a liberal.[27] It was probably in her course with Hemmeon that Wisdom first encountered professional social work. Unsatisfied with the library material available for an essay entitled "Poverty and Pauperism" on the history of the English "social service movement," she arranged a meeting with Richard Lane, general secretary of the Montreal Charity Organization Society. Lane not only supplied her with research material but, through his encouragement of her interest in the agency, also set her off on a lifelong career.[28]

If Hemmeon introduced Jane to socialist ideas, they were not the only new ideas she was encountering. Clipped speeches, offprints of articles by Stephen Leacock written after she left McGill, and newspaper accounts of Professor Ernest W. MacBride's addresses on evolution were also saved among her personal papers. We do not know if Jennie attended the February 1906 McGill appearance by African-American leader Booker Washington, described as "a tremendous gathering of students and a most memorable piece of oratory." We do know, however, that in October 1906, Jennie heard Rudyard Kipling speak at RVC. She was not entirely impressed, as she described him as a "small, spare, ugly man older than I expected."[29] University and Montreal's intellectual opportunities both reinforced Wisdom's view of the world and, at the same time, presented some challenges.

Even though she was now away from home, family remained a source of comfort, support, and worry. In Jane's first year in Montreal, Katie joined the staff of the Presbyterian Ottawa Ladies College but appears to have been a frequent visitor to Montreal, and the two girls spent the Christmas vacation together.[30] In 1904, younger sister Bessie was able to join Jane at RVC. Perhaps Katie and brother Roy's earnings made this possible, and I have long suspected the financial contribution of Aunt Jessie McQueen, recently returned to Sutherland's River after teaching in British Columbia, who, twenty years later, Jane would take to England. Like Katie and Jennie, Bessie became involved in the McGill YWCA and gained a reputation for hard work in her studies. A Saint John paper heralded her academic success, noting the previous success of Katie but saying nothing of Jane, and a McGill student publication poked fun at her work ethic:

> Six freshette undergrads,
> Very much alive,
> Bessie died of overstudy,
> Then there were five.[31]

For Jennie and Bessie, money was always tight. University sports events could cost as much as 50 cents and, unless complimentary tickets were available, they went without. It is unknown if Jennie's residential bursary lasted more than one year, and it remains unclear how the Wisdoms managed at all with both Bessie and Jennie at college. By the spring of 1906, the strain was too great for everyone. In March, acting RVC warden Susan Cameron helped Jane arrange for a summer position as a lady's companion for Louisa Archibald Wilson's mother, Harriet Cheney Archibald, offering her intimate insight into elite anglophone Montreal society.[32] Jennie thus spent the late spring and early summer in Vermont and Cascapedia, Quebec, and may have come back for her final year with some contribution to her educational expenses. Cameron thought, at the end of December 1905, that Bessie was showing "nervous strain" from her work, and endorsed the decision for her to remain home for the 1906–07 academic year as "means and strength [were] both over strained." From England, Hilda Oakeley also supported the decision that Bessie return for her final two years to graduate with the class of '09.[33]

Oakeley's interim replacement, Susan Cameron, was one of two Maritime women who taught at Royal Victoria College during the Wisdom girls' tenure. Only Katie benefited from direct contact with the other, Annie Marion MacLean. MacLean was the daughter of a Baptist minister. Born in 1870 in Prince Edward Island, she graduated from Acadia University, earning an AB in 1893 and an AM in 1894. She then enrolled in sociology at the University of Chicago, where she was awarded both a PhM (1897) and PhD (1900). Her doctoral work on the Acadians of Nova Scotia is lost, but she pursued her master's research on women and work for the rest of her career. In 1900, after being perhaps the first Canadian to receive any kind of formal social work education at the New York School of Philanthropy, she moved to Montreal and taught history and economics at RVC. Katie Wisdom would have been one of her students. She left Montreal after one year to become professor of sociology and economics, and dean of women, at Stetson University in Florida. Between 1907 and 1910, she and a team of researchers put together the important 1910 publication *Wage Earning Women*. Although McGill did not have a sociology department until 1922, Annie Marion MacLean offered her RVC students a direct, early link with the Chicago School of Sociology and the New York College Settlement.[34]

Susan Cameron was also from Saint John, and graduated from McGill with an MA in 1899. Her academic reputation earned her the position of first English tutor at RVC. She was appointed a lecturer in the Department of English from 1902 to 1912 and assistant professor until 1918. When Hilda Oakeley left RVC in 1905, Susan Cameron was named acting warden until the January 1907 arrival of new Warden Ethel Hurlbatt.[35] Cameron played a leadership role in the Girls' Club and Lunch Room, and the University Settlement, and served as vice-warden until, in 1918, she married University Bursar Walter Vaughan. Widowed in 1922, she returned to serve as acting warden in 1928 and was named warden in 1931, a position she held until her retirement in 1937. Cameron may not have known the Wisdoms in Saint John, but there is no question that she took a personal and lively interest in them upon their arrival in Montreal and that she maintained a close relationship with Jane throughout the 1930s. She appears to have taken particular pleasure in her relationship with Relief Williams, Katie's daughter, who later resided at RVC in the 1930s.

Jennie's time at RVC gives us some sense of her character. In the *Old McGill* 1907 yearbook, beside a serious photo of Wisdom, is the quote "True as the needle to the pole." In January 1904, Hilda Oakeley wrote Mary Bell Wisdom about Jennie's health and how she was getting along. Mrs. Wisdom had told Oakeley that "Jennie was not very strong," but Oakeley thought that Katherine and Jennie, who had spent the Christmas vacation together in Montreal, were both looking well. Oakeley told Mary Bell that it was in Jennie's character always to "err on the side of doing too much, never the opposite" and that it was "students such as she is, who help to build up the character and spirit of College life and work, which we most want to create." Oakeley concluded that she had originally been interested in Jennie as "a sister of Katherine. Now I know Jennie, and am, of course, interested in her, for herself."[36]

The most candid assessments of Jane Wisdom's character probably came from Cameron, who, as acting warden, recorded character notes on most of the college girls. Many assessments were not generous but Jane's certainly was. Jennie demonstrated "self reliance in a nature already anxious and responsible. Capable, self-exacting, but not harsh or austere – solid though not brilliant, orderly and methodical with excellent disposition and influence." Bessie did not fare as well. Cameron observed that Jane's "same influences … working on a nature less strong and more artistic have produced a slightly pathetic type – gentle and a little inclined to self-pity but is likely to strengthen."[37]

Just before graduation, Cameron wrote a final assessment of Jane's character, hinting at the financial anxiety she carried. Cameron wrote that Jane was "as last year but still further developed by study, reflection and alas sorrow. Looking ill and sad and more responsible than ever. Will probably improve in health after the final exams and enjoy peace of mind with the self respect of wage earning."[38] While Cameron confidently foretold of future careers for other graduates, there was no such suggestion for Jennie, other than the obvious point that she would need to earn her living.

Cameron also referred to Jane's tremendous sadness. On 13 November 1906, at the age of twenty-four, her brother Roy died of typhoid fever in Port Arthur, Ontario, where he had been working nearby on a railway survey. According to one obituary, the young man had "shown great aptitude for engineering work." When his parents in Saint John were notified of his illness, Freeman Wisdom started immediately for northwest Ontario but word of Roy's death arrived when he reached Montreal. Free was at least able to accompany Katie and Jennie back to their home in New Brunswick. When Roy's body arrived, it was accompanied by Rev. Daniel Fraser, now principal of Montreal's Presbyterian College, who later attended the funeral and preached a memorial sermon to his former congregation. The sermon may have given comfort to the family and it spoke to Jane's interest in service. Rev. Fraser claimed that a "life's usefulness" was not to be evaluated by its "length but by the good that was done."[39]

By 7 December, Jane had returned to Montreal and was preparing for exams, but her life had by no means returned to normal.[40] The memorial service's message of "life's usefulness" coincided with graduation, and she was, no doubt, thinking about her own future purpose. The idea of evaluating a life based on "the good that was done" resonated with Wisdom. It reinforced messages she had received from her upbringing regarding Christian service, her interactions with Hilda Oakeley and the culture of female service among McGill alumnae, and her philosophy courses dealing with British idealism and citizenship.

The role and significance of British idealism have been a matter of debate among Canadian historians. In *A Disciplined Intelligence: Critical Inquiry and Canadian Thought in the Victorian Era*, A.B. McKillop emphasized the importance of John Watson of Queen's University as Canada's greatest Christian idealist. Sara Burke also recognized the centrality of idealism in her study of the development of social service at the University of Toronto until the 1920s, while historians Barry Ferguson, Nancy Christie, and Michael Gauvreau have downplayed its importance in favour of new political economy and social evangelism. Idealism, with its focus on progress, social responsibility, and concern for others, attempted to reconcile individuality with the need to find meaning within a wider collective community. It encouraged adherents to realize their "higher selves" by serving others, thus fostering a collective form of liberalism.[41] Susan Pedersen has argued that female students "already accustomed to subordinate personal desire to various definitions of 'duty' were especially susceptible to the idealist movement and gave it a 'new lease on life'." At RVC, the link was direct, for Oakeley's Oxford tutor had been Edward Caird of Balliol, who was at the centre of the British movement and, according to Oakeley, transformed philosophical study to active citizenship.[42] Through the influence of Oakeley, the women of RVC were interested in *both* Christianizing and Canadianizing the growing population, combining Anglo-British democratic values and Protestant idealism. The unquestioning and unreflective emphasis on assimilation to this culture was remarkable in a predominantly Catholic city, which was also the largest French-speaking city in the world outside France.

The tradition of service for female undergraduates at McGill dated back to 1889, when the first women graduates of McGill formed the Mu Iota Society (it changed its name the following year to the Alumnae Society). In May 1891, the society began a Girls' Club and Lunch Room. The provision of a decent and affordable place where young working women might have lunch and a club that might provide a more uplifting and respectable environment than lonely rooming houses or commercial entertainment was a reform current in many American cities at that time.[43] The Lunch Room was a success, but the response to the Girls' Club was decidedly more tepid. During the winter months, evening classes were offered in singing, dressmaking, cooking, English literature, gymnastics, and Bible study, but, with the exception of singing and Bible study, offered by the Anglican Circle of King's Daughters, attendance was very low.[44]

The poor response to the Girls' Club must have been especially disappointing because the alumnae hoped to establish a settlement house. The settlement movement originated in London, England, in the 1870s when an East End clergyman began to encourage Oxford and Cambridge students to "settle" for their vacations or for a period after graduation in the city slums to see conditions for themselves and to live among the poor as neighbours. Toynbee Hall was the first settlement house, and it was quickly followed by others, both sectarian and independent from religious organizations. Americans in London visited the settlement houses and brought the idea first to New York, then to Chicago and Boston. In 1886, American college graduate Jane Addams visited Toynbee Hall. Upon returning home to Chicago, she established Hull House in 1889 with other female friends. Hull House was a mixed-sex institution (future Prime Minister William Lyon Mackenzie King was among its residents) but others, such as the University (male) and College (female) settlements of New York's Lower East Side, remained single sex. The settlement ideal upheld and celebrated the notions that "all should share in community" and that social divisions might be overcome through rich and poor residing in an interdependent community. Volunteer middle-class settlement workers would live in poor urban districts. Through friendship and personal relations, they hoped to share knowledge and culture with their working-class and often new immigrant neighbours. Keeping with the spirit of British idealism, settlement workers hoped to find meaning in serving these communities, experiencing a kind of solidarity in living for others.

As early as 1895–96, addresses on settlement work "by outstanding leaders from the United States" were hosted by the Alumnae Society. In December 1899, the society hosted prominent settlement worker Graham Taylor of Chicago Commons.[45] The topic of establishing a college settlement came before the Alumnae Society again in December 1901. McGill alumna Helen Reid led the discussion, and Hilda Oakeley proposed that the society "take some steps in a practical direction" by sending delegates to represent RVC on the newly formed Montreal "child saving committee." A year later, the question was first officially raised about "altering the character" of the Girls' Club and Lunch Room by moving it to another neighbourhood where larger work was needed. It was "the general feeling of the meeting" that while the Lunch Room had filled a need and continued to service those working in the area, if the Alumnae Society sought the "practical results" possible in a college settlement, it would need to relocate from a business area to a "district of workers' homes."[46]

As the work with factory girls faltered, there was simultaneously an increased emphasis on work with children. Jennie Wisdom's arrival in Montreal in 1903 coincided with the establishment of the King's Club for boys and girls. Work with children had begun as a special Christmas event but expanded as a practical means to assimilate immigrant children and, by proxy, their families into English-Canadian Christian culture.[47]

With this expanded interest in children, the Alumnae Society continued to question if the Girls' Club and Lunch Room was the best use of its efforts. During this uncertain time, Jennie Wisdom was a student volunteer at the Saturday lunch.[48] But the number of meals served continued to fall and the cost of operating continuously increased, so, in January 1905, the society decided to discontinue the Lunch Room. The Alumnae Society continued the King's Club and Christmas work among children.[49] Almost immediately, the Protestant Board of School Commissioners was approached for the use of Dufferin School as premises, moving the Alumnae Society's focus east towards boulevard Saint-Laurent. This area was what the *McGill News* would later describe as "the heart of Montreal's foreign quarter, on the western fringe of the 'red light district,' and in the notorious No. 5 police district."[50]

The idea of the settlement remained the most constant theme at regular monthly alumnae meetings as settlement-like programs developed under the auspices of a Neighbourhood Club. Support was building outside the Alumnae Society: the Women's Canadian Club hosted prominent activist Lillian Wald of the New York Henry Street Settlement, who spoke in December on the "Social Value of the Settlement."[51] The McGill University Neighbourhood Club Workers' Committee representative, librarian Elizabeth G. Hall, addressed the alumnae in February 1909 on what "has already been done by the way of a foundation for a University Settlement." She also spoke on settlement work in Boston, suggesting earlier experience there.[52]

In early 1909, the McGill Young Men's Christian Association formally joined the Neighbourhood Club, bringing men into the project. One of the men, Mr. Williams, a McGill graduate – presumably Katie's fiancé – wrote a play performed in aid of the building fund. Another fundraising project was the establishment of an alumnae bulletin. The periodical was intended to keep in touch with out-of-town graduates and to help solicit support in the society's social service work.[53]

Finally, in January 1910, the Alumnae Society and McGill University Neighbourhood Club created a Settlement Committee. The Montreal Local Council of Women invited Sadie American, executive secretary of the American National Council of Jewish Women, to lecture on settlement work to assist in the foundation of the local project. American's Montreal lecture coincided with an upswing in general interest with the settlement house movement. Jane Addams's international bestseller, *Twenty-Five Years at Hull-House*, was first published that year, and 1910 saw the opening of the University Settlement in Toronto.[54] The invitation of a prominent American Jewish woman to promote a settlement project strongly tied to Protestant cultural elites is remarkable, and it did not go over well with all settlement supporters. Although Susan Cameron considered the talk "good," she did not think it was likely "to bring an actual settlement much nearer. The audience was largely Jewish, in sympathy with the very Jewish speaker."[55] She was wrong, however: two weeks after Sadie American's talk, the Settlement Committee arranged to rent a house facing Dufferin Square.

The move towards the settlement and the development of allies outside the Alumnae Society were connected to the arrival of James A. Dale in Montreal. Dale became the most important man to support the project. Months after Jennie Wisdom graduated, Dale was hired as McGill's first professor of education. In her characteristically candid and pessimistic fashion, Susan Cameron wrote that "One hopes well for the new chair but the wisdom of the selection seems more than doubtful."[56] Dale, who was educated at Mason College (Birmingham) and Merton College (Oxford), was a central figure in English Montreal's reform community until his departure to the University of Toronto in 1920. He played a leading role in the settlement but also in creating the McGill School of Physical Training, the McGill Department of Social Service, the City Improvement League, and the 1912 Child Welfare Exhibition. The Montreal Social Workers' Club began in one of his classes, and his emphasis on community-based education meant that his influence extended beyond the university. One admirer described him as "a scholar who is not scholastic, and an idealist who is not an ideologist, a professor who is not professorial." In England, he had been one of the founding members of the Workers' Education Association and worked with the Oxford Extension Delegacy from 1902 to 1908. Some accounts also state that he spent some time as a resident in England's most famous settlement, Toynbee Hall.[57]

With the important exception of Dale, the financial support of Dr. Milton Hersey, and the moral support of Protestant clergy, women seemed to dominate the enterprise.[58] Jennie Wisdom was among these women. She had returned to Montreal in January 1909 and, through her alumnae connections, began volunteering with a club for girls aged twelve to sixteen. When the settlement elected its first executive committee, Wisdom was in the position of recording secretary. She remained active in both these capacities for the next two years and, along with a Victorian Order of Nurses nurse, was one of the initial residents, boarding at the settlement September 1910 through June 1911.[59]

Wisdom had previous experience with this kind of undertaking, having already stayed at New York's most important women's settlement, the College Settlement in the Lower East Side, for June 1910. This transnational experience was common. Both the Alumnae Society and the Montreal settlement movement had many ties to international networks. At RVC, both Hilda Oakeley and Ethel Hurlbatt linked college women to British movements. Active associate members of the Alumnae Society included J.A. Dale's wife Margaret Butler, a graduate of the University of London, and Elisabeth Anthony Dexter, a Columbia graduate and the wife of Charity Organization Society (COS) secretary R.C. Dexter. All were experienced in social work and settlements before coming to Montreal.[60] Richard Lane, the Montreal COS general secretary between 1902 and 1910, became interested in social problems after living in London's Oxford House Settlement and later the University Settlement in New York. The same was true for Dale in London and for Howard Falk, the nephew of Toynbee Hall's namesake, who came to Montreal in 1919 with residency at Christadora House in New York City on his resumé. Settlement experience fundamentally influenced the direction of these people's professional careers in social work. Furthermore, between the mid-1890s and the 1920s, nearly every prominent settlement worker in the United States and Britain spoke in Montreal. While Jane Addams never did visit, notwithstanding her invitation, American settlement worker Sara Libby Carson spent several months in the city.[61]

It should, therefore, not be surprising to find the Montreal settlement within the mainstream of settlement practices and thought. A fundraising brochure from 1911 reveals how the settlement presented its mission. The emphasis was clearly on children rather than adults, helping those from fifteen different nationalities and many creeds "to become good, intelligent, friendly citizens. Such citizens, realizing the privilege and responsibility of citizenship, will become the City's greatest asset." Along this line, additional work was done with mothers and infants. But there were always tensions and contradictions. This work was not supposed to be charitable, but, although the pamphlet boasted that every children's club paid its own way, donations were needed for facilities and the salaries of two paid workers. Ten years later, a promotional article would describe the settlement's "great task" in the seemingly contradictory objectives of interpreting "Canadian standards and ideals to the foreign-born" and assisting "the people ... towards self-expression."[62] This broad mandate was frustrating for people such as Susan Cameron, who felt that "many things are not satisfactory about this rather undefined institution and that there is something dangerous in the attitude of persistent optimism of the leaders."[63]

For others, such as Dale, the objects were absolutely clear: help neighbours, promote "true and strong Canadian citizenship" in all children, create a study centre to launch an investigation of modern urban problems, and provide a residence and club for all interested in social work. Dale envisioned the settlement as

> a centre for the student of social and economic conditions. Just as in England students of great social reforms have found their inspiration in the settlement centres so may it be here. It was in the settlement clubs of London that conditions leading up to the Workmen's Compensation Act, the Child Labor Act, the Poor Law, and many such reforms were studied in actual conditions. So may the university student here take advantage of the social conditions of Canada. Practical examples of life among the poorer classes – the very living of life of the people to be helped – may be taken advantage of.[64]

While the University Settlement was not going to become the centre for social reform in Quebec, given that it excluded the majority population, Dale was at least successful in bringing together individuals in the English-speaking community who were interested in social work. Beginning in 1913, the Montreal Social Workers Club offered a series of winter lectures by various workers connected to McGill, the YMCA, the COS, and the settlements.[65]

Efforts to develop citizenship were intended to be "entirely non-sectarian." Many children of the neighbourhood were either Jewish or Roman Catholic, and it was important that all children be able to "take full and free advantage of the facilities offered ... entirely protected from interference with their religious faith." Back in 1910, RVC Warden Ethel Hurlbatt had reminded the Settlement Committee of its duty "to safeguard certain characteristics" of the society, particularly the settlement's non-sectarianism. The Girls' Club and Lunch Room, with its Bible study, hymn singing, and extensive celebration of Christmas, could not sustain this claim, nor could its successor. When, in 1908, the suggestion was made that Christmas not be celebrated, a worker defended the sectarian practice, pointing out that "the children seemed to be expecting it."[66] Indeed, notwithstanding religious beliefs, the prospect of toys, sweets, and a banquet may have been cherished by many. The non-sectarian ideal was in constant conflict. Public perception mirrored the title of an article in the *Herald* proclaiming "University Settlement, Where Real Christian Work Is Done." Still, the settlement attempted to put forward its non-sectarian face by emphasizing the presence of Christian and Jewish volunteers and the participation of Chinese children in its programs.[67]

The early years of the settlement were rocky and peaked in 1914 with a great division between Dale's idealism and those more interested in assimilation, who included the wife of the primary donor. The compromise was for both warring sides to approach Jane Wisdom, now living in New York, to offer her the position of head resident. She declined.[68]

The University Settlement was not the only Montreal settlement attempted or created at this time. In the spring of 1911, another group of English-speaking Montrealers launched the Iverley Settlement on Richmond Square, and recruited head resident Margaret Tree, who had ten years' experience in mission work in South London, providing yet another direct link to the British movement. With its emphasis on non-sectarian service, it had the support of prominent English-Montreal philanthropists such as Herbert S. Holt, Jeffrey Burland, Sir Hugh Graham, and Frederick Meredith.[69] Moreover, it had the crucial financial support of at least some of the city's English-speaking Catholics in a rare example of Catholic–Protestant co-operation. This included Blanche Duchesnay Wotherspoon, who subsidized the settlement with her late husband's estate.[70]

Not all Montreal settlements were even nominally non-sectarian. In the fall of 1912, just months after the establishment of their first settlement house in Toronto, the Presbyterians established Chalmers House in the city's working-class East End. Chalmers House was one of thousands of denominationally supported settlements to be established in North American cities and was organized by Canada's settlement house pioneer, Sara Libby Carson. Led by Carson and Wisdom's former Saint John minister, Daniel Fraser, now the principal of Presbyterian College and founding chairman of Chalmers House's Management Committee, a building was leased and three "New York experts" arrived to take up residence. These "ladies" were instructed to organize "gymnastic and club work" that was to be "almost entirely focused on the women and children of the district."[71]

From the outset, Fraser hoped that the settlement would provide an opportunity for theology students to come into contact with workers and immigrants and learn directly about social problems. It had an evangelical social service mission that Fraser conceived as a response to immigration and the relocation of many congregations to the suburbs. In following their members, these congregations left the city "centre barren of any religious influences." In the absence of religious influence, Chalmers House sought to meet the "physical, social and intellectual needs of the community."[72]

There was a strong emphasis on Canadianization; indeed, these settlements played a role in the Anglo-Canadian nationalist project. As with the Iverley Settlement, there was no apparent contradiction in Chalmers House's being directed by an immigrant, in this case an American Quaker. The "immigrant problem" strictly referred to the working class. A photo in an early annual report was subtitled with the caption "I pledge allegiance to my flag, and to the British Empire for which it stands, one nation indivisible, with Liberty and Justice for all." This nationalist theme was reinforced inside by children's club names that included patriotic and royal titles, such as the Queen Mary Club, the Patricia Club, the Royal Young Canadians, the Young Citizens Club, and the Patriots' Athletic Club. Citizenship training was emphasized through democratic practices, with all clubs holding "regular business meetings on the self-governing plans" with elected officers. Even young children were exposed to these ideas, as the "tots" in the kindergarten not only had the opportunity to learn "songs, games and simple forms of handwork," but also "the lessons of courtesy, obedience and self-control."[73]

Except for their façades of non-sectarianism, Chalmers House did not differ greatly from the University or Iverley settlements. Like the University Settlement, Chalmers House had the co-operation of public bodies. For example, the Protestant School Commissioners granted the use of the yard at Lansdowne School and the municipality provided a grant for a summer milk station. The solely English-language publicity used rhetoric direct from the settlement movement, celebrating "co-operation" and the "personal opportunity of knowing our neighbours in a neighbourly fashion, ... working out with them the problems of life."[74] By 1923, Chalmers House boasted a resident staff of five and seventy-five volunteers, and about 800 families represented through 1,461 "registered members." The 1917 establishment of St. Columba House, a second Presbyterian Montreal settlement in the working-class district of Point Saint Charles, further attests to the movement's growing momentum.[75]

The tradition of female social service was at work at Chalmers House, with its all-female staff. There was frequent turnover among the women, and relatively few appear to have been college graduates. The lack of locally trained personnel meant that many residents had no previous connection to Montreal and Quebec upon arrival, but house residents Charlotte Whitton and Ethel Dodds would come to dominate Canadian social work during the interwar years.[76]

English-speaking Montreal operated other organizations that possessed some settlement-like aspects. The Old Brewery Mission offered community programs and an evangelical social service staff in residence, in addition to a hostel for homeless men. Although it was not residential, the Nazareth Street Boys' Club, established in 1908 and later renamed the Griffintown Boys' Club, offered various community programs.[77] More intriguing was an informal settlement, the Montreal Mission for Friendless Girls, established by reformed prostitute Maimie Pinzer Jones in rooms rented on Ontario Street West, within blocks of the original location of the Girls' Club and Lunch Room. This project offered tea, club space, magazines, and emergency shelter, and was supported by Pinzer Jones's American reform connections, including reformer Lillian Wald in New York.[78] The existence of individual projects such as this alerts us to the possibility that many service missions existed in the city.

The more orthodox settlement movement continued to grow after the First World War, although Chalmers House shut its doors in 1925, following the creation of the United Church of Canada. During the 1920s, two additional settlements were established in the city, the Negro Community Centre in Little Burgundy in 1925 and Neighbourhood House on Laval Street in 1927. Both settlements were instigated from within their own communities by founders who may have felt unwelcome by other institutions. Although Neighbourhood House was officially non-sectarian, almost all its membership was Jewish and it was financed by the Federation of Jewish Philanthropies. It is doubtful if this institution achieved any more detachment from Jewish values than the University Settlement did from Protestant Montreal.[79]

What is most remarkable about the Wisdom girls' experience at McGill and later replicated in the settlement movement in Montreal is the extent to which the majority French-speaking population was rendered completely invisible by the records. Indeed, with a children's club named after the British monarch and the high visibility of the Imperial Order of the Daughters of the Empire, one might never imagine that Montreal was not an English-speaking city. This was indeed a world of two solitudes. With the sole exception of Katie's observation of McGill–Laval students rioting during the South Africa War, one could easily imagine her living in a linguistic world no different from Saint John, New Brunswick. There was no mention of Montreal's French-speaking inhabitants except in Daniel Fraser's suggestion that Montrealers were perhaps slower to address the immigrant problem because of their preoccupation with "the question of the relations between the English and French populations."[80] Throughout her life, Jane Wisdom clipped articles from newspapers, many of which ended up in the McGill University archives. It is interesting that the final clipping in her collection covers the 1969 McGill français demonstration, a movement to bring McGill University, the bastion of English-speaking Montreal, into francophone society.

Jane Wisdom had a long involvement with the settlement movement. She was among the first residents of the Montreal University Settlement, and an active volunteer and member of the Board of Management. After she left Montreal, in New York, she lived in both the Rivington Street College Settlement and Brooklyn's Trinity House. In Halifax, the Community House was among her proudest achievements, and in Glace Bay, the establishment of community-based playgrounds would offer her particular satisfaction. Throughout her long career, she never strayed far from the values of female social service she acquired as an undergraduate. By embracing both the co-operative neighbourliness of the settlement movement and scientific philanthropy, Wisdom reminds us that these two branches of welfare service were never as distinct as subsequent historians might have us believe.

Chapter Three

Montreal: Charity, Philanthropy, and Social Service, 1903–1912

Until after the Second World War, Montreal was Canada's largest city and its commercial and financial centre. At the turn of the twentieth century, it attracted tens of thousands of immigrants – primarily British – to jobs in its vibrant industrial and transportation sectors. Montreal historian William Atherton boasted that between 1901 and 1911, Montreal moved from being the ninety-sixth to the twenty-sixth largest city in the world, achieving a place between Boston and Brussels in terms of population size. It held the honour of being the largest metropolis among the self-governing Dominions of the Empire and the largest French-speaking city outside France. But Atherton, and reformers like him, were also preoccupied with the consequences of rapid growth: urban poverty, poor housing, and child welfare.[1] Montreal cannot be overlooked as being central to understanding the development of social welfare in English-speaking Canada. It was the subject of early Canadian sociological investigations such as Herbert Brown Ames's 1897 *City Below the Hill* and social novels such as *A Little Life* and *Looking Forward*, which described "districts that would have fairly turned the stomach of an East Londoner, or a denizen of the Cowgate."[2] Jane Wisdom took advantage of emergent opportunities within the Montreal English-language reform community's interest in scientific philanthropy to launch her career in professional social service. While it is almost impossible to catch glimpses of her activities at this time, exploring the groundwork of English Montreal's charitable and philanthropic organizations uncovers the roots of social service and its early integration into American formal and informal philanthropic networks, and introduces individuals who had a profound effect on Wisdom's career.

Montreal's day-to-day power relations reflected Canada's colonial past. While not all anglophones were wealthy, Montreal was economically dominated by an English-speaking minority. The Anglo-Protestants of Montreal were unlike their compatriots in Toronto, whose experience has been too often universalized to the distortion of English Canadian history. Anglo-Protestant Montrealers, for example, tended to be Anglican rather than Methodist, and Montreal Methodists were not wealthy, but among the poorest Protestant denominations in the city.[3] As the Methodist Church was the denomination most closely association with evangelical reform and the social gospel in Canada, a weak Methodist Church in the city meant English-speaking Montrealers may have been less influenced by the social gospel than their Toronto compatriots. The social gospel was present, but English Montrealers were just as likely to be attracted to charitable reform through calls for progressivism, and were in keeping with major trends in the North American voluntary charitable associations. For example, the Montreal Society for the Protection of Women and Children was organized in 1882, only seven years after the New York Society for the Prevention of Cruelty to Children.[4] Montreal also took the lead in Canadian service organizations such as the Victorian Order of Nurses. In 1914, for example, 71 of its 232 nurses in Canada – or nearly one third – were working in that city.[5] Montreal's English-speaking philanthropic reform community was closely associated with the local women's movement and shared its personnel, tactics, and frustrations.

The centrality of Montreal to English Canadians must be kept in mind in understanding the close connection between Maritimers such as Jane Wisdom and the city. It may have been with considerable regret that, after graduating in May 1907, with Bessie back at McGill, Jane Wisdom returned to Saint John to help keep house with her mother. Without resources for domestics, Mary Bell Wisdom may have needed a daughter's labour. Katie remained in Montreal, combining her position teaching at the Trafalgar Institute, a Presbyterian elite private school for girls, with graduate courses in French, while Bessie finished her degree at Royal Victoria College. In March 1908, Bessie wrote her Saint John family that she would like to find a teaching position for the summer, but if "Jen has dreams of a job in the holiday, I would enjoy nothing better than keeping house."[6] The Wisdom girls understood that a daughter's obligation did not end with a completed BA. When Freeman and Mary Bell moved to New Glasgow, Nova Scotia, in January 1909, Jane was finally free to return to Montreal and pursue her own career. Years later, she recounted: "At the time there was not much for a woman to do in the line of a profession outside of teaching and nursing, and neither appealed to me. While I was studying, I learned of the history of the English movement of social service. This country had no background in this area. I was taking inspiration from England and to some extent, from the United States."[7] As Wisdom moved towards a career in social service, she was aware that she was participating in an international movement. She also understood that social service, as it existed in Canada at that time, involved no specific training. In the view of many, a social worker's services did not differ substantially from those of a nurse or a nun.

On 15 January 1909, at 9:30 a.m., Jane Wisdom reported to the Montreal Charity Organization on Bleury Street, where she had been engaged as one of its first paid visitors. With almost no orientation, she started her first case investigation that same afternoon, and, within eighteen months, had risen to the position of assistant general secretary.[8] For three years, Wisdom worked at English-speaking Montreal's most important welfare agency. While her specific actions were often invisible to the historian's eye, at the time, she had front-row seats to witness English Montreal's position at the crossroads of British and American scientific charity and the particular role women played in its development. While Bessie and Katie followed a traditionally female occupation and taught school, Jane Wisdom took advantage of what appeared to be a new opportunity for women.[9]

In fact, social service at this time was less a new career than it was an extension of work already being performed by religious women and female volunteers. Unlike New Brunswick, Quebec did not have a poor law. There was no statutory state responsibility requiring communities to care for their indigent paupers. In Quebec, poverty was deemed a moral rather than legal issue. Charity was administered primarily by confessional institutions and private societies. These organizations sometimes received municipal and provincial grants, and they tended to provide residential care, small cash grants, or aid in kind such as food, coal, and clothing. In addition to this thriving informal and voluntary sector, there were also modern bureaucratic solutions, such as the Municipal Department of Social Assistance and the Charity Organization Society.

But most charity in Montreal was ad hoc and private, and took place at the level of the individual. Certainly, the harsh winter climate prompted individual compassion from many citizens. British immigrant Hilda Oakeley recounted that "housing may be an almost more imperative need than food in the Canadian winter."[10] When professional social service worker Francis McLean arrived in Montreal in 1900, he observed that the "seasonal idea of 'charity' has a pretty strong hold here" and that "almost any one of the right religion, and who does not appear before the board of a society in a drunken condition, is sure of getting relief, which invariably means a package of groceries each week, and a quarter ton of coal or a quarter cord of wood each three weeks, whether there be one or six in the family." On the other hand, McLean noted elsewhere that while relief was abundant during the cold weather, during the summer, it was "extremely difficult to secure anything."[11]

In addition to individual private actions, national societies abounded. The St. George's, St. Andrew's, and St. Patrick's societies, serving the English, Scottish, and Irish communities, all dated back to 1834 and originated with charitable objectives. A Germany Society was established in 1835, the Irish Protestant Benevolent Society in 1856, Young Men's Hebrew Benevolent Society in 1863, and the St. David's Welsh Society in 1884. By 1914, there was also a Newfoundland Society, the Société Suisse de Montréal, the Scandinavian National Society, and the Jersey Society, in addition to established kin societies among the Chinese community.[12] Significantly, the most important national society for francophone Catholics, the Société Saint-Jean-Baptiste, did not engage primarily in benevolent activities, as this work was left to the parish. In almost all cases, philanthropic objectives reinforced and were integrated with social activities. This was not the case only for national societies. One of the great annual events of the Montreal anglophone elite was the Charity Ball, where descriptions of attendees and their dresses received much more attention than did the object of fundraising.[13]

As Montreal was Canada's largest city, it is not surprising that there was a large number of private agencies and institutions serving various needs. William Atherton claimed that in 1914, Montreal was home to 150 churches and 72 public and private hospitals and asylums.[14] With important exceptions, charitable institutions and agencies were strictly divided along confessional and usually linguistic lines. These divisions were not only bureaucratic but also reflected distinct cultural and theological attitudes and responses to poverty. In her study of religion and charity in Boston, Susan Traverso has argued that while Protestants had a more "individualistic view of social relations," holding that "the market economy provided opportunities for economic independence for men and perhaps women," Catholics and Jews were more likely to see capitalism as a "system of dependency than independence. They did not see self-sufficiency as either possible or necessary."[15]

The largest philanthropic infrastructure was associated with the Catholic Church, but even this community was fragmented, as distinct institutions, orders, and agencies often served the Montreal French- and English-speaking Catholic communities. The most important association for both communities was the St. Vincent de Paul Society, which operated at the level of fifty-four parish conferences. Professional, secular social workers generally approved of the society's approach, which emphasized confidentiality and personal visitation before the provision of relief. At the parish level, most congregations operated parochial sewing circles that sewed clothing for children of the poor. They hoped it would encourage these children to attend school and be well dressed for first communion. Religious orders such as the Sisters of Providence and the Grey Nuns visited the poor in their homes, and parishes such as St. Helen's offered the special services of two nuns from the Congregation of Daughters of Wisdom to visit the parish poor. The 1911 *Handbook of Catholic Charitable and Social Works in Montreal* also noted that food was distributed at almost all convents, colleges, and institutions to a regular clientele.[16]

Within Montreal, the Catholic Church and its various orders operated scores of specialized facilities covering every aspect of health care and social services from birth to death. To educate the laity about local social problems, the Jesuits organized English-speaking Catholics into the Catholic Social Study Guild and French-speaking Catholics into L'école sociale populaire.[17]

With few exceptions, French-speaking institutions were all under the direction of the church. Three important exceptions were Notre-Dame and Sainte-Justine hospitals and Assistance Publique, organized by lay French Catholic leadership in 1904. Originally directed at women and children, Assistance Publique offered shelter to residents of Montreal regardless of nationality but "especially French Canadians," probably much in the same way that institutions such as the Royal Victoria Hospital, also open to all races and creeds, was strongly associated with the anglophone community.[18]

The general wealth of the English Protestants also fostered the development of a wide range of institutions and agencies for this confessional and linguistic community. Although some organizations, such as St. Margaret's Home, had religious institutional ties, most associations were voluntary, ad hoc, and autonomous. Many of these institutions dated back to the 1820s, but the second half of the nineteenth century saw rapid expansion of charitable enterprises with the establishment of seven hospitals and twenty-one charitable institutions, such as the Victorian Order of Nurses. Within the first decade and a half of the twentieth century, another flurry of activity created the Children's Memorial Hospital, the Brehmer Rest Preventorium, the Montreal branch of the Canadian National Institute for the Blind, the Girls' Cottage Industrial School, and the Women's Directory in 1914.

The third sphere in a city profoundly divided by religion and language was the Jewish community. Here was yet another parallel set of institutions and agencies to help this heterogeneous community. The most important was the Baron de Hirsch Institute, organized in 1863 as the Young Men's Hebrew Benevolent Society. By 1914, Montreal's Jewish community boasted several women's auxiliaries, the Herzl Free Dispensary, and the Hebrew Sheltering Home. In 1915, the community would lead the way in interagency co-operation with the establishment of the Federation of Jewish Philanthropies.[19]

While it would be partially true to understand the Protestant, Catholic, and Jewish communities as isolated and distinct in their welfare interests, the day-to-day reality was much more complicated. There were points of ordinary contact between the relatively small English Catholic middle class and the dominant English Protestant community at institutions such as McGill, where Anglo-Catholics were permitted to attend, and in common memberships at the elite male social clubs of Sherbrooke Street. The Victorian Order of Nurses was described as "undenominational," as was the Society for the Protection of Women and Children, the Royal Edward Institute for tuberculosis, and the City Improvement League established in 1909, which also incorporated French and English Catholics and representatives of the Jewish community. Another example of cross-confessional and linguistic co-operation was the establishment of the Montreal Children's Aid Society in 1908. Its first meeting was held at the home of Senator Frédéric and Caroline Dessaulles Béïque, but this was after a campaign begun in 1905 by the Montreal Women's Club. The objective of this Children's Aid Society was the establishment of a juvenile court, achieved in 1912.[20]

Even co-operation within confessional groups such as the English Protestant community could be difficult to achieve. There was considerable parochialism among the various agencies, and many supporters were quite isolated from others interested in similar social welfare concerns. A contemporary remembered that the boards of Montreal private agencies were strictly vested in their own interests and unwilling to co-operate with others. This led to intense protectionism over what various agencies considered their responsibility or territory. In 1914, for example, the Society for the Protection of Women and Children rejected a request from the Montreal COS for its support in the establishment of a court of domestic relations because it considered this an encroachment of its own work.[21] Important exceptions to this insular parochialism were rare male philanthropists such as Jeffrey Burland and Herbert Brown Ames, a significant number of the male medical community, and a much larger number of women who integrated their concerns relating to welfare, suffrage, and reform. Women such Helen R.Y. Reid possessed a vision of the city that connected the various streams of welfare action into one integrated purpose.

Helen R.Y. Reid is one of the most important, if neglected, figures in the history of social service in Canada. Reid was a Unitarian from an influential Montreal family connected through marriage to the politically prominent Stephens family. Born in 1869, Reid was among the first class of women to attend McGill University, and she pursued post-graduate studies in Germany and Switzerland. Her father, Robert Reid, operated Montreal's most important marble and granite works, and her mother, Eliza A. McIntosh, founded the Montreal Women's Club in 1892, an organization that grew to nearly 2,000 members and included a subsection focused on social reform. Helen Reid had independent means, and devoted herself full time to various reform causes, travel, and golf. She rose to national importance through research for the National Council of Women, and took on local leadership in the Victorian Order of Nurses, especially during the 1909–10 typhoid epidemic, when she introduced medical social work to Montreal. During the First World War, she was general director of the Montreal Canadian Patriotic Fund, where she oversaw as many as 800 volunteers and employees and monthly payments of $75,000 without ever drawing a salary.[22] Reid's connections extended beyond national boundaries, and she was a regular attendee at American social work conferences. Her international friendships and connections were also crucial to the careers of Canada's most famous social worker, Charlotte Whitton, and, perhaps not surprisingly, Jane Wisdom. Reid exemplifies the amateur professional social worker. Her significant contributions and leadership were all without either formal training or remuneration but she was nevertheless a leading advocate of specialized practical education.

Reid was among the supporters of the organized charity movement. The road to the establishment of a COS in Montreal was long and difficult, plagued by what the Montreal Local Council of Women's 1900 annual report described as "apparently insurmountable obstacles." An earlier attempt, concurrent to other North American cities, had been made to create an Associate Charities Organization under the leadership of Rev. Dr. Barnes, a Unitarian minister, around 1883, but it quickly failed. One of the first priorities of the newly established Montreal Local Council of Women (MLCW) in 1893 was the establishment of a COS. Indeed, Montreal members such as Julia Drummond, wife of the president of the Bank of Montreal, were prominent at the national level in promoting the establishment of scientific philanthropy, the goal of the organized charity movement.[23] A dynamic committee of the MLCW composed of well-connected women began a study of local conditions, including charitable societies. They used their transnational connections to discover how poverty was being dealt with in the United States, Australia, New Zealand, Japan, the British Isles, and other European countries. The report, authored by Helen Reid, was submitted to the national council, and was followed up in Montreal by two subgroups, a Philanthropy Group and a Social Study Club under the direction of Carrie Derick of McGill. The emphasis on prevention, not just responding, was evident in the Social Study Club's program of studies for 1899, which examined topics such as the causes of poverty, the distribution of wealth, "children of the state," the education and housing of the poor, "the family," women as wage earners, and domestic service.[24]

In October 1899, several women from the MLCW decided to strategically co-operate with a group of local influential men and formed a committee to campaign for a COS. Together, they used the press to influence public opinion, and met with various charitable societies to quell concerns of territorialism and rivalry. One month later, a meeting of francophone and anglophone elites organized a public meeting to which the representatives of various charitable societies were invited. In a nice moment bridging both British and American links, on 12 December 1899, her Excellency, the Countess of Minto, wife of the governor general, along with prominent American social reformer Dr. Graham Taylor of Chicago, attended the founding meeting. Montreal Mayor Raymond Préfontaine held the chair, and there were a number of speeches in both English and French, including one by Julia Drummond. While it was unusual for a woman to speak at a mixed-sex public meeting in Montreal, Drummond's speech "really clinched the day," according to popular memory.[25] She argued that for the Montreal COS to be a success, three conditions were necessary. First, women must be involved. Second, its governing board had to be composed of businessmen. Finally, she stated, "everyone should make use of it." Hence, it was carefully ensured that the society would be non-sectarian and include both anglophone and francophone Montrealers. Indeed, the organizers had paid a great deal of attention to ensuring that the speakers' list reflected the diversity of the city. Senator Frédéric L. Béïque, Dr. Emmanuel Lachapelle, and Jean-Damien Rolland, local manufacturer and politician, spoke as French Catholics, while anglophone Catholics were represented by manufacturer and politician Charles F. Smith and former Montreal mayor Sir William Hingston.[26] Without question, the minority English Protestant community was dominant, but the original incorporators of the COS, while all members of the elite, crossed religious, linguistic, gender, and political divisions. The influence and role of the MLCW were obvious; the first board of directors featured seven of its representatives, including Drummond and Reid.

The creation of a non-sectarian organization in Montreal was a remarkable accomplishment, and the fact that it was incorporated in both French and English suggests the initial intention of reaching out to the entire community. It never lived up to this founding aspiration, although it officially remained a non-sectarian organization until 1921, serving the Catholic, Jewish, and, disproportionately, Protestant communities. The language of operation was English, but it employed a French secretary, published frequently in both English and French, and, at least before the war, shared links with Catholic institutions and leaders. Like most charity organization societies, it began as a non-relief-giving organization, leaving the provision of direct assistance to other organizations. Its explicit objectives were to eliminate "duplication and begging," connect those "worthy of being helped" with assistance, and provide advice to other organizations interested in preventing pauperism. However, the COS soon became a relief-giving agency, thanks in part to its being used by the city of Montreal to distribute its growing aid budget.[27]

In 1899, American COS leader Mary Richmond admitted that the COS's focus on the individual caused it to exaggerate "those causes of poverty that have their origin in the individual," such as "drunkenness and licentiousness ... thriftlessness, laziness, or inefficiency." At the same time, she noted that those involved in the settlement movement exaggerated causes of poverty that were "external to the individual," such as "bad industrial conditions and defective legislation. ... Settlement workers are likely to say that the sufferings of the poor are due to conditions over which the poor have no control." She admitted that the truth lay "somewhere between these two extremes; the fact being that personal and social causes of poverty act and react upon each other, changing places as cause and as effect, until they form a tangle that no hasty, impatient jerking can unravel."[28] Through the individual investigation of cases, the COS would prevent indiscriminate charity and offer help to those deemed deserving.

The focus on the individual rather than on larger social forces explains the Montreal COS's preoccupation with specific issues such as begging. The elimination of beggars from Montreal streets appears to have been a prime means of gaining popular support for the COS. Julia Drummond claimed that "Montreal had the unenviable reputation of being like Naples, a city of beggars," and was quoted as having turned away either seventeen or thirteen penitents in a single day. She continued, "Enquiry into the case of the suppliant was, as a rule, impossible. One had either to turn a deaf ear, or salve one's feeling by a dole. In either case, no help was given. In the latter, charity defeated its true end which is to prevent and eliminate pauperism."[29] Begging also preoccupied Francis McLean, the first general secretary of the Montreal COS. He made a direct connection between the absence of available public relief and the difficulty of reducing house-to-house begging. One general secretary of the COS explained licensed street begging as "a custom which came to us from the Latin countries."[30] Permits were to be granted only to "deserving" beggars who were unable to work as a result of poor health, disability, or infirmity.

McLean did not think that a strict scientific philanthropy principle was feasible in Montreal, given the absence of any public relief. The organized charity ideal that only "helpable" individuals be assisted could not be realized when there was no poorhouse to act as the ultimate safety net for the unredeemable pauper. According to McLean, Montreal licensed begging as a cheaper alternative to institutional care.[31] The COS responded to the begging problem by issuing bilingual cards outlining sources of institutional help, instead of directly providing money or food. The card directed men to the COS office on Bleury Street during the daytime. In the evening, it listed one of seven night refuges that offered meals and lodging for men or women, often for token fees.[32] It is significant that across the linguistic and religious divide, there was a consensus that providing "something for nothing" encouraged pauperism. Minimal fees were charged at most facilities, or, in the case of the Protestant House of Relief, work was expected in exchange for necessities. In March 1914, another option appeared for destitute men when the City of Montreal opened the Meurling Refuge. The city's movement into welfare was gradual and ad hoc. At the most basic level, it provided shelter for the homeless in the city's jails. Over the winter of 1909–10, Montreal police housed approximately 22,000 "guests."[33]

Statutory support from the province in aid of the poor was almost completely discretionary. With no laws compelling state responsibility, charity matters were "entrusted" to the churches with discretionary, non-statutory local support. Prisons and penitentiaries were the only institutions in the general area of charities, and correction maintained exclusively by the province. Individuals who, in other jurisdictions, would be classified as paupers, in Quebec were criminalized under the Vagrancy Act. Francis McLean maintained that among those in jail "were also a certain proportion of senile imbeciles who cannot be legally committed to hospitals for the insane, and who therefore remain in jail, being recommitted every six months, if there is no room for them in benevolent institutions." Quebec law required municipalities to pay one half of the per capita cost for the maintenance of any insane person committed from its district, but any other support was elective. Similarly, the municipalities *could*, but were not compelled to, support dependent and delinquent children. This was permissive rather than mandatory legislation, and if municipalities undertook the financial burden, did they have statutory means of forcing the province to share costs? In 1902, representatives of the Montreal COS accused the province of refusing this responsibility, increasing pressure on Quebec's metropolitan centre, where most of the children lived. Charitable institutions might receive annual grants from the province but these were also discretionary and even described as "insignificant." For example, in 1901, provincial grants amounted to less than $45,000. These were shared among seventy-eight charities throughout Quebec. Meanwhile, the city of Montreal dispersed close to $70,000. The same year, Quebec granted nearly half a million dollars to its lunatic asylums and reformatories.[34]

The de facto responsibility placed on the city led in 1904 to the establishment of a municipal assistance department. Twenty-seven-year-old Albert Chevalier was hired as its director, a position he would retain for more than thirty years. The civic department served as a referral agency, a source of annual grants for private charities, and an advisory body for municipal authorities. Chevalier associated himself with the American charity movement, attending and speaking at its annual conferences. He was interested in suppressing street begging, sympathetic to the scientific philanthropy model that eschewed sentiment in exchange for rational, organized, and coordinated assistance, and was especially enthusiastic about working with the Montreal COS to form a public–private partnership with the agency. Regardless of religious affiliation, requests to the city for relief were investigated and processed entirely by the COS.[35] But, notwithstanding the professional associations of Chevalier, municipal involvement in charity had an amateur or voluntary flair. Like the various city churches, City Hall also had a 'poor box' where free-will offerings could be donated.[36]

The province did not completely turn its back on welfare matters. In 1915, Quebec introduced an Amusement Tax, collected by the municipality from tickets and revenue at places of leisure, the proceeds of which were divided between the municipality and the province. Montreal needed the money because, by 1913, the city was making annual grants of $105,996 to local privately and religiously operated institutions. It was spending an additional $391,716 for relief of the city's destitute, primarily funnelled through the COS. The city was also directly involved insofar as it had some funds available to return indigents to their home communities. In a wonderful example of church and state co-operation, in 1905, street begging was made illegal in Montreal unless one had a permit signed by the mayor, a clergyman, or a Justice of the Peace.[37] Presumably, most of these permits were signed by clergy, as they would have been the most accessible to those in need.

Although charity in Montreal was primarily voluntary, there were some professionals working in the area. Visiting nurses, city missionaries, deaconesses, and nuns performed tasks that were indistinguishable from what would later be picked up by professional social workers. Visiting nurses at the Diet Dispensary did much more than medical work. They attended the sick in their homes, brought nourishing food, and sought ways to keep families together. In 1906–07, there were two women working out of the Old Brewery Mission: a "Nurse Deaconess" and "Visiting Deaconess."[38]

There may not have been much popular understanding of the difference between social work and traditional religious work or nursing for women. A cousin of Jane Wisdom, attending McGill in 1911, referred to Wisdom as engaging in "missionary work." Montreal social service workers were also associated with medical institutions. Montrealers Elizabeth Helm of the University Settlement and Rufus Smith of the COS attended the Canadian Health Association Conference in Toronto in September 1912, where there was a specific social workers' section a full decade before any such professional conference existed for social workers in Canada. It has already been mentioned that at least one Catholic downtown parish arranged for nuns to visit its poor; the Anglican parish of St. George also employed a visiting nurse with similar responsibilities.[39] Jane Wisdom's entry in the 1911 census also suggests some confusion. In June 1911, while working on a COS project that later became Montreal's first Hospital Social Service Department, Wisdom temporarily moved into the Westmount receiving home for a convalescence home. The census enumerator listed her occupation as a "maid."[40]

It is doubtful if men involved in social service were ever confused with domestic servants, in part because they were more likely to be found at the executive and administrative levels, rather than working directly with individuals in need. Consider, for instance, the Montreal Charity Organization Society's appointment of Francis McLean when it opened its office in May 1900. This ambitious young American would play a central role in the development of American social work until the Second World War, and he reinforced Montreal social service links to New York. McLean was born in 1869 and graduated from the University of California, Berkeley. Among his undergraduate courses was French, so, unlike many Americans who were to follow in Montreal, McLean probably had at least a rudimentary understanding of the French language. Upon graduation, he began work as a journalist before pursuing what one biographer referred to as a "self-directed education in social work" at Johns Hopkins, Columbia, and University of Pennsylvania, much of the time living at the University Settlement in New York City.[41] In 1898, he became assistant general secretary of the Brooklyn Bureau of Charities, and he returned there in 1905 after a sojourn to Chicago, establishing an important link between the Brooklyn agency and Montreal. McLean spent only two years in Montreal but, as the COS's founding director and as someone who would play a central role in the professional development of family social work in North America, his influence was substantial.

McLean's later career led him to the New York Russell Sage Foundation, and, in 1911, he organized the National Association of Societies for Organizing Charities (later known as the Family Service Association of

America). His Montreal connections were evident, as Montrealers were among the most visible Canadians to be involved in both these US-based organizations. Between 1910 and 1922, he was also the associate director of the Russell Sage Summer Institutes; as such, he had contact with hundreds of social workers, including Jane Wisdom.[42]

As discussed earlier, McLean was preoccupied with the absence of a poorhouse and direct public relief, and the effect this had on private charity in Montreal. He believed not in distributing relief but, rather, in making it unnecessary through individual family rehabilitation. Family rehabilitation was supposed to take place through casework, the careful investigation of each case's particular circumstances with a subsequent plan to restore the family to independence and self-support. Relief was a temporary and makeshift solution until the plan could be realized. According to the 1901–02 annual report, the COS distributed relief in 885 of the 1,031 cases it investigated.[43] The problem for McLean was that, without a public almshouse as the "final refuge," private charities in Montreal could not rigorously discriminate between the deserving poor and the undeserving pauper: all needed food, shelter, and fuel. Rather than being able to carefully investigate the roots of individual family problems and implement specific solutions, Montreal private charities found themselves "unwholesomely centered around elemental material problems of bread and fuel."[44]

In McLean's second annual report, he emphasized the need for friendly visiting: behind the "salaried officers of the Society," there "must be the score upon score of volunteer visitors, each visiting one or two families, but visiting with a definite purpose in view, with a definite recognition of the problems involved and their solution."[45] Friendly visiting was a cross between traditional, voluntary, religious obligations and the emergent scientific investigation of casework. The element of friendship was supposed to convey the importance of solidarity and co-operation apparent in the social settlement movement. In 1899, Mary Richmond characterized it as "intimate and continuous knowledge of and sympathy with a poor family's joys, sorrows, opinions, feelings, and entire outlook upon life." Wisdom's first position with the COS was as a "paid Friendly Visitor," and, throughout her career, she often reverted to the term "friend" as a description of what she did."[46]

In June 1902, McLean was replaced as COS director by another American, Richard Henry Lane. Lane played a pivotal role in Jane Wisdom's life. Born in Vermont in 1870, he was a graduate of Middlebury

College. Upon graduation, he left for London, England, where he lived at the Anglican Oxford House Settlement for several years. During his eight years in Montreal, Lane was less of a bureaucrat than McLean and continually emphasized the compassionate and even sentimental aspects of charity work. Having enrolled in the 1901 New York School of Philanthropy's special summer school, he did possess some formal training. Yet, he explained his motivation to enter social work with a reference to George R. Sims's mawkish ballad "Billy Rose," which "appealed to him to such an extent that he declared he would give his life's work to the poor."[47] At the meeting of the newly created Canadian Conference of Charities and Correction in October 1903, he argued that while organized charity should strive for efficiency and suppress pauperism, "the sympathetic side of the work should not be ignored." A deeply religious Anglican, he was also characterized as "a man of refined taste," and, as such, was invited into many prominent homes, where he acquired patrons for his work. He was certainly the only welfare professional I ever came across in Montreal English-newspaper social columns. After his death in 1910, his mourners emphasized his "kind manner in dispensing charity [, which] made the sufferer feel that they were being helped by a friend."[48] Lane's personal style challenges any simplistic dichotomy between sentimentality and a commitment to scientific charity, as he, like his protégé Wisdom, clearly embraced both.

Montreal's population growth placed a corresponding demand on the COS. In 1908, the year before Wisdom arrived, society dealt with 3,552 new cases, secured temporary employment 14,367 times, and found permanent employment for 207 individuals. Direct emergency aid was distributed 27,187 times, medical treatment was provided in 147 situations, 418 paupers were returned to their homes elsewhere in Canada or deported, 375 individuals were committed to charitable institutions or hospitals, and 23 people were buried. Overall, the staff conducted 6,508 visits.[49] While these numbers demonstrate the tangible contribution the COS was making to the city, COS activities did not solve the overall problem.

In light of the demands on the organization, changes at the executive level must have been difficult to weather. A third American, Rufus D. Smith, succeeded Lane. Born in 1884, the same year as Wisdom, Smith was a graduate of Cornell and came to Montreal from the sociology department at the University of Pittsburgh, where he had been an assistant professor. Upon his departure from Montreal, he returned to academe, joining the staff of New York University, where he remained for the rest of his career, teaching politics and government, and serving eighteen years as provost.[50]

The fourth general secretary of the COS, Robert Cloutman Dexter, was Canadian-born and served in Montreal from 1914 to 1918. Born in Shelburne, Nova Scotia, in 1887, he was a graduate of Brown and later returned to Clark University, where he received a PhD in 1923. Like Helen Reid and subsequent leader Howard Falk, Dexter was a Unitarian, which placed him outside the mainstream of Montreal Protestant culture. In 1918, he left Montreal to undertake Red Cross work in the United States, and, in 1920, was appointed general secretary of the Associated Charities of Atlanta.[51] Dexter brought with him a remarkable wife, Elisabeth Anthony Dexter, a graduate of Bates College and Columbia University who earned a PhD from Clark in 1923. Elisabeth Dexter worked as a social and settlement house worker before marriage, and published in American colonial women's history. She shared her husband's work with the Unitarian Service Committee, and was probably an asset to Dexter during his time in Montreal. Elisabeth Dexter spoke at least some French.[52]

It is interesting that the early general secretaries were all Americans, with the nominal exception of Dexter, who left Canada at an early age. Richard Lane's familiarity with London and his decision to become a naturalized British subject may have pleased some of his anglophile patrons, but it is doubtful if any of the general secretaries had a great appreciation for the specific Montreal context. In 1922, one local volunteer argued the necessity of McGill University's committing to a serious social work program, since the American student had to "unlearn much that applied to his own country and to begin at the very beginning in studying Quebec's problems."[53] There was also some recognition of the usefulness of French language ability. While the COS employed a permanent French secretary, F.X. Turgeon, it was unclear if any of the general directors except McLean knew any French. Nevertheless, four general directors in eighteen years suggest relative stability within the organization; turnover within social service organizations could be extraordinarily high. The subsequent success of McLean, Smith, and Dexter in the United States indicates that Montreal was not regarded as some isolated, backwater posting. Instead, it could be used as a stepping stone by ambitious men who had their eyes on some greater prize.

Although the Montreal COS might claim some success, the idea of scientific philanthropy itself was contested. In 1909, an article on the women's page of the *Montreal Herald* complained that "generosity which hedges its gifts with precautions and provisos seems to me too cold-blooded to deserve the warm sweet name of charity at all." The article presented a dialogue between a group of philanthropic workers whose individual gifts of money were diverted to seemingly inappropriate luxury items, such as a canary and a cage, the first instalment on a baby carriage, or a hired carriage drive. The story ended with the question of whether it was "possible to starve for other things beside food." The sanctioning of non-essential items to poor families who did not earn them was clearly anathema to the organized charity movement, but the appearance of the story suggests that not everyone shared this view.[54]

Another criticism of the COS appeared on the front page of the *Herald*, concerning Mrs. John Elvery and her four children, who had been homeless for a month. Mrs. Elvery explained that she had approached the COS for help several times and was told only that she should find a house. In the month without a home, her husband was put up at the Brewery Mission, but his wife and children were given only a few days' lodging at the Salvation Army and six nights in jail, and were forced the rest of the time to sleep on a bench in downtown Dominion Square. The *Herald* journalist took it upon himself to place the family directly into Richard Lane's hands. Presumably in light of adverse publicity, the society offered more tangible material assistance in place of useless advice.[55]

The organized charity movement also had positive publicity. Inspired by the success of educational exhibits throughout the Western world, the first big health exhibit in Montreal was organized in 1908 by the Montreal League for the Prevention of Tuberculosis. Credit for the exhibit is given to the Ladies Auxiliary and the leadership of Charlotte Smithers Learmont, with grants from the province and the city. In November 1908, an estimated 55,000 people attended and viewed displays, witnessed demonstrations, and heard special lectures on medical, domestic, and educational aspects of tuberculosis. The exhibition and lectures were primarily in English, with the École Ménagère de Montréal, founded in 1904 to promote housekeeping skills, being the only obvious francophone participant.[56]

The success of this event inspired a much larger and much more inclusive exhibition four years later. Montrealers such as Professor J.A. Dale attended the famous New York Child Exhibit of 1911, and their enthusiasm fuelled the momentum for the 1912 Montreal Children's Welfare Exhibit. Learmont, once again, appears to have been at the forefront as head of the charity and philanthropy section of the exhibit. In fact, along with the professional organizer brought in from New York City, the English-language press gave Learmont full credit for the exhibition's success.[57]

Although the French- and English-language press would give different emphases to the exhibit's "true" leadership, from the beginning, linguistic, religious, and gender divisions were bridged under the City Improvement League, the Société Saint-Jean-Baptist, the Fédération Saint-Jean-Baptiste, the Local Council of Women, the St. Patrick's Society, and the Baron de Hirsch Institute. Everything was presented in English and French, and there was also a conscious effort to reach out to other linguistic communities through clinics and lectures in Yiddish, Italian, Russian, and Chinese.[58] The exhibition was supported generously by all three levels of government, with the city, Quebec, and Ottawa all contributing $5,000 each towards the $25,000 budget. Montreal's astronomical level of infant mortality – said to be comparable only with Chile's and Russia's – was the thematic focus. Among some of the most impressive displays were photos of baby hearses lining up at the Côte-des-Neiges cemetery, maps of "black districts" with especially high mortality rates, charts of mortality rates with graphic images of "ghost baby borders," and moving pictures.[59] The publicity techniques of the Progressive movement were never subtle. How the Montrealers who were the objects of this educative publicity responded is open to question. The *Herald* reported the case of an exhibit attendee who reportedly screamed and fainted after encountering a photo of her own home entitled "Haunts of Gangs." Upon being relieved, she countered that her home was a "happy and comfortable one" and unsuccessfully attempted to tear down the offending picture.[60] Although exhibit propaganda targeted the middle class as much as the popular classes, attendance reached 300,000 visitors, which means that a large proportion of the city participated.

The local Montreal organizing committee engaged Anna Louise Strong to coordinate the event. Strong, who would later gain renown as one of the great American radicals of the twentieth century, was at the time associated with the Child Exhibit Office of the National Child Labor Committee and was employed in organizing exhibits throughout the United States. Born only a year later than Jane Wisdom, Strong represented an entirely different response to contemporary societal problems. By the end of the First World War, Strong had abandoned social service and turned to journalism and radical politics, joining the Communist Party and eventually moving to the Soviet Union and, later, China.[61]

From her headquarters at the Monument Nationale theatre, Strong and her team of paid and unpaid assistants were able to attract thousands of exhibit volunteers, including 20,000 children as participants, and the estimated audience of 300,000 during the thirteen days the exhibit was open. Visitors participated in a 'healthy baby' clinic, viewed a model home and kitchen, watched cooking demonstrations, and were educated against patent medicine and impure children's clothing.[62]

The exhibit was a local, provincial, national, and international event. The Canadian Conference of Charities and Correction, an ambitious name for an organization that, since its 1898 inception, had been largely based in Toronto and sought to bring together various organizations and people involved in charity, arranged to meet for the first time outside Ontario. It met in Montreal to coincide with the exhibit, and attracted delegates from Winnipeg to Halifax. These included prominent local reformers such as Julia Parker Drummond, Carrie Derick, Édouard Montpetit, Charlotte Smithers Learmont, and Helen Reid, and current or future national leaders such as J.J. Kelso, J.S. Woodsworth, Howard Falk, and Ernest Blois. There were also international visitors, such as Kier Hardie, leader of the British Labour Party, and unnamed prominent American sociologists and social workers linked to the New York Russell Sage Foundation.[63]

International philanthropic connections were not new. Members of the Montreal English Protestant and Jewish philanthropic community, and civic employee Albert Chevalier, attended meetings of the National Conference of Charities and Correction. English-speaking Montrealers were also active in the National Association of Societies for Organizing Charities. In 1913–14, Smith was appointed to the organization's executive committee, and, the following year, Helen Reid and Montreal lawyer Charles M. Holt were added. Reid and Holt remained on the American executive throughout the war, and the only three Canadian cities that were members were Montreal, Halifax, and Winnipeg.[64] Some of the same individuals were also active in the emerging pan-Canadian movement. In 1912, for example, Julia Drummond was elected vice-president of the Canadian Conference of Charities and Correction and served on the executive with Elizabeth Helm of the University Settlement.[65]

Nowhere in the child exhibition or at the Canadian Conference of Charities and Correction can Jane Wisdom's presence be seen. The sudden death of Wisdom's mentor, Richard Lane, began a period of great uncertainty and change, both personal and professional. When Lane's health failed in June 1910, Wisdom was called back early from her training course in New York to temporarily co-administer COS operations, "with some of the Committee to fall back on when too hard pressed." That December, Lane died. Wisdom and two other colleagues were left to carry on with "tears in their eyes" while a new general manager was found.[66] At the time, Wisdom was assistant general secretary of the organization, and may have been involved in every aspect from coordinating volunteers and running the office to individual case investigations. The future of the COS may have seemed uncertain; one editorial in the *Montreal Star* implored that the society "not be permitted to wane or decay."[67]

Wisdom's personal life was also in flux. In June 1911, Katherine married Harry Williams, a young Anglican lawyer who taught commercial law at McGill.[68] Meanwhile, Bessie had graduated and taken up a teaching position outside Montreal at the Dunham Ladies' College. The same month Katherine married, Wisdom moved out of the University Settlement. Three months later, she left the Montreal COS to take a position as assistant to Effie McLeod's father, Professor C.H. McLeod, at the Canadian Society of Civil Engineers. I have no idea why Wisdom left the COS at this time, but it occurred six months after the arrival of new director Rufus Smith, a contemporary, whom she had met previously during her New York course. Between Lane's death and Smith's arrival, she had been sharing leadership. It is difficult to imagine that her move was completely unrelated to this change, in light of how much she had adored Lane. Lane's emphasis on personal relations, respect, and sympathy had provided Wisdom with a way of conciliating her position as a COS investigator and a resident of University Settlement. She may also have been physically exhausted, as her health and stamina were never strong. In November 1909, Jane had contracted diphtheria and ended up in the Alexandria Hospital.[69] It is equally possible that her departure may have been for financial reasons. In 1909, Wisdom was making only $35 a month, and continued to help support her parents in Nova Scotia.[70] Her financial responsibility may have actually increased, notwithstanding Katherine's "good" marriage, as her sister's wage contribution to her parents would have ended. Then, tragedy again struck the family. In June 1912, just short of her first anniversary, a pregnant Katherine was widowed when Williams died of typhoid fever. Her daughter, Relief Williams, was born in January

1913 in New Glasgow, where Katherine had returned to her parents' home. Six years later, Katherine Wisdom Williams would re-enter paid employment, first teaching at the Halifax Ladies College and then, in 1922, the Mount Allison Ladies College and School for Girls, eventually teaching French at the university. Relief would become one of the most important people in Wisdom's life.

When Katherine left the city, it is possible that Wisdom was now open to new possibilities outside Montreal. In November 1912, a month after the Child Welfare Exhibition, Wisdom received an employment offer from the Brooklyn Bureau of Charities to take charge of two districts for the annual salary of $1,000. She wired her acceptance and informed her father of her decision, noting that the "position may not be permanent but has many advantages."[71]

Jane Wisdom left a city where the basic issues of poverty were unresolved as it faced the ongoing pressures of immigration and economic instability. The English-speaking charitable leadership, under the influence of currents from both Britain and the United States, adopted a COS model that emphasized individual solutions through rational and planned rehabilitation and material support. This leadership, which included a significant number of Americans at the executive level, joined national and international networks, and adopted modern publicity and bureaucratic practices. The values of co-operation, solidarity, and community taken from settlement and religious beliefs did not entirely disappear but were melded together with scientific philanthropy. In a city marked by deep linguistic and confessional divisions, there were some efforts to overcome differences through the COS, but these aspirations were never realized. The de facto language remained English, and the de facto culture, Protestant. Within the Montreal movement, women took a visible leadership role, notwithstanding their marginal legal status in Quebec. The conspicuous position of women contrasted with the invisibility of the state, as private organizations and the churches were left to deal with the devastating consequences of urban poverty in a rapidly expanding city. Jane Wisdom witnessed the initial years of the Montreal COS. Some of the people and influences she encountered in its midst would remain with her throughout her life.

Chapter Four

New York City: Private Agency Work, 1910–1916

New York City, 1910. Was there any place in the world that both symbolized and generated more excitement? The largest city in the United States, New York was undergoing dramatic population and spatial growth, technological change, and immigration. While the vast majority of contemporary immigrants to Montreal were British, New York City immigration was much more diverse, although still European. The post-First World War mass migration of African Americans north and the large influx of Spanish-speaking people from Latin America had yet to occur. Still, the population of metropolitan New York City in 1910 was more than 4.7 million, with 2.3 million living in Manhattan and 1.6 million in Brooklyn, a borough of the city since 1898. With the city's total population greater than those of Quebec and Ontario combined, it is not surprising that residents of New York City would be preoccupied with poverty and social conditions and that there would be abundant opportunities for social service employment. When historian Linda Gordon created an historical network of influential American women involved in social reform and welfare in the early twentieth century, 57 per cent of those who met her criteria were based in New York City. Moreover, she noted that New York was not only the headquarters of many important organizations, but that the city was leading in the development of public services, municipal regulation, and demonstration projects. These organizations and activities created particular opportunities for female involvement and leadership.[1]

Jane Wisdom first travelled to New York City to receive professional training in areas of social service that were unavailable in Canada. Therese Jennissen and Colleen Lundy have recently called attention to the American influence on Canadian social workers, as "they belonged to US professional associations, attended US conferences, contributed to US journals, and relied on US accreditation bodies."[2] More importantly, early social workers depended on American educational and employment opportunities.

Wisdom arrived in a city that, according to the 1910 census, identified 2,256 social workers – a considerable under-enumeration, since the social work community contained more than 4,000 workers in the private sector alone. It is impossible to know how many social workers would have been employed in Canada in 1910, but three related categories – "asylum and hospital employee," "religious worker," and "charitable institution worker" – appeared in the 1911 Canadian census. The investigative casework Wisdom had conducted in Montreal may still have been regarded generally as volunteer labour. Alice Parkin Massey, in her 1920 book outlining career opportunities for Canadian women, included "Social Service" but noted that, while the need was great, workers found it difficult to find positions with acceptable salaries.[3] This ambiguity was evident in the 1921 Canadian census, where paid social workers employed by outside institutions may have fallen into the category of "professional pursuits, not otherwise specified," but they did not merit their own specific occupation until the 1931 census, when social work, for the first time, was listed as a distinct occupation. In 1931, twenty years after the first American census data were available, the Canadian census listed 792 women and 381 men employed in the vocation. Their absence until this point is quite remarkable, as the census appears to have classified every other conceivable profession. This testifies to the profession's marginality and charity's strong association with traditional institutions. With the emergence of social work as a distinct profession came an increased emphasis on specialized training, techniques, and knowledge.

Social work, as it was practised in the second decade of the twentieth century, was closely linked to what we would today consider private agencies and hospitals. Although this was its primary arena, social work was expanding into the public sphere with the development of early welfare programs, such as mothers' allowance. The occupation was mainly women's work, but it often took place in a bureaucratic context where the ultimate authority rested with a man. Certainly, social work, at least in New York City, appears to have been better paid than teaching or nursing in Canada, two of the other occupations open to educated women at this time. Nursing students received

$8 to $12 a month plus board, and graduated nurses earned $50 to $75 a month. The best-paid Protestant female at the Montreal High School for Girls could receive a maximum of $77 after many years of service, and a first-year public-school teacher might start at $45 a month.[4] In contrast, in December 1912, Jane Wisdom was hired in New York as a district secretary for the annual salary of $1,000 a year, or $83 a month. This was a significant improvement over what she had been earning in Montreal.[5] No doubt, the prospect of a higher salary in New York complemented goals for professional development. A salary of $83 a month was decent pay for a woman. Moreover, unlike teaching and nursing, social work offered some degree of workplace autonomy. Direct supervision was not possible when workers were out in the community or in the homes of their clients. But, as historian Daniel Walkowitz has perceptively pointed out, the class position of social workers was somewhat murky. Unlike teachers, the 1910 United States census placed social workers in the semi-professional category. Even the title caused problems. The term "social worker" was adopted to differentiate between those engaged in amateur, ad hoc, personal and religious charity work and those working for private or public philanthropic organizations. It also served to emphasize that this was paid, rather than voluntary, work. Social workers placed themselves in a unique situation: what other emergent profession referred to itself so explicitly as "worker"?[6]

Like nursing, social work continued to have a strong association with voluntary and informal women's work, and so its transition to a particular form of paid employment encountered obstacles in gaining recognition. Many historians have noted the difficulty social workers had in making the public understand "the transition from benevolent charity worker to paid social worker." The new profession was further marginalized by the perpetual question: what skills did social workers possess, precisely?[7] Were not the qualities of a good social worker closely associated with the "natural" attributes of a good woman? Nurturance, sympathy, compassion, discretion, kindness, and moral suasion were personal characteristics and surely could not be taught. Nancy Christie has noted that in the early 1930s, while actively involved in the debates about social work training, Wisdom argued against enforcing overly academic requirements for admission to social work programs, lest that "discourage those who 'follow the glean,'" drawing her words from the New Testament injunction that Christians "follow the glean, until we become like Christ."[8]

Character and specialized knowledge dominated debates about social work education through the 1930s. The first development on this road to specialization was the adoption of scientific objectivity. Dawn Greeley, in her study of the New York Charity Organization Society, has observed that the charity workers of the 1880s and 1890s had no concern about "the appearance of objectivity," and "made little attempt to disguise their contempt for men who failed to support their families." The emergence of social scientific understandings of the nature of poverty located it not only in individual failings and morality but, more importantly, in social and economic structures such as seasonal labour markets, poor housing, ill health, and lack of educational opportunities. The landmark text in the development of specialized social service knowledge was Edward Devine's *Principles of Relief* (1904). Here, the Columbia professor and general secretary of the New York COS emphasized the problem of poverty rather than pauperism. This reflected a de facto shift that had already occurred within most private relief agencies attempting scientific charity in the last decade of the nineteenth century. Devine saw poverty as an economic, not moral, problem. Importantly, he rejected the old rigid COS notion that "giving relief pauperized recipients and created a permanently dependent class"; instead, he believed that giving relief helped those in need during difficult times and could lead to family rehabilitation.[9] Devine's influence was critical, and *Principles of Relief* was widely distributed. The copy in the McGill University library, for example, predates the establishment of the school's social service program. In emphasizing poverty rather than pauperism and science rather than morality, Devine argued that social work had a preventive mission. He placed the emerging profession within the context of broader Progressive-era movements for social change.[10]

Progressives were confident that social problems resulting from poverty, immigration, urbanization, political corruption, industrialization, and monopolies and trusts could be dealt with through the application of scientific methods: problems could be identified, studied, analyzed, and solved. As their name implied, Progressives believed in progress, but they also had unfaltering faith in social harmony and were willing to intervene in the lives of others, either through private charity or expanded government. Historian Shelton Stromquist has drawn attention to their "imagined" social category of "the people," which was "broadly conceived and undifferentiated by class interests" and upheld a "common good." They believed that individuals were created by their environments, and if you altered the environment, you could change the person. They thought it was possible to reform capitalism to make it more human and take into consideration the needs of communities.[11] Although not all Progressives were Christians (or Protestants), many were influenced by the social gospel and married evangelical Protestant duty and faith with scientific principles. The social gospel identified justice issues such as poverty as "sins of society," and asked adherents to seek salvation through building "the Kingdom of God on this earth." This doctrine certainly conformed to Wisdom's own Christian world view of equality and harmony, although she would remain cautious about the expanded state until the First World War.

The New York COS Summer School for Philanthropic Work opened in 1898. In 1904, the New York School of Philanthropy, the Boston School of Social Work, and the Chicago School of Civics and Philanthropy were established. In 1906, the University of Pennsylvania began a summer program, and in 1907, the St. Louis School of Philanthropy opened its doors.[12] Notwithstanding the establishment of specialized courses, many eventually linked to established universities, the question of social work's professional status garnered much debate. Perhaps the most famous volley was medical educator Abraham Flexner's 1915 address before the National Conference of Charities and Correction, in which he argued that social work was not and would never be a profession, as social workers possessed no specialized knowledge or skills. Walkowitz rightly identifies this accusation as becoming an obsession in social work debates for the next twenty-five years.[13]

The loudest response to Flexner's dismissal of social work came from Mary Richmond in her 1917 publication *Social Diagnosis*, which outlined a precise methodology for the profession. Unlike Devine, who came from social science, Richmond's background was in the COS movement. Her perspective rooted social work not in social activism and reform but, rather, in practical efficiency and objectivity. She touted individual-focused casework methodology as the particular professional skill social work had to offer. Casework came to be heavily associated with Richmond and would be the focus of Jane Wisdom's career.

Historian Regina Kunzel has defined casework as "a step-by-step procedure of collecting information about a client's experiences and background, or 'investigation,' followed by 'diagnosis' and 'treatment' of the client's problem." It was supposed to be confidential, impartial, and objective. While casework usually involved workers' imposing their norms on clients, it also had the potential to assist clients, as it focused attention on all aspects of a family context. According to Linda Gordon, good individual caseworkers had the potential to bring "flexibility, creativity, and empathy beyond the strictures of agency policy."[14]

This individual-focused approach shared much with contemporary understandings of history as an "ideographic" or individualizing discipline compared to the emergent social sciences such as sociology, economics, political science, and anthropology, which were characterized as "nomothetic" or generalizing disciplines.[15] Social work, like history, shared an approach that emphasized inductive reasoning, where patterns were supposedly found, not made. Most importantly, history and social work shared a commitment to objectivity, with both the historian and the social worker playing the role of neutral or disinterested judge whose ideal was even-handedness.

It is strange that no historian I have encountered has forged the direct link that Mary Richmond made in her 1917 study to connect casework methodology with "modern approaches to history" by placing central importance on "social evidence." Richmond claimed that "social evidence, like that sought by the scientist or historian, includes all items which, however trifling or apparently irrelevant when regarded as isolated facts, may, when taken together, throw light upon the question at issue." Urging all social workers to read Charles V. Langlois and Charles Seignobos's 1898 *Introduction to the Study of History*, Richmond discussed the importance of inference. She also argued that social workers must use a range of sources for evidence, such as oral testimony; expert evidence; documentary evidence; character evidence; immigration, civil, and employment records; city directories; and newspaper files. Again, Richmond drew a direct comparison between social work and history by noting that "the social worker and the historian cannot and need not reject an item of hearsay evidence," but, rather, should use caution and make an effort to trace the idea to the original observer. Richmond urged social workers to consider the possible bias of witnesses and sources, and even asked her reader to consider what "we mean by the word fact."[16]

The primacy of history was also evident in Edward Devine's *The Principles of Relief*, the common text used in professional training before Richmond's 1917 publication. This classic study had an entire section dealing specifically with the history of relief in the United States and Great Britain. It also contained a model section of seventy-five individual case studies outlining the history of each family and the measures taken to provide relief. By studying individual cases, new caseworkers were supposed to gain practical knowledge; their goal was to become omniscient, objective narrators who could investigate cases, create interpretative narratives, and draw conclusions. This was the only section of Devine to be annotated with student marginalia in the original volume I consulted at the McGill library. But if casework was based on a form of history, it was not the prestigious kind based on nations and war; it was the other tradition of amateur storytelling that, Bonnie Smith has argued, was strongly associated with women.[17] The investigation of the family and the economic history of an individual household were lowly subjects indeed. While men teaching in the professional programs were associated with policy and addressing social problems writ large, the practical knowledge of early female social workers was built through casework: an historical understanding of individuals, households, and various ways of dealing with the poor.

In 1909, Mary Richmond arrived in New York to work at the Russell Sage Foundation. The Russell Sage Foundation was established in 1907, following a $65 million endowment provided by Russell's widow Olivia Sage for "the improvement of the working and living conditions in the United States." Although the terms of the endowment were focused on the United States, the ambitious group of men and women at its New York centre had transnational aspirations. Mary Richmond, as head of its Charity Organization Department, quickly solidified her place as the United States' most important social worker through the organization's resources and her very public profile. The Russell Sage Foundation could not distribute funds to the needy. Instead, it funded research into poverty, social work education, and charitable infrastructure support. Richmond's powerful department within the foundation was reinforced by field secretary Francis McLean, former general secretary of the Montreal Charity Organization Society. The other full-time employee within this department, Margaret Byington, had important social science and industrial connections. Byington's origins were also in the charity organization movement, as she had been a district agent for the Boston Associated Charities. She also had a social science background, with an MA from Columbia in sociology and economics. In 1907, Byington was hired by the Russell Sage Foundation-funded Pittsburgh Survey, the American counterpart to Charles Booth's investigation of London poverty, *Life and Labour of the People*. Byington authored the survey's most famous volume, *Homestead: The Households of a Mill Town*, and established the notion of an "American standard of living."[18] While it is perhaps easy to present Devine, the progressive social scientist, and Richmond, the practical COS worker, as professional opposites, as many historians of social work have done, the figure of Byington represents an interesting mix of the two streams. With a foot in both traditions – the activist, reform-oriented, preventative version of social work emerging from social science and the pragmatic version emphasizing casework – Byington had much in common with Jane Wisdom and would join Richmond as a mentor.

Devine, Richmond, McLean, and Byington all worked in the same building, the United Charities Building, which housed many of the city's, state's, and country's most important charity and reform agencies. They all taught at the New York School of Philanthropy. Although it is simple to sort them into two separate camps, one focused on broad social reform and the other focused on individuals, their work was intertwined. Unlike more radical settlement workers such as Jane Addams who directly entered politics, Devine remained scrupulously non-partisan. The activist bent of his New York Charity Organization Society and the New York School of Philanthropy was moderated by Richmond, who emphasized practical action for the individual, without dismissing the impact of environment.[19] Richmond was influential in another way, and one of her responses to what she believed to be the overly theoretical tendency of the New York School of Philanthropy, before its reorientation in 1912, was the establishment of a summer institute organized for experienced workers who desired formal training.

In June 1910, the Russell Sage Foundation's Charity Organization Department organized the Summer Institute, an intimate, month-long seminar emphasizing case conferences, investigation, treatment, relief, and administration. Both Richmond and McLean described these institutes, which were operated by the Russell Sage Foundation until 1925, as their most satisfying teaching experiences.[20] Again, so as not to exaggerate the gulf between Richmond and Devine, it is worth observing that until the publication of Richmond's own text, she used Devine's *Misery and Its Causes* (1909) as the course's primary textbook. Operating six days a week, the summer institute was proposed as "a new experiment in supplementary training." The number of participants was limited to twenty, there was no fee to attend, and graduates received a certificate from the New York School of Philanthropy. Publicity emphasized the institute's practical orientation.[21]

In the first institute, sixteen women and four men participated. One was Rufus D. Smith, future general secretary of the Montreal Charity

Organization Society. Another was Frank Bruno, a Congregational minister who came under the influence of Richmond. He would later take a leadership role in the American profession as a civil rights activist and a pioneer of theoretically based social work as director of the George Warren Brown School of Social Work in St. Louis.[22] None of the women rose to equivalent professional renown. Jane Wisdom's name did not appear on the original list of twenty participants. There must have been a last-minute withdrawal, however, and Richard Lane, general secretary of the Montreal COS, sent Wisdom to New York to take the course.

Wisdom was one of the four students assigned to Mary Richmond's group and so received intense immersion in the professional practice of casework. Almost immediately, Wisdom declared that she "adored" Richmond. She wrote to her mother that she forgave Richmond "for being an American because she really is nice enough to be a Canadian." After a two-hour private interview with Richmond at the end of the course's first week, Wisdom wrote: "I do not know when I ever enjoyed such a talk. She is so sane and big-minded and yet so perfectly simply and lovable in her manner. She fairly inspires one."[23] The warmth of Richmond's personality played as large a role in Wisdom's understanding of casework as any discussion of specific methodology.

This relatively small group not only had close daily contact with Richmond and McLean, but a later report intriguingly offered that the participants had "unusually good opportunities for getting well acquainted" and that "there were a number of social gatherings in private houses and several social outings which cannot be part of this record."[24] There is a photo of eight women participants at Coney Island that included Jane Wisdom, her friend Sara Dissoway, and Mary Richmond, which Wisdom's humour could not help but title "Interim Relief." At the end of the session, Wisdom felt that she had come away with several good friends. She reported that "we felt as if we had been working together for years and some of us were actually blubbering (including Miss Richmond herself)."

These new friendships may have been cemented by shared residence among the out-of-town women at the College Settlement in New York's Lower East Side. Opened in 1889 by female graduates of Smith College, next to Hull House in Chicago, this was probably the United States' most famous settlement house. Located in a largely Jewish neighbourhood, it offered a wide variety of children's and women's educational and recreational activities, and connected sociological studies to local living and labour conditions.[25] This is where Eleanor Roosevelt taught dance lessons, Royal Victoria College instructor Annie Marion MacLean stayed in 1900, and American suffragist Alice Paul lived while attending her own course at the New York School of Philanthropy. Settlement workers regarded members of their community as citizens and active participants, rather than as clients and passive program recipients. Modern concepts regarded as relatively recent innovations, such as solidarity, community capacity building, and active consultation, were at the core of these settlements' objectives, even if they often failed to realize their egalitarian and democratic impulses. As a result, the College Settlement was also a centre of support for the Women's Trade Union League (WTUL), an attempt at cross-class organization led by progressive, middle- and upper-class women reformers with the purpose of supporting "industrial feminism." The WTUL and settlement house link was especially prominent during the 1909 and 1913 garment workers' strikes, which swept New York City. The head resident of the College Settlement was an enthusiastic participant at strike meetings. Historian Annelise Orleck has noted that virtually every middle-class woman who came to support the WTUL had previous experience with social reform and philanthropic activities. Nearly all had come to the WTUL through some association with settlement houses after "disenchantment with traditional welfare work," where charity was given but broader reform was not made.[26]

When Jane Wisdom lived as a temporary resident on Rivington Street in 1910, the College Settlement's headworker since 1898 was Elizabeth Sprague Williams. Through participation in a range of social reform activities, she promoted self-discipline and initiative taking, values thought necessary for a capitalist, liberal, democratic society.[27] Again we see, in the College Settlement, that there was no clear division between those who sought solutions to urban poverty through individual responsibility and those working for broader social reforms. Wisdom's intense involvement with the Montreal University Settlement would have meant that she was already familiar with the ideals of the College Settlement and may have meant that her time there was especially significant.

Did Montreal seem small and provincial to Jane Wisdom after her short time in New York City? On her return, she wrote that "everything did seem most awfully still and quiet at first and the buildings look so flat but things are getting to be more natural now. I'd rather work and live in Montreal but I want to go to New York."[28] Certainly, family and work demands in Montreal kept Wisdom occupied. In May 1911, fellow Summer Institute student Rufus Smith arrived at the Montreal COS as the new director. This new supervisor, with his graduate education, may have been a stark reminder of the qualifications Wisdom lacked. The efforts made at informal continuing education by Montreal reformers J.A. Dale and Helen Reid for Montreal charity workers may have seemed insubstantial after the excitement of being among the so-called "elect" at the first New York Summer Institute. Some time in the fall of 1912, Wisdom decided that she required more training "in order to help people more adequately." She let it be known to her New York friend Sara Dissoway that she was interested in returning to New York City for work and study.[29]

Wisdom was unusual in her access to any professional training before the war. Only one other Canadian can be identified as having attended the Summer Institute, Winnifred Forsyth of the Eastern District, Toronto, in 1912. Social worker Laura Holland, a contemporary of Wisdom's, born in 1883, followed another path. A nurse trained at the Montreal General Hospital, she served overseas and, after the war, took specialized social work training at Simmons College. Clare Gass, another Nova Scotian a few years younger than Jane, also nursed overseas during the war and used her background to launch a career in medical social work. With the advent of Canadian social service programs during the war and immediately after, travelling to the United States for education became an option rather than the only choice. Going to the United States did not end with the introduction of Canadian programs, however. In 1918, for example, founder of the Institut Notre-Dame-du-Bon-Conseil Marie Gérin-Lajoie attended the New York School of Philanthropy as a summer student.[30]

While Wisdom's pre-war training may have been uncommon, her presence in New York was not. There were a number of Canadians working in the city in the field of social work. One of Wisdom's fellow residents at the College Settlement was a visiting nurse from Toronto. The assistant headworker at the Lower East Side University Settlement in 1911 was Montrealer Solomon Vineberg. Ontario-born Anna Ruddy founded the Home Garden Settlement in 1898, and Quaker Sara Libby Carson worked for the Canadian Presbyterian Church to establish a chain of settlement houses, including Canada's oldest, Toronto's Evangelia House, established in 1902.[31]

Montreal and New York had especially strong connections. A stream of people from the United States spoke in Montreal on social service issues. One was Sadie American, whose 1910 talk was so crucial to the establishment of the Montreal University Settlement. The following year, Ernest K. Coulter of New York City addressed a large Montreal audience on the subject of the juvenile court. May Reid, a graduate of Brandon College who taught casework at McGill until 1931, had practical experience with the Brooklyn Bureau of Charities before teaching. She later returned there once her McGill position disappeared.[32] Elizabeth Helm, former head resident at the Montreal University Settlement, appears among the list of participants at the 1914 meeting of the New York City Conference of Charities and Correction. During the 1920s, welfare experts such as Ethel Taylor, director of the Department of Children's Case Work of the New York-based Child Welfare League of America, were invited to Montreal to conduct organizational surveys and reports.[33]

Montrealers who saw their city as Canada's metropolis felt a particular bond with New York. At a time when intercity travel was associated with the train, the two cities were unusually well connected, and Montrealers often possessed intimate knowledge of the goings-on in New York. Wisdom was not in New York at the time of the tragic Triangle Shirtwaist Factory fire in March 1911 but she was there during the 1913 garment workers' strike. The move to New York City placed her at the centre of North American urban culture and the core of the emerging social work world.

Wisdom's entry into New York professional casework did not mean a complete break with her settlement house background, and the two worlds crossed more than the historiography might suggest. When she moved to Brooklyn in 1912, Wisdom lived with eighteen other women in two houses at the Holy Trinity Parish House, an Episcopalian settlement located on Pierrepont Street in the well-to-do Brooklyn Heights neighbourhood. In 1915, Wisdom described the other women in residence as a mix of teachers, librarians, social workers, students, and church workers who participated in programs in exchange for reduced accommodation expenses.[34] Holy Trinity Parish House was established in 1911 and provided social services for women, girls, and children by operating clubs, offering employment training, and running a summer home on Long Island. Wisdom herself led a mothers' club. Around the corner was Hall Memorial House, the male counterpart, with distinct program offerings and its own residence.[35]

Although the Holy Trinity House was a religious settlement in a wealthy neighbourhood, it would be a mistake to dismiss it as a buttress of conservatism. The Holy Trinity Church had a radical edge inspired by the social gospel and was led by John Howard Melish, rector from 1904 to 1949. Before coming to Brooklyn, Melish had been a chaplain at the University of Cincinnati. Upon arrival, he threw himself into social justice causes associated with labour and housing reform. Melish was one of the speakers to appear at the famous Hippodrome amphitheatre meeting on 6 December 1909, when 7,000 gathered in support of the striking textile workers. Melish also opened the 1914 New York City Conference of Charities and Correction with a prayer with no mention of Jesus, suggesting accommodation or at least sensitivity towards the Jewish membership. He would later gain notoriety during the Cold War when his congregation tried to dismiss him and his son for their political beliefs.[36] In 1911, Melish explained, "Our parish stands for a social Christianity, for the reconciliation of opposing classes, for brotherliness, friendship, for the improvement of this life by means of the vision and strength of the heavenly city." He maintained that the settlement house was "one expression of this social mission." In a clear expression of the social gospel, he went on to say that the parish hoped to "reconcile the Church and settlement, by showing the Church that the settlement is an expression of the social Gospel inasmuch as its end and aim is that of Christ 'to be among men as one that serveth,' and by showing the settlement that the Church can be disinterestedly concerned about the community, and that all true service must include the ministry to religious needs." When Melish arrived from Cincinnati, he was able to convince the parish that it needed to make connections to the local working class, as he feared a "growing hostility of organized Christianity" if the church became a middle-class institution.[37]

This activist interpretation of the social gospel was more radical than what Wisdom had been exposed to in Saint John and Montreal Presbyterian circles, but its message of service appealed to her as she integrated this new world with her family. In October 1915, Wisdom was joined at the Holy Trinity Parish House by her sister Bessie, who had accepted a position at the nearby Brooklyn Bedford Children's Library. Wisdom remained connected to her family in other ways. Cousins sailing in and out of New York for Europe were met, and some members of the extended family appeared to be living in the area.[38]

Professional and personal lives frequently overlapped. In 1914, Jane Wisdom shared her accommodation at the Holy Trinity House with at least three other employees of the Brooklyn Bureau of Charities. Social notes recorded during her first winter in Brooklyn list attendance at plays, dance performances, music recitals, art galleries, churches, the 1913 "Votes for Women Ball," and the Women's Industrial Exhibition at Grand Central Station. This social life mirrored her professional life in terms of being female-centred, with outings shared by old Montreal friends and recent New York colleagues.[39] Wisdom's New York was very much a woman's city. Women co-workers, women clients, women-run church settlements, and women mentors provided continuity with her college experience.

Wisdom's employment in December 1912 with the Brooklyn Bureau of Charities (BBC) profited from earlier, well-established contacts. She was approached by Sara Dissoway, a fellow student at the 1910 Summer Institute, now employed as a district secretary with the BBC. Wisdom's personal references were Mary Richmond, Rufus Smith, and Francis McLean, a former employee of the BBC linked to both Montreal and the COS Summer Institute. On 30 October 1912, the BBC executive commit-tee approved the appointment of Jane Wisdom on a provisional basis as secretary in charge of Red Hook and Fort Greene districts for $1,000 a year.[40] The following May, Wisdom was transferred to take charge of one of the BBC's largest and poorest districts, Williamsburg.

When Wisdom arrived in Brooklyn in late 1912, the borough was emerging among urban reformers as New York City's "biggest prob-lem on the social side," with a rapidly growing, immigrant residential population. In an article in the leading social service journal *The Sur-vey*, Francis McLean described Williamsburg's transformation "from a quiet residence section to a new East Side." Between 1900 and 1910, Brooklyn's population growth outstripped Manhattan's, in large part because of the completion of the Williamsburg Bridge in 1903 and the Manhattan Bridge in 1909. (The Brooklyn Bridge was completed nearly thirty years earlier, in 1883.) Brooklyn's school registration of 254,097 students in 1910 was only 18,115 less than Manhattan's. Williamsburg boasted the most densely populated blocks in New York City. In 1917, the block between South 2nd and South 3rd streets housed over 5,000 people and was probably the most densely populated neighbourhood in the United States.[41]

The particular issue for those concerned about urban conditions, however, was that private relief and charitable agencies were much less developed in Brooklyn than they were in Manhattan. Wisdom would later describe Williamsburg as a "factory district with a large foreign population" comprised largely of Poles, Italians, and Germans. The personal photos she took and kept all her life showed busy streets lined with pushcarts and crowded sidewalks. These photos always placed people in the foreground and captured children in formal poses at the BBC, in dilapidated rear tenements, or candidly on the street. From Wisdom's first visit to New York, the city's people interested her as much as its buildings, theatres, or stores. Wisdom's time in Williamsburg coincided with the setting for Betty Smith's novel *A Tree Grows in Brooklyn*, which begins in that neighbourhood in the summer of 1912.[42] Here, an Austrian-Irish-American family living in an ethnically diverse neighbourhood of Italian and Jewish neighbours faced constant hunger and scrimping. They scavenged, bought stale bread and smashed pies, and got by with the weekly use of a pawnshop for cash. The poor-quality housing, irregular employment, alcoholism, and widowhood would have been familiar to Wisdom and her clients. The wrenching poverty described in Smith's portrayal of Williamsburg also offers insights into the continuing power of the political machine of Tammany Hall and the importance of free, partisan, leisure activities.

The BBC was the most important private agency in Brooklyn. It had its beginnings in the Union for Christian Work in the City of Brooklyn, established in 1866 and reorganized as the Brooklyn Bureau of Charity in 1878 in close affiliation with the New York COS. Alfred Tredway White was a leading supporter. Although he had a sustained interest in housing conditions and was credited by Jacob A. Riis for the ideas behind his important book *How the Other Half Lives*, he also epitomized the BBC in his emphasis that relief should be provided only in exchange for employment and "training" in the woodyards, laundries, schools, and workrooms operated by that organization. The BBC was not only concerned for the city's poor; it also sought to terminate corrupt public relief distributed to the poor in their homes, which was thought to "aggravate and perpetuate pauperism."[43] Although the BBC was supposedly non-sectarian, in the early twentieth century, its culture and staff were, in fact, firmly rooted in the Anglo-American and Protestant world. The agency worked together with the Brooklyn Children's Aid Society, the Brooklyn Society for the Prevention of Cruelty to Children, the Association for Improving the Condition of the Poor, and the Catholic St. Vincent de Paul Society. Before 1909, there was a distinct Jewish branch of the BBC, but this group reorganized under the name of the United Jewish Aid Societies and thereafter operated separately.[44]

In 1910, the BBC was divided into three offices, open six days a week from 8:00 to 5:30. The agency's services included operating a registry of charitable recipients, the investigation of new individual or family relief cases, and the provision of "temporary employment and industrial training." In addition, the BBC offered district nursing services, legal advice, household training, nurseries, and lodging for homeless men and women "in return for work," as well as accommodation for young children and their mothers.[45] The same year, in the Williamsburg office, there were 907 different applications for help. Annual reports of the BBC reflected the contemporary preoccupation with quantification. Clients were broken down by ethnicity and race, number of years in the United States, marital status, age, and family size in charts, tables, and graphs. These numbers are interesting as they suggest a perhaps exaggerated preoccupation with recent immigration. In 1911, for example, more than 40 per cent of the cases investigated by the BBC concerned 'white' Americans, and if those categorized as either Irish or German were added to this group, they would have accounted for more than 66 per cent of clients whose race or ethnicity were identified.

In July 1908, the BBC opened a new branch for the northern district on Marcy Street in Williamsburg, adjacent to the Carnegie Library and the Williamsburg YMCA. The first floor provided office space for the caseworkers and visiting nurses and a waiting room for clients, while the second floor was used as a day nursery and kindergarten for young children while mothers worked. Some of the mothers may have been employed on the third and fourth floors where there were a dining room, kitchen, workroom, and public laundry area. Rather than take in laundry to their overcrowded homes, women could bring their customers' laundry to a central place provided with tubs, soap, and hot water in exchange for a small daily fee of ten or fifteen cents, which went towards the cost of fuel and other expenses. The BBC building was topped with a roof playground where local children could play safely off the busy city streets.[46] It was from this building that Wisdom worked for most of her time in Brooklyn.

Wisdom's arrival at the Brooklyn Bureau of Charities coincided not only with a brand-new building but also more generally with the renewal and modernization of the organization. After sixteen years, General Secretary Rev. William I. Nichols resigned in April 1912. Nichols held very conservative nineteenth-century beliefs about relief and pauperism, and the agency, while progressing "in the area of family rehabilitation work," emphasized temporary employment in exchange for relief. The *Survey*'s announcement of Nichols's departure critically appraised that he may have "overemphasized" the usefulness of this kind of work in rehabilitation. This was certainly reflected in Nichols's final annual report. While he admitted that the "trend of modern charity ... is giving unprecedented attention to methods for the prevention of distress, by the discovery and removal of its underlying cause," he concluded with a plea for "consecrated disinterested volunteers." Nichols noted that the use of paid workers "curiously" coincided with the trend among charity organizations to distribute material relief and thereby abolish "one of the chief purposes of the founders of the charity organization movement. Much now is said of securing pensions for the poor, both from private benevolence and from public funds," but, according to Nichols, who clung to a fear of pauperism, this would do "more harm than good. They foster dependency rather than independence."[47] There is some evidence that even in the autumn of 1913, Jane Wisdom still shared this perspective. When testifying before the New York State Commission on Relief for Widowed Mothers, Wisdom defended her expectation that a poor widow with three young children work outside the home on the grounds that it was better for her to "make the effort on her own part."[48]

But the culture around charity work, particularly within the BBC, was changing. In August 1912, clergyman Nichols was replaced as general secretary with an academic, Dr. Thomas Riley, founder and director of the School of Social Economy in St. Louis, Missouri. In April 1913, he was joined by Margaret Byington from the Russell Sage Foundation, who was employed as supervising district secretary. As noted earlier, Byington bridged both the academic and practical streams of social work with casework experience and academic qualifications. Her widely distributed pamphlet, *The Confidential Exchange, A Form of Social Cooperation*, published during her time at the Russell Sage Foundation, meant that she was well known in the relief agency network.[49] Byington also believed that relief meant more than providing the basic necessities of food, clothing, shelter, and heat. Resources were required for "sundries," by which she meant the newspaper (so that the labourer could be an informed voter), and money for church, books, school supplies, dispensaries, dental clinics, and even flowers for the window and an attractive dress for a daughter. Byington's study of the steelmaking community of Homestead had led her to think about the "physiological and psychological effects of certain limitations of expenditure."[50]

The arrival of Riley and Byington resulted in immediate change. Riley increased the number of paid caseworkers from twenty-one to thirty-four, and introduced a new reporting system. He instituted new administrative and bureaucratic practices, including standardized forms to be completed by each district secretary, which, no doubt, expanded the workload of these women.[51] He also closed the lodging house for women and consolidated the central laundry and workroom as greater focus was given to the nine reconfigured relief districts. Each subdistrict was now run by an experienced secretary who was, in turn, assisted by a visitor-in-training. The exception was Williamsburg, the largest district, which boasted three assistants. With its greater emphasis on family-based casework, the BBC had new staffing needs.

Clearly, one of Riley's greatest challenges in his reformation of the BBC was dealing with working conditions for investigators and a high staff turnover. Many women worked only a short time before marriage or a lateral move to another agency or career. Salaries were an issue. When Wisdom was hired in 1912 at the annual salary of $1,000, she was the highest paid of the female district secretaries, although her salary was considerably below that of her supervisor, Byington, at $2,100. All employees were granted a two-week vacation after one year of work, and district secretaries received four weeks after two years. Additional benefits for district secretaries were ad hoc. When a district secretary who had been with the BBC for three years required a serious operation costing $300, she was given the funds, a leave of absence, and one month's salary. The working environment may have also been characterized by a strong sense of collegiality between the district secretaries and caseworkers. In her November 1914 report to the board, Byington noted that "a strong feeling of comradeship in the district staff" was "a valuable asset in counteracting the sense of discouragement that comes with the present pressure."[52] The constant demands of the work should not be underestimated. A small team of women, restricted by inadequate funds, bureaucratic rules, and limited time, could not adequately resolve the seemingly endless demands for help among the city's poor.

Wisdom and Byington appear to have been especially close. Upon her departure in 1914, Byington explained to Wisdom that she was leaving in part because she wondered how long she could "stand physically the strain of the work here (not that I've worked any harder than you have)." She expressed her love for Wisdom and her anxiety that Wisdom would "find the physical strain too great. *Please* be a little more selfish, a little less conscientious (– advice for a superior to give) but you really ought to save your strength for the fine sympathetic work you do. Please let me feel even next winter that I may have a little share of your time and thought and please forgive me if I seem to be a deserter."[53]

There were many "deserters," and Byington would have been well aware of what her departure meant for the remaining staff. Constant turnover meant that filling vacancies with workers "whose enthusiasm, intelligence and training would be adequate for the responsibilities devolving on them" was a constant challenge. Of the nine additional workers hired in 1913–14, eight were college graduates and the ninth had a teaching certificate and was a graduate of a special course at the University of Wisconsin. In addition to this general background, three of the nine workers had completed the specialized first-year course at the New York School of Philanthropy. But employees were constantly leaving for other agencies. For example, in November 1909, one former BBC district secretary became the general secretary of the Associated Charities of Pawtucket, Rhode Island. Another left to take a position with the National Red Cross.[54]

To address this problem, the BBC may have emphasized opportunities for ongoing professional development. It should be remembered that this search for educational opportunity was part of what drew Wisdom to New York in the first place. In 1912, for example, the agency introduced a policy of granting a leave of absence without pay for workers to attend the Charity Organization Institute with the understanding that they would receive higher salaries upon their return. The following year, two employees were granted leave with pay for the same course. Byington's arrival in 1913 marked the start of weekly training classes, and, in February 1915, Mary Richmond addressed a meeting of district secretaries.[55] Other opportunities were based in the local community. In 1913, for example, there was a fifteen-week lecture course run by the New York School of Philanthropy on "Elementary Problems of Modern Charity," held at the Brooklyn Institute for Arts and Sciences. Another opportunity for professional development was the annual New York City Conference of Charities and Correction, meant to supplement the national and state events. Wisdom was listed among the large number of attendees in 1913, 1914, 1915, and 1916, but I do not know what other opportunities she may have pursued. Names of other participants form an impressive list of social work pioneers, such as Florence Kelley, Lillian Wald, Mary Richmond, and W.E.B. Dubois.[56] The focus on education may also have been a pragmatic response to dealing with an inexperienced staff. The expansion of staff to forty-two district workers in early 1915 meant that a number of the new hires were not experienced, placing yet another burden on the exhausted veterans. In 1915, there was an especially high level of experienced worker turnover, including Byington's departure to the American Association for Organized Charities.[57]

Working conditions dramatically worsened in 1914 with widespread economic depression. There is a marked difference in board and executive minutes, which, before 1914, centred on such individual case problems as the administration of Red Cross money for a *Titanic* widow and trust money for at least one child whose mother was killed in the Triangle Shirtwaist fire.[58] The BBC became more broadly concerned with homelessness and the problem of unmarried mothers, which it sought to remedy most often by finding domestic service positions in the country, where mother and child could stay together. Along with economic depression in 1914, the outbreak of war in Europe brought unemployment, especially in the docks, and "widespread suffering." BBC President Alfred T. White noted that "the strain on the staff ... was necessarily severe," despite an increased staff of caseworkers; "the burden of making wise decisions in each case fell back in multiplied measure on the experienced heads of departments and district workers." This meant that every BBC caseworker was responsible for 100 families.[59]

In response to this crisis, the district secretaries were able to provide only partial investigations; relief was given because workers were not able to fully investigate the situation of families since so many new cases were presenting themselves each day. The scientific method of careful, individual, casework investigation was not feasible. The BBC was carrying almost as many cases as the New York COS, which had many more investigators and helpers. Because the workload of district secretaries had increased so dramatically, Riley proposed that the Executive Committee grant each district secretary an extra month's pay as a bonus. In January 1915, the board approved a pay increase to $88.33 a month for the four most experienced district secretaries, including Wisdom. The financial crisis was covered in part by a special $10,000 grant from the Rockefeller Foundation and an extraordinary community solicitation.[60]

Thomas Riley estimated that, normally, unemployment was the cause of only about a quarter of families seeking relief, but that in 1914, it had played a much more dramatic role. Those who were usually able to turn to support from kin and friends presently did not have this option. Fully three-quarters of families assisted turned to the BBC as a result of unemployment, sickness, old age, or "feeble-mindedness." Responsibility for finding employment could fall on district secretaries, who regularly contacted employers in their areas for hiring possibilities. The BBC also expanded its workrooms for women, establishing facilities for making clothing for Belgium, where workers earned 90 cents a day plus their lunch and had the privilege of "short hours" so that they could also attend to their domestic duties. The supervisors believed this program had the additional advantage of teaching much-needed sewing skills; providing suggestions of nourishing, "simple," and economical meal ideas; and assisting in the Americanization of immigrant women while reducing their housebound isolation.[61]

In the fall of 1915, Jane Wisdom wrote to her aunt that she was "not going to overwork this year for anybody or anything."[62] It is difficult to believe that she was able to keep this promise. Her position as district secretary was multifaceted and demanding. Her most important duties focused on the supervision of district casework investigators, as well as conducting her own family investigations at clients' homes. In the morning, she kept office hours at the district office but in the afternoon, she might be found anywhere in the area. Historian Karen Tice has noted the importance of standardizing methods of observation and interpretation to the emerging profession. The volume of Wisdom's work is suggested by the amount of funds the district secretaries distributed to needy clients. In 1913–14, for example, the Williamsburg district expended $6,003.70 in aid, with only the Bedford–Bushwick and Flatbush neighbourhoods spending more. Relief expenditures for 1914–15 in the Williamsburg district increased to $8,203.94 as economic depression set in.[63]

I could not locate any file for which Wisdom did the casework, but insights into her clients may be drawn from a collection of five Brooklyn photographs. An amateur photographer, Wisdom snapped informal shots of people in motion, and composed portraits of neighbourhood children in squalid, rear-tenement yards and at the pristine Williamsburg District office. These photographs were not for annual reports or agency publicity, and they are neither sensational nor sentimental. Likely taken to accompany letters for family and friends, the images illustrated her life in the city. Wisdom's street scenes are bustling: rather than telling tales of moral danger, they reveal the exotic commotion of pushcarts, market stalls, and men, women, and children who sold, shopped, and browsed. In the background, store signs are in Hebrew script, old men wear Jewish prayer shawls, and women cover their hair with scarves, the camera at such a distance so as not to let the subjects know they are on display. In three posed photos, groups of children have a variety of complexions, suggesting Wisdom's ideal of harmonious, cross-ethnic community relations. The children are clean and decently clothed (one boy is shoeless), and although the rear tenement is dirty, it is also domestic. Clean laundry hangs on lines; a washtub dangles out of a crowded apartment window; a mother watches out a window; and, among the children, an older girl rests her arms tenderly around younger children. There is no sense of voyeurism: the children are collaborating, either grinning directly at the camera or running to participate in a group photo. Wisdom is clearly not trying to reproduce the iconic work of photographers Jacob Riis or Lewis Hines; rather, she captures joy, community, and the use of BBC facilities.[64] While photographs of children as victims were often used by reformers to generate emotion, the children Wisdom captured on film have dignity, humanity, and the ability to act for themselves.[65]

The faces of individuals in these photos balance the barrage of impersonal numbers provided in the BBC's annual reports regarding the use of local facilities and programs Wisdom had to supervise. In 1914, for example, the annual report noted that the Williamsburg laundry was used by thirty-one women for a total of 1,585 working days, noting that these women were able to earn $9 to $12 a week. The BBC in Williamsburg also operated a local nursery, offered the services of a district nursing staff, and undertook special projects. In October 1915, Wisdom reported making a round of addresses to local women's church groups about the need for organized charity. She wrote that "there are so many little organizations you see and they have got to work together to some extent or they do more harm than good." Educational initiatives could also be directed towards clients. For example, Wisdom may have been involved in creating the model demonstration flat that opened in the summer of 1914 under the joint auspices of the Committee on Housing and the Williamsburg District.[66]

In early October 1913, after only four months in Williamsburg, Wisdom faced intense examination by the New York State Commission on Relief for Widowed Mothers regarding relevant cases in the district for the year and a half before she arrived. We see that she was constantly collaborating with doctors and visiting housekeepers, and negotiating not only with her clients but also their relatives. She revealed ethnic prejudices when she argued that Italian households required less money for food than Polish homes. More broadly, we see her failure to make contact with clients and address their needs. Based on her testimony and that of Sara Dissoway, the commission concluded by stating the "absolute inability of the Brooklyn Bureau of Charities to care in a suitable and adequate manner for the families of widowed mothers looking to it for assistance."[67]

There is no question that the volume of work was overwhelming for social workers at the BBC. In addition to addressing the needs of clients, the job also entailed supervising the community committee, whose individual members performed the voluntary service role that had earlier been played by individual friendly visiting – when volunteers formed direct and ideally intimate relationships with the agency's clients. In 1916, Wisdom's now-former assistant Mary Shenstone published an article describing the demographic changes that had occurred in Williamsburg with the influx of working-class immigrants and the exodus of the older, middle-class "American" population. According to Shenstone, "Williamsburg now seems a foreign city, with crowded streets, push-carts, rough-looking Poles, and dirty-faced Italian children. Within the last two years, three of the old churches closed their doors and one has been turned into a synagogue." Unlike the nineteenth-century city where rich and poor were more likely to share common residential neighbourhoods, the modern industrial city was characterized by residential separation along class and ethnic lines. For organizations charged with serving the non-sectarian community, where there were parallel Jewish and Catholic parish-based associations, there was a great store of potential middle-class volunteers with a "great scarcity of ... workers in some districts and a great abundance in others." Wisdom and her team appear to have dealt with this problem by encouraging former residents of Williamsburg to volunteer in their home neighbourhood.[68]

The 1912–13 Williamsburg District Advisory Committee was composed of eleven individuals: three men, one with the title of doctor, and eight women. During the 1913–14 year, the committee grew to twenty-one, with fifteen women and five men. While many members had Anglo-Celtic surnames, the addition of two religious Catholics, Father J. Cysmowski and Sister Rebecca, suggests a small attempt to broaden the community base. This trend was continued in 1914–15 when the advisory committee, again predominantly female, added Miss Ida I. Kelheimer and Rev. O. Silvestri.[69] The presence of a single Polish, German, and Italian surname on the district committee was perhaps tokenistic, but the belief in community participation was constant throughout Wisdom's professional career.

Although Wisdom had great confidence in the community, she had much less faith in formal politics. Her experience in Brooklyn, perhaps reinforced by the widespread municipal corruption she had witnessed in Montreal, made her skeptical that public welfare and pensions could ever be completely removed from political interference.[70] Proponents of private charity regarded its insulation from patronage as one of its primary virtues. Wisdom could not imagine public assistance isolated from political graft. Lessons learned about political corruption, favouritism, and patronage and waste in the distribution of Civil War pensions made many social reformers in the United States wary and suspicious of government. At the same time, one of the principal objectives of the Progressive movement was to end political corruption. Tammany Hall, the Democratic Party's system for buying and controlling votes in New York municipal politics, was perhaps the most infamous example. From Williamsburg, Jane Wisdom had a front-row seat to watch the dominant political machine. Many social reformers in New York actively sought ways to free public-welfare spending from political interference. The establishment of the New York State Board of Charities was one strategy to minimize the power of the local Democratic Party.[71]

Along with presumption of corrupt local governments came the correspondingly naïve confidence that private charities were somehow objective and desired only to distribute relief to the deserving. It was in this context that many early social workers opposed public pensions. Politicians and much of the public were not so cynical. In 1913, a widows' pension bill was introduced in the New York State Assembly. The proposed legislation generated much debate within the Executive Committee of the BBC. It questioned the need for state relief, as many widowed mothers were being served by private charities; such a public pension would be "the entering wedge to more extended public relief." The leadership of the BBC did not condemn the proposal outright, but, rather, resolved that no pension legislation should be introduced without a public inquiry.[72] A subgroup of the New York State Commission on Relief for Widowed Mothers later spent some time examining the work of the BBC, and Wisdom and General Secretary Riley spent two afternoons before them. Fifty years later, Wisdom remembered the commission as "antagonistic" towards private and volunteer social agencies. She also remembered the "long heated discussion that social workers had when Mothers' Allowances were being discussed for New York State. This was during the politically corrupt 'Tammany Hall' gang. Some of us workers were against the allowance at that time because we couldn't see how these corrupt politicians would be able to understand the problems of our mothers, especially the immigrant mothers, some of whom couldn't even speak English."[73]

In this memory, there are several interesting points. The first was that Wisdom placed herself in the company of Mary Richmond, who strongly opposed state mothers' pension to widows.[74] Wisdom and Richmond were not against supporting these needy women and their children. Instead, they believed that the private agencies with which they were associated were in a better position to allocate funds; they were in the more neutral and objective position, untainted by political patronage, corruption, and influence peddling. Obviously, there was a strong element of self-interest involved at the prospect of losing control over the distribution of money, but, to be fair, this self-interest coincided with a concern about the loss of volunteerism and community responsibility. In any case, their concern about the loss of influence public welfare would bring to private agencies was correct. Susan Traverso, in her study of Boston, concludes that with the growth of state-based welfare, and as private agencies "relinquished" their relief functions, they tended to "retreat from the politics of public welfare." Adopting the role of "professional providers of social services," they lost social and political sway. Wisdom and Richmond would have also known that private charity tended to be more generous to recipients than public provisions and, some claimed, did not have the same tarnish of public dependency.[75]

Second, Wisdom's recollection emphasizes that mothers' pensions were fiercely debated among social workers and that there was not one, unified, professional line. The diversity of opinion matters a great deal here. Different social workers saw pensions as either much-needed assistance or harmful to their clients. Wisdom's particular choice of words was interesting. Notwithstanding claims of distant objectivity, she refers to the clients as "our mothers," suggesting both a maternalistic and protective attitude. Certainly, one of the potential pitfalls of an allowance scheme identified by Wisdom and her colleagues was the lack of accompanying casework or counselling support. Through casework, Wisdom placed the individual or family in a larger economic, social, and moral context, and sought individual solutions to people's problems. In the end, arguments against public pensions did not prevail, and the committee ultimately submitted a liberal report recommending state pensions for widows.[76]

As a precursor to her 1964 reflections on mothers' pensions, Wisdom also recalled the state of the profession at that time: "The purpose of the worker was the same then as today, to help people, but the challenge of the worker was different. We had to tackle the problem of great poverty. There is still poverty today but not in the same sense as then. Poverty was common and accepted then, but as students became interested in social conditions they wanted to know just why such conditions existed." There is little doubt that Wisdom was permanently affected by the poverty she had witnessed first in Montreal and later in Brooklyn. During the 1940s, she sympathetically dismissed claims that housing conditions in Glace Bay, Nova Scotia, were the worst in North America with the memory that even its worst places did not match what she had seen elsewhere.[77]

It is also evident that she could understand that period only through the filter of her subsequent experience and eventual commitment to the necessity of state support. Even during her four years with the BBC, she changed a great deal, distancing herself almost completely from fears that unearned charity pauperized its recipients. Again, remembering this time fifty years later, she continued, "Some workers became almost radical in their desire and efforts to help the welfare program. All workers were forced to realize that they couldn't make the world change over night. The work was doubly difficult then because much was left to voluntary effort. The government had not yet begun to take a part in this work."[78] I do not think Jane Wisdom was speaking of herself when she referred to the radical project of some workers, but I do think it was personal experience that forced her to admit that dramatic change was unlikely to be immediate.

Wisdom's departure for Halifax in the spring of 1916 went virtually unnoted in the official agency minutes, except for a comment at an October board meeting that the bureau had lost some of its "best secretaries." This discreet observation must have included Wisdom.[79] She recalled that when initially asked to go to Halifax, she responded that she could not "leave her important work." After subsequent pressure and persuasion that she could serve the profession better where there was a great scarcity of trained workers, she acquiesced. Going to Halifax also brought personal satisfaction, bringing her closer to her aging parents, her sister, her niece, and her extended family.

From New York, Wisdom was able to participate in, and follow, debates about emerging professional practices. She had the unique opportunity to work with some of the most powerful leaders in her field, the very people who were developing the new technique of professional casework. She worked regularly with a diverse group of clients,

Chapter Five

Halifax: Bureaucratization, Emergencies, and the Progressive State, 1916–1921

If New York City was the heart of the philanthropic world and the home of the emergent profession of social work, Halifax could easily be dismissed as both a geographic and cultural periphery. Certainly, Halifax had become geographically marginal by the second decade of the twentieth century. Like Saint John, the development of a continentally based industrial economy demoted the resource-extraction industries of "wood, wind, and sail." Halifax found itself no longer at the centre of a vibrant North Atlantic maritime economy, but at the terminus of railway lines. This geographical isolation was temporarily altered during the First World War, when Halifax's port played an important role in supplying England with resources and material.

But the consequences of urbanization that were encouraging reform movements across North America in the early twentieth century were also present in Halifax. Location and population size had not isolated Halifax from the influence of progressive thought and reform. The smaller scale of industrialization and trickle of immigration meant that specific urban problems were different from those in cities such as New York or Montreal, which was experiencing enormous rates of growth. Between 1901 and 1911, the population of Halifax grew only from 41,000 to 47,000, which meant that it actually fell from being Canada's fifth-largest city to a distant eleventh place, and the city's total population was less than Jane Wisdom's district of Williamsburg in Brooklyn. Nevertheless, many Haligonians were closely integrated into a North American network of reform, and the extraordinary local tragedy of the 1917 explosion, which killed close to 2,000 people, and left around 9,000 persons injured, pushed the city at least temporarily into the centre of continental reform networks. Jane Wisdom's residence in Halifax between 1916 and 1921 coincided with the development of a number of new private, semi-public, and public agencies created to address various welfare needs. Rather than a simple progression of private to public, wartime Halifax and Wisdom's career showed the simultaneous coexistence of these various forms, the change in the boundaries of what was thought possible, and, finally, the disappointment of tremendous potential unrealized. Wisdom's experience in wartime Halifax made her a Progressive, one who now regarded the state as a potential ally in solving individual and community problems.

When Jane Wisdom arrived in Halifax in 1916, she would have immediately recognized similarities with the city of her youth. Like Saint John, Halifax also operated under a poor-law regime accompanied by private charities and institutions generally organized along confessional and ethnic lines. As a poor-law province, Nova Scotia had no direct public provisions for outdoor material assistance, and depended on private charity to assist the deserving poor in their homes. Those who did not have immediate kin or sympathetic friends and those whom private agencies did not wish to assist had to resort to the municipal poorhouse. The poor law, in fact, encouraged the proliferation of private charities in Halifax, who had overlapping clients and some of whom acted as indirect agents of the state as recipients of municipal grants.[1]

Halifax also shared similarities with Montreal. Unlike Catholics in most North American cities outside Quebec, Halifax Catholics mirrored the full economic social structure of the Protestant community with a large middle class and its parallel social and institutional structures. This shaped the local reform movement, since many progressive impulses and campaigns were closely aligned with the Protestant social gospel. In 1891, Pope Leo XIII issued an encyclical *Rerum Novarum*, which offered a critique of capitalism as destructive to communities and individuals and provided a means by which progressive Halifax Catholics might find common cause with their Protestant neighbours in campaigns against prostitution and in support of child welfare and improved industrial conditions. They would find women's suffrage, Sabbatarianism, and temperance less appealing causes.

Even before the war, all Nova Scotians witnessed every level of government's expanding their areas of welfare concern. In 1911, Nova Scotia introduced a Workmen's Compensation Act to compensate employees working in specified industries who were injured or killed on the job. The federal government was expressing some interest in the entire area of insurance, as it collected private insurance information on all residents as part of the 1911 national census.

Federally and provincially, the concern was often general child protection. In February 1912, the province appointed Ernest H. Blois as Superintendent of Neglected and Dependent Children and Chief Probation Officer. Blois would be a key figure in Nova Scotia social service until 1947. Born in Hants County in 1878, he attended Dalhousie University for two years, taught school, and, in 1901, joined the staff of the Halifax Industrial School.[2] While he was remembered by his friend and protégé Fred MacKinnon for a "life of public service devoted to social justice," contemporary social worker Ethel Bird described him in 1915 as a "huge 6ft 5in police probation officer," obstinate, and her "bête noire" in the campaign to establish a central charity office in Halifax.[3] But Blois was extremely well connected in the North American welfare community. In 1912, the United States government created the Children's Bureau; the following year, Blois and R. H. Murray of the Society for the Prevention of Cruelty were requested by the federal Department of Justice to "to investigate and report upon the establishment, maintenance and working of the Children's Bureau in the United States." They toured various American cities, attended a national convention of the American Humane Association, and, finally, visited the Children's Bureau in Washington. On their return trip to Halifax, they visited the Russell Sage Foundation in New York City. They judged the private agency to be "carrying on greater work than that in Washington."[4] Wisdom, about to embark for Brooklyn at the time, would probably have agreed.

The confidence that Blois and Murray possessed in private agencies reflected their experience with Halifax. Although the American social work press would later characterize pre-war Halifax as either "backward" or "conservative," with rates of infant mortality twice that of New York and Boston, the city did not lack for private agencies trying to improve general conditions. Inspired by either the international currents of Protestant evangelicalism or Catholic social action, institutions such as the Halifax City Mission of the 1850s had links to the London City Mission in England; organizations such as the YMCA and YWCA, both active in Halifax by the 1870s, were international movements. Halifax established its own variant of the Association for Improving the Condition of the Poor in 1866, following the New York society established in 1842. The Society for the Prevention of Cruelty was created in 1880, only five years after the original New York society and two years before its Montreal counterpart got off the ground.[5] These Halifax male organizations were arguably Protestant counterparts to the male, parish-based, worldwide St. Vincent de Paul Society, which came to Halifax in 1853, followed by its female counterpart, the Children of Mary, a year later. Catholic religious orders such as the Sisters of the Good Shepherd were engaged in "rescue work" among female offenders internationally, and the Salvation Army, which arrived in Halifax in 1885, pursued a range of charitable evangelical endeavours, as it did in other cities throughout the Anglo-American world.

Perhaps because of the strength of these Christian charitable agencies, scientific philanthropy was slower to come to the city.[6] When Wisdom arrived in Halifax, the organized charity movement could be best described as fledgling. Historian Christina Simmons has noted that conservative forces such as the Jost Mission acted within the framework of "19th-century women's Christian charity," where help for the poor was firmly embedded as an expression of religious faith, well into the twentieth century.[7] But it is surprising that Halifax was one of the few large cities in Canada that did not have a coordinating body; neither was this a top priority for a generally very active Local Council of Women before the First World War.[8]

Other local reformers were connected to North American welfare networks and felt the reverberations of many North American social service trends. A local correspondent occasionally contributed to the monthly American *National Bulletin of Charities and Correction*. Halifax had yet another link to the main current of North American social work through Arthur James Johnstone, a Dartmouth journalist, who became well known for his writings on the Halifax explosion. Johnstone was the first Canadian who can be identified as having attended the Chicago School of Civics and Philanthropy (which, in 1920, became the University of Chicago's School of Social Service Administration) when he enrolled in the 1911 summer program.[9]

No individual in the reform community had more links to American organizations than lawyer Reginald Vanderbilt Harris, the engine behind the city's 1911 "civic revival." He was a key to understanding the challenge that broad-based reform faced in Halifax, for although he was described "very clever" and "clear sighted," he was also hampered by "*very severe* prejudices" towards Roman Catholics and too outspoken to be popular. Sectarian prejudices were a serious hindrance to community work. In at least one case, the Local Council of Women stated that its support of one of his schemes was conditional on the assurance that "religion and politics shall not be brought into the question."[10]

The civic revival was modelled on a Boston campaign, which had had the support of the Russell Sage Foundation and the social service journal *The Survey*. The main speaker of the revival was "evangelist" John L. Sewell, who emphasized co-operation and coordination of voluntary agencies and municipal government. In a well-attended public address hosted by the Catholic and Protestant charitable societies, Sewell made the link between co-operation and efficiency, quoting material issued by the Russell Sage Foundation's charity department. Halifax needed a "united charity council" where delegates of various organizations could meet together, run a coordinated registration bureau or "confidential exchange" to prevent duplication, and organize preventive work along the lines of health, housing, and education.[11]

But no concrete action was taken. The Halifax Local Council of Women periodically raised the issue, and Harris attempted to keep the issue alive through journalism and ongoing links with the New York Russell Sage Foundation. The Halifax civic revival had coincided with the June 1911 establishment of the National Association of Societies for Organizing Charities with Francis McLean as its first head. Although this new association was technically distinct from the Russell Sage Foundation, it shared personnel, space, and funding.[12] Its expertise in organizing and coordinating charitable societies meant that it was soon involved in Canadian cities, notably Winnipeg, Toronto, Montreal, and Halifax.

International circumstances, not local activity, finally brought results. Hostilities in Europe seemed distant in Brooklyn but it preoccupied Halifax. Canada's 1914 entry into the war prompted local feminist activists such as May Best Sexton to resurrect coordinated charity in a wartime context, calling for greater efficiency as "a means of conserving resources." The city refused to finance the effort but local activists, under the influence of the American Association of Societies for Organizing Charities, arranged for one of its professional organizers to come to Halifax to lay the groundwork for something permanent.[13]

In December 1915, American Ethel Bird finally arrived in Halifax.[14] By then, the war had become the focus of civic life, and it was difficult for a neutral American to make an easy transition to wartime Halifax. Those bringing Bird to Halifax with the intent of establishing a Bureau of Social Service found themselves having to vie for attention and resources. Competing causes included fundraising for the Victory Loans, the Red Cross, cigarettes for soldiers, and, most importantly, the Canadian Patriotic Fund (CPF). The CPF was the national voluntary charity charged with providing soldiers' families with monthly grants to supplement their meagre military pay. Within the CPF, local practices varied. Unlike the CPF in Montreal, which employed the principles of scientific charity – namely, investigative casework and co-operation with the city's COS – the Halifax CPF distanced itself from any connection with charity. The grants to soldiers' families were portrayed as entitlements, and this put the CPF into direct conflict with an organization trying to introduce scientific charity based on careful casework and investigation.[15]

Bird had some idea of the importance of the war but was unprepared for the difficulty it would pose for local organizing. Before she arrived in Halifax, Ethel Bird stopped in Montreal, where she visited the local CPF office, which she described as "the most wonderful volunteer organization I've ever been privileged to see." A contemporary social work publication also praised the Montreal office for combining the "business-like system of an insurance company ... with the human insight of modern social work." Here Bird met the indomitable Helen Reid. Reid was administering a fund of $1.5 million to supplement separation allowances for soldiers' families and was supervising some 600 to 800 local volunteers. She was also overseeing a professional statistical and financial department along the lines of scientific charity, a movement she had supported and been involved with since the 1890s.[16]

Halifax had no such groundwork. During her time there, Ethel Bird established an office in the Halifax Dispensary, gave more than twenty lectures before various local groups, and undertook actual casework with some families and individuals.[17] She found many aspects of the city frustrating. Harris insisted that Bird not stay at the local YWCA, as he felt it would affect her "prestige," and presumably that of the bureau he was trying to establish. Members of the advisory board provoked a variety of reactions. She identified Agnes Miller Dennis, wife of a Conservative senator and publisher of the *Halifax Herald*, correctly – as a networker and a useful ally. But Bird had trouble with two of the most influential members of the advisory board: Blois, mentioned earlier, and May Best Sexton, whom she described as "a very clever woman, ... and one of the most strident and impossible I've seen in a long time!" On another occasion, Bird wrote that Sexton enjoyed speaking too much; "she simply *lives* for the limelight," she wrote.[18]

Throughout Bird's time in Halifax, she was in constant correspondence with both Margaret Byington and Francis McLean of the New York-based American Association of Societies for Organizing Charities and acted as a general go-between for various American foundations and societies. Bird and McLean arranged that Byington be invited to Halifax to speak in late February with the hope that her visit would be the impetus for the creation of a permanent new welfare organization.[19]

Byington's visit was a success, with good attendance at various meetings and the establishment of a permanent bureau and board.[20] The new board was remarkably similar to the original advisory committee, with a representation of Catholics and Protestants, businessmen and politicians, men and women. Taking a lead from other cities that had chosen a reputable businessman to be chairman of the board, the bureau elected prominent local financier H.R. Silver to this position. The constitution also looked remarkably like that in other North American cities. It emphasized that the Bureau of Social Service was not as much for relief granting as it was for promoting "harmonious cooperation" between charitable societies, investigating cases of need, and reducing duplication and waste through the maintenance of a confidential registry. The bureau promoted independence for families in need, sought to eliminate begging, and advanced "the general welfare of the poor by social and sanitary reforms, by industrial instruction, by the inculcation of habits of providence and self-dependence."[21]

In May 1916, the Bureau of Social Service announced it had hired a trained Nova Scotian, Jane Wisdom, as its first permanent secretary. Both the *Halifax Herald* and the *Echo* highlighted the new secretary's alleged Nova Scotian identity in headlines.[22] The significance placed on the new secretary's being (if somewhat indirectly) a Nova Scotian challenged Bird's earlier observation that she had "not the slightest hint (except in one or perhaps two cases) that her coming from the States mattered." In fact, hiring a Canadian was regarded as essential during wartime, at a point when the United States had not yet entered the fray. Insider versus outsider status may have mattered more than Bird understood. Nevertheless, she left with good friends in the city and returned there in December 1917.[23]

As noted earlier, Wisdom came under considerable pressure to leave her work in Brooklyn and accept the Halifax position. She received several letters from H.R. Silver and Reginald Harris, who emphasized the importance of getting a trained worker with local connections. With an eye to post-war reconstruction when family rehabilitation work would need to be organized "along modern lines," and the fragility of the Halifax initiative, the men approached Wisdom's boss at the Brooklyn Bureau of Charities and her former supervisor Margaret Byington to persuade Wisdom to reconsider her initial rejection. Byington's influence appears to have been especially important, and she enthusiastically recommended Wisdom to the Halifax committee, praising her ability to create "lovely personal relations with people she was trying to help."[24] Local connections were an advantage to Wisdom, as she already knew some community members and was sensitive to local culture and institutions. She had relatives and close family friends in the city, and the curate of St. Paul's Anglican Church, Samuel Prince, who would take a leadership role in Nova Scotia welfare through the 1950s, was in the class behind her at Saint John High School. Certainly, her sense of local politics was better than her predecessor's. Rather than being an itinerant society organizer, Wisdom had experience with managing ongoing relations with boards, volunteers, and clients. She began her publicity for the bureau with exaggerated praise of Halifax's general interest in social service. She publicly characterized the city as progressive rather than conservative, drawing attention to its employment of a school nurse, a tuberculosis nurse, and a policewoman.[25]

Wisdom began a busy year of establishing scientific philanthropy in Halifax, and created welfare networks that would soon take on demands beyond anyone's imagination. When Wisdom started in June 1916, she did so at a salary of $1,200 a year, only slightly more than she had earned in Brooklyn, but initially bore a much smaller caseload. But individual casework was only a part of the position; she appears to have spent considerable time speaking publicly and gathering supporters to women's, church, and community groups.[26] Although the Bureau of Social Service was originally intended to be primarily a means to coordinate local charities, hiring a professional social worker changed this objective. Wisdom described herself as a "thorough-going believer in the modern theory of keeping a family together and making the individual home the unit of influence and training," so her philosophy did not necessarily coincide with existing charitable residential institutions such as orphanages, refuges, and asylums. Her unequivocal confidence in casework, whereby social workers "improve the home and brought it up to the proper standard," meant that she needed assistance. With this in mind, Wisdom quickly set about recruiting volunteer friendly visitors.[27]

In the Bureau of Social Service's 1917 annual report, in reference to the war, Wisdom described her activities as "Home Defense Work" for Canada and Halifax in particular, as it supported "the mobilization of all the social forces in the community against the inroads of poverty and its allies – the enemies of civilization for which our men are laying down their lives on the battle fields – the enemies which threaten the very homes of our fighting men themselves."[28] While she admitted that war improved general conditions with full employment, a regular income among military men, and aid from the CPF, Wisdom reminded supporters that there continued to be serious problems. She drew attention to the elderly and the particular problems of "tuberculosis, mental and physical disease of every kind, poor housing, high rents, illiteracy, ignorance, incompetency (domestic and industrial), intemperance and moral defects." She attributed welfare problems to both societal and individual origins. With this in mind, she identified the work of the bureau as creating opportunities for health, education, work, recreation, and spiritual development. The Christian duty of the community should not end with addressing cold and hunger; rather, she implored organizations "to locate the deeper trouble behind the hunger and cold, or whatever the symptoms may be, and where it can be found, to work as a doctor does after diagnosis, to remove the cause and prevent contagion." By 1919, she was prepared to state that Halifax had moved "from the old idea of charity to philanthropy ... to the thing we call 'social justice.'"[29]

If, by the end of the war, Wisdom spoke of "social justice," with her arrival in Halifax, she was already moving squarely into mainstream progressive culture. No doubt, war conditions, an expanding government, and personal patriotism encouraged her to reconceptualize the state as a positive force for regulation and social harmony. The war also accelerated the process described by historian Robert Wiebe –"the ambition of the new middle class to fulfill its destiny through bureaucratization" – and this could be found at "the heart of progressivism."[30]

Between July 1916 and September 1917, Wisdom organized a confidential index of clients, conducted campaigns about poor wartime housing and tuberculosis, and undertook individual casework in areas that ranged from providing working girls with country vacations, to keeping families together after a father died, to finding interim accommodation for an evicted family. Fundraising was also a perpetual task. In the quantifying fashion of the day, Wisdom listed that for the first fifteen months, she had opened 281 cases, conducted 386 office interviews, made 1,728 visits, and assisted people of Canadian, Irish, Newfoundland, English, French-Canadian, West Indian, Scottish, Italian, and Russian descent.[31]

Wisdom was also networking within the emerging, national, Canadian social work community. In the fall of 1917, she travelled to Ottawa to attend the Canadian Conference of Charities and Correction, the Annual Meeting of the Canadian Association for the Prevention of Tuberculosis, and the Annual Congress of the Canadian Public Health Association. She returned convinced that the dominant agendas of child welfare, immigration, "feeble-mindedness," and tuberculosis were relevant to local conditions.[32] But the general preoccupations of the Canadian social service community were about to be displaced by dramatic local circumstances, which placed family rehabilitation at the core.

On 6 December 1917, Jane Wisdom arrived early at her office with a headache. Unable to get down to work, she left her office and went down the hill to busy, commercial Barrington Street in search of Aspirin. At 9:04, she was safely on the street, three kilometres south of the area of the harbour known as the Narrows, when two ships collided, setting off one of the largest, pre-atomic, man-made explosions. The "Halifax explosion" killed almost 2,000 people, left 10,000 homeless, and instigated a mammoth relief and reconstruction effort that would distribute $26.5 million through the Relief Commission in its first twenty months and bring Halifax to the forefront of international welfare circles.[33] Wisdom was, fortunately, not in her office, where the plate-glass window imploded on her desk.[34] On the day of the disaster, Jane Wisdom was the only trained, practising social worker in the city.

To a remarkable degree, Wisdom's Saint John schoolmate Samuel Prince has dominated understandings of the relief and construction efforts following the explosion. *Catastrophe and Social Change, Based on a Sociological Study of the Halifax Disaster* was his Columbia PhD thesis, supervised by eminent sociologist F.H. Giddings and published in 1920.[35] Prince argued that social disintegration following the disaster created the conditions for social change. This understanding of the explosion as a rupture has distorted the continuity that characterized social service in the city before and afterward. Scientific charity and social work casework had been taking place at the professional level for two years before the Halifax tragedy.

Indeed, by December 1917, the Halifax social service and reform community was already well integrated into the American and central Canadian charitable network, with pre-existing personal and associational links. This was evident in the scores of social work professionals who descended on Halifax from throughout Canada and the eastern United States. Ethel Bird returned to work for the Investigation Department of the Halifax Relief Commission, along with professional workers from the American Red Cross, the New York Charity Organization

Society, the Montreal Charity Organization Society, the Toronto Department of Public Health, the Winnipeg Welfare Commission, the Montreal Patriotic Fund, Boston Associated Charities, and the Association for the Improvement of the Condition of the Poor of New York, who were all working under a set of shared assumptions and familiar with a similar operating procedure.[36] The professionals who came to Halifax were both ordinary female caseworkers and men recognized as leading the profession. Wisdom probably already knew Nova Scotia-born R.C. Dexter, general secretary of the Montreal COS, and Garfield A. Berlinsky of Montreal's Federation of Jewish Philanthrapies, but this may have been the first time she had met Howard Toynbee Falk, then of Winnipeg, who was appointed chief of staff at the request of the American Red Cross.[37] Falk was three years older than Wisdom, related to several prominent English reform families, and would play an important part in her life for the next thirteen years.

The American Red Cross arrived in Halifax under the command of John F. Moors, president of the Boston Associated Charities, who had previously been in charge of Red Cross operations after the 1914 Chelsea and 1908 Salem fires. Moors was assisted in coordinating rehabilitation work by C.C. Carsten, general secretary of the Massachusetts Society for the Prevention of Cruelty to Children. Both men had been influenced by Francis McLean, who had first professionalized disaster relief for the Red Cross after the 1906 San Francisco earthquake. Using the principles of scientific charity employed by McLean in San Francisco, explosion relief followed a policy of centralization, coordination, treating individuals as part of family units, and all records being cleared through a single registration bureau. Adherence to a bureaucratic system, an emphasis on efficiency, and a preoccupation with preventing fraud brought considerable criticism, as compassion, empathy, and charity were not always apparent to suffering and frustrated victims.[38]

On 6 December, organizational expertise in the city was held by the military, churches, labour unions, businessmen, and women volunteers. Initial relief impulses were simultaneously efficient and chaotic. Putting out fires, preventing secondary explosions, finding and caring for survivors, combating a blizzard, and issuing calls for assistance preoccupied those in charge, and, as historian Jacob Remes has demonstrated, took place at the ad hoc and informal community level.[39] While formal relief efforts were organized throughout the Maritimes and in Boston, Haligonians emerged from their shock and organized themselves. At a meeting of City Hall on the morning of 7 December, Clara MacIntosh, sister of Reginald Harris, offered to use her Voluntary Aid Detachment and St. John Ambulance Corps connections to conduct a primary registration of those who were still in their homes around the devastated area. Wisdom, who had slipped into the meeting late, did not realize that MacIntosh had already floated this idea informally to others and she was concerned that MacIntosh's proposal ignored other groups of women volunteers.[40] In this situation, Wisdom was both the only one with social service training and the only person who was an employee of the local leadership stepping up to take responsibility. Wisdom was in a delicate position: she did not want to contradict her employers, yet she sought to provide efficient help. She and the bureau's secretary immediately installed themselves in the mayor's office and began organizing the cases. On that afternoon, volunteer help came from Salvation Army workers, who took over the desk.[41] Wisdom recalled that the aim of this first relief was to "try and fill all urgent needs with a minimum of record," but admitted that even in the emergency period, "practically every name and address was kept." Almost immediately, Wisdom organized "material relief applications" for the distribution of food and coal orders upon either personal application or the report of one of the workers. Within twenty-four hours, a food distribution system was established in the devastated area and depots were available for clothing and blankets. The St. John Ambulance Brigade later reported that "Miss Wisdom and Mrs. Freeman [the secretary] did most excellent work ... working like others without proper meals and with very little sleep." Throughout the initial period, Wisdom "carried on to the point of exhaustion," and was later remembered by one of the relief commissioners as "a woman sent by God for that work." Personally, she recalled the "numbness."[42]

On Monday, 10 December, Wisdom was seconded to the American Red Cross as power shifted from City Hall to that organization. Self-appointed local amateurs were replaced by American professionals in the Red Cross who acted as behind-the-scene advisors, nudging control away from local politicians and into the hands of unstable and sometimes fractious citizens' committees. Money, resources, and, ultimately, legislation removed decision making from the local level. The first chairman of the Rehabilitation Committee, prominent local banker Dougall MacGillivray, lasted until Christmas Eve, and he was replaced with J.H. Winfield, the general manager of Maritime Telephone and Telegraph. There was also the suggestion of a power struggle between the existing Bureau of Social Service and the post-explosion committee structure. The Halifax Commercial Club, presumably through the initiative of Reginald Harris, suggested that an enlarged Bureau of Social Service handle "all the goods that have arrived in the City and ... have sole authority to issue orders."[43] He was remarkably naïve about what was about to happen.

Samuel Prince later wrote: "The Halifax disaster was one of the first of great extent which has occurred since the principles of relief have been authoritatively written. No other community has experienced their applications so fully or so promptly."[44] In practical terms, this meant the centralization of authority, records, and distribution of relief, and the "early abolition of mass treatment" with an emphasis on family-based casework. This set the rehabilitation committee with the enormous task of "discovering on a case by case basis what every individual family needed" for the almost 6,000 registrants by the end of the first month. Laura MacDonald, author of *Curse of the Narrows*, noted that the disaster was also "the first time in the American Red Cross' experience that people would be compensated monetarily for disaster-related losses" – a daunting prospect, as material losses alone were estimated at $35 million.[45] In the aftermath of the explosion, private and public donations from around the world poured into Halifax. A plan was required to distribute funds fairly and on the basis of need.

The American Red Cross was in Halifax only for the immediate emergency period. When it closed its offices in mid-January, operations were transferred by statute to the federal government's Halifax Relief Commission. The commission was a public/private hybrid, with its funds originating from both government and private donations, and operating under federal statues and with government appointments. It conflated the categories of state and society already under pressure of war stringencies. The commission was organized into four areas: rehabilitation, reconstruction, medical, and finance. Wisdom, who had been working with the temporary committee, was transferred to the Halifax Relief Commission and worked with the Rehabilitation Department until 31 December 1918. She began her position as general supervisor of District Work, answering inquiries for missing relatives and the unidentified dead, and coordinating the scores of volunteer and professional caseworkers who flooded the city.[46] Manitoba-based Howard Falk, one of Canada's leading social workers, was appointed chief of Case Work and Records until March 1918, when Wisdom assumed control of operations along with supervision of the five relief districts' casework. Wisdom may well have been the public face of operations while Falk was in charge, as Falk later boasted how he worked from bed while sick with phlebitis. After Falk left Halifax, Wisdom's position remained titled as General Supervisor of Case Workers and Staff rather than the more formal "Chief" held by her predecessor. According to one newspaper article, however, "even the length of the title does not give any adequate idea of the extent and variety of the work performed." Problems and difficult cases that could not be solved by caseworkers landed on her desk. In August 1918, the Rehabilitation Department brought together other units into a general Social Service Department, and Wisdom was named director until this department closed in 1 January 1919.[47]

Falk criticized the decision to use Wisdom rather than appoint another "Chief." At one point, the commission inquired whether another man, Dr. Horace L. Brittain, Director, Bureau of Municipal Research, and acting superintendent of the Toronto General Hospital, was available to replace Falk, but it does not appear to have contacted anyone else. Falk assessed Wisdom as "competent and able" to act as supervisor of the districts and train new workers, but he doubted the ability of any one person to undertake this work in addition to managing medical social workers and the records department.[48] He believed the Halifax reconstruction effort would have a tremendous impact on the future of Canadian social work, and he saw the position of Director of Rehabilitation as pivotal. The American Red Cross concurred, contending that "the progress of social work in Canada may ... be vastly advanced by the thorough-going completion of the work."[49]

But Wisdom was a success, in large part because of her ability to get along with a wide range of people. She worked closely with parallel organizations such as the Sisters of Charity, who supplied many volunteer caseworkers and with whom it appears she had a particularly warm relationship, and earned their admiration as a "benefactress of the Poor."[50] Not a great deal of personal correspondence exists for this period but that which does suggests that Wisdom also had warm personal relationships with both Acadia University president George B. Cutten, who served as the director of the Rehabilitation Department, and G. Fred Pearson of the Reconstruction Committee.[51]

Rehabilitation efforts, however, were frequently a source of great frustration and anger. Those waiting for compensation often resented the rational, bureaucratic, and detached perspective of professionals. Those who had losses and injuries felt entitled to public funds; this was not private charity but redress. From the very beginning, there was a real and perceived preoccupation with preventing fraud and waste, which could happen at the expense of immediate distribution of goods to the needy. Part of the problem was the sheer size of the undertaking. In January 1918, there were seventeen clerks working for the Rehabilitation Committee, dealing with 13,844 registrants via an elaborate index system of coloured cards. There were also at least twenty-six professional social workers from across Canada and the United States; these outsiders were portrayed as particularly insensitive to local needs. By March 1918, there were still twenty-seven social workers working with the Rehabilitation Committee, most of them untrained but local. These caseworkers were supported in the maintenance of their files by thirty-four clerical workers.[52]

As a deliberate strategy, local amateurs were hired as case investigators, and they received on-the-job training from experienced workers. Falk believed it was better to "depend upon Haligonians, or at least Nova Scotians, than to depend indefinitely on the services of workers from other cities." This policy meant that there were more investigators hired than would have been the case if they were dealing only with experienced social service workers.[53] Not everyone agreed with this policy. Haligonian Constance Bell, who worked for five months as an untrained visitor, felt that the great lesson of the disaster was the need for permanent, trained, social service workers. She observed: "Many local workers went at the thing enthusiastically and with a keen desire to help, but ... in spite of the antagonism which exists in Halifax towards trained social service workers, if a strong corps of such men and women, say three times as many as there were, had been available much of the trouble that arose would have been avoided." In her experience with the Rehabilitation Department, the professionals, unlike local helpers, never lost their temper or became inefficient through fatigue: "No one who has not worked for a long time with those wonderful women can realize how invaluable they were. ... Things would have been better with a strong central executive and sufficient number of *trained* social service workers."[54]

Some untrained visitors, such as Gwendolen Lantz, subsequently launched careers in social service.[55] Other locals may have been untrained but were no strangers to such work. For instance, Bessie Egan had three, concurrent, paid positions: agent of the Society for the Prevention of Cruelty, a church outreach worker at the port of Halifax, and visitor for the Halifax Association for Improving the Condition of the Poor. She could not be considered inexperienced. There were also those who might be considered quasi-professional social service workers, such as local schoolteachers, nuns, public health nurses, Salvation Army and Y workers, and even clergy.[56] The face of contact after the initial emergency period between claimants and the bureaucracy was almost exclusively female. Some of the resentment towards these professionals may have stemmed from the expectation that these women be caring and compassionate, placed against the reality of their commitment to set rules and regulations.

The bureaucratic organization that accompanied disaster relief, especially the work done by social workers, was both necessary and the lightning rod for discontent among survivors; claimants were slow to receive aid as claims were carefully investigated, verified, and processed.[57] The foundational premise of casework was that each family be treated individually, which meant that, notwithstanding efforts of centralization and standardization, caseworkers had a great deal of discretion. The Rehabilitation Committee described its mandate as "the delicate and difficult problem of bringing separated and broken families back to a state of self-support and independence," and pledged to prevent disabled adults and children from becoming permanent dependents. The Rehabilitation Committee took responsibility for all social services needed by any family in the city, except for families already known to the St. Vincent de Paul Society.[58]

This division alluded to the complex issue of rehabilitation that the Relief Commission faced. Some cases were relatively straightforward. Widows and orphans received monthly pensions, housekeepers were hired for widowers, the blind were educated, houses were rebuilt or repaired, and furniture replaced. At the most mundane level, good Samaritans who had offered up their coats to the injured had them replaced. Most cases, however, were extraordinarily messy. The influx of resources with reconstruction meant that both potential recipients and those with goods to offer were looking to make money, sometimes by means of scams or fraud. Anonymous letters of secret bank accounts sent by jealous neighbours had to be investigated, along with suspicions of clients who registered several times under different names.[59]

Even more complicated was achieving the objective of family rehabilitation through scientific philanthropy's practice of addressing the underlying issues of distress. In the initial registration form required of all households, applicants were required to state "PLANS FOR FUTURE: Family's estimate on what it needs and its plans," suggesting that each household had to be involved alongside the investigators in defining objectives. The problem was that much suffering was exacerbated but not actually caused by the disaster. Waves of influenza hit Halifax from December 1918 throughout 1919, and, although this clearly had nothing to do with the explosion, clients already vulnerable by weakened health, unemployment, or poor housing were cared for with Relief Commission resources. More difficult were the cases of those families and households who may or may not have already been known to relief agencies before the explosion and had a precarious existence due to pre-existing underlying problems such as poor physical or mental health, marital conflict, alcoholism, old age, and underemployment. The explosion pushed these households over the edge, but the influx of resources also offered the possibility of solving long-term problems.

Wisdom and her caseworkers wrestled daily with the issue of their responsibility as stewards of Relief Commission funds in terms of what it meant to rehabilitate affected families. Certainly, some cases received special treatment, such as a young woman whom the American social workers especially "liked," as they arranged for a private donor to finance a trip to Boston to have her fitted with a particular artificial leg so that no precedent would be created. This particular respectable, working-class adolescent ended up as a social work success story. Her tuition at Mount Saint Vincent College was paid for with commission funds and she went on to a MA at Dalhousie, a PhD from the University of London, and a college teaching career in the United States.[60] In other cases, initial generosity had an expiration date, especially if a family continued to demand more. An unusually aggravated Jane Wisdom wrote about one case that "Our understanding is that Miss M – is not now suffering from any disability other than impatience."[61] The October 1918 suicide of a teamster with four children under twelve living with his wife in the emergency housing on the Exhibition Grounds prompted Wisdom to review the file. The family's rental accommodation had been badly damaged and their goods lost by the explosion, so, through March 1918, the family was supported by the commission with food, coal, and a cash settlement of over $200. When the man was injured at a post-explosion workplace accident, social workers creatively found a way of temporarily channelling additional money to the household as retroactive compensation for taking care of an infant niece, and also secured a small private donation. But this was not enough. The normally empathetic Wisdom concluded that the man was intemperate, that the wife had often been required to support the family, and that they had "[l]ived in wretched conditions prior to the explosion. ...

Condition, if anything, improved since the explosion."[62] The family very well may have been better off, but the breadwinner was unable to cope. The newspaper report laid the blame on the explosion, not on the man's running a wheel over his foot.

One of the most important critics of casework-based charity after the explosion was Senator William Dennis, publisher of the *Halifax Herald*. Although his wife Agnes Miller Dennis was closely aligned with the organized charity movement, his newspaper published extensive criticism of bureaucracy and delays. In early January, Dennis agreed to a two-week moratorium on publishing criticisms of relief work in exchange for a statement about how workers would eliminate repeated interviewing of those who had suffered losses. One of the most laborious parts of the bureaucracy was the repetition of information collecting: household members constantly had to repeat their circumstances. An extreme case was that of the Watson family, which had to deal with fifteen different caseworkers in the first year.[63]

A leading critic of scientific charity was Dartmouth journalist Arthur Johnstone, whose criticisms were especially cutting in light of his formal social work training. Populist Judge Ben Russell also condemned the efforts as suffering from "an overdose of 'business efficiency' and social service pedantry."[64] A leading Catholic priest in the city was concerned about the "needless and tactless investigation" that sufferers had to endure, while others targeted the "tendency on the part of social workers, or whoever the people are who visit and supervise the victims of the explosion, to intimidate and bulldose these poor unfortunates."[65] Many Haligonians would have considered the investigations a considerable breach of privacy. The standard form of the secondary registration requested information on every aspect of the household, including number of relatives and church, union, and organization affiliations. Since the residents of the devastated area were primarily working class, the form assumed that each household would have a number of breadwinners, so it requested information on what each was doing presently and any earnings. There was also much grassroots discontent in the community. Letters to the editor of the *Halifax Chronicle* complained that "red tape" interfered with relief, and public meetings were organized to protest the fact that those who had suffered were not represented on any committee.[66] The case files regarding pension claims also indicate that clients were not simply passive victims. Rather, they persistently pressed their cases to federal politicians, and refused second-hand clothing or clothes not culturally suitable for mourning.

Some also stormed into the Relief Commission office in active pursuit of their own interests.

The most infamous case of claimant discontent was the Settle sisters, who went so far as to publish a pamphlet claiming that the commissioners were "robbing the sufferers." Emma Settle and her sister had been clients of the Bureau of Social Service before the explosion. After the explosion, Emma Settle, either through post-traumatic stress or the instability of the vulnerable, appears to have become "violently insane," issuing threats against various caseworkers and medical staff. At the time, Settle was clearly the bane of the Rehabilitation Department. When caseworker Beth Walker designed a mock coat of arms as a parting gift for Wisdom, she included the image of "Emma Settle Rampant," playing off the traditional lion rampant. Settle's character also appeared in a starring role representing the relentless client in a workplace sketch written for a private party. Almost fifty years later, Wisdom recounted the memory of hearing the real Emma Settle yelling in the hall of the main office, "Wisdom, Wisdom, I want Wisdom, Let me see the Wisdom of all ages."[67]

While claimants' frustration was understandable, it is clear that professional social workers cared deeply about the suffering they witnessed. Wisdom, who, at an early meeting, called for the "great need for action in the way of awards to disaster sufferers," was perhaps overly optimistic that this could be balanced with efficiency.[68] There are also glimpses of the professional social workers as advocates for their clients. During the summer of 1918, Wisdom petitioned Fred Pearson, chair of the Reconstruction Committee, for particular attention to the replacement of an elderly woman's furniture. He replied affirmatively in a letter marked "Personal." With patronizing good humour, he wrote that "we should endeavor, as far as possible, to meet your views in return for your consideration towards us. Some years ago I was very sympathetic myself toward maiden ladies, but I have got over that recently, and it is my sincere desire that you will some day undergo the same cure."[69] Wisdom was not alone in her concern for claimants. In a skit titled "Resume of What You Are Escaping," written by Beth Walker when Wisdom left the Relief Commission and returned to the bureau, there is a flood of demands from clients and caseworkers. Walker has social worker Dorothy Judah barging in: "Shut up, you ass, I want to talk to Jane. See here, Jane, this woman has got to have this money or I'll resign." In actual practice, Walker attempted to use her friendship with Wisdom in cajoling her to a favourable recommendation for her cases. In one case, a formal report was followed with a handwritten note: "Aw, go'wan, *please* get them their furniture."[70]

In March 1918, Wisdom was already reflecting upon her disaster experience as having "broadened and deepened" her own world view and encouraged her confidence in the possibilities of community. Ideally, this type of social service could "lead a community into ways of justice and brotherly kindness," but it could also bring the needy together so that they might assist each other. This rhetoric cannot be dismissed as impersonal or bureaucratic.[71] It was the humanity present in the relations between clients and caseworkers that generated a great deal of discretion. Wisdom and other caseworkers held significant power over clients, whom they could favour with a particularly generous award (or nice table) or punish with nothing or accusations of fraud.

Among the diverse projects that Wisdom oversaw was the establishment of the Community House, a social settlement established with a $4,000 donation from American Christian Scientists. As early as 1911, Halifax reformers had called for a settlement house in Halifax, and, following the explosion, the Presbyterians and Methodists identified a pressing need. Wisdom, with her Montreal, Manhattan, and Brooklyn settlement experience, was an enthusiastic supporter, and spoke of it as "a remarkable opportunity for social work." By October 1919, the settlement claimed a membership of approximately 400 and hosted a variety of activities, such as kindergartens; dance; cooking and dressmaking classes (conducted by Wisdom's cousin Kate Cunningham); various girls', boys', and mothers' clubs; moving pictures for children and adults; a library; and Saturday-evening dances for adults.[72]

By the summer of 1918, both the renamed Halifax Welfare Bureau and the Halifax Relief Commission vied for Wisdom's services. The latter claimed that "we find it quite impossible to get along without Miss Wisdom." To a degree, Wisdom may have been doing double duty the entire time. In the press, she was associated with the Welfare Bureau rather than the Relief Commission, and she delivered its 1918 annual report, although she was on the payroll of the commission at the time. Wisdom's association with both the Relief Commission and the Welfare Bureau was intended to provide continuity of care during the transition period when the commission closed and the bureau took over its family rehabilitation casework in exchange for $5,000. The Welfare Bureau's fiscal circumstance improved further when the Christian Science Church donated nearly $5,000 in unspent funds. Wisdom's work for the Relief Commission was recognized upon her return to the bureau on 1 January 1919 with a $500 bonus – a considerable sum, equivalent to four months' salary.[73]

While the initial response to the explosion focused on rehabilitation, by 1919, ongoing local relief activities again conformed to broader national concerns, such as health, welfare, and child protection. Both in Halifax and nationally, there was a much greater openness to state intervention and an expanded expectation of political leadership. As a result of war losses and the belief that "Nations Are Built of Babies," the Dominion Department of Health, established in 1919, added a special children's division the following year. Since health was a provincial jurisdiction under the British North America Act, federal action was generally limited to information and coordination of various local agencies. Its most important coordination effort was an October 1920 meeting, which led to the creation of the Canadian Council on Child Welfare (CCCW), an Ottawa-based volunteer agency supported by federal subsidies. Historian Tamara Hareven has characterized this organization as combining the functions of two American organizations: the private and voluntary Child Welfare League of America, and the public United States Children's Bureau.[74] Indeed, the CCCW absorbed the children's division of the Canadian Department of Health, confusing the public/private divide further as it became the most important welfare organization in the country under the leadership of Charlotte Whitton.

In Halifax, when Wisdom returned to the bureau, it was with an understanding that she would continue to oversee family casework for the Relief Commission.[75] Although the bureau received support from a wide swath of religious and secular volunteer associations, privately, Wisdom saw the bureau as fragile. Because of her experience and the growing demand for social work skills, Wisdom frequently received other job offers. When she came to Halifax in 1916, she had also been offered a position with the Montreal COS as casework supervisor, an offer repeated in 1919 by Howard Falk. Following the explosion, Wisdom received an invitation from the American Red Cross to lecture in its New York Study Course on Home Service. Through her connection with Acadia University President George Cutten, she was also offered the position of acting dean of women in March 1919. The latter position may have tempted her the most, but Wisdom ultimately declined it. She wrote to her sister Katherine that Acadia could "get someone else to fill the bill here although it is a big opportunity for someone like me (if I *do* say so) but the whole thing might all fall to pieces in Halifax if

I don't stick to the job there for at least another year." She continued using the language applied to families in casework after the explosion: "We're not reestablished or rehabilitated yet as an organization. I really only put in a bare year and a half on that job."[76] The bureau itself claimed that the explosion had stimulated general interest in welfare in the community. It drew particular attention to "Miss Wisdom, under whom the Bureau is enlarging its usefulness every day, her unfailing tact and gentleness having won over many who were at the outset entirely opposed to what they wrongly considered the work of the Bureau. Steadily and efficiently, she has gone on her quiet way, and hit her mark." The challenges of "rehabilitation," however, continued, with the departure of Wisdom's friend Beth Walker from the Community House, the sudden death of agency leader Ebenezer Mackay in January 1920, a downturn in the local economy, and new community responsibilities, such as participation in the Local Council of Women and the Halifax Women's Club. All this left Wisdom exhausted.[77]

Wisdom had not long returned to the Welfare Bureau when she was called upon for another form of service. Her recognized credentials as the city's "trained social worker" and her father's Liberal Party connections qualified her to be the first woman to be appointed to a provincial commission in Nova Scotia. In 1919, Premier George Murray struck a commission with the mandate of investigating "Assistance for Needy Mothers with Children and Minimum Wage and Factory Conditions for Women." Mothers' allowances, minimum wages, and working conditions for women were very much in the public eye as coalitions of feminists, progressives, and labour leaders promoted social support for the most deserving of the community's poor – the respectable, widowed mother. They worried about the impact of long hours, low wages, and harsh conditions on the physical and moral health of Canada's next generation of mothers, the young girls working in factories before marriage.[78]

The proposal for a government inquiry was launched in April 1919 at a moment when the political clout of the labour movement and reform groups was especially high. The commission, established in November 1919, was composed of five members. Wisdom was the only woman and, at first, the only individual with any social research experience until an original appointee was replaced with Ernest Blois, then Provincial Superintendent of Neglected and Delinquent Children. Historian A.A. Mackenzie told a history undergraduate in the 1970s that Wisdom believed her appointment to be tokenistic: "she felt herself to be only a nominal member appointed as a sop to the rising tide of post-war feminism."[79]

She may very well have been a token appointment, but she was unquestionably also a knowledgeable one. In the area of mothers' allowances, she even boasted particular expertise, having presented at three meetings of the New York State Commission on Relief for Widowed Mothers in October 1913 and having seen first-hand the political corruption associated with Tammany Hall.[80] By 1920, however, she was "all for it," her position altered, no doubt, from her experience with the non-partisan, quasi-public Relief Commission. She no longer held that private agencies had a monopoly on doing things properly, had gained trust for the state, and had become an enthusiastic supporter of mothers' allowances, and the same arguments (actually the exact same words) of the Nova Scotia report appeared in Montreal throughout the interwar period.[81]

The commission first dealt with the issue of minimum wage and working conditions for Nova Scotia female factory workers. It visited Halifax, Truro, Amherst, Yarmouth, and Windsor, where many of the most important employers of women were located. In the sparse surviving, scattered, informal notes, there are details of workers' wages, living arrangements, and other expenses. Very much in keeping with contemporary concerns, Wisdom noted quality of lighting, cleanliness, adequacy of fire protection, and the state of toilets in various factories.[82]

In April 1920, the commission issued a cautious report, based largely on the Manitoba and Saskatchewan mothers' allowance acts. No recommendations, however, were implemented until March 1930. It was up to Wisdom, as the only female member, to defend the commission's recommendations at a May 1920 meeting of Halifax's Local Council of Women. The commission had recommended a maximum forty-eight-hour week for all women workers, except those engaged in domestic service or agricultural labour. Some council members felt that this exception would exacerbate the shortage in available domestics, but Wisdom explained that although the "government did not mean to discriminate," it was "not prepared as of yet to fix hours for these two classes of workers," suggesting that the commission's report was made to comply with government policy.[83]

The recommendations on mothers' allowances followed in April 1921 and were very much in line with what was happening in other provinces at the time. The commission recommended a monthly payment to widowed mothers of more than one legitimate child under the age of sixteen who were, in the ubiquitous phrase, "fit and proper persons." As in the case of the minimum wage board, the actual program was not introduced until 1930.

Between the two government reports, Wisdom showed signs of restlessness and a desire to expand her world. Reflecting her broadening professional network within Canada, she submitted several short notes and articles to the new national journal *Social Welfare*.[84] Rather than lose her services, the bureau offered an eight-week leave, and board members took up a private collection of $132 to support Wisdom on a trip to England. After cashing in her Canada War Loan bond, Wisdom, accompanied by her aunt Jessie McQueen and her friends Helen and Josie Crichton, sailed from Halifax in July 1920. The Crichton sisters had taught at the Halifax Ladies College where Wisdom's sister Katherine had been employed and "Jo" had been in charge of records at the Relief Commission. Together, the travellers toured art galleries and churches, saw plays and dance, heard music, and shopped. Wisdom's professional interests led her to the offices of the London COS, where she took out a subscription to its *COS Review*. She also heard Hilda Oakeley's friend and leading British proponent of family allowances, Eleanor Rathbone, speak on "National Family Endowment: Its Relation to Wages and Prices." We see here a direct link between the British experience and the Nova Scotia report.[85]

By the time Wisdom returned to Halifax in September of 1920, the city had slid into a serious recession. The planned expansion of the Welfare Bureau was curtailed: during the winter of 1920–21, fifty new families a month came to the attention of the bureau, and revenue did not meet expenditures. With three trained workers on staff and a full-time stenographer, the bureau launched a fundraising campaign in May 1921, stating that "unless this present appeal meets with generous response, the work of the Bureau must be seriously curtailed if not abandoned." In a private report to a leading city fraternal organization, the bureau's treasurer reported that expenses exceeded income by $2,000 and that, without a generous public response, it would be necessary to spend the Christian Science endowment.[86]

In the midst of this uncertainty, Wisdom resigned in June 1921, citing the need to rest. She may have been considering a renewed offer to become acting dean of women at Acadia, a quasi-academic position that would have included some lecturing, but her lack of a graduate degree meant that while the "pull" of academic life was strong, its long-term prospects would still be uncertain. In the many tributes that accompanied her departure, the repeated theme of her pleasant relations with clients, board members, and fellow workers was emphasized, as was her efficiency and tact.[87] While efficiency might be a professional quality, tact and kindness reflected personality. A goodbye luncheon included the city's entire Protestant welfare establishment, and the commissioners from the Halifax Relief Commission.[88]

Wisdom's sojourn in Halifax coincided with remarkable welfare expansion, intensive bureaucratization, and openness to an enlarged state. Neither the war nor the Halifax explosion alone blew Halifax social services into the twentieth century or modernized nineteenth-century charitable institutions. While it was slower to do so than other North American cities, Halifax had already begun to embrace scientific charity and was integrating itself into the North American welfare mainstream before the emergency of 1917. The delayed start had much to do with the fact that associated charities were not a priority for the Local Council of Women, which was occupied with other matters. When organized charity came to Halifax, the original rocky start was largely thanks to personality clashes, territorial factionalism, confessional jurisdictions, and the patriotic support of war campaigns; it was not generally about principles or opposition to methods. Institutional, associational, and personal connections existed before the explosion. When social workers flooded Halifax from elsewhere in Canada and the United States, they found themselves in a place that already shared many of their common assumptions and ideas.

Notwithstanding the backlash against scientific philanthropy from some clients, the war and the specific circumstances of the explosion fostered a new openness to state programs and social service intervention. It marked a turning point for Wisdom, who, through experience, lost her fear that public welfare would be partisan. Respect for expertise and, as a consequence, bureaucratization flourished. This did not mean that religious and private initiatives disappeared; rather, it is important to recognize their coexistence. Jane Wisdom, rooted in the private sector but temporarily seconded to an emergent public agency, played a central role in developing new state programs such as minimum wage for women and mothers' allowances. In Halifax, the face of the interventionist progressive state came in the form of young, female social workers in their twenties under the leadership of a woman in her early thirties.

Montreal and Cape Breton: Social Work Training and Professionalization, 1921–1939

The ideal of apolitical professionalization was one of the core tenets Jane Wisdom held as she entered the interwar period. Although she had arrived somewhat late to progressivism, a commitment to apolitical expertise sat along with her other core beliefs such as social harmony, individualism tempered by strong social bonds, and the necessary coexistence of voluntary associations and an active neutral state. Her unwavering commitment to professionalism drew her into debates during her graduate studies at the McGill School for Social Workers and its successor, the nascent Canadian Association of Social Workers. Issues of professional identity, accreditation, claims of expertise, appropriate educational background, and specialized knowledge, especially regarding casework, generated heated discussion in which Wisdom often participated. Social work was not alone in emphasizing practical experience as part of training; in medicine and law, hands-on experience played a vital role in accreditation. However, the practicum of social work in charity agencies and philanthropic institutions was much less prestigious than what took place in hospitals or lawyers' offices. The combination of the lack of supervision by certified professionals in the field, its association with unpaid work, and the fact that those supervising were most likely to be female offered little prestige. As someone influenced by progressive ideology, Wisdom fundamentally believed that her expertise was apolitical, although she was active in professional interventions to use expertise to shape public policy.

The professionalization of social work was a matter of ongoing, significant debate. In the interwar period, the emergent profession of social work faced two particular challenges. In the first place, it was strongly associated with women. Like other relatively new and emerging female professions such as nursing, librarianship, and dietetics, social work attempted to gain stature and standing before the public and within the university. But it was difficult to persuade the general public that there was skill and expertise involved in solving family problems; this required more than just the supposedly natural feminine attributes of common sense, caring, and compassion. Second, claims of technical expertise were hampered by the ongoing presence of amateur volunteers. How were paid, trained social workers different from untrained and unpaid co-workers? Indeed, the boundaries were often messy, and attempts to differentiate could prove embarrassing. Esther Wilson Kerry worked as a prominent Montreal "lay worker" but qualified for trained status by both practical and academic standards: she had attended the McGill School for Social Workers and, in 1939, completed an MA thesis in sociology and philosophy on the "Role and Function of the Volunteer in Social Work."[1] During the First World War, amateur philanthropist Helen Reid headed the Montreal Canadian Patriotic Fund, one of the largest volunteer organizations in the country. Neither woman conforms to preconceptions about amateurs. The head of the Montreal Family Welfare Association once quipped that both volunteer and professional "worked side by side performing much the same tasks. The difference, if any, was that the volunteer helped raise the money to defray the paid worker's salary."[2]

The interwar period, and especially the economic collapse of the 1930s, also provided amazing opportunities for the fledging profession. The number of individuals willing to identify themselves as professional social workers in a Canadian professional organization increased from a charter group of 200 in 1927 to over 600 by 1939. One contemporary social worker described the Depression as having the impact of a hurricane on the new profession, as private welfare agencies were ill-equipped to administer relief and deal with greatly expanded need, scarce resources, and a shortage of caseworkers. The inability of private agencies alone to cope with expanded demand led to the parallel expansion of public welfare services for the unemployed, and professionalizing social workers joined those looking to the state for new solutions and more generous allowances.[3] With limited results at the time, community-based social workers, such as Wisdom, intervened in public policy debates as part of their professional identity. They thereby participated in laying the groundwork for the post-war welfare state.

Jane Wisdom returned to Montreal in 1921 to undertake graduate studies but she never finished her MA thesis in historical political economy.

Her uncompleted thesis testifies, in part, to interesting tensions between theoretical social science and social work's practical casework methodology. Theory, research, and practical work were increasingly juxtaposed, as specialists focused on one stream or the other. The social scientific methods Wisdom adopted were broadly conceived and served to mediate between naïvely sentimental and harshly punitive responses to poverty. Much has been written about the influence of social science on social work, and it undoubtedly played a central role in the interwar educational debates about the best preparation for the profession. Historian Marlene Shore has written comprehensively about the rise of social sciences, especially sociology, at McGill, while Nancy Christie's work has emphasized the continuity of older influences such as religion, service, and gender expectations.[4]

In the fall of 1921, at age thirty-seven, Wisdom returned to McGill. She enrolled in a two-year MA in economics. During the first year, she took courses in economic theory, labour problems, money and banking, public finance, political and social theory, and the history of England since 1794. While a graduate student, she also taught the newly created Department of Social Service's foundational course, "Treatment of Poverty." The opportunity to teach while studying may help explain the attraction of returning to university at such a late date, although Wisdom's exact motivations remain unknown.[5] She had expressed a previous attraction to academic life, and was likely aware that, as a woman, her prospects for advancement into executive positions were increasingly limited without the MA degree. Alternatively, she may have been frustrated with the research methodologies of the Nova Scotia royal commissions or inspired by the graduate work of former schoolmate Samuel Prince. The decision may also have been entirely personal, reflecting a desire to leave Halifax as many of her colleagues had done after reconstruction or to return to the familiarity of friends in Montreal.

For her thesis, Wisdom focused on the coal towns of Cape Breton. This topic made sense in light of her own "Nova Scotianess," the related labour unrest, and the presence of Nova Scotian economist and self-described socialist Professor J.C. Hemmeon.[6] Hemmeon had been a pivotal figure for Wisdom as an undergraduate, launching her towards an intellectual interest in poverty. By the 1920s, he was encouraging his students to read Harold Laski (who had taught at McGill from 1914 to 1916) and the British socialists Sidney and Beatrice Webb. His sympathy towards the working class was clear in his representation of labour on arbitration and conciliation boards. In the 1930s, he participated in the Fabian-inspired League for Social Reconstruction, served on the executive of the Montreal Branch of the Canadian Civil Liberties Union, and became one of the leading proponents of the McGill Social Science Research Project.[7]

Wisdom began her studies in economics and history, as McGill did not inaugurate its pioneering department of social science until the following year. A decade and a half later, her only niece, Katherine's daughter Relief Williams, with whom she was particularly close, also pursued graduate work in history at the same university. Williams was one of the first women to complete an MA in Canadian social history, writing a thesis on early social welfare in Nova Scotia.[8]

After a year of coursework, Wisdom arrived in Cape Breton in the late spring of 1922. Her research coincided with one of the most important strikes in Cape Breton, the last brilliant flash of the Maritimes' post-war labour revolt. When the United Mine Workers (UMW) contract expired at the end of 1921, the coal companies were looking for massively reduced wages. The conciliation board recommended, in January 1922, a 30 per cent wage cut. Most of the union executive believed the offer to be the best one possible, given the post-war recession, but it was rejected by the rank-and-file members, who immediately implemented a cut in production and eventually went on strike. The August strike, ultimately settled with government intervention, fostered a divisive left/right split and radicalized local District 26.[9]

Wisdom, in her own words, became "embroiled" in the problems of the miners. She set about recording her impressions of contemporary events through a daily newspaper column on the front page of the *Sydney Post*. Between 10 August and 15 September, she published twenty-four columns generally sympathetic to labour, under the pseudonym "Observer." Her connection to this paper, strongly associated with the governing provincial Liberals and the coal companies, was probably through news editor H.B. Jefferson, who had been with the staff of the *Halifax Herald* during the explosion.[10]

The pseudonym "Observer" was significant. In Mary Richmond's 1917 classic text on casework, *Social Diagnosis*, she differentiated between a witness and a trained observer. According to Richmond, the latter "belongs to natural science; the former is primarily a law term. The observer is trained to accuracy, is on the lookout for facts tending to uphold or discredit some hypothesis; ... the observer uses controlled experimentation as his method, approaching his subject with impersonal detachment; whereas the witness has no method, is liable to personal bias, and is accurate or not according to his native powers of observation and memory." The fact that these columns were written anonymously forsook Wisdom's claim to recognized expertise. There was no acknowledgement of her training or influences or the relationship this might have had with what she saw or heard. She introduced herself to her readers as female, not of Cape Breton but with the "blue blood of Nova Scotia flowing in her veins."[11]

Jane Wisdom believed in pursuing reform through sequential actions: the identification of a problem, empirical enquiry, legal reform, and implementation. Insofar as she thought research necessary for action, she was influenced by the social survey movement. The social survey movement was originally linked to England and the studies of Charles Booth, but Wisdom's professional relationship with Margaret Byington in Brooklyn brought her in contact with the most important American study, the Pittsburgh Survey, and Byington's volume *Homestead*.[12] The Pittsburgh Survey was influenced by emergent social science methodology; however, there were other traditions, and Wisdom was likely to have been familiar also with the series of amateur surveys focused on moral conditions conducted under the auspices of the Canadian Methodist and Presbyterian churches. Eight cities, including Sydney, Nova Scotia, were investigated in 1913–14. The surveys brought together evangelicalism with social service through a focus on problems associated with urbanism and immigration, and offering the church as a solution. Alan Hunt's observation that we need to recognize similarities between social science and moral–religious surveys is a useful reminder that both traditions aimed to inspire community action.[13]

Wisdom went to Cape Breton not as a social worker but as an academic and social scientist. Still, her past casework experience coloured everything she saw and did. Her use of the newspaper to reach a popular audience fell within a pre-established social work tradition. While some proponents of casework emphasized scientific objectivity, others, such as Wisdom's mentor Mary Richmond, believed this did not preclude preserving human interest and empathy. The New York COS, for example, explicitly trained its staff as "cub reporters" to write engaging casework stories for public newspapers. Like many social scientists coming from a practical background, Wisdom found herself walking the line between objectivity and advocacy. Occasionally, she experimented with giving textual space to her objects of study, openly questioning whether the miners would share her perspective and conclusion.[14] For example, when Wisdom compared housing in Glace Bay and Brooklyn, she reasoned that "the miner would seem to have some advantages over the city dweller," because he was free from "wretched rear hovels and basements [and] the squalor of a city slum." Nevertheless, she concluded her column by asking, "Wonder what he thinks about it?," thereby permitting space for an alternative perspective or at least ongoing dialogue.

In a different column, an interview with the Marxist editor of the *Maritime Labor Herald* led her to observe: "I suddenly find I am actually envious of the editor[.] [I]f I could only be as certain as he that the remedy for social ills is at hand, how comfortable it would be after all." This middling position, between social science and "humanitarian narrative" aimed at generating sympathy through details, should be one familiar to many historians, who, for most of the twentieth century, have found themselves placed in a similar position.[15]

Forty years later, Wisdom recalled: "At first I had more courage than knowledge of [the social effects of the strike]. It was quite a study." Her columns contained many features of the normal social survey, such as attention to geography, population, racial and ethnic composition, economic life, recreation, housing, and health, but it ignored other usual preoccupations, such as crime and prostitution. Moreover, although she covered a range of expected topics connected to the masculine world of the strike – co-operatives, unions, the press, and the coal company – almost all the columns wove back to women and the household. The final two columns drew explicit attention to the situation of young women and wives in a predominantly male resource economy. Finally, Wisdom's observations of the Cape Breton coal towns in the 1920s testify to historian Ellen Ross's claim that women's accounts were more "aural than visual."[16] Wisdom emphasized conversations, the act of listening and being told. This was not to the neglect of tactile observations, the feel of the fog, the throb of industry, or attention to the decent, respectable character of the inhabitants. She also rejected the authority of statistics. Her first column slipped in numbers about coal production, but she embraced the humanist perspective in her statement that "figures signify but little in human terms to the majority."[17]

Wisdom's stated agenda was to uncover "real facts and real folks,"[18] and the range of community contacts was indeed broad as she positioned herself as the neutral observer, adhering only to liberal democratic values such as tolerance and order. Her understanding of ethnicity was essentialized. She noted that Glace Bay was a "cosmopolitan town," but also drew attention to the fact that four of the fifteen pages in the local telephone directory were "devoted to Mc's and Mac's alone." Women and children were described as "friendly" and "pleasant faced," and she frequently praised the reserved nature, hospitality, and honesty of the Scots. Wisdom applauded the principle of free press, and the fact that so radical a paper as the *Maritime Labor Herald* could publish in Canada. She also shared some of Margaret Byington's skepticism about narrowly focused budget studies, and, playing with John Stuart Mill's notion of the "economic man," worried about a female counterpart, "a new bogey, that of the economic woman." Although she was generally sympathetic to the union, the limits of her support became apparent with the UMW's decision to call a 100 per cent walkout, including the mine pumpmen and firemen, which put the infrastructure of the mines at risk. Wisdom wrote that while "the conduct of a strike can be quite honorable," there were accepted rules in strikes, just like in "white man's rules of warfare," which did not extend to the permanent destruction of property.[19] She permitted no space for opposing perspectives in her conclusion that "the declared policy of the union justified some government action," although she did not explicitly support the government's decision to call in the militia.[20]

The attention Wisdom paid to households was perhaps the most striking aspect of the series. Even at a moment when community life through class solidarity was most apparent, she reminded readers that miners and their families lived their lives at the level of the individual household. Near the beginning of her columns, Wisdom asserted that, based on her conversations with the women of the households, they had believed that there would be no strike and that a settlement was imminent. Her willingness to believe this claim was based on the fact that the women had set no emergency provisions aside. Two weeks into the strike, Wisdom was prepared to link unstable public life with unstable households: "Household and domestic arrangements in the mining town are observed to be disorganized to a large extent already. With no regular working hours and the air full of uncertainty, meal times and sleeping times are 'any old time.' It is well to remember that people are living already under abnormal conditions and may be expected to react in abnormal ways to the events of these days."[21]

Wisdom, like other progressives, was also willing to overlook significant class divisions. She frequently pointed out that public opinion sympathized with the miners, since almost everyone in the community was related or connected to someone in the mine. These connections meant that "the strata of society here are not marked off in hard and fast ways."[22] She credited the generally good living conditions of the miners to their own efforts and values, referencing their neat homes, productive gardens, and healthy children. She emphasized household solidarity in noting that "even the most harassed woman would not for a moment admit that the men folk are not justified in going out on strikes." While Wisdom did not think the workers and the company were inevitably at odds, she observed that, among the women, there was "acceptance of the creed that the worker and the company have opposing interests." Wisdom's understanding of society, informed by her religious upbringing, emphasized its organic, interconnected nature. She rejected the inevitability of conflict and constantly identified examples of co-operation. Outside the household, Wisdom was interested in community organizations and had particular praise for the British-Canadian Co-operative Society.[23] She also extolled the 1920 introduction of the Dominion Coal and the Dominion Iron and Steel Company's Industrial Relations Department, which emphasized safety and accident prevention, reducing labour turnover, and an "employee service" program to promote home ownership.[24]

She had less confidence in the Canadian state's ability to resolve industrial conflict. Wisdom depicted the Industrial Disputes Act as a failure and counterpoised it with the potential of new organizations such as the League of Nations.[25] She touted the possibility of an interventionist state in protecting the consumer, both in preventing labour stoppages and in inspecting and regulating the price of milk.[26] Wisdom was even prepared to expand this absolute belief in co-operation and collective bargaining beyond the economy. Social harmony would thrive in her vision of society: "Where representatives of big industries meet with representatives of city government, with Boards of Health and School Boards, with Rotary Club representatives and social welfare representatives generally, each and all conscious of civic obligation, practical results would surely follow."[27]

Jane Wisdom's columns also presented a list of basic human rights that were influenced by the emergent field of psychology. Her description of the "irreducible minimum" for normal living was inspired by American economist and reformer Edward T. Devine. She outlined that every person was entitled to work, health, education, recreation, and spiritual development.[28] The latter was a theme in several columns, and Wisdom conceived of churches as playing a central role in coal towns. She noted in one column that both the UMW and local churches were supported by the "check off," and that almost every miner agreed to a

25-cent weekly deduction to his church. She also drew attention to the frequent use of biblical quotations in miners' speeches and pointed out that the bible was present even in the offices of the radical *Maritime Labor Herald.*

With no notice, the newspaper series abruptly ended. Wisdom returned to Montreal, where she continued to teach in the social work program and work on her thesis. Her self-styled identity as "Observer" meant that she had no real commitment to what was happening in these communities and was free to return to her academic life. But teaching, ill health, and, eventually, full-time employment interfered with the thesis's completion, and Professor Hemmeon soon handed the topic over to another McGill MA student, the much younger, male, and academically conventional Eugene Forsey. Forsey's thesis, which launched his own impressive career as a teacher, political advisor, and public figure, was grounded solidly in political economy and public life. There were few interviews with ordinary people and little attention to household or associational life. Instead, it offered careful attention to tables, figures, and statistics. In the introduction to a published version of the thesis, Hemmeon noted that Forsey's thesis was completed "solely in the object of learning the facts; that he began his investigation with no initial prejudices, and with the hope that he might be able to do something toward the solution of a very difficult and complicated problem." In light of English Montreal reform circles' support of Cape Breton miners, it is difficult to believe that either student or supervisor was actually neutral. Even so, like Wisdom, they both believed that investigation could ameliorate the situation and had great faith in collective bargaining and co-operation.[29]

Forty years later, Wisdom described her primary interest as "standing up for underprivileged people." She continued: "We were taught in the early years to be more scientific minded in our studies. This, I think, is the biggest change that has occurred in the movement. We were told to deal with facts, not to let our hearts run away with our heads. Consequently we were called hard-hearted, and we were probably the only ones who really cared at this time. What we were trying to do was find facts that explained the conditions affecting people and to throw some light on their behaviour."[30] The newspaper series written in the summer of 1922 cannot be considered hard-hearted any more than it can be considered objective. Elements of the new social sciences were present, but the perspective was first and foremost grounded in Wisdom's practical casework experience. This explains her conviction that the centre of Cape Breton coal communities was not the mine but the home. Historian Peter Novick has noted that with the emergence of policy-oriented social sciences after the First World War, "there was a migration out of history on the part of those with a more activist inclination." Wisdom's abandoned thesis may have been part of this trend. She soon accepted full-time work in a private welfare agency, but she continued to participate in the evolution of the profession as an instructor of casework. Indeed, her pivotal teaching position at the McGill School for Social Workers from 1921 to 1924 bridged a period of turbulent change at McGill.[31]

The earliest years of English-language social work education in Montreal had predated Wisdom's return to Montreal. In the spring of 1913, Helen R.Y. Reid began her campaign to establish some kind of training program for social workers in the city. Her original conceptualization was modest. It involved courses such as practical hygiene and social economics, what we would recognize today as internships with local agencies, and supervised case discussions under the local COS. Reid described the program as being specifically for women, designed to promote expertise and efficiency among professionals and volunteers.[32] This female and vocational conceptualization of social work made sense, given Reid's own involvement with the Local Council of Women and her familiarity with working with volunteers. It would characterize the McGill program and eventually bring it into conflict with university bureaucracy.

Meanwhile, the University of Toronto was also contemplating the issue of social work education. With the onset of the First World War, nationalists argued that a specialized knowledge of Canadian problems required Canadian training. But it was not at all clear what this meant. British and American social work training appeared to be developing in different directions. The recent amalgamation of London's COS Institute and the London School of Economics resulted almost completely in the abandonment of casework; the new program focused on training policy experts and bureaucrats through academic disciplines and theory. On the other hand, American schools, influenced by the Russell Sage Foundation, were evolving with what scholar Lorna Hurl has described as "minimal attention to the social sciences and philosophies, concentrating instead on specific social problems and casework methodology."[33]

Toronto supported the British model and launched the Department of Social Service, albeit with an American founding director. In 1920,

McGill's J.A. Dale assumed the directorship until the program came under the influence of another British immigrant, E.J. Urwick, formerly of the London COS Institute and the London School of Economics. What historian Sara Burke identified as the "Toronto ideal" emphasized, often unsuccessfully, the importance of young men's participating in social service work, going back to the original ideal of British settlement house work for male Oxford undergraduates.[34] The University of Toronto's British, theoretical, and male-centred approach differed from the more American, vocational, female-dominated program at McGill.

Both schools, however, agreed with the need for Canadian programs. The lack of qualified Canadian social workers meant that, according to the YMCA immigration secretary, "Americans were taking the jobs by default." These Americans were often transient, and wasted considerable time in becoming familiar with different federal and provincial legal structures. In 1922, the president of a private Montreal casework agency complained about the lack of local expertise:

> In every instance the caseworker in question had admitted that conditions in this Province were so unusual that it was necessary for one who had obtained his training in the States to unlearn much that applied to his own country and to begin at the very beginning in studying Quebec's problems. Three highly trained social workers engaged in Montreal in recent years ... all expressed themselves in identical terms, "I have had to unlearn all I knew – I would not have believed conditions could be so different." This is a shocking waste of time, especially as the average American social worker makes but the briefest stay in Montreal, and is replaced by another "Learner."[35]

Americans in particular found it difficult to negotiate Montreal's bilingualism and religious politics, and the very limited role of the state. The need for Canadian programs was further underlined by the real concern that Canadians who took their training in the United States would not return home but, like Jane Wisdom, accepted better-paid jobs there. While Montreal came strongly under US influence, the first cohort of Montreal professionals contained a large number of British immigrants (sometimes via the United States) and Americans with British experience. J.A. Dale, Howard Falk, Dorothy King, G.B. Clarke, and John B. Dawson all would have spoken with a pronounced British accent, and American-born Richard Lane gained his foundational experience in London settlements.

During the war, Helen Reid seized the opportunity created by a sizable bequest following the death of Julia Parker Drummond's son, Lieutenant Guy Drummond, to introduce what she called 'practical sociology' to McGill. Sociology and social work were two sides of the same coin, as the study of society was intended to effect change through social work. Reid distinguished between theoretical and practical sociology, the latter referring to efficient social service. Others, such as Professor J.A. Dale, the dean of applied sciences, unnamed members of the board of governors, and supporters among the Co-operating Theological Colleges who believed such a course would be appropriate for divinity students, joined her. Indeed, the Governing Board of the Co-operating Theological Colleges agreed to donate $2,000 per annum, with similar sums promised by the university's Graduate Society. Wealthy Montrealer Elsie Meighen Reford personally agreed to subscribe $200 per annum for the preliminary period.[36]

In early 1918, with the support of Principal William Peterson, the subcommittee for the proposed School of Social Service and Training hired J. Howard Toynbee Falk as founding director on a three-year contract at a salary of $3,500. The choice of Falk reflected the subcommittee's desire for practical experience and reputation over academic qualifications. Falk held no university degree, having spent two years at Balliol, Oxford, before going into business and emigrating to Canada. He was the nephew of Arnold Toynbee, for whom London's most famous settlement house was named, and the brother of Oswald Toynbee Falk, an economist and stockbroker who has been given credit for originating many of the ideas developed by his close associate Maynard Keynes.[37] After settlement house and public health reform experience with the COS in New York City, Falk was asked by J.S. Woodsworth, Canada's most prominent social gospel minister and subsequent founding leader of the Co-operative Commonwealth Federation, to become the first director of the Winnipeg Associated Charities. Subsequently, Falk was appointed secretary of the provincial Welfare Commission and the Manitoba Mothers' Allowance Commission before being seconded by the American Red Cross to act as chief of staff of the Rehabilitation Committee following the Halifax explosion. The McGill committee had the opportunity to meet personally with him on his return to Winnipeg.

Falk was a complex personality whose character cannot be isolated from his influence on Canadian social work. It is clear that, notwithstanding his professional success, many people found working with

him difficult. A McGill University thesis completed in 1957 offers unattributed harsh assessments of his character, ascribing to him an "almost
childlike need for public recognition." The unnamed source claimed
"he was at once charming and tyrannical; he was most attractive to
women, and he used his power over them to accelerate his purpose
time and time again. Those women who knew him well outside the
family circle admired him greatly and none suspected him of subtle
manipulation."[38] Ernest Blois of Halifax, who rarely forgot anything,
somewhat disingenuously later recounted that after the explosion, Falk
had not made "a good impression for some reason I cannot account
for." He was a man of strong prejudices and great ambition. Charlotte
Whitton, who may have been among the women initially charmed by
Falk's personality, claimed privately that he "hated the French and
never showed, in my judgement, the patience or the understanding of
their position in Quebec that he should have."[39] This fault may have
come to light later, but Falk certainly made a good impression on the
hiring committee in 1918. Peterson assured Falk he had nothing to
fear about "antagonizing the different denominations" of the affiliated
Theological Colleges because of his Unitarian connection, but Peterson,
like historians Michael Gauvreau and Nancy Christie, may have over-
estimated his acceptability to the Anglican, Congregational, and Presbyterian Theological Colleges.[40]

From the beginning, those behind the McGill social work program – a
group of women, the Theological Colleges, and certain supportive academics – underscored the practical nature of the program, emphasizing
its prospects for increasing efficiency within local charitable agencies.
Even political economist Stephen Leacock originally supported the
program's vocational emphasis. In November 1918, he wrote to Falk
that "the subjects treated should be as *definite* and as *practical* as possible. General courses about *Society* and *Sociology* handed out in ten or
twenty lectures are mere nonsense." Instead, students should have an
introduction to economic theory, municipal government, and industrial
history. Falk agreed with the importance of practical training to the social work program; he analogized that "social agencies are to a school
for training social workers what a hospital is to a medical school." The
Social Service Advisory Committee emphasized that the "department
must expect to have to train a great variety of types from the young
woman who just graduated to the middle-aged woman with little education and no experience outside domestic duties." But the problem
from the beginning was that English-speaking, Protestant Montreal

social agencies had few trained and experienced workers and were poorly equipped to supervise students in casework.[41]

The Department of Social Service was launched in September 1918, began its Training School in 1919, and, in 1922, was renamed the McGill School for Social Workers. Originally, it was not associated with any faculty, although its students could attend arts lectures. Admission standards were vague. The one-year program was intended for those who had at least high school matriculation; yet, entry was to be offered to those who could "show reasonable evidence of being able to benefit from the course offered." If educational requirements tended to be nebulous, qualities of character were more specific. The program's announcement solicited those with "tact, patience, sympathy, poise, cheerfulness and that something which we may term 'religion' and which 'calls' a person into social work." The prioritizing of character over educational background would be a source of ongoing tension for those connected to social work training. In its annual report, Chalmers House, the Montreal Presbyterian settlement, emphasized that McGill's new department would offer "practical training," even noting that certain patrons were offering financial support to "young women in our churches who have the spirit of social service and the necessary education and essential human sympathies for success in this work."[42] This report, issued under the leadership of Daniel Fraser, principal of Presbyterian College and an old family friend of the Wisdoms', indicates that the Theological Colleges initially accepted the female nature of the new program.[43]

The full-time, one-year, certificate program launched in 1919 offered courses on heredity and environment, the treatment of poverty, child welfare, public hygiene, crime and delinquency, social legislation, research methods, and the administrative practices of social work. Lectures did not begin until 5:00 p.m. so that working students could enrol. A significant emphasis was placed on "inspections and field work." The program was cast as ideally "'post-graduate work' with the most desirable student having a college education, three to five years in teaching, business or nursing." Age restrictions were in place such that students under twenty-one and over thirty-five were to be admitted only for exceptional reasons. Personality continued to be regarded as important: according to a program description, "it is the human qualifications which distinguish the effective from the ineffective." Professors Stephen Leacock and Carrie Derick, voluntary philanthropist Helen Reid, and professional practitioner John B. Dawson, general secretary of the COS, all served on the faculty in the early years. Students had a placement with the COS during the first term and then worked with a more specialized agency during the winter.[44]

Jane Wisdom began lecturing during Falk's last year at the school, taking over the foundational course on casework that had been offered by Dawson. She was engaged for fifty lectures for the sum of $350.[45] She was a sensible choice: Falk had strained relations with the financially important Theological Colleges, and Wisdom, no doubt, carried the personal recommendation of Daniel Fraser, who sat on the Committee of Management. Like her predecessor, she used Mary Richmond's *Social Diagnosis* as the primary text, and we know something of Wisdom's content for her course called "Treatment of Poverty" through the surviving exams. The first term provided an overview of the history of responses to poverty in Europe and North America, with particular emphasis on the differences between older forms of charity and current practices. The influence of Mary Richmond was present, as students were asked to either illustrate "how confusion between a fact and an inference" might lead to an inaccurate diagnosis, or to articulate what a social worker needed to accomplish in her first visit to a family. The second term continued these themes, also emphasizing "social diagnosis" (gathering the kinds of information necessary to assist families and individuals), legal frameworks, and the necessary components of a case file.[46]

As English-speaking Montreal developed a social work program at McGill, parallel events were developing in the majority French Catholic community. In 1919, Marie Gérin-Lajoie initiated a social action course for women that also emphasized objectivity and the scientific methods associated with casework. In 1931, together with the Congrégation de Notre-Dame and in affiliation with the Université de Montréal, Gérin-Lajoie opened the École d'action sociale, which attracted nuns and bourgeois women to its program. The École d'éducation familiale et sociale, another initiative by Gérin-Lajoie, opened in 1936. It trained social workers and working-class women outside an academic milieu, and offered courses to assist in coping with poverty by acquiring skills in nutrition, sewing, hygiene, and budgeting. These programs were entirely distinct from the Université de Montréal's newly autonomous École des sciences sociales, économiques et politiques under the leadership of Édouard Montpetit. At Loyola College and in conjunction with Notre-Dame Ladies' College, the Loyola School of Sociology and Social Service offered English-language Catholic instruction between 1918 and the early 1930s.[47]

Changes outside the university were also having an impact on the McGill program. From November 1920, Falk worked part-time as general secretary of the new Montreal Council of Social Agencies, blurring the lines between the university program and the Protestant Montreal welfare organizations. This arrangement, however, worked neither for Falk nor for McGill. Christie and Gauvreau have pointed to the alarm raised among university conservatives by an "uncontrolled acceleration in the direction of vocational training in social work" and women's increasing power within the university, a perspective epitomized by Stephen Leacock. In February 1922, he initiated a crisis with a memorandum proposing to reorganize the department with a more theoretical emphasis on social conditions, higher academic standards, and supervision by social scientists. Falk and his allies opposed this reorientation. Sociology as an academic discipline was controversial among some colleagues. For example, moral philosopher and professor William Caldwell articulated that sociology, with its discussions of "social disease, housing, immigration, the family; the latter involving as it did the question of divorce," was unsuitable for immature undergraduates.[48] The idea of protecting young men and women from academic discussions of controversial subjects while permitting them exposure to real-life problems through casework was, of course, ludicrous.

Falk also felt frustrated by what he perceived as McGill's lack of support, noting he had been recruited to build a practical program. His version of the department's origins expunged the role of women and the Theological Colleges; instead, he attributed its establishment to Principal Peterson, Professor Dale, and R.C. Dexter, general secretary of the COS. Consequently, he connected the program's current difficulties to Dexter's and Dale's departures at the end of 1918 and Peterson's debilitating stroke in early 1919.[49]

In the end, Falk resigned from McGill and was replaced by a "theoretical" sociologist, Prince Edward Island-born Carl Addington Dawson. Although Dawson was a "theoretical sociologist," he also had practical credentials: theological training, experience as a Baptist minister, and a background in civic reform. He arrived at McGill in the fall of 1922, and, as Christie and Gauvreau have argued, the program continued to emphasize practical techniques. As before, Jane Wisdom continued to teach casework from Richmond's *Social Diagnosis* until April 1924. Wisdom herself maintained a long-lasting, warm, respectful, and collaborative relationship with Dawson throughout the interwar period, and he may have offered stability rather than dramatic change.[50]

But Dawson's joint appointment as assistant professor of sociology in the new Department of Social Science and as director of Social Study and Training was also a break with the past.[51] The first part of his appointment led to the establishment of the first sociology department in Canada. This new department, established in 1925, not only emphasized theoretical concerns but also distanced the social work program from its religious and social-service roots.

The conflict between sociology and social work became even more pronounced in 1930, when McGill received the staggering sum of $100,000 from the Rockefeller Foundation for a research project on "social science and human welfare." This was the first large-scale social science research project in Canada, and, although multidisciplinary, it focused on sociology. Its concentration on unemployment at the local and national levels meant that Montreal social workers had access to some of the best research in the country. The Social Science Research Project attracted a group of dynamic scholars who moved the discipline of sociology even further away from social work. To administer the project, McGill hired an economist named Leonard Marsh. British and young (he was twenty-four years old!), Marsh was a graduate of the London School of Economics. He had recently worked under William Beveridge, the British economist who would be largely responsible for the direction of the post-war British welfare state. At McGill, Marsh directed the Social Science Research Project for its entire eleven-year run. The project also incorporated newly hired political economy lecturer Eugene Forsey, who was just twenty-five and still working on his PhD dissertation.[52]

Meanwhile, at the McGill School for Social Workers, throughout the 1920s, there was a disjuncture between curriculum and the school's stated objectives. While it emphasized the practical value of fieldwork under the supervision of competent professionals, that fieldwork was not always available. In 1925, the program changed to a two-year diploma course. By 1929, the majority of students were university graduates but the program remained somewhat ad hoc and makeshift. Enrolment at the school was also almost entirely female, despite Dawson's efforts to recruit men. In 1925, he wrote that "a real need also exists for men in this field. Executive heads of important agencies, community leaders and boys' workers will be required in the near future, and it is hoped that more young men might enter the school next year."[53] The centrality of student placements to professional training also raised problems for Jewish students not always welcome in

Wisdom's mother, Mary Bell McQueen Wisdom. (Family Papers, privately held)

Wisdom's father, Freeman Wisdom. The two photos were probably taken around the time of their marriage in 1880. (Family Papers, privately held)

Jennie and Bessie. There is no date associated with the photo, but it might correspond with their high school graduation in 1902. (Family Papers, Privately Held)

Residence room at Royal Victoria College, around the time that Wisdom lived there. Note the Union Jack pillowcase and the number of photos throughout the room. (Hilda Oakeley, "Higher Education for Women," *Canadian Magazine* [October 1904]: 503)

University Settlement House, 1910, across from Dufferin Square. From reprint broadsheet of the *Montreal Standard*, marking the opening of the project. Jane Wisdom was among the first residents. (JBW Papers)

A young Jane Wisdom working with a girls' group at University Settlement, 1910, reprint. This is a rare image; Wisdom was more comfortable behind the camera than in front of it. (JBW Papers)

In this image, taken by Wisdom in 1911, she photographs two Irish, elderly sisters who had been evicted from their home and landed on the door of the Montreal COS with all their goods in a cart. They were taken to St. Bridget's Refuge. Of all the cases she encountered, why did she take and keep this image? (JBW Papers)

"Interim Relief" is a social work pun that captures a moment of leisure when the women of the 1910 Summer Institute visited Coney Island. Wisdom is bottom centre. Social work pioneer Mary Richmond wears the black hat and Wisdom's friend Sara Dissoway ("Dizzy") is back right. (JBW Papers)

Postcard Wisdom sent to her father of Holy Trinity Parish House on Pierrepoint Street, Brooklyn, where she and Bessie resided. The door is marked with an arrow. (JBW Papers)

Photograph taken by Wisdom of children on the front steps of the
Williamsburg District Office of the Brooklyn Bureau of Charities. These photos
were saved among a meagre, personal, professional archives. (JBW Papers)

Photograph taken and kept by Wisdom of Schermerhorn Street, Brooklyn, near the headquarters of the Brooklyn Bureau of Charities. (JBW Papers)

Wisdom's personal archives included this image of Williamsburg Street, Brooklyn. An explanation on the back states: "foreign district (mostly Polish)." The street shots are informal and capture people in motion. (JBW Papers)

In this image of a rear tenement in Williamsburg, Wisdom has the children posed, looking directly at the camera. A latecomer on the right runs to be included. (JBW Papers)

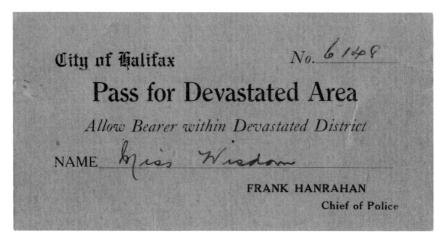

Pass permitting Wisdom to enter the district devastated by the Halifax explosion. (JBW Papers)

A glimpse of workplace culture through American social worker Beth Walker's design of a mock coat of arms for Wisdom, with the motto "Sauvez les Peuples." Disgruntled relief applicant Emma Settle appears lower left. 1) "Ship [identified as the *Mt Blanc*] couchant on azure sea, argent on bar" in a canton a cross gules; 2) Azure, a loaf of bread couchant; 3) Ships on sea azure; 4) Argent, a "devastated" house Volant; 5) Vert, Emma Settle rampant; 6) Gules St John's Ambulance Arms; 7) a boot argent. (JBW Papers)

Workplace culture extended beyond the office and the clients' homes. Photo taken by Wisdom of caseworkers and the office staff of the Halifax Relief Commission enjoying a picnic at nearby Cow Bay beach. Back from left: Beth Walker, Jessie Forbes, Elizabeth Woodward, Miss Caldwell. Front from left: Evelyn Bolduc, Jo Crichton, Jean Faulkner, Gertrude Blakeney, Dotty Murray, May Reid. (JBW Papers)

Wisdom's photo of the Exhibition Grounds' temporary housing for those made homeless by the Halifax explosion. The block on the left was named for Massachusetts Governor Samuel McCall. Note the visibility of the not-so-private privies. (JBW Papers)

Wisdom's photo of the Community House funded by the American Christian Scientists. The smaller building was the temporary primary school constructed by the Halifax School Board on the Exhibition Grounds. (JBW Papers)

The Community House operated this playground at the Exhibition Grounds. Here African-Nova Scotian and "Syrian" boys play with girls of European descent. In 1918, Jane Wisdom's unusual image would have been considered inappropriate for fundraising/publicity purposes. As controversial then as it is revealing now, the personal photograph captures her ideal of community and co-operation. (JBW Papers)

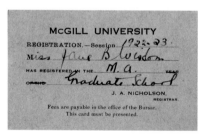

Universities were less bureaucratic in 1922–23. In July 1921, Wisdom's plans were not settled, yet she began her MA coursework at McGill University that October. (JBW Papers)

A foster mother with WDM foster children, the birth-mother holding her own child, and that child's grandmother sit in the back garden of a suburban Montreal foster home. Jane Wisdom captures the directory's mission of assisting efforts of clients to keep and support their children, and to nurture often damaged relationships within their own families. (JBW Papers)

Wisdom was registered as member No. 27 in the Canadian Association of Social Workers, 1927. (JBW Papers)

In February 1941, Wisdom travelled to Montreal and, while there, had a passport photo taken. Was this to comply with wartime measures that required a passport to travel the CPR's train that cut through Maine, or did she have other plans? (JBW Papers)

An eighty-seven-year-old Jane Wisdom at Sutherland's River, October 1971, living with her niece Relief Williams Mackay and her family. (JBW Papers)

Montreal "Protestant" private agencies. The social work profession and its ideals of community service conformed to ideals associated with Jewish femininity in Montreal, and, in 1926, female Jewish students comprised a disproportionately large percentage: about one-fourth of the class. Their placements depended on the willingness of Protestant agencies to accept them for work experience, and only one unnamed agency was willing to do so. The school's Management Committee occasionally discussed the "appropriate" number of Jewish students after 1926 in light of post-graduation local opportunities, and, although no formal quota was introduced and it was "the wish of the Committee" that the school be open to all, "irrespective of creed," the chilling effect of this discussion was reflected in a drop in Jewish enrolment.[54]

Jane Wisdom, in her position as a general secretary at a private casework agency, always supervised female Protestant social work students, and seems to have had a particular talent and generosity at mentoring them. Frances Montgomery, who would go on to a prominent national and international career in social work, came into contact with Wisdom during her student placement. Montgomery cited Wisdom as a major influence, claiming that "if Jane had not employed and encouraged me; I would not have become a social worker." A significant cohort of social workers did program fieldwork or found early employment with Wisdom in Montreal, and individual mentoring during practicums may have been more influential than what happened in the classroom.[55]

In January 1930, the Joint Board of the Theological Colleges informed the McGill principal that it would be discontinuing its $2,000 annual grant to social work. The timing was inopportune: even with the subsidy, the school was running a deficit and understaffed. Resources were scarce with the onset of the Depression, and the university would soon raise tuition, cut academic salaries, and remove telephones from professors' offices.[56] Meanwhile, a Faculty of Arts committee reviewing all programs unanimously recommended that the school be closed, citing intellectual and fiscal reasons. According to the report, the program did not belong in a university, for not all students or courses were at an appropriate level.

Principal Arthur Currie initially approached Helen Reid about the possibility of receiving funds from the Montreal Financial Federation of Charities to cover the school's annual deficit, reasoning "we get nothing from the federated charities, and I really think we had better stop the school and let the Federated Charities make arrangements to train the social workers." Reid replied in anger and sarcasm that she had never anticipated that McGill be "included among our Federated Charities," and queried if the principal had also approached the bar and the medical associations for support of the law and medical programs. Reid argued that she would "far rather see Sociology as a Department restricted for the present," as "sociologists occupying professorial chairs are in constant danger of becoming too academic – they are too far removed and unlike the doctor and lawyer in this respect – from practice and experience in the field!" Tension between Reid and Currie escalated as he described the school as a foundling left on his doorstep "with only enough clothes to last it for a year. Those whose child it was, having gotten rid of it, withdrew their help." He acknowledged that the Theological Colleges had continued their grants until the past year but noted that the graduates' grant and personal female subscriptions "were very quickly withdrawn" once the program began.[57]

Principal Currie was away from the university from December 1930 to May 1931 when many crucial decisions about the future of the school were being initiated. Acting in his place was Carleton Stanley, newly appointed assistant to the principal. Stanley was a classics scholar who, according to historians Paul Axelrod and John Reid, "denounced the erosion of moral philosophy, the decline of classics [and] the emergence of applied psychology" within the university. From his perspective, social work had no place in the university, and, later, as president of Dalhousie University (1931–1945), he was able to ensure no social work program opened there. An unattributed file note in the McGill archives commented that Stanley "was mainly responsible for ... shedding the School."[58]

The report of the school certainly received Stanley's critical assessment. The initial assertion that "professional education in social work takes its place beside education for doctors, lawyers, ministers and engineers" was annotated with the condemnation "ridiculous and false," and he felt it was significant that the head of the Toronto program had not been permanently replaced after Dale's 1925 retirement. Stanley concluded "that more and more educated men should be giving their attention to social questions. But it can be denied that men can be educated by exclusive attention to social questions, and under the guidance of others who have received this excuse for an education." In light of the predominantly female student body, it is difficult not to see that his conclusions reflected his own sexism, conservatism, and elitism.[59]

In early August 1931, the McGill Board of Governors, whose membership overlapped with the local Protestant philanthropic leadership, voted unanimously to immediately close the school. There would be no new students admitted in September, although students in their second year would be provided with courses to finish their program. Principal Currie, in his remarks to the board, argued that the school's practical training tended "to weaken concentration of resources and attention upon the essential business of a university, which is the discovery and propagation of knowledge." Reid, who was heavily implicated in both social work and nursing, had enough resources for only one campaign, and decided to throw her support and fundraising efforts behind the nursing program, which was saved. Others tried to save the social work school. In November 1931, the Montreal branch of the Canadian Association of Social Workers wrote to McGill, requesting it reconsider its decision. But Currie refused, responding that "the training in case work, the practice part, and all aspects of the professional side, must be undertaken by the Social Agencies themselves, or by other auspices."[60]

It is almost impossible not to see that a large part of the school's problems was its close proximity to women. Three programs targeted by the university – child study, nursing, and social work – were conspicuously female occupations. Although social work may have begun among the male divinity students, women played an important role as settlement-house and church workers. Reid and Falk emphasized the practical value of training female caseworkers for agencies, in contrast to the University of Toronto's (unfulfilled) aspiration of forming policy-producing bureaucrats.[61]

After the school closed, applications continued to arrive, and efforts were made to be as humane as possible to employees made redundant. Principal Currie successfully petitioned the United States' Consul General to permit the now-unemployed May Reid to return to her pre-1924 position at the Brooklyn Bureau of Charities.[62] But English-language social services in Montreal were left in crisis. During the worst of the Depression, there were no facilities to train members of an occupation with increasing scope for employment. This particular context presented a unique opportunity to debate appropriate training for the profession and to evaluate the balance between natural aptitude and acquired skill.

In February 1932, Jane Wisdom chaired a committee of volunteers, professional workers, and prominent businessmen who met to consider ways to train anglophone social workers in Montreal. The task required cultivating community support and developing academic and financial plans. Business may have supported rational social service as a means to promote efficiency and cut waste, but it was less enthusiastic about the professionalization of social work if it required the investment of scarce resources. From Ottawa, Charlotte Whitton observed that the Montreal group had to overcome the prejudice of its "wealthy clientele, that 'any person of judgment' with a few months' training should be able to take a job in social work."[63] Indeed, Wisdom's own experience only twenty years before had her showing up at the office at 9:30 a.m. and handling her first case that afternoon.

Although there were rumours in the Canadian social work community of an independent school headed by Wisdom, she, in fact, shared local leadership with close friend Dorothy King, supervisor of casework for the Montreal Family Welfare Association and the actual future director of the new school. A British immigrant, King was two years older than Wisdom and had attended London University, and would eventually hold an MA from the New York School of Social Work, and a BA and MA from New York University's School of Education.[64] Like Wisdom, King has been identified by historians P.T. Rooke and R.C. Schnell as part of Charlotte Whitton's "circle." They certainly worked together, but it would be a mistake to see Whitton as having control of the relationship, and the two sharing a similar world view. Both King's and Wisdom's experience was rooted in individual casework, not bureaucratic politics, and Whitton expressed private disappointment when both women at various times failed to act according to her wishes.[65]

Wisdom and King formed the core of the group trying to put together a new social work school with virtually no resources at the worst of the Depression. They assumed responsibility for seeing the remaining students through their final year, and proposed a new curriculum and financial basis upon which a new training school could open. The two women regularly sought the advice of Dawson, and constantly nurtured informal relations with McGill after formal connections were severed. Both women got along with Principal Currie. When he was asked to comment on proposed names of the new school's board of directors, Wisdom's had an approving checkmark beside it while other names were crossed out.[66] The fact that Currie could comment on potential director and lecturer names alerts us to the ongoing ties between the independent school and McGill.

Indeed, the Montreal School of Social Work could not have opened in October 1933 without McGill support. The university had three members of its staff on the board of trustees: sympathetic allies J.C.

Hemmeon, Carl Dawson, and Leonard Marsh. The school originally occupied rooms in the same building as the School for Graduate Nurses,
and the university offered students certain library privileges. Another
example of the close affiliation between McGill and the new school was
convocation. The 1935 ceremony was held at McGill's Moyse Hall and
the graduation address was offered by the dean of arts, who had been
so influential in the McGill school's closing. Arm's-length suited the
university well, as proven by the university's dismissal of an early proposal that King, Wisdom, and Whitton be named school lecturers. The
dean of arts felt that, with the possible exception of King, these women
did not meet the academic requirement "for any formal affiliation with
the University."[67]

When the new school opened, it offered a two-year program of lectures and supervised fieldwork aimed at college graduates. The Committee on Admission reserved the right to admit students who did not
meet normal qualifications, but emphasized an "appropriate" equivalent if they did not possess a degree. Conscious of the school's success
being linked to its ability to recruit male students, the committee drew
attention to "the need for well-trained men to act as leaders in the field
of social work." Consequently, it asserted, "special attempts will be
made to attract suitable male students."[68] Wisdom remained involved
with the school for its first six years as honorary secretary and a member of the board of trustees until she left Montreal in 1939.

The precarious and almost slapdash nature of the Montreal school
inadvertently protected it from internal schisms emerging elsewhere
within the social work profession. Montreal remained rooted primarily in Mary Richmond's diagnostic treatment procedure and inductive methods. This approach paid attention to environmental factors,
sought cause-and-effect relationships, and increasingly emphasized
individual mental hygiene and nascent psychiatry. King's association
with Columbia University linked Montreal and the diagnostic school,
with its emphasis on Freudian analysis. Daniel Walkowitz, however,
prudently warns us "not to mistake the rhetoric of psychiatry for its
operative reality; psychiatry was much less influential than social work
historians and many psychiatric social workers have claimed."[69] The
other emerging school of social work in the interwar period was the
functional approach, closely associated with the University of Pennsylvania, which emphasized an individual's capacity to change and the
centrality of the relationship between the social worker and client as
a vehicle for change. It encouraged the client – with the help of the

worker – to find solutions for him/herself rather than be dictated solutions by the welfare agency. This approach was more closely associated with Wisdom's own practice, and was a direction that most of those who worked under her followed. The coexistence of both schools in Montreal without evident conflict suggests that the issue of survival was at the forefront.

Even before Wisdom found herself immersed in the challenge of organizing a school in the early 1930s, she had become involved in social work education and professional standards at the national level. The origins of a national professional association began among the male leadership, under the guidance of Dale, during the 1924 meeting of an American association held in Toronto. Additional meetings were held at the 1925 Canadian Council on Child and Family Welfare's Ottawa conference, and, on 20 March 1926, a meeting in Montreal launched the Canadian Association of Social Workers (CASW). The prominence of men in a predominantly female profession was striking, as was the unilingual English and secular nature of the membership, notwithstanding the Montreal location of its founding meeting. The CASW identified its goals as promoting professional standards, training workers, cultivating public opinion through publishing, maintaining an employment service, and conducting research. Senior membership was limited to those older than twenty-four years of age who had two years of study in an approved school of social work and four years of professional experience. Junior members were required to have the educational qualifications and not be under the age of twenty-one. Wisdom and contemporaries such as Whitton, Falk, and Dale did not technically qualify for senior membership, so a grandfather clause was introduced whereby charter membership could be sought before the end of 1927 "on lesser qualifications than those stated above." Although men formed the initial executive of the organization, prominent women such as Wisdom, Whitton, King, Ethel Dodds Parker, Bessie Touzel, Nora Lea, and Mary Jennison also signalled their support to the profession through active involvement.[70]

Concurrent with the national organization, an affiliated Montreal branch of the CASW was established in February 1927. It focused on the continuing professional education of its members, and, in the 1926–27 year, offered lectures by experts such as Édouard Montpetit of the Université de Montréal and Whitton. Like its national counterpart, its membership list is striking. In September 1935, the Montreal branch boasted ninety-one members, but only seven were men and not one francophone or religious name appears on the list. Obviously, the membership did not reflect Montreal's population or the membership of those working in social service. Wisdom served as Montreal branch president from 1936 to 1938 and accepted other responsibilities at the national level. She represented Quebec on the national executive in 1930, acted as national vice-president from 1942 to 1944, and served on the 1946 program committee.[71]

The Canadian association ran parallel to the American association; the creation of the CASW did not mean that Canadian social workers, especially those in the East, broke continental links. Social workers such as Wisdom remained active in the North American professional network. When the American Association of Social Workers met in Boston in May 1930, at least twenty-six delegates came from Montreal, including Wisdom. In June 1935, 6,000 social workers from across the United States and Canada attended the annual meeting in Montreal, in conjunction with fifty-three other organizations, including the American Public Welfare Association and the National Federation of Settlements, Community Chests, and Councils. While the 1935 meeting exposed local prejudice and social tensions regarding race and creed, it offered many Canadian social workers contact with powerful American activists and social reform trends. Speakers ranged from Eleanor Roosevelt and Frances Perkins (US Secretary of Labor) to the radical Mary van Kleek of social work's rank-and-file movement.[72]

One of the CASW's most important activities was its biennial national conference. Rather than draw people from across Canada, it was national only insofar as it met in a variety of cities with primarily local attendance. The forum encouraged ongoing professional development, as practising social workers shared research based on their particular expertise. For an emerging profession with no standard background, this opportunity was important for both knowledge sharing and networking. The first conference, held in Montreal in April 1928, promoted training and research, and these two themes remained central in subsequent meetings. In Montreal, Wisdom presented a paper, "Adoption as Preparation for Life," and her presentation on illegitimate children at the 1931 Quebec City National Bilingual Conference "was one of the most eagerly followed papers of the Conference."[73] In the latter paper, she argued strongly for a revision of Quebec laws to ensure proper guardianship for children born outside marriage. Wisdom also attempted some research on immigration and delinquency, using her agency records, but research projects were put on the back burner by

the 1930s, as her interests increasingly focused on training and professional standards.

Wisdom's two largest contributions to the national professional organization were in the areas of social work education and ethics. Just as the
crisis was developing at McGill, the CASW established, in conjunction
with the Canadian Council on Child and Family Welfare (CCCFW), a
joint committee to examine social work education and training. The co-
operative national effort gained momentum and was a response to both
the specific Montreal crisis and the dramatic Depression-related expansion of public social services, which tended to be less professional than
private agencies. The University of British Columbia had established
a social service program in 1929, and there were prospects for a new
program at the University of Manitoba. The national twelve-person
committee, chaired by leading social worker Ethel Dodds Parker and
convened by Charlotte Whitton, had Wisdom representing the CASW,
and Dorothy King, Howard Falk (now in Vancouver), and Ernest Blois
serving as delegates for the Canadian Council on Child and Family
Welfare.[74] Wisdom, King, Whitton, and Reid regularly met informally
outside the committee structure – the result of the geographic proximity of Montreal and Ottawa – to discuss social work training, so their
influence was stronger than that of dispersed committee members in
Vancouver, Toronto, or Halifax. Their ideas did not necessarily result in
concrete action, however. Wisdom and Whitton tried unsuccessfully to
float the idea of social work's following the example of law and medicine with academic qualifications set and controlled by the universities,
and to make social workers themselves responsible for issuing professional certification after a period of practical work and a set exam.[75]

The final report was shaped by reaction to the 1931 findings of the
Community Welfare Council of Ontario, which had conducted its own
investigation into the education and training of social workers. Its recommendations were explosive: it suggested an exclusive concentration on undergraduate social sciences, followed by graduate studies
in applied social science, in place of casework training. Moreover, the
report not only rejected the tradition and influence of the humanities
and practical training, but it also argued that a single, Toronto-based,
"well equipped School of Applied Social Science will meet the present needs of the Province of Ontario and probably of the Dominion
of Canada." The report used the rhetoric of science to completely ob-
scure and distance social work from its feminine and religious past.
It was echoed in a *Social Welfare* article by C.W. Topping, the first and

only sociologist at the University of British Columbia between 1929 and 1954, who linked social science with masculinity. Topping looked to the social sciences to turn out graduates who would "become daring and constructive social engineers rather than 'wipers of bloody noses.'" Whitton, Reid, and Wisdom, however, argued strongly for the humanities in preparation for a career in social work, and Wisdom still advocated a broad and general education. "We want the girl with education and a cultural background to begin with," she wrote, arguing that candidates for the profession could later "cover the ground themselves in the 'ologies' and social sciences."[76] Whitton attempted to leverage her position by arguing that if the proposals of the Ontario report were adopted, she, like "Jane Wisdom, Dorothy King, Falk, Judge Blois, and many others like Laura Holland, etc.," was prepared to resign from the CASW.[77]

The final CASW–CCCFW 1932 report began with the repeated assertion of the need to educate the public that "social work is really a profession demanding special background and equipment." None of the committee members had much specialized training themselves and, since no specifics were provided, I am left imagining "equipment" to mean printed forms, pens, and sensible walking shoes. In the 1930s, Wisdom lacked the basic technological skills associated with a typewriter, and relied on clerical support for her official correspondence. The authors of the report made the analogy to nursing, arguing that their profession in Canada was in a similar position to nursing before Florence Nightingale. The committee concluded that social work's problem was the lack of a standard of academic admission, and proposed that "ANY" undergraduate arts degree would do. They also preserved the tension between specialized training and personal attributes by emphasizing the important of "personality, character, emotional balance, and maturity of outlook." Programs had to combine academic and practical work, offer instruction by individuals with experience in the profession, and emphasize learning by doing.[78]

A second way that social workers sought to have their profession recognized was through a code of ethics. Doctors had the Hippocratic Oath, but social workers had no such code to guide professional standards. In May 1933, Jane Wisdom became the first chair of the CASW National Committee on Ethics. She had taken a leadership role on the issue locally, leading branch discussions on confidentiality and whether volunteer workers should have access to case records. Limited progress was made in formulating a professional code, but the goal of the committee was perceived more generally by Wisdom to be "the build-ing up [of] a *profession*." A local study group in Montreal took on the subject as a discussion theme, and Wisdom argued strongly that ideas about ethics must emerge from practitioners in the field rather than be imposed from the top down.[79] She focused on confidentiality, impartial-ity, and objectivity as the foundation of ethical social work. Wisdom's leadership on the committee once again highlights the contradictions of this emerging profession. She was recommended for the position be-cause of her character, personality, and reputation for solid judgment rather than for having any particular expertise. In arguing Wisdom's suitability for the post, Dorothy King noted that, "apart from the social work experience, she is a person to whom some of us turn naturally for help in questions of an ethical character, partly because of her fair-mindedness, her ability to seize on the principles underlying the imme-diate situation and her own very high standards of personal conduct." Wisdom's commitment to establishing professional standards of ethics was ongoing. In 1938, she helped hammer out a national code for Ca-nadian social work that began with a preamble emphasizing the lack of prejudice "to race, color or creed," signalling a consideration of rights that would continue to expand after the war.[80]

Professional responsibilities, for Wisdom, also meant preparing and presenting briefs to interwar government committees, as politicians and bureaucrats explored the idea of an expanding state. In 1928, she participated in the Ottawa Conference of Delinquency, which brought together social activists and government policymakers to deliberate on ending British child immigration to Canada. Her past experience with a government commission in Nova Scotia made her a valuable asset at the Montreal Council of Social Agencies' 1931 presentation to the Quebec Social Insurance (Montpetit) Commission and the same organization's 1938 appearance before the federal Royal Commission on Dominion–Provincial Relations. The latter looked into the impasse in federal–provincial relations, power, and financing exposed by the Depression.[81] Wisdom was also the senior member of the CASW's Committee on Progressive Programme, a group organized to promote social changes based on social workers' expertise.[82] This activist group brought together leftists within the national social work community and action-oriented left-liberals such as Wisdom.

The demands of employment and the extracurricular responsibili-ties of building a profession were exhausting for Wisdom, who, from childhood, never enjoyed good health. In 1925, Helen Reid had warned

Charlotte Whitton that Wisdom was "not physically strong enough to force the pace" that heading an agency demanded. Serious illness led her to take a leave of absence from work in February and March 1928. She recovered with her sister Bessie at Grasmere Bermuda, a location favoured by the wealthy Montrealers who populated her volunteer agency board. Following the crisis at the McGill school in August 1932, when questioned about Wisdom as a candidate for CASW national president, Charlotte Whitton quickly dismissed the suggestion: "Jane Wisdom is in no condition at this time to carry the responsibility of this office."[83] Whitton was correct: Wisdom took another leave of absence from work from November 1932 to May 1933, recuperating in Sutherland's River, Nova Scotia, with sister Bess. When she returned to Montreal in spring 1933, she was told by her doctor to "slow up," advice that would have been very difficult to follow, considering desperate social conditions in Montreal and ongoing community and professional responsibilities. At the first annual meeting of the Montreal School of Social Work in April 1934, Charlotte Whitton as speaker was described as "all confidence" while Wisdom, as honorary secretary of the school, was deemed by her old mentor Susan Cameron Vaughan as "somewhat pathetic ... like a ghost."[84]

Professional identity for early female social workers such as Wisdom was reinforced by social networks and friendships. Friends referred to Wisdom as JBW and to Dorothy King as DK, as formal initials became affectionate nicknames. Other elements of Wisdom's social life, such as her participation in the McGill Alumnae Modern Literature Group, her membership at the Presbyterian Church of St. Andrew and St. Paul, and her charter membership in the Maritime Women's Club of Montreal, all would have brought her into contact with her employers at the social agency where she worked. Professional networks and friendships were mirrored also in housing arrangements. Single professional women not living with their families had few options, as there were relatively few small apartments in Montreal at the time, salaries for women were low, and both time and labour were scarce for housekeeping. For example, writer Jessie Georgina Sime lived for nearly twenty years in the downtown Mount Royal Hotel. When Wisdom returned to Montreal as a graduate student, she lived in a francophone neighbourhood off Parc Lafontaine. Thereafter, her work and home life were usually rooted in the anglophone West End, with the exception of a September 1936 move to Hutchison Street to a Mme. Frechette's for what Wisdom described as "board and French!"[85]

It is easy to see a pattern of accommodation based on friendship and professional relations. I found no personal correspondence that might suggest a permanent home address, and only intermittent listings in the Montreal City Directory. For some of the first eight years, she appears to have boarded with Halifax friend Helen Crichton, now Grant, and shared an apartment and, later, a house in the anglophone suburb of Notre-Dame-de-Grâce with the newlywed couple. From 1930 to 1932, and then again from 1934 to 1935, Wisdom's residence is listed as the University Women's Club, an association and residential facility. In 1932–33, Wisdom is listed as boarding in the household of W.H. White, secretary of the YMCA, and, in 1935–36, with Helen Reid, two Montrealers with prominent social work connections. I suspect a third connection, as the 1936–37 directory lists Wisdom as staying with a widow, Mrs. Marcelle Gaudion, who shared the family name with Mrs. E.H. Gaudion, superintendent of the Montreal Welfare Services Department. On only one occasion during her eighteen-year return to Montreal is Wisdom listed as having her own home. In 1938–39, her last year in the city, Wisdom lived in an apartment on downtown Crescent Street, and shared a home with cousin Catherine Hebb, a doctoral student at McGill.[86]

Wisdom's occasional residence at the University Women's Club of Montreal is especially interesting. The club was organized in 1926 with 240 charter members, Wisdom among them. Members had to have obtained a degree from a recognized university, and paid a $25 entrance fee and an annual membership subscription of $15. Unlike the two other prominent Montreal English-language women's clubs, the Themis and the Monteregian, the University Women's Club, after March 1927, offered accommodation. It purchased a large house on Peel just north of Sherbrooke, with twelve bedrooms and two bathrooms on each floor, a lounge, a private room for parties, a card room, and a dining room that opened to the garden. The club, adjacent to Premier Lomer Gouin's home, offered a prestigious and convenient downtown address. Residents had more privacy and flexibility than they would have as boarders, and, at the same time, were freed from housekeeping duties.[87] A variety of meal plans was offered, and many residents went away for the summer months, an option Jane Wisdom pursued several times. In 1935, rooms were available from $35 to $50 a month, and three meals a day could be had for an additional flat rate of $42. In addition, residents could entertain at the club and "put up guests." For example, in 1931, when Charlotte Whitton spoke to local workers about the need for professional training, Wisdom organized a private luncheon at the club and arranged for Whitton to stay there.[88]

The blurry boundary between Wisdom's professional and private life was mirrored by the unclear line between social work as an acquired set of skills and social work as a natural disposition or series of character traits. Although social work sought to cast itself as a profession based on the techniques of casework and a professionally specific set of ethics associated with confidentiality, impartiality, and objectivity, these same qualities were closely aligned with individual character. Historian Linda Gordon has pointed out that through casework, "individuals brought flexibility, creativity and empathy beyond the strictures of agency policy."[89] As with other caring professions, it is difficult to argue specialized expertise in terms of acquired skill when "natural" qualities of character and personality were regarded as more important. This was epitomized in a 1952 tribute written by Frances Montgomery on Wisdom's retirement. It vaunted not her technical expertise or professionalism but, rather, her "educated heart [which] ... opened avenues of help to clients, social work students, practitioners, boards, and communities in various regions," the inspiration she offered to those in the profession, and her values.[90]

In 1928, Porter Lee, director of the New York School of Philanthropy and one of the most influential social work educators in North America, lamented that with professionalization came a "greater interest in social work as a career than as a Cause. ... Social workers, conscious of a relatively new form of expertness, are sometimes more interested in their programme and methods than they are in the human lives which those programmes and methods affect." In a published response, Wisdom cautioned against "the jaded social worker" who was unable to negotiate the idealism and functionalism the job required. She argued that it was each social worker's professional responsibility to regularly tap into "the everlasting sources of life's inspiration," whether that meant nature, art, religion, intellectual pursuits, or friendship.[91] Wisdom insisted on the unity of professional technical expertise and humanistic values, as she negotiated the tensions of an educated heart balancing between idealism and functionalism.

Efforts to professionalize through national and international associations, set standards of training, and common professional ethics offered opportunities for social workers to articulate community needs and shape local, provincial, and national futures. The profession faced challenges as it continued to be associated with women and unpaid work, and found it difficult to negotiate the difference between acquired skills and character. Wisdom rejected any division between expertise and professionalism and core human values. She tried to span the growing division between "practical" sociology and the emerging academic discipline, and was instrumental in keeping some social work training alive in English Montreal during a period of crisis. Wisdom's own social work practice ultimately led her to abandon a formal academic path, a choice that was mirrored by McGill University. After the Second World War, McGill cautiously accepted overtures from social work, and cemented the relationship in 1950.

Chapter Seven

The Women's Directory of Montreal and Private Agency Work, 1923–1939

In March 1923, while Wisdom was still in the hospital recovering from surgery, a former college classmate approached her to become the executive secretary at a private welfare agency for Protestant, first-time, single mothers. The discreetly named Women's Directory of Montreal (WDM) would be the focus of her life over the next fifteen years. It would draw her into specialized casework, private-agency culture and politics, and the larger question of female citizenship and its meaning for unmarried mothers, agency volunteers, and board members. Wisdom was both an employee of the agency and someone with power and responsibility over agency cases. This leads us to question: to whom was she ultimately responsible? The Women's Directory's donors and her employers, or the directory cases?

Because of their so-called moral transgression, the unmarried mothers who sought the directory's care lacked normal claims to respectable femininity. Yet, the agency, under Wisdom, gradually adopted what can be regarded as "redemptive citizenship," which included economic autonomy and an emphasis on belonging and community. Danielle Gauvreau has cautioned us not to exaggerate the importance of mothers in Quebec. Not all women became wives or mothers, and few mothers had large families. Nevertheless, historians such as Andrée Lévesque, Denyse Baillargeon, Magda Fahrni, and Marie-Aimée Cliche have amply demonstrated the prominence of married motherhood in public discourse. In particular, Lévesque, Cliche, and Marie-Paule Malouin et al. have examined the situation of women who became pregnant outside marriage. They emphasize the extent to which these women were made invisible. Cliche draws attention to at least three secret drop-off points in the Quebec City area for infants to be passed anonymously to the various religious orders and Hôpital du Sacré-Coeur. This covert process was designed to protect the honour of the disgraced woman's family and to prevent infanticides.[1] One sees this desire for invisibility even in government commissions. Most Canadian provinces explicitly rejected British Columbia's decision to provide support through mothers' allowance programs to the mothers of children born outside marriage. The report of the Quebec Social Insurance Commission in 1933 did not even raise this possibility or acknowledge that there was a group of impoverished women attempting to raise children in these circumstances. Although concealment, secrecy, and denial were undoubtedly the dominant approaches, they were not universal. What Jane Wisdom called, borrowing progressive philosopher John Dewey's term, the "experiments" of the WDM represented a significant alternative.[2]

Wisdom's return to Montreal had coincided with a greatly altered landscape for Montreal charity, the result of both local and transnational influences. Locally, the war, through the Canadian Patriotic Fund, a private charity charged with supporting soldiers' families, had extended exposure to efficient and rational charity beyond the Charity Organization Society. While, in some communities, such as Halifax, the fund had approached disbursements as an entitlement, in Montreal, it operated like a charity, underpinned by notions of deservedness, rigorous investigation, and careful documentation. Ethnic alliances changed as well. Various expressions of French-Canadian, English-Canadian, and British nationalism, and the related conflict over wartime conscription, fractured the rapport between English and French Montreal elites. As a result, even the pretext of a universal coordinated charity had to be abandoned. "Mutual isolation" between the city's English- and French-speaking populations would increase during the 1920s as tenuous elite links dissolved.[3]

The economic crisis of the 1930s brought together English-speaking Protestant, Catholic, and Jewish charitable communities, but there were only rare and limited instances of coordination across linguistic lines. Co-operation between the WDM and the Société d'adoption et de Protection de l'enfance à Montréal, established to promote adoption within the French Catholic community, was one such example. The population of the Island of Montreal grew dramatically from 724,000 in 1921 to 1,117,000 in 1941, with the percentage of francophones increasing by 2 per cent and anglophones declining from 27 per cent to 24 per cent of the population.[4] As the largest French-speaking city outside France,

Montreal remained economically dominated by an English-speaking minority.

While Montreal had a powerful and visible English-speaking elite, the rest of the province, and certainly its civil legal structure, was shaped by French custom and culture. Married women were legally considered minors, with no right to work outside their homes unless their husbands granted a permit and no right to own real estate or be members of commercial partnerships or civil associations. Legal roots were reinforced by influential, conservative Catholics who encouraged married women to submit to patriarchal family conventions. Non-aboriginal Quebec women older than twenty-one years of age could vote in federal elections after 1918, but not until 1940 was the franchise extended in provincial elections. During the interwar period, the Dorion Commission, established in 1929, re-examined the legal position of women within marriage. It reported back in 1931, but few changes were made. The most significant reform involved married women employed outside the home finally obtaining the right to receive their own salaries. Women's legal status could result in grey areas. When the Women's Directory of Montreal sought incorporation in 1918, its lawyer wondered if "authorities might require the authorization of their husbands to sign such a declaration." However, since some of the husbands were overseas on military service, he "decided to try to put through the petition without taking this precaution."[5] Remarkably, the incorporation was granted, even though these women had no legal rights to create the association. In this particular case, a group of privileged women asserted their sense of entitlement outside the legal context, and it was not questioned.

The same patriarchal influence that shaped the law towards women had distinct consequences for children born outside "the bonds of marriage." Adoption had no legal status in Quebec before 1924. After that point, only "illegitimate" and full orphans were eligible. The province had no formal role in protecting children's interests when "natural guardianship" failed or lapsed. It was almost impossible to force an unwilling father to admit paternity, which left full responsibility for support to the mother. Legally, neither parent was connected to the child unless maternity or paternity was acknowledged voluntarily or judicially. Any "natural" child could claim maintenance once maternity or paternity was acknowledged, but a "*declaration de paternité*" was a secondary legal action that could be initiated only after the mother was legally appointed guardian. Legal proceedings were expensive and intimidating, and the scope of the law was not always clear. As a result, some children whose families did not conform to a patriarchal structure had no one legally responsible for them. Under Wisdom, the WDM spent its financial "nest egg," which it carried forward from before amalgamated fundraising, on obtaining legal rulings. The directory's volunteer legal advisor was occasionally called into service to advise Canadian organizations on the complexity and distinctiveness of Quebec law in this area.[6]

Although the family and the church remained paramount in caring for Quebec's vulnerable populations, there was no denying an expanding state in the post-war period. In 1914, the city of Montreal reached out to one group when it established the Meurling Municipal Refuge, which provided immediate shelter and relief to homeless men. The Quebec Public Charities Act, implemented in 1921, gave the province the right to inspect institutions and provide grants to residential charitable facilities. The grants were funded by a municipal tax collected on all amusements, half of which was transmitted to the province, and a hospital tax on all meals over 35 cents. Eventually, profits from legal liquor sales were also added. All sources generated much-needed cash for both Montreal and the province, but funds were allocated only to residential institutions, thereby preserving the Catholic religious norm that privileged this form of assistance.[7] This mattered especially for the care of children, and it ran contrary to the increasing English-North American practice of deinstitutionalization and the move towards placing children in foster care. Throughout the 1920s, the Protestant and Jewish communities lobbied city and provincial governments for support, but were unable to dislodge their commitment to residential institutional support. It was only during the 1930s, with the expansion of charitable support on all state levels, that Quebec addressed the issue of social assistance through the Montpetit Commission. In 1936, Quebec became the last province to join the Old Age Pension federal cost-sharing program. It was not until 1937 that it adopted a Needy Mothers Assistance Act to extend monthly support to certain widows with children.[8]

The head of the Montreal agency charged with dealing with Protestant and non-sectarian family welfare argued that Quebec's legal structure made it particularly ill-suited to face the crisis of the 1930s. He pointed out: "There is no Minister of Public Welfare, no Superintendent of Neglected Children, no provision for municipal or provincial hospitals, no Mothers' Allowance or Old Age Pensions, no municipal outdoor relief except in the city of Verdun, though Montreal operates an excellent municipal refuge for homeless men." Large municipalities took over the administration of federal unemployment relief from private charities only in 1933.[9]

Although the Quebec state was a reluctant participant in welfare, Montreal remained the richest city in Canada. In both 1910 and 1930, over 40 per cent of all directors of Canada's leading companies called Montreal home. Abundant private wealth continued to dominate Montreal's charitable structure, especially within English-speaking communities. Desmond Morton has noted that although wealth and power were concentrated in Montreal, municipal administration remained poor. Toronto had only 72 per cent of Montreal's population but 120 per cent of its tax revenue. In 1930, 86 per cent of the revenue available for the amalgamated council of Protestant charities came from the Financial Federation, rather than from government sources such as the province or local municipal governments.[10] The astonishing wealth of certain individuals and the grave inequality of Montreal society meant that philanthropists wielded considerable power – power that had to be negotiated by professional social workers and those in need.

The most prominent professional social worker in Montreal when Wisdom returned was social work educator Howard Falk. As a networker and organization builder of some renown, his arrival in Montreal had instigated a January 1919 English-language meeting of Protestant charity representatives and a delegate of the Montreal Federation of Jewish Philanthropies. Local anglophone groups had rejected an invitation to join the national Protestant-dominated Dominion Council of Social Services in the hope that Protestant, Jewish, and Catholic organizations might come together to form a "Central Committee for Co-operation." This cross-confessional anglophone alliance was finally achieved in 1940.[11] The 1919 meeting resulted in the creation of the Montreal Council of Social Agencies in April 1920. This umbrella organization, which coordinated certain services and fundraising, ran parallel to the Federation of Jewish Philanthropies previously established in 1916.[12]

One of the survey's most important revelations was the uneven scale of private and corporate giving. The 1919 survey of eighty Protestant associations concluded that 7 per cent of individual donors contributed 60 per cent of the funds collected by all agencies, and 12 per cent of firms gave 76 per cent of corporate donations. Businessmen almost unanimously supported the establishment of one, joint, fundraising campaign. They were eager to eliminate the "multiplicity of appeals" by parallel efforts that wasted time and money. In November 1922, twenty-seven English-language Protestant agencies came together for a common fundraising campaign and subsequent division of these resources through a "Financial Federation." English-speaking Catholics made a similar move in 1930 with the creation of the Federation of Catholic Charities. Francophone Catholics followed in 1932 with the Fédération des Œuvres de charité canadiennes-françaises.[13]

Falk guided the COS, which had held onto the pretense of looking after francophone Catholic families and coordinating all Montreal charity, towards its reorganization in 1921 as the Family Welfare Association. Thereafter, it focused solely on relief in the English Protestant and non-sectarian communities. He was also instrumental in recruiting G.B. Clarke, a former colleague from Winnipeg, to head this new organization in 1924.[14] Among the many organizations that came to together to form the Montreal Council of Social Agencies was the Women's Directory, established in 1915.

Just as the Women's Directory gave no indication of its purpose through its name, its clients are almost impossible to bring into focus. There is one exception: a series of labelled photographs that include three women staring straight into the camera, with babies and toddlers on their knees. One photo shows a young woman with two older women in a St. Lambert suburban backyard garden. Nothing in the image indicates the supposed unusualness of the grouping, but the young mother holding her baby on her knee is not married, and, while one older woman is the child's grandmother, the other older woman is the foster mother with whom the baby lived. Foster mothers were typically older, often residing in working-class Montreal suburbs such as Verdun, St. Lambert, or Greenfield Park. Recruited by word of mouth, they were vetted to ensure the suitability of their character, and received a minimal allowance in exchange for their work. To be eligible, these working-class households had to be able to maintain themselves without the foster payment to prevent homes from becoming mercenary commercial establishments.[15] Indeed, in another photo, Wisdom points out that a foster mother and father had brought their own two foster children to the downtown clinic in their own car. Without this context, the photos would be indistinguishable from snapshots in so-called respectable family albums.

The young women who appeared in this collection of photos were 1930s clients of the WDM. The charitable agency helped first-time,

English-speaking, Protestant, unmarried mothers to keep their babies by providing health care, financial support, employment placement, and supervised foster care. Most of the women were between seventeen and twenty-two years old, Anglican and Canadian-born, employed as domestics, and of "ordinary" intellectual capability, but many were older or younger, and came from a wide variety of circumstances.[16] Jane Wisdom took, and, interestingly, kept, the photos, perhaps as personal mementoes, perhaps as a record of her professional achievements. Certainly, no such photos ever appeared in the agency's published annual report. For someone preoccupied with cases' confidentiality, they afford a rare glimpse at real people.

In her position as general secretary for the agency from 1923 to 1939, Wisdom was supported by a small staff of female professional caseworkers, nurses, office employees, student interns, paid foster mothers, volunteers, and a board of managers that linked the agency to some of Montreal's most influential Protestant families. The Women's Directory was not only a charitable organization; it was also a women's organization with female clients, female professional staff, female volunteers, and, with a few exceptional early years, a female board of managers. Dealing with the consequences of misused, or what they understood as inappropriate, female sexuality was sensitive women's work. By working within a closed female world, the WDM perpetuated the myth that these women were abnormal. At the same time, the directory was also regarded as innovative. It offered specialized care and high-quality service, and Wisdom may have been the first to offer counselling to unmarried fathers in Canada. In 1952, one nationally prominent social worker reflected that, in the 1930s, "the standard of help [at the WDM] was in advance of much child welfare practice today."[17]

Almost all the scholarship on unmarried mothers in Quebec before the Second World War has focused on the French Catholic institutional model, which necessitated giving up infants to religious institutions. It does not apply to the Women's Directory, however. The WDM was influenced by a combination of professional social work standards and, after 1925, American philosopher John Dewey's ideal of democratic, participatory citizenship. The WDM helped women after confinement by boarding them with their babies so that bonding and nursing could take place. They then tried to keep mother and child together by negotiating reconciliation with the mother's own family. If this was not possible, they tried to provide employment for mothers, and sought to subsidize and supervise foster care for their children for up to five years. Following Dewey, the WDM emphasized traditional liberal ideas such as individual enhancement or "the claim of every individual to the full development of his capacities."[18] This development required "direct and active participation" in the community and, ultimately, the democratic process. Private agencies had to adjust to the realities of an urban, industrialized age and equip clients to deal successfully with these challenges. This relatively small agency was regarded as one of the most progressive experiments in the field of "illegitimacy" in Canada. In focusing on a single agency, we are forced to confront the myriad and simultaneous currents of thought at work within Montreal charitable agencies.[19]

Certainly, there were significant silences in the reports, and the ideals of "wholesome family life," at least in public, remained unquestioned. Nothing was ever mentioned about sexual coercion, either in the form of incest or rape. But the WDM from 1923 to 1939 offered a selected group of women who met its criteria an opportunity to keep their infants. However, change in social work conventions was fast-paced, and the WDM's reputation as progressive was short-lived. By 1939, professional conventions increasingly regarded mothers who had children outside marriage as psychologically rebellious. Agencies, the WDM among them, encouraged women to pursue a "second chance" at normative, heterosexual behaviour by hiding their pregnancies and giving up their infants for adoption.

The Women's Directory of Montreal did not start out as progressive. It was modelled on the Women's Directory of Philadelphia, an agency established in 1894 by doctors Charlotte Abbey and Rebecca J. Cole. Cole is an especially interesting participant. She is recognized as the second African American female physician and the first Black woman to graduate from the Woman's Medical College of Pennsylvania.[20] The Women's Directory of Philadelphia sought to address the high rate of infant mortality for children born outside marriage, and to "redeem" women who had gone astray through the power of motherly love. Historian Sherri Broder has described its origins as being in an anxiety over "baby farming," the practice of taking in young infants for profit, often ending up with a high mortality rate. This moral panic was further reinforced by "representations of fallen women, mercenary caretakers, and nonmaternal, dangerous and possibly murderous destitute mothers."[21] As was the case in Philadelphia, commercial infant-boarding houses in Montreal were a focus of concern for anglophone female reformers, as were foundling hospitals, such as the large Catholic institutions or the Montreal Maternity and Foundling Hospital. The women reformers saw foundling hospitals as encouraging unmarried mothers to abandon their infants, even as they acknowledged unmarried mothers had few options to ensure their babies' survival. Even in 1929, the WDM estimated that half of all Montreal infants born outside marriage died.[22]

The women who established the WDM were harsh in their attitudes towards unmarried mothers. One lecture read by an agency founder in 1917 noted that 50 per cent of prostitutes were unmarried mothers; she thereby linked having a child out of wedlock with the worst form of female deviance. But even this harsh condemnation was leavened with the recognition that "illicit sex relations" were "as sinful in a man as in a woman."[23] The Women's Directory of Montreal was launched in 1915 with three objects. The first was to keep the unmarried mother and her child together. The second was to "bring the father to the realization of his paternal responsibilities," which tended to mean financial help rather than forcing what was regarded as an inappropriate marriage. (The putative father had already revealed his poor character through engaging in extramarital sex.) The third was to train "the unmarried mother so that she may fulfil her parental obligations usefully and happily."[24] Initially, this final point emphasized placing mothers in domestic service, but the goal of economic autonomy grew in the interwar period as professional social workers adopted frameworks that expanded to citizenship and community.

The original constitution and bylaws of the agency gave very strict parameters about eligibility, and these both benefited and plagued the agency for its entire existence. First, there was a sectarian qualification. Only Protestant women could be helped. Second, the directory assisted unmarried women only with their *first* "illegitimate" child. Should a second transgression occur, or should the woman be married and the husband deny responsibility, the woman was directed to the Family Welfare Association. The women who entered the agency's care had to do so willingly. They had to agree that they were going to try to keep their child after birth, and that they would participate in individual programs to become autonomous or "rehabilitated." Originally, no help with confinement was offered if adoption plans were made. The women could not be widows or divorcees and had to be of sound mind and body, so that they were capable of self-support. If, after five years, self-sufficiency was not achieved, the child would be handed over to the Montreal Children's Bureau.[25]

While the impetus for the Women's Directory in Philadelphia came from the female medical community, in Montreal, it was strongly associated with female, amateur social reformers. Before the First World War, there were few female physicians in Quebec. The most prominent was Grace Ritchie England, who was prominent in the WDM's early years. Organization meetings began in early 1911, with strong links to the Montreal Local Council of Women and the local Charity Organization Society. There was also considerable overlap with women who participated in Montreal's settlement house movement. When the agency opened in 1915, it was decidedly amateur, and the primary attention offered to mothers was developing their potential as domestic servants. An ill-conceived plan to establish a training house to improve the "total ignorance of the rudiments of housework" among the mothers was abandoned within a year as a financial disaster.[26]

In 1916, twenty-six-year-old Lucy Phinney, an Anglican from Boston, Massachusetts, was hired as the general secretary of the organization. Phinney was a graduate of Radcliffe and had three years' experience as both a volunteer at Denison House, a settlement in Boston, and a paid worker with the Boston Society for the Care of Girls, where she had undertaken a study of unmarried mothers. Before she was seconded to become general secretary of the Committee of Sixteen, Montreal's voluntary commission looking into prostitution, in 1918, she attempted to introduce professional standards to the WDM. These efforts were reinforced by a subsequent general secretary, Canadian-born Flora McNeill, who also had experience in the settlement house movement. In a 1921 report, Falk considered the Women's Directory to be one of only four organizations in Montreal performing actual casework; that is, doing individual investigation into the particular circumstances of each case and proposing an individually appropriate plan of action.[27] Other charitable organizations offered standardized aid not tailored to individual circumstance.

While work with the young women was conducted on an individual basis, no written historical sources survive that recognize these women as distinct. Composite data on age, religion, and "nationality or racial origin" of the women who arrived as clients were published in annual reports. In the early 1920s, these statistics emphasized that 38 per cent were immigrants – almost all from Britain – and that nearly one-third of the women had arrived in Canada in the previous five years. Almost all the women worked in domestic service, and their average age was 21.8 years. Over the interwar period, the average age of the young women dropped and the clientele was increasingly Canadian-born. The 1938 report was broken down by occupation. It noted that of the fifty-eight women with occupations who entered the agency's care that year, thirty-eight were in domestic service, five were waitresses, five were factory workers, two worked in offices, and the remaining eight were schoolteachers and graduate nurses. Wisdom attributed the predominance of domestic service workers in the agency to the occupation's low wages, which did not permit women to pay for their own amusement, and the isolated nature of the work, which led girls to "seek companionship … and recreation on their days off."[28]

While the women who came to the agency in need of help are known to us only as statistics, the women who volunteered as board members, office workers, and visitors were neither invisible nor anonymous. Before the Financial Federation, fundraising was probably the volunteer's most important work. In his 1919 report, Falk noted that "the money-attracting power of an individual" was the first consideration in selecting a new board member. "Society women" were useful recruits to agencies but it worked both ways: one Montreal agency director reported that women were "anxious to get on our board, because a place on the board is a step up on the society ladder."[29] Membership in the early years entailed petitioning special support from the local council, running charitable bridge games in private homes, throwing raffles, and presenting theatrical performances and lectures. In 1917, for example, volunteers raised $3,470, half through entertainment and half through personal subscriptions. In 1919, the directory engaged a professional female "collector" to solicit funds. She worked for a salary but also earned a percentage from the donations received. This method was clearly successful: the directory brought in more than $7,000 in subscriptions, compared to the $137 raised through bridge and raffles.[30] The same collector was engaged the following year, and personal subscriptions rose to nearly $9,500.

Most personal donations still came from the households of active volunteers. For example, during the 1920 campaign, WDM president Mary McDonald and her husband each donated $200, as did executive member Maud Norsworthy and her husband. Beyond individual donations, the Executive Committee also organized a series of successful lectures with an impressive list of contemporary authors that included W.B. Yeats. Stephen Leacock may have given his service for free, as his wife, Beatrix Hamilton Leacock, was a member of the Auxiliary Committee. With the introduction of the Financial Federation in 1923, the board was "released from the problems of money raising" and transformed into what Jane Wisdom called a "thinking and working Board."[31] The directory occasionally had fundraising obligations, but, overall, the Financial Federation provided a dependable source of revenue, and the labour-intensive activities of organizing charitable bridge games or lectures were over.

A "thinking and working Board," intimately involved in the operations of the agency, had to overcome the prejudices of certain agencies. There were Montreal boards that refused to meet with their chief executive officers, since, as their employees, they were "socially inferior," or because of traditions "established many years ago, when social workers and domestic servants were graded together in the social scale." The board of the Women's Directory met with its staff. Lucy Phinney is an interesting example of overlapping volunteer and professional identities. While she was a paid professional employee of the WDM, she was also chair of the Social and Moral Reform Committee of the Montreal Women's Club and secretary of the Montreal Committee on Feeble-Mindedness.[32] Was she still regarded as an employee by board members of the WDM when they encountered her in a different capacity? Clearly not, for when Phinney left the directory for the Committee of Sixteen, she was appointed to the Executive Committee of the WDM in a volunteer capacity.

Phinney was not the only one to carry multiple identities. Dorothy Judah, a district agent for the Montreal Charity Organization Society, also participated in the creation of the directory and was an unpaid member of its Executive Committee from 1915 through 1917. Directory employee Mildred McCombe, a trained nurse and graduate of McGill's public health course, resigned upon marriage; as Mrs. Allan, she accepted a place on the organization's Executive Committee.[33] There was also the case of Miss Elsie Bowden, described in the annual report as a volunteer worker. She appears to have worked full-time for the WDM without pay. In her study of the anglo-Montreal elite in the interwar period, Margaret Westley recounts the story of an unidentified Montreal debutante who was volunteering full-time for a charitable agency and was eventually offered a regular paid position. According to this anecdote, she had to turn down the opportunity. A paid position would have embarrassed her family, possibly suggesting that her father could not comfortably support her. Social conventions, such as those pertaining to married women working after marriage, or to women of a certain class working for pay before marriage, could affect whether one was considered a professional or a volunteer. In Elsie Bowden's case, there was no difference in the work she actually performed. The slippage between professionals and volunteers may also have resulted from the lack of formal qualifications for either. In 1922, Mary Hitchcock McDonald observed that the "average worker in the average social agency in Montreal has been so completely untrained that 'well-meaning amateur' was an obvious designation."[34]

Volunteers could also provide continuity, local knowledge, and stability during periods of rapid professional turnover. In the general secretary's report for 1923, Jane Wisdom noted that, with the exception of one employee, the entire staff had been appointed since the last annual meeting. Wisdom understood that office staff turnover hampered long-term follow-up work with mothers and children, and that this follow-up could be maintained only through the work of committed volunteers. Volunteer participants could also provide local knowledge and connections for professional staff members new to Montreal. In 1918, for example, a leading volunteer arranged "many informal meetings at which the General Secretary had the opportunity of explaining the work, the aims and ideals of the Directory."[35] Without this local contact, it is not clear that the general secretary would have been able to identify *whom* it was important to meet or if she would even have been able to secure a successful meeting. The support and facilitation of a permanent, connected community member were vital to the success of the organization, and the leadership of the WDM was among the most visible of those who urged McGill to establish a local social work program.[36]

When the directory began in 1915, it largely depended on a system of domestic service placement for the mother and her baby, and in the ability to find employers willing to accept unmarried mothers with infants for live-in situations. This made the social connections of the board and Auxiliary Committee especially useful. With increased emphasis in the early 1920s on casework methods that pursued "individual re-establishment," and the use of foster homes for the child until the mother could provide her own home, the role of volunteers became more diversified. Volunteers were intimately involved in casework. In 1922–23, before Wisdom's arrival, the Executive Committee met weekly, and, on the first and third Wednesdays of the month, the general secretary reported on active cases, concealing names to offer limited privacy. On the second and fourth Wednesdays, broader management issues were discussed. This weekly contact ensured that volunteers had a deep understanding of the organization's daily operations. A 1924 report of the board of managers commented that Wisdom considered it "an essential part of her duty to instruct the members of her board in the principles of case work." Nearly forty years later, one member of the executive, Esther Kerry, remembered Wisdom's "warmth and interest in people and in helping them" when she "conveyed her feeling for casework." The ongoing education of board members was also evident in conference attendance. In 1924, for example, the president accompanied the general secretary to the National Conference of Social Work and the Inter-City Conference on Illegitimacy, both held in Toronto.[37]

By 1928, Jane Wisdom called it "an accepted fact that only trained workers can do consistent social case work." Still, she maintained that the volunteer continued to play a vital role, participating in the Financial Federation campaign, driving automobiles, and providing clothes, furniture, Christmas stockings, recreational funds, and general assistance in the office.[38] Access to automobiles seemed to be especially appreciated at a time when this was beyond the means of both professional workers and agencies.

So, who were the volunteers at the WDM? Annual reports provide the names of 221 women involved in the directory between 1915 and 1939. Of this group, 18 were single, 10 were widowed, and 193 were married. It is possible to identify the maiden names for 124 of the married women, which suggests their generally upper-class origins, through their fathers' presence in biographical guides such as the *Who's Who*, the *National Reference Book of the Canadian Newspaper Service*, and social registers such as *Dau's Montreal Blue Book*. Echoing Christina Simmons's findings in Halifax, these women were upper middle class, but they did not come from the city's wealthiest families. In a study of the members of the Montreal Council of Social Agencies, Anne MacLennan describes them as "financially comfortable" but not among the very richest. This was generally true of women in the WDM, although some did belong to the elite. Among these was Lady Julia Drummond, English Montreal's most prominent female reformer and the widow of a Bank of Montreal president. She supported the foundation of the directory, offered her residence for the annual meeting in 1924, contributed to the agency, attended annual meetings, and served as the honorary president between 1915 and 1939.[39] Other titled women included Lady Edith Brooks Gordon, wife of the president of Dominion Textiles and a director of the Bank of Montreal for twelve years, and Lady Martha Waitriss Thornton, second wife of the president of the Canadian National Railways.

Women whose husbands were involved in the financial sector were most heavily represented. More than fifty women were married to men with links to insurance and brokerage firms or banks. This was even true for one of the rare, single, career women associated with the directory. Dorothy Heneker, a volunteer from 1917 to 1920, trained as a lawyer, but, as a woman, she could not be admitted to the Quebec bar until 1942. She found employment handling women's investments for a leading financial house before she developed an international career with the International Federation of Business and Professional Women in Geneva, Switzerland.[40] At least twenty-five women had links through marriage to the legal profession, and many were related to doctors and engineers. Beyond the professions, the WDM attracted the wives of a number of industrialists, including the Morgans and the Birks, both prominent Montreal retailers. Interestingly, there were no women identified as married to clergy, although several of their adult children or daughters-in-law were active members. In nineteenth-century Montreal, even religious orders who worked with unmarried mothers were tarnished by their association, and it is possible that this charity remained too controversial for ministers' wives concerned about their own reputations.[41] The wives of several men with prominent public careers were linked to the directory. Beatrix Leacock was the wife of author Stephen Leacock. Between 1926 and 1931, the directory also attracted Helen Savage Claxton, wife of future federal Liberal cabinet member Brooke Claxton, and Margaret Yuile Heeney, wife of A.D.P. Heeney, future Secretary of State for External Affairs.

Beyond the networks of husbands, there was also a significant degree of immediate kinship. There was considerable overlap in surnames and birth/maiden names; at least 145 of the 221 women may have been related to at least one other volunteer with the directory, as sisters or sisters-in-law, mothers, daughters, aunts, and nieces.

Religion could also be a source of connection or exclusion. Of the forty-one women for whom religious affiliation was determined, twenty-six were Anglican, twelve were Presbyterian, one was Congregationalist, and two were Roman Catholic. This distribution generally reflected Protestant denominational size in Montreal. The Catholic women's presence is interesting, especially that of Corinne Roy Terroux, the sole francophone, whose husband was associated with the politically influential Brooke Claxton and Frank Scott circle.[42]

Most women were not involved with the WDM for very long: fifty-three women were visible on only one annual report, eighty-three women were involved for between two and four years, sixty-four were involved between five and ten years, and only twenty-one were involved for more than ten years. This turnover, at times explainable by death or removal from Montreal, seems fairly consistent with what Anne MacLennan found for her study of the 1930s, where 60 per cent of the women were involved with the central organization for less than six years.[43]

The majority of female volunteers lived in the area known as the Golden Square Mile. Many also lived in Westmount, with the remaining few scattered throughout Notre Dame de Grâce, Hampstead, and Outremont. In addition to these general residential patterns, participation was often heavily concentrated on certain streets. Thirteen women, for example, lived on Redpath Crescent, residing in the opulent new houses built in the early teens high up the mountain. Another eight women lived just below on McTavish Street, adjacent to McGill University. In Westmount, many lived on Belvedere and Belmont and lower down the mountain on Clarke Avenue.

Finally, many women shared networks of belonging to other organizations or causes. For example, seven had links to Montreal settlement houses, and Kathleen Fisher, Grace Ritchie England, Grace Murray Skelton, Margaret Wherry, and Julia Drummond were all involved in the suffrage campaign. Thirteen volunteers at the directory were also members of Montreal's most prestigious women-only club, the Themis Club; thirty-seven were members of the Women's Canadian Club; at least twenty-five were members of the IODE, and at least ten were involved in the Junior League. At least eight women were also members of the Women's University Club (six of them involved for more than six years). Some women volunteers also served on the Montreal Council of Social Agencies, and twenty-five names are shared with the 1919 subscription list for the COS financial campaign.

The overlapping, interwoven, and concurrent networks of the 221 volunteers remind us that their voluntary participation in the Women's Directory of Montreal was, for many, just one small facet of their busy lives. None of this considers the personal motivation of participants in choosing to devote their time and resources to this particular cause, although it is evident that recruitment networks based on kin, husbands' occupations, and neighbourhood played a role. The Women's Directory, as it evolved in the 1920s, may have been especially attractive to women who considered themselves part of a "smart set," educated, socially progressive women concerned with women's issues more broadly. Mary Alice Hitchcock McDonald, who originally approached Wisdom to head the WDM, for example, was married to George C. McDonald. He was the founder of the prominent Montreal accounting firm McDonald Currie, one-time president of the Canadian Chamber of Commerce, and a member of the 1934 provincial Commission de l'Électricité. She had graduated in 1905 from Royal Victoria College, been treasurer of the University Settlement House in 1912, and spent part of the war in England to be near her wounded husband. A 1937 article describes her as being very much a team with her husband.[44] She was sophisticated, cosmopolitan, and intelligent, as were many of the women involved. With their various degrees of commitment, the 221 WDM women alert us to be wary of narratives about welfare and charitable organizations that emphasize professionalization to the complete neglect of the ongoing role of volunteers. Although professional social workers were the pre-eminent agents of the welfare state, they were supported by an army of volunteer foot soldiers. While the Women's Directory certainly demonstrates that professionalization of social work changed the role of these female volunteers, they nonetheless remained indispensable.

Part of the reason that the volunteers were so valuable was that Wisdom was overextended and occasionally in poor health. In her early years at the WDM, she attempted to balance the day-to-day operation of the agency with research and publications on the subjects of illegitimacy and immigration in Montreal. She kept in close contact with the stream of American welfare experts brought to Montreal to investigate and rationalize English Protestant charities. A 1924 report commissioned by the Financial Federation quoted the Nova Scotia Commission on Mothers' Allowances. Since this was certainly not the most prominent social document in North American reform circles, it seems likely that Wisdom herself had provided the American author with documentation. She communicated with other coordinating agencies and initiated the move to consolidate many of the organizations serving Montreal's English-speaking Protestant children into adjacent offices located in the Montreal Forum building. Board members and donors were also encouraged to develop this coordination through joint annual meetings promoting cross-agency understanding and synchronization.[45] This was a clear response to Falk's 1920 criticism about the isolation and territorialism of most agencies, whom he described as "'babies' of their Boards. ... [It] was the very dickens to get them interested in what the others were up to."[46]

Wisdom not only made links between various agencies, but she may have had a particular interest in building bridges with Montreal's francophone and Catholic social agencies. In 1930, when Montreal's English Catholic community organized itself into a coordinated council similar to the English Protestant Montreal Council of Social Agencies, the new Catholic Welfare Bureau included an Unmarried Mothers' Division explicitly based on the model of the Women's Directory. After WDM legal advisor John Kerry wrote a pamphlet, "The Legal Status of the Unmarried Mother and Her Child in the Province of Quebec," published by the Ottawa-based Canadian Council on Child Welfare in 1926, Wisdom repeatedly requested that it be translated into French. She conveyed to the Ottawa organization that, while teaching an extension course at McGill, she "had inquiries on this point from some of the French nurses and Sisters." Her 1931 paper given to the first bilingual national conference of the Canadian Council on Child Welfare was translated into French, and, quite remarkably, was still being discussed in 1956 in at least one francophone Catholic institution.[47]

It was a constant challenge to reconcile Quebec's legal structure and a charitable financing model that assisted residential facilities with the conventions emerging from the relatively new profession of social work. During the interwar period, the WDM took on between 100 and 200 cases each year and provided intense casework for an average of two years. With an annual budget by the late 1930s of between $21,000 and $26,000, this was very expensive work, even if $4,000 was generated by the mothers to help cover foster-home payments. The agency financially supported mothers during the year after the child's birth and supervised foster homes, should the mother not be available to look after the child and establish economic self-support.

By the early 1920s, individual casework was firmly established and there were signs of the start of a long-term shift from an environmental to a psychoanalytical orientation.[48] Under Wisdom's leadership, the WDM never let environmental explanations disappear. She insisted on the relevance of economic opportunities, lack of parental supervision, and a changing popular culture that promoted "false ideas of personal responsibility and false ideas of that to which all youth is entitled – happiness and pleasure." There were widespread popular concerns that the new youth culture was trading in older middle-class values of self-control, responsibility, and duty for immediate gratification and freedom. Such anxieties were clearly at work when Wisdom saw cases of individual girls' "poor judgment." Environment also helped explain the significant presence of British immigrants among the clients. Rather than inferior immigrants, these women were recast as vulnerable young women, "strangers in a strange land" whose isolation from society led to their downfall.[49] At the WDM, American philosopher and psychologist John Dewey had greater influence than Freud. Dewey emphasized interpersonal relations and participation in cultivating useful citizens. Following his lead, the agency believed it was creating programs that gave mothers responsibility for their lives, and offered them a chance to be autonomous but not isolated.

By the mid-1920s, the WDM was offering unmarried mothers something more than the nineteenth-century evangelical reform solution of rehabilitation through motherhood. Instead, it promoted casework methods that pursued "individual reestablishment and the use of foster homes for the child until the mother could provide her own home." The speed of this shift is noteworthy: only four years before, the agency was preoccupied with eugenics and domestic service. When the WDM began, it publicly stated that 50 per cent of unmarried mothers in Montreal were feeble-minded. In the early 1920s, IQ tests were routinely given to all clients. The 1922 annual report made the remarkable claim that 70 per cent of the women were "mentally deficient." This preoccupation with mental capacity, however, disappeared almost instantaneously and coincided with Wisdom's arrival. By 1926, the director of the Mental Hygiene Committee of Montreal was able to write the agency's director that this preoccupation "has had the unfortunate effect of overemphasizing what is after all only one and a relatively unimportant factor in disordered behaviour." Moreover, IQ tests, still being conducted, revealed that the women served by the WDM compared quite favourably "with the capacity of groups in similar walks of life, not necessarily showing any behaviour deviations."[50]

With a new emphasis on individual casework study, the agency put considerable energy into occupational readjustment, vocational training, and employment, treating each case separately rather than providing a standard solution for all.[51] Domestic service positions, where unmarried mothers could keep their children, were no longer regarded as the ideal placement; Wisdom identified such work with poor pay and social isolation. Instead of being seen as keeping women safely within the restrictive confines of a family, domestic service became portrayed as leaving young women especially vulnerable: the low wages meant they were unable to pay for their own recreation, and the nature of the work meant that they were frequently alone in the house or over the weekend. Instead, women were encouraged to choose occupations that were better suited to goals of independence and self-support. This was especially difficult to achieve in the early 1930s, when the Depression reduced wages for Montreal working women. Moreover, women's health and well-being were touted as being as important as the child, as this physiological security was essential to autonomy. The emphasis on the individual could have the strange effect of concealing the obvious centrality of gender to the agency's work. Mission statements that emphasized the "obligation to the individual human being" who came for assistance were articulated along with the stated "obligation to the community of the future."[52]

Following John Dewey's ideas, community and social networks were regarded as key to restoring "the girl to normal lines of thought and endeavour." "Self-respect" and "self-control" were to be achieved not only through self-support, but also by interactions with people of "good will" and "standards." In one annual report, church affiliation was emphasized in the same paragraph as agency office visits. One corner of the WDM was described as "a little 'parlour'" with a small lending library. This offered "an excuse for a little visit when no other business would necessitate one."[53] Links were made with "wholesome" female associations, such as Big Sisters, Girl Guides, the YWCA, and settlement houses.[54] The agency's 1930 annual report expressed the "need for building up a healthy social life by every means at our disposal for children and adults alike." The welcome for clients at the agency was supposed to be mirrored in foster homes; it sought foster mothers who were "capable of extending a kindly welcome to the mother, thus affording us the opportunity of setting up a safe and helpful connection with normal and wholesome family life." No doubt, this ideal was not always met, but social workers noted the frequency of mothers' visits. It was hoped that children would benefit in similar ways: not being isolated in an institution meant they could have "status in the community" by going to neighbourhood schools alongside "those born in happier circumstances."[55]

John Dewey's name never appears in the WDM's annual reports, but his influence on the agency was everywhere. Jane Wisdom frequently gave books by Dewey as Christmas gifts to student interns. Frances Montgomery, who began as a clerical worker at the agency before deciding on social work, returned to the WDM as an intern, eventually went on to teach social work, and had an important international career with the United Nations. She was introduced to Dewey by Wisdom in the form of a Christmas gift, a tradition Wisdom repeated several times over the next fifteen years. Montgomery and Phyllis Burns, another of Wisdom's protégés from the WDM, became leading proponents of the Functional School of Canadian social work in the 1940s. Associated with the University of Pennsylvania and its director of social work, Jessie Taft, who herself had been a student of Dewey, this approach centred on collaborative, practical therapy. Rather than emphasize social norms, functionalist casework encouraged clients to build their "will."[56] Although the functionalist therapeutic relationship has been associated with those favouring professional social action, Daniel Walkowitz has argued that it "did not translate into open political positions." Still, its egalitarian premise that caseworkers "helped" rather than "treated" encouraged "an identity of interests between caseworkers and clients."[57] Although coming from psychiatric social work, the principles were completely consistent with Dewey's ideas.

The expressed desire to assist the "life of these mothers and children as individuals in the community" came almost directly out of Dewey's writings on the development of citizenship and participatory democracy. The language of the directory's annual report also emphasized its "experimental" nature, a term Dewey also used. Published reports attempted to educate its readership that it, too, had obligations of citizenship, as Canada was a signatory of the League of Nations Children's Charter. Wisdom's 1930 annual report scolded the Quebec government, stating that "no part of a nation which has subscribed to the Children's Charter at Geneva can permit these conditions to go unheeded in the future."[58]

At the same time, like Dewey's writings, the WDM denied power relations and inequities. The social worker was described as a "friend and counselor of misguided girlhood," rather than a professional with considerable discretionary power and access to resources; a parallel disregard of power was at work in Dewey's democratic classroom, which denied the power of the teacher.[59] Another contradiction was the discrepancy between the supposed emphasis on individual support and guidance, and what was ultimately regarded as the universal solution. While the WDM adopted a language of autonomy, individualism, and community, its work always terminated with clients' marriage. Notwithstanding that most of those working at the agency had rejected it, marriage was regarded as the ultimate solution for women. Ideally, the clients did not marry the fathers of their children, as these men had already proven themselves unworthy by their earlier irresponsible actions.[60]

The Women's Directory of Montreal prompts us to think about the different levels of citizenship available to women in Quebec in the interwar period. Yolande Cohen has argued that during this time, charitable organizations offered women a privileged place of public involvement through negotiation. Their contribution as citizens was based on public participation that ran parallel to electoral politics.[61] For example, although denied the provincial vote at the time, Jane Wisdom spoke before both provincial and federal commissions. She was refused direct democratic participation but still was involved in shaping social policy through her professional knowledge and her experience with government commissions in other jurisdictions. She spoke out regularly about the limitations of the Quebec Public Charities Act, which provided funding only to those children placed in institutions, and pointed out that the lack of birth registrations meant that Quebec had no accurate idea about the size of its problems. In 1930, the WDM went on record with the Attorney General's office in protesting "any laxity in the enforcement of the Laws of child abandonment," and, in 1938, demanded that the province introduce better guardianship and adoption laws.[62] In Wisdom's 1931 address to the first bilingual national conference of the Canadian Council on Child Welfare, she proposed that the province establish a department responsible for child welfare. The petitioning by Wisdom and others of the Montreal Council of Social Agencies did effect change. In 1931, agencies such as the WDM received the institutional crèche allowance from the Children's Bureau for support of care in foster homes. This government grant became a vital source of income. In 1938, the WDM's annual revenues were composed of $16,000 from the Financial Federation, $4,000 from mothers to assist in boarding fees, and $4,000 from the publicly financed Quebec Public Charities Act.[63]

Finally, as a Dewey-style liberal with social democratic leanings, Wisdom joined the Canadian Association of Social Workers' Progressive Programme. This national committee emphasized social action by focusing on the state as a means of acquiring respect for the social work profession. It attracted some of the leading "radicals" in the Canadian profession, such as Bessie Touzel and Dora Wilensky.[64] This was all towards influencing policy at a time when she was denied the provincial vote. Wisdom did not separate social welfare from social policy.

At its best, the WDM occasionally nodded to what Dewey called "the messiness of the moral life." Annual reports reminded readers that "unmarried mothers are not the only ones who thus fail in life's struggles."

During the height of the economic crisis of the early 1930s, reports almost sympathized with young women who ended up pregnant, seeing them as "defrauded of their right to work, to love and to mate" and drawing attention to the high number of postponed marriages brought about by unemployment. The extreme economic situation also necessitated "some compromise with regulations" if the overall goals of "sanctity of human life and respect for the individual" were to be achieved.[65]

At this time, women in Quebec had ambivalent positions as citizens. They were able to vote in federal elections, able to speak before legislative committees, able to petition and meet with politicians, yet they were denied the provincial franchise, and married women were unable to enter contracts in their own name. It was in this context that the WDM not only provided material support and relief for first-time unmarried mothers, but also attempted to cultivate in them "virtues of democracy" and participatory citizenship. Rather than isolation and concealment, the WDM emphasized an engaged, active citizenry, dense and diverse networks of associational life, and action centred on the public good. Here, the volunteers who assisted the agency and the women they served might even have had something in common. According to Dewey, democracy is not "simply and solely a form of government," but a social and personal ideal. In other words, it is not only the property of political institutions, but inheres within a wide range of social relationships.[66] As well as the liberal notion of the capacity for choice, individuality and freedom also required the ability to reflect and revise goals.[67] Indeed, one interpretation of Dewey is that he believed that individuality was a result of social relations.

This enmeshed relationship between individualism and community was completely consistent with Wisdom's world view. Dewey, who also had settlement house experience, provided the link between older ideas of moral character and environmental factors in fostering poverty or deviance and newer psychoanalytical approaches. The WDM began its existence as a redemptive charitable organization but it soon became more complex in its aspirations.[68] Although most of the professionals and volunteers associated with the agency in the interwar period were privately informed by a strong religious faith, the secular influence of modern social science led the focus away from "rescue work" and personal salvation of the "sinner." Deliverance, to these professional women and the volunteers who assisted them, meant creating the conditions for an autonomous, self-respecting individual supported by a network of associations and family. The occurrence of pregnancies

outside marriage was deemed "grave" and "irregular," and this delicate attempt not to judge without evidence reflected a confidence that
first-time unfortunates could be rehabilitated as citizens.[69]

Still, the women clients themselves are silent. Through their actions,
we know that each year during the interwar period, between sixty-three
and ninety-five Protestant, first-time unmarried mothers in Montreal
turned to the WDM after the birth of their child. It is difficult to know
how many births took place in Montreal outside marriage, but it is reasonable to assume that the WDM was involved with only a small frac-
tion. Other pregnant women chose other options, such as going it alone
or giving up their children. The directory also rejected others when
they turned to it for help. Some mothers were accepted and co-operated
when social workers sought to re-establish them with the means and
autonomy to raise their own children. More than likely, these were the
same young women who agreed to have their pictures taken, staring
directly at the camera while proudly holding their child, or those who
later sent Wisdom follow-up photos of healthy, happy, older children.
In the late 1940s, one former client invited Jane Wisdom to the wedding
of her daughter – a momentous occasion marking a new generation of
respectable heterosexuality. This invitation must have held particular
meaning for Wisdom, perhaps as a certificate of success, for she kept it
among her carefully culled professional mementoes.

There are also suggestions that some clients did not co-operate. Some
ran away, abandoning their children in foster houses. Some refused to
contribute to the cost of boarding their children, or became pregnant
again. These women were not given a second opportunity. Limited resources were provided only to those thought to be "deserving." Those
who made the cut were entitled to everything – more than what the
law allowed – as they moved towards a respectable womanhood based
on self-support, self-respect, and engagement with society. In the new
space between redemptive citizenship and charity, these attributes
were both the reward and the rehabilitation process.

A caseworker at the agency in the early 1940s recounted the warmth
of most interactions with clients and emphasized the tremendous brav-
ery of the young women who came in for help. Beneath the agency's
respectability, there may have been a culture of discreet dissent and direct action. During the Second World War, agency caseworkers offered
birth control counselling on the side, and the entire staff was among the
earliest supporters of a failed American unionization drive to organize
social workers when it came to Montreal.[70] The appeal of unionization

may have spoken to democratic and political sympathies, but it also may have reflected staff unhappiness.

By the mid-1930s, the WDM was under assault, a casualty of the trend towards psychological social work. Wisdom was a member of a Montreal Council of Social Agencies' 1935 survey subcommittee on "Certain Other Agencies," which concluded that the directory required "clarification and definition" in terms of its functions and services. The survey reflected this new direct conflict between traditional social work philosophy and psychology.[71] If the directory's objective was to reha-bilitate the unmarried mother with her "accompanying psychological problem ... then it would appear that *all* unmarried mothers need the specialized service." The report noted, for example, that in 1933, the WDM accepted only 91 of the 182 applications it received; the remain-ing half was left to other charitable agencies. It concluded that "it is dif-ficult to appreciate the line of distinction between an unmarried mother which the Directory accepts for intensive service, and unmarried moth-ers who become clients of the Family Welfare Association, as service cases, or of the Children's Bureau." That only certain women could be recipients of casework – or were thought to be deserving – reflected a moral and philosophical perspective rather than a psychological one. While the directory may have been concerned with medical care and protection of infants, the report reasoned that other agencies could just as easily accomplish these goals. Its services were described as "costly duplication." The report recommended that all child services for En-glish Protestant Montreal be amalgamated into one Children's Aid So-ciety, an objective realized ten years later. As the WDM faced massive reorganization, a depleted Wisdom looked towards leaving the agency. The agency's objectives had gradually changed. The idea of keeping mother and child together seemed increasingly old-fashioned, even if the death rate for illegitimate infants in Montreal continued to be four times that of children born into a marriage. Concerns about infant mor-tality now had to be balanced against considerations of psychology.

Betty Kobayashi Isserman, who worked for the WDM in 1942 as a caseworker, reflected the agency's change in philosophy. She had clearly accepted dominant ideas and pathologized unmarried mothers, although she did not completely abandon a social critique based on eco-nomics and environment. In a 1948 professional article, she wrote: "We know that unmarried mothers are usually emotionally immature, that they have come from families that have given them little affection and security, that often there is neurosis present, or at least neurotic trends."

She concluded, however, that if unmarried mothers were to keep their children, Canada needed low-cost daycare, maternity homes, foster homes, and staff to supervise them. In order to prevent pregnancies outside marriage, Kobayashi Isserman echoed Wisdom's sentiments of the early 1930s, declaring that Canadians had to "make it possible for young people to marry early and assume family responsibilities. We have to help them rear their children in sound homes without fear for the future." But the mission of the WDM changed. It came to think that long-term placement for children in foster homes was "very bad," and that adoption was "a good solution in many situations. We might say adoption is best in all cases where the mother chooses a more normal life for her child than she can provide or where the mother is mentally and physically unable to rear her child or for mothers whose children represent guilt or shame." The past practices of the WDM had let mothers retain legal custody without parental responsibility and had provided an "out" for mothers who could not make quick, definitive decisions.[72]

On 1 November 1935, immediately after the survey report was released, Wisdom notified her board of her resignation for the spring of the following year. She was persuaded to change her mind until March 1938, when Wisdom informed the president that she was retiring. She arranged for Muriel Tucker of the Canadian Welfare Council to be her replacement and, to ease the transition, had her appointed as assistant general secretary. Tucker became the new general secretary in July 1939 when Wisdom left, sent on her way with a reception and a travelling case from her friends at the Financial Federation. Looking back six years later, Wisdom wrote: "My heart is still in that field, but I was exhausted when I left it."[73]

As a private agency, the WDM brought together a broad range of women: predominantly working-class clients, career-focused social workers, and solidly upper-middle-class married volunteers. Although the paid staff may have shared a relatively common political and philosophical approach, this was not necessarily the case for the volunteers who permitted the agency to exist. For most of its existence, the WDM simultaneously articulated an almost Victorian romanticism towards maternalism and the redemptive possibility of "mother love," adopted modern scientific medical care for infants, and espoused modern notions of justice in foundational premises such as "No family should be broken up on the ground of poverty alone."[74] The premises that a young, single mother and her baby were a family and that single mothers should have supported choices have contemporary echoes. In 1935, Wisdom wrote that the directory refused "to class unmarried mothers as 'bad girls' as if they alone of all human beings had failed to be 'good.' Our best stories are those which will never be told in annual reports or on any public occasion."[75] Indeed, Wisdom, her staff, and the volunteers who devoted time to the WDM were sympathetic at a time when few others were. There were limits, however. Wisdom and the WDM under her leadership had a relatively narrow definition of which women were eligible for help and redemption. In the balance between serving clients and maintaining support from the community and agency volunteers, she was willing to go only so far.

Chapter Eight

Glace Bay: Exploring Public Welfare, 1940–1952

Jane Wisdom's departure from Montreal in June 1939 could not have been better timed for an historian interested in the intersection of an individual life and the history of Canadian social welfare. Her relocation east coincided with the most dramatic shift in twentieth-century social welfare. Canada's entry into the Second World War that September both transformed the role of the state and fundamentally altered attitudes towards welfare and citizenship rights. Wisdom's return to Nova Scotia also offers the opportunity to focus on a particular provincial jurisdiction struggling with the modernization of an antiquated welfare regime. Everywhere in Canada, war facilitated increased government intervention in all aspects of life. It broke down barriers between public and private, and encouraged a rights-based language of entitled citizenship. During this period of great change, Wisdom moved to Glace Bay to modernize municipal welfare services within a poor law regime. Her career had been closely tied to voluntary private agencies, so this foray into the public sector was a significant departure. Some historians have portrayed the post-war welfare state as the construction of bureaucrats, politicians, intellectuals, labour, and citizens. Jane Wisdom's experience refocuses our attention to the grassroots, where the state was simultaneously built by policymakers and jury-rigged locally to respond to actual need. Wisdom was a community-based social worker who both promoted and shaped the emergent welfare regime as it was practised in all three levels of government.[1]

The municipal welfare state, as it first emerged in Glace Bay, Nova Scotia, was not anonymous or impersonal. Public employees, like private charity workers, maintained a great deal of arbitrary and discretionary power that could be employed either generously or parsimoniously, and welfare workers continued to work within the existing framework of "deserving" and "undeserving." The public and private welfare streams were permeable, with a great deal of 'back and forth.' Some agencies fell somewhere in between, such as the Children's Aid Society, which, though private, was largely supported by public funds and governed by provincial legislation.[2] Professional standards of social work, such as concern for client privacy and emphasis on training credentials, came to the public sector through practices developed in private agencies where patronage was less of a factor in gaining employment. But the private and public sectors also had distinct employee profiles. Public sector workers tended to be older, so Wisdom was typical in this respect. As a woman, she was unrepresentative; this was the one area of welfare services dominated by men.[3]

In June 1939, an exhausted fifty-five-year-old Jane Wisdom returned to Sutherland's River, Nova Scotia, for what she described as a "period of rest and informal study of general living conditions in smaller communities and rural areas." She accounted for the next eighteen months as a time of living and travelling in eastern Nova Scotia when she became "more familiar with the point of view of farmers, fishermen and miners – and their families – in that section of the Province."[4] She was firmly among family again at Sutherland's River, with all its rewards and obligations. Her sister Bess had married in 1932 and was farming there with her husband Dwight Burns. Her niece Relief Williams had married Alex Mackay in 1939, and they and their growing family moved to Sutherland's River after the war to join her mother Katherine, who had retired there in 1941. Notwithstanding often demanding family responsibilities, Wisdom attended the Canadian Conference on Social Work in Toronto in May 1940, worked several days on wartime national registration under the National Resources Mobilization Act, began exploring various employment opportunities, and, in spring 1941, sat the federal civil service exam for a position at the Employment and Claims Office in New Glasgow.[5]

Although the prevailing focus was war, communities in Nova Scotia continued living with the legacy and the burdens of the Depression. Some contemporaries argued that unemployment in the province had been more chronic than in other places in Canada, noting that in Halifax, Glace Bay, and Sydney, half of those on relief had been so for more than two years in 1937.[6] The taxation structure of the fundamentally unchanged Nova Scotia Poor Relief Act meant that the burden of the economic crisis was carried almost exclusively by municipalities or poor districts, the smallest and most impoverished level of government. The Department of Public Health was responsible for provincial "charitable" institutions such as the Victoria General Hospital in Halifax and the Hospital for the Insane in Dartmouth. It also received the annual reports of the Inspector of Humane Institutions on local poorhouses. During the 1930s, both mothers' and blind persons' allowances were implemented, and the Nova Scotia government began participating in the federal–provincial cost-sharing program to provide old age pensions for the poor. The director of Child Welfare (and director of Mothers' Allowance and Old Age Pensions) was still E.H. Blois, who, in addition to administering the Children's Protection Act, was responsible for the province's twelve Children's Aid societies.[7] These meagre programs reinforced older ideas about the "deserving poor," still defined to include vulnerable children, widows with children, the elderly, and the blind. Deemed worthy, they were provided for at a minimal level through a mix of federal and provincial funds. These ideas persisted in other provinces but were especially pronounced in Nova Scotia as a result of the combination of poor law statutes and the stagnation in executive leadership. The assumption remained that those in distress would be assisted by family, friends, churches, or the community before becoming a public burden. In Cape Breton Catholic communities during the Depression, this encouraged the growth of self-help alternatives through a co-operative movement in housing, retail, and banking.[8] Through pooling resources and eliminating the middleman, this movement sought to lift the bonds of poverty through collective action.

Under Nova Scotia's poor law, local districts were supposed to raise funds to support indigents "with settlements." After 1923, "settlement" was defined as two years of consecutive residence. Amendments to the provincial poor law and the Town Incorporation Act in the early 1920s reorganized poor districts. Each town was deemed to be a separate poor district, with town councils acting as Overseers of the Poor, usually through a standing committee. It raised its funds through the taxation of ratepayers. This system had barely served the needs of the poor during good times, but, during the 1930s, when the number of people who could not support themselves grew, the inadequacy of the system was apparent. Historian E.R. Forbes notes that the general poverty of Maritime provincial governments meant that the region did not get its share of Depression matching-grant programs: the provinces did not have the money to leverage the available funds.[9] In Nova Scotia, local governments such as Glace Bay that chose to offer aid at an adequate level went deeply into debt.

Nova Scotia's structural welfare problems concerned Wisdom. Immediately after her return to Nova Scotia in 1939, she published an article on the Nova Scotia poor law in *Canadian Welfare* that revealed an emerging systemic critique. Using evidence from her niece's master's thesis on welfare in colonial Nova Scotia, she argued that the 1763 act "proved to be a very good reproduction of the Elizabethan Poor Law of England."[10] This critique was further developed in a 1945 article in Dalhousie University's *Municipal Affairs*. Here, she wrote that "the administration of the Poor Relief Act of Nova Scotia is admittedly in a state of some confusion," and, within the 249 poor districts in the province, there was "wide variation [in] the public obligation laid upon them by ancient provincial enactment." She went on to note that "the functions or duties of the overseers may be described as traditional rather than statutory" and that few overseers knew or understood the legislation under their charge. According to Wisdom, the meaning of 'indigent' was unclear. The local overseer was "left to fall back upon his own imagination and that of local councilors for a definition." Even the purpose of relief was open to interpretation. It could be to "relieve destitution," "grant subsistence," or "supplement income." She concluded by emphasizing that attaching responsibility to a specific community conflicted with Canada's national economy, as Canadians no longer lived in a fixed agrarian society: "Mobility of labour is an essential factor to-day, and the application of settlement laws is anything but appropriate."[11] The provisions and funding scheme for public welfare were failing badly.

The restructuring of funding was very much a matter of public discussion, given the May 1940 report of the Royal Commission on Dominion–Provincial Relations, also known as the Rowell–Sirois Commission. The commission, which Wisdom had testified before in Montreal, had been charged with investigating the finances and the legal structure of the British North America Act. The 1940 report cited problems with the misallocation of resources and responsibilities. The British North America Act gave the bulk of revenue to the federal government, and the expanding areas of welfare, health, and education were the domains of the provinces. While strongly defending provincial autonomy, the commission recommended a "national minimum standard of social services." This was to be accomplished by transferring responsibility for unemployment and contributory old age pensions from the provinces to the federal government.[12]

The rethinking of welfare arrangements was not happening only at the federal and provincial levels. In July 1940, Wisdom received a letter from her friend Dorothy King, who was assisting at the Canadian Welfare Council while Charlotte Whitton was on holiday. King had received a letter of inquiry from the Town of Glace Bay, Nova Scotia, requesting advice about the appointment of a professional social worker to solve its crisis in municipal welfare services.[13] Wisdom accepted the assignment of researching and writing a background report.

At the end of the 1930s, Glace Bay had especially complex problems. The *Montreal Standard* labelled it "the biggest and dirtiest town in Canada."[14] By 'dirtiest,' the newspaper was drawing attention not only to its coal-mining heritage but also to its poverty. With a population of 25,000 dispersed over more than twenty-six square kilometres, Glace Bay was a single-industry town marked by its predominantly Scottish population and dependence on coal. A de facto "man's town" with few economic opportunities for women, it had, in fact, few openings for men outside the mine and a small, retail, middle class marked by a significant Jewish population. Its three strong institutions, the Dominion Steel and Coal Company (DOSCO), the United Mine Workers of America (UMW) union, and the churches, influenced almost every aspect of life. The town council was controlled by labour, and, by 1940, the mayor, "Dan Willie" Morrison, had served for sixteen of the last eighteen years. He had also been UMW District 26 president since 1927. In the 1940s, Glace Bay elected the Co-operative Commonwealth Federation at both the federal and provincial levels, and the union owned the local newspaper. Wisdom noted the odd juxtaposition of Glace Bay culture, which she described as a mixture of Scottish traditions characterized by Gaelic church services, and the "ideology of the new democracy of labour."[15]

At one time, Glace Bay was a company town, with company houses and company stores. While company stores were not rebuilt after they were destroyed by arson during the 1925 strike, by 1940, the coal company remained a landlord for many houses but no longer sought to provide housing for all. One of the main ways the company still held sway over Glace Bay was through "checkoffs." These deductions from weekly pay envelopes covered everything from domestic coal and miners' supplies, to UMW dues, to approved voluntary contributions to churches and the local sport centre. The checkoffs also included highly controversial medical care paid by the miners, with weekly deductions in exchange for access to local doctors and hospital care.[16] Wisdom was especially critical of this program, writing in 1943 that "so much of the workers' money is spent on medical services with so little to show for it."[17] The Dominion Coal Workers Relief Association operated contributory plans that covered sickness, death, and dependent allowances for miners and their families. These were jointly financed by the miners, the coal company, and the province. The coal company's and union's importance in organizing local services was not, in the words of one 1940 observer, "a substitute for planned community effort and support or public welfare measures." It may also have been responsible for the failure of local, private, charitable services. For example, the Victorian Order of Nurses could not sustain itself because it was not included in the checkoff.[18]

Along with mine shafts, church spires marked the landscape. Glace Bay in the late 1940s had sixteen churches, two Salvation Army halls, and four convents. Other than the churches and the union, there was virtually no private voluntary sector. The Catholic Charities Association, along with the Sisters of St. Martha, operated a program in which they visited mothers and housekeepers in their homes. The United Church operated a settlement house at Passchendaele.[19] In association with the Catholic Church and its community-development actions through the Antigonish movement, Glace Bay boasted a healthy co-operative sector with credit unions, co-operative housing projects, and co-op stores. But, unlike most Catholic communities, there was no local St. Vincent de Paul Society. Parishes were regarded as having vague "obligations" to their members but, in fact, responsibility for the poor often fell to the Miner's Relief Association and the Town Poor Committee. The Antigonish movement, a church-led campaign aimed at empowering Nova Scotians through co-operatives and adult education, and especially spokesman Father Jimmy Tompkins, had considerable influence over Catholic organizations such as the Glace Bay branch of the Maritime Council of Catholic Nurses.[20]

While confessional associations served their particular communities, they also divided the town. Sectarian differences almost evenly split the town, with a slight Protestant (or, more accurately, a non-Catholic) majority. Going against predominant stereotypes, Wisdom later described the Catholic population as "progressive in its conception of social welfare," but lamented the way the non-Catholic majority reinforced sectarian divisions by blocking community-wide efforts. As a result, Glace Bay was rather like Montreal in its provision of private services. There was no community-wide Family Welfare Association in Glace Bay, no private, secular charitable organization serving the community needs, and relatively few volunteers for non-sectarian agencies such as Children's Aid. In 1940, the local Board of Trade advocated for a community chest, not to address philanthropic concerns but to resolve complaints that merchants were constantly being called upon to support ad hoc charitable appeals. The relatively small middle class supported a number of male and female service clubs such as the Knights of Columbus, the Red Cross, the Rotary, the Kinsmen, the Imperial Order of the Daughters of the Empire, and the Kinnettes. However, these organizations tended to limit charitable projects to specific appeals from recognized personnel, such as the school nurse for eyeglasses or assistance to a particularly needy family.[21]

But the role of the small middle class was complicated. Jane Wisdom's work in Glace Bay caused her to reject many of the beliefs she had held two decades earlier, as class differences further divided the town and thwarted community action. She lost some of her faith in the progressive liberal notion of the "common good" as strikes and prejudice fragmented the community. "Class interests" divided the coal miners and the "white collar people" who ran the service clubs. The wealthiest group of all was the doctors, who made $15,000 to $20,000 a year through the miners' health checkoff system. In a 1943 article, she concluded that it was "difficult to find the common denominator for social planning in such a population where there is more social stratification and extremes in wealth and poverty. It seems almost easier to think internationally than to get people down to local co-operation and action outside their own particular group."[22]

With rigid internal divisions, outside organizations removed from local sectarian and class constituencies sought to assist Glace Bay. In 1937, the Rockefeller Foundation initiated a three-year program that created the Cape Breton Island Health Unit. After the Victorian Order of Nurses left Glace Bay in 1938, Metropolitan Life Insurance nurses attended to policyholders until November 1950.[23] This particular configuration of a strong union, a relatively small middle class, and, with the exception of churches, virtually no cross-class civil society meant little interest in voluntary social planning and no private charitable agencies. Miners were willing to support class-based politics, electing a labour mayor and town council and helping to elect the first Co-operative Commonwealth Federation Member of Parliament east of Manitoba, Clarie Gillis, in 1940. The efforts of the Sisters working for the Catholic Charities Association, public health workers, and the small staff of Children's Aid Society could not create what Wisdom would have considered "community," even as their work was supplemented by provincial employees associated with mothers' allowance and old age and blind pensions.[24] Notwithstanding a restrictive and outdated legal structure, any action required the reluctant state.

But local government had little leeway under the poor law, which limited resources and recipients. In Glace Bay, for example, the duties of the Overseer of the Poor were subsumed by the Town Poor Committee, one of eleven standing committees of the labour-controlled Town Council. The committee was composed of six councillors and, in 1940, held irregular meetings. There was no privacy. The names of applicants for relief were reported in local newspapers. As a union town, Glace Bay, unlike other Nova Scotia jurisdictions, rejected sending indigents to a poorhouse or county asylum and, instead, offered meagre outdoor relief in its residents' own homes. The town clerk administered all forms of relief, which was divided between payments to institutions such as orphanages, hospitals, and the Children's Aid Society, those on the Poor Roll who were paid cash monthly, and those who required emergency aid in the form of food, rent, coal, or clothing. There was no routine procedure to check the validity of names on the Poor Roll, and, once names were added, they were seldom removed.[25] The roll was composed largely of elderly people ineligible for government pensions, widows with dependent children ineligible for mothers' allowance, and unemployed women. The vague criteria were tolerated because of the Poor Committee's sense of helplessness at being able to deal fairly with all applicants. Cash payments to those on the roll were not large, amounting to only eight to ten dollars per person per month. Much more generously, Glace Bay offered unemployed men assistance on a work-relief basis. Men were paid the equivalent of the miner's shift union rate for unskilled labour ($3.71 a day). During the 1939–40 financial year, this program supported 167 heads of families and 70 single men. Unlike other welfare costs, the heavy expense of this unemployment program was, until 1940, shared by the province and federal government. There were no provisions to assist unemployed women, so they were simply added to the Poor Roll, contributing to the general confusion and sometimes conflation of public relief with help for the unemployed. The miners' union in Glace Bay meant relatively decent support for unemployed men, but the untenable burden of social expenditures for local government was one of the conclusions of the 1940 Rowell–Sirois Commission report.

Debt and a desire for cost cutting through efficiency and the elimination of fraud had led the Glace Bay Town Council to contemplate hiring a municipal social service worker in 1939, and the salary for one had been included in the 1940 town budget.[26] In the late 1930s, the town had been issuing special debentures to cover spiralling relief cost. In March 1940, the Poor Committee, after consulting with the provincial director of Old Age Pensions, went public with its plan to hire a properly trained social worker. It was this person's responsibility to investigate cases and recommend steps to prevent individuals and families from becoming permanent charges of the town. Relief matters had become too time-consuming for the town clerk and required skills beyond what the Poor Committee possessed. Moreover, help was requested when the Poor Committee was not in session, and, therefore, it recommended that a "mature women, preferably a registered nurse who has had some public health experience," be engaged. The fact that Glace Bay was still completely untouched by the social work profession's demand for specialization is a useful reminder of how marginal the profession remained outside certain circles. Both Glace Bay hospitals had employed social service nurses in the late '20s and early '30s, so there was a reason for the community to be aware of their expertise. Many municipal Poor Roll cases originated in health problems or in the delicate moral issue of "recidivist unmarried mothers."[27]

The Poor Committee was aware from the beginning that the personality of the woman hired mattered a great deal to the success of the experiment. Discretion, sympathy, efficiency, and record keeping were all qualities that Glace Bay people associated with the nursing profession. It was also assumed that the worker should be local. This would not only provide scarce employment for a town woman but would also ensure political sensitivity to community standards. Because Glace Bay was lacking a family welfare association, the committee hoped that a municipal social service worker would make private, individual charity more efficient and would supervise hospital and institutional payments.[28] The assumption that this was women's work was completely taken for granted.

From the start, the Poor Committee had a particular person in mind: Jean Guthrie, the town's school nurse. The local school board, not wanting to lose a valued employee, objected to this arrangement. Local Children's Aid Society worker Elizabeth Torrey, the only local layperson with any training in social service, suggested approaching the Canadian Welfare Council in Ottawa for assistance, insisting that such an administrative position was better suited for a professionally trained social worker.[29] That Jane Wisdom's long-time friend Dorothy King received Glace Bay's letter unquestionably altered Wisdom's life. King suggested to Canadian Welfare Council director Charlotte Whitton that Wisdom travel to Glace Bay to assess the local situation and advise the Town Council on an appropriate course of action. Wisdom was living relatively close to Glace Bay, and was already somewhat familiar with the community because of her incomplete MA thesis research. Glace Bay's town clerk, D.J. Macdonald, later explained that the council and Poor Committee knew they required help, "but the majority [did] not understand the qualifications and scope of the work covered." There was insufficient coordination of unemployment relief, hospitalization, children's aid work, and temporary relief efforts.[30]

Wisdom's availability was fortuitous not only because of her professional expertise and experience but also, according to Whitton, because she knew the area, was "extremely sympathetic, and moreover, [came] from Pictou."[31] Once again, the tension between professional qualifications and individual character and background was apparent. As someone with Nova Scotian credentials and a reputation for getting along with a wide variety of people, she was suitable for this sensitive task. Wisdom was advised that the local lobby for a professional social worker primarily consisted of Elizabeth Torrey of the Children's Aid Society, Sister John Hugh of the Catholic Charities Association in Bridgeport, Nova Scotia (also a graduate of the Toronto Department of Social Science), and the town clerk. From the start, others were skeptical of the need for a professional person, a sentiment Charlotte Whitton attributed to the stereotypical cautiousness of Nova Scotians and their ignorance of the new profession.[32]

When Jane Wisdom began her investigation in late October 1940, she had not been to Glace Bay since her 1922 MA thesis research. She met with Children's Aid social worker Torrey, the Cape Breton's Mothers' Allowance supervisor, the local medical officer, and representatives of the Protestant and Catholic communities. According to local press reports, she made a favourable impression on the Glace Bay Council. After two days in the community, the usually cautious Wisdom was enthusiastic, writing to Whitton that "the opportunities here are simply manifold."[33]

After spending a week gathering all kinds of information, Wisdom returned to Sutherland's River to begin writing the report, learning to type on her newly acquired typewriter. Almost from the start, she expressed self-doubt over her "lack of techniques and experience" in community studies and fretted that her conclusions would be incomplete. In trying to conform to professional standards of detachment, Wisdom struggled to separate her "own personal reactions" from scientific social work, maintaining that she "did try to be 'objective.'"[34] By the middle of November 1940, in correspondence to Whitton, Wisdom was endorsing the establishment of a town office to coordinate welfare services in the community. She specified that this would depend greatly on finding "the right person" to introduce professional standards to Glace Bay. Poking fun at herself and her profession, Wisdom chided herself for a lack of distance from the problem: "I am afraid I am committing the sin of 'identifying myself' with the client – I do feel concerned for them – which shows how rusty I am as a social worker!" On a more serious note, Wisdom candidly warned Whitton of potential problems with top provincial bureaucrat Ernest Blois. Wisdom suggested he was territorial and controlling, and might impede local municipal projects not under his immediate direction.[35]

Almost as soon as Wisdom's initial report came in, Whitton asked Wisdom if she might "consider at all, taking a chance at Glace Bay," suggesting that her appointment might be politically popular with Blois, with whom any municipal officer would have to work.[36] Indeed, Wisdom had a long connection with Deputy Minister Blois, dating back from her time working in Halifax almost twenty-five years earlier. It is also likely that she knew Fred MacKinnon of the Child Welfare Division, who was being groomed to replace Blois upon his impending retirement. In late 1940, MacKinnon had just returned to Nova Scotia after being sent by Blois to the School of Social Service Administration at the University of Chicago. Although MacKinnon was twenty-eight years younger than Wisdom, they shared a similar background and he was born and raised about five kilometres from Sutherland's River. He certainly would have known her family. To Whitton's inquiry of possible interest, Wisdom cautiously replied that "it is the only kind of social work job I'd want to tackle now. If the appointment was not too permanent and the right person doesn't appear in the flesh. I MIGHT consider it."[37]

But the report dragged on and Wisdom procrastinated. In February 1941, she travelled to Montreal to write and to assist the terminally ill Helen Reid. Finally, from Reid's home, Wisdom telephoned Whitton to say she was interested in a six-month contract in Glace Bay. Whitton then began negotiating. She informed Glace Bay that Wisdom was willing to come for the mere cost of her maintenance, an offer not endorsed by Wisdom, who had ongoing family financial responsibilities.[38] In fact, Wisdom was worried about money, describing herself in January 1941 as "almost dead broke ... having taken a longer year off than I originally intended with insurance premiums to meet etc etc."[39] But money was not the only obstacle to Wisdom's appointment. One problem was religion, as confessional interests had to be balanced. Both the mayor and town clerk were Presbyterian, as was Wisdom, and a number of Catholic councillors had suggested Catholics for the appointment. In addition, Deputy Minister Blois thought that Wisdom was too old for the position (she had expressed the same concern herself) and was perhaps too indecisive by nature. Ageism was common throughout social work, and it was often difficult for women older than fifty to find positions, as agencies requested candidates in the specific range of thirty-five to forty-five. There were different standards for men from those for women, and sexism was at play in discrimination against older women. In correspondence with Blois, Whitton pointed out that Wisdom was younger than he was and proposed that, after an initial, short appointment, a younger, more energetic person might take over the position. Wisdom herself felt that a necessary practical qualification was the ability to drive a car, a skill she did not possess. However, Wisdom did have familiarity with the community, a history of successful co-operative relationships with Catholic agencies, and the general respect of provincial bureaucrats. Negotiations continued throughout the winter. In May 1941, it was finally decided that on 1 June, Jane Wisdom would go to Glace Bay for six months to establish a municipal welfare office.[40] The position was a step down in terms of pay and status but Wisdom may have felt that, as an older woman, she had little choice.

The entire experiment nearly went off the rails before Wisdom even arrived. Over the May long weekend, D.J. Macdonald, the enterprising town clerk behind the welfare project, tragically died. Wisdom arrived in Glace Bay without her biggest supporter at Town Hall. Public opinion was cautious. One newspaper editorial expressed concern that relief would be administered in a "mechanical" manner, and warned that it was important the worker be "a person of tact and sympathy." Shortly before her death in 1975, Jane Wisdom recounted that "they had never seen a social worker in the place ... so I had to tell what a social worker was."[41] One of her former social work-placement students, Gertrude O'Brien Hilchie, who was living at the time in Glace

Bay, remembered a similar challenge and "the wonderful adjustment she made ... Everything at the WDM [Women's Directory of Montreal] was done so correctly and scientifically, and in Glace Bay she was thrust into such a hurly burly. I remember her shaking her head one time and saying 'Shades of the WDM.'"[42] There was quite a difference between courting Montreal and Westmount matron board members and pacifying male town councillors in Glace Bay.

At the end of the first month, Wisdom wrote to Whitton that her welcome had been tepid. Community members "told me so at the very beginning 'it was D [Macdonald]'s idea and he was all for it' – that is WHY I am accepted. There was no preparation made for me." Setting up office where the Unemployment Relief Office had operated, she shared a telephone with the next office.

She continued:

> I'm having a truly novel experience and hope I'll have originality enough to discover the filling procedure. I have learned so much that already I feel I only scratched the surface before in every direction. I'm cultivating the "Poor Committee" individually and collectively and at this stage am working with and through them and the Acting Clerk. I've begun on the current temporary assistance cases which are bothering them most and along with them taking up the "poor roll" lists as quickly as possible – checking with the provincial departments, miners' relief and the Catholic charities, but there is almost nothing to begin from. I can collect a name from the financial accounts and sometimes it is just "J McDonald" – no sex – age – status – address or Christian name! Even the people around the office or the Committee who know (or did know) are often lazy about personal data but I'm gradually building up an index for general use. There are depositions for the Poor Roll but they have to be dug out and the same about commitments and Town wards. I think the Poor Committee are very hopeful types to work with and like lots of others they are full of divine discontent about much of the present system.[43]

The Glace Bay municipal dissatisfaction with the status quo meant that in June 1941, Jane Wisdom became the first full-time, professional social worker hired to administer local welfare in Nova Scotia. From her office on the second floor of Glace Bay Town Hall, with a view of the ocean and pit ponies, there was no distinction between what elsewhere would be considered public and private concerns. The Sydney newspaper explained that she would keep "a file on all cases ... so that private organizations would be able to secure information on needy cases whenever they planned to distribute assistance."[44]

Glace Bay was facing difficult times in June 1941. Low wages and rank-and-file discontent had led to a "slowdown strike," causing strife within the union. The town was suffering from a serious wartime housing shortage, but Wisdom was able to rent an apartment from a schoolteacher for the summer. Glace Bay was different from Montreal: she observed that the men generally smoked cigars and the women chewed gum and wore white shoes but no hats. Unlike her previous professional space, her new office was slightly chaotic. It was "very dirty," her pencils disappeared, the man in the adjacent office was "friendly but not very sober," and, in addition, she had to deal with the town hall janitor's cat, who was a nuisance.[45]

But Glace Bay should not be seen as a quaint, parochial backwater removed from the problems that had plagued Montreal. Wisdom was shocked by the town's potential for violence and anti-Semitism. Her arrival in Glace Bay coincided with the vicious double murder on 17 June 1941 of seventy-five-year-old Hyman Brody, one of the founders of Glace Bay's Jewish community, and his wife Chibalaya. The two were among the town's most prominent merchants and real-estate holders, and were brutally shot in their home by a tenant, police sergeant Arthur Frost, who was arrears in his rent. According to RCMP reports, Frost had expressed "anti-Semitic leanings," and the murder horrified Wisdom for the rest of her life. Most astounding was Frost's ultimately successful defence: although he had served as a police officer for almost twenty years, he suffered from neurasthenia as a result of overseas service during the First World War. In less than two hours, the jury found him not guilty by reason of insanity. Glace Bay was not Montreal, but Canada's largest town shared problems with its largest city.[46]

Wartime conditions also brought unique circumstances to Glace Bay. The uncertainty associated with coal mining and production was lessened as it became an essential war industry, but cases of family poverty resulting from mining-related accidents and health problems remained. War brought full employment to the mines, ending years of Depression hardship, but only for able-bodied men and their families. Glace Bay also experienced very high levels of enlistment, which meant widespread family dislocation and new federal support programs such as Dependents' Allowance flowing into the community. In addition, the town itself served as a defence area. Within the town boundaries were two army encampments and various defence installations, and just outside town limits was a newly constructed airport built primarily for military requirements. Problems created by war were different from those that had instigated the creation of a municipal welfare office, but they, too, threatened family stability and necessitated new forms of economic and social assistance. Wisdom's original appointment was extended indefinitely, and, within two years, she had concluded that "the demands upon the 'Town Social Worker' have far exceeded the statutory limits of actual municipal responsibility under provincial legislation." By the end of the war, Glace Bay's experiment had attracted the attention of Halifax. The Canadian Welfare Council in Ottawa received unofficial inquiries for other social workers who might follow Wisdom's example.[47] The war and reconstruction placed increasing demands on Nova Scotian municipalities, which continued to carry the burden of care.

Wisdom started working for Glace Bay during a time of change for certain Nova Scotia welfare programs. The section on public welfare written for the 1944 Nova Scotia Royal Commission on Provincial Development and Rehabilitation was shown to Wisdom in its first draft. There can be little doubt that she enthusiastically supported author George Davidson's conclusion that "the poor relief system in Nova Scotia is outmoded and outdated in every sense of those words ... nothing short of a complete recasting of the present Poor Relief Act will suffice to provide a reasonably adequate legislative basis for general services to needy persons in the Province."[48] While such criticisms of the Nova Scotia government were just, they must be kept in some kind of perspective. Historian Janet Guildford has noted that the report's condemnation of Nova Scotia services was "tempered by the dismal record of most Canadian provinces." The report read: "On the whole, Nova Scotia's services would probably rank among the top four of the Provinces of Canada – equaled or surpassed only by those to be found in provinces which are blessed with more adequate financial resources."[49] In 1944, Nova Scotia established a Provincial Department of Public Welfare and there were new federal programs to administer, but the structure of local support for the poor still did not change.

As a result, the new welfare office in Glace Bay spent a great deal of its time involved in education, advocacy, counselling, and information work, responsibilities usually filled by the private voluntary sector in most Canadian communities. After her first year on the job, Wisdom explained to the Canadian Welfare Council in Ottawa that "there is great variation in the application and interpretation of [the Poor] Law as between the different towns and municipalities. Much of my work has been to analyse the current 'case load' and interest the [Poor] Committee in working out policy. As one has to begin without records other than financial and committee minutes (of undetermined date very often) the task is very time-absorbing." Building contacts and understanding "local conditions and attitudes" began with focusing on the Town Hall before moving out to the wider community.[50]

The municipal office also served as an important liaison between the town, the province, the federal government, and the military. It distributed dependents' allowances in the community and helped coordinate government and military departments with the Children's Aid Society, charitable institutions, and the juvenile court. This was an especially important role, as rules and programs were rapidly changing. In 1946, Wisdom described her job as a "clearing house for information," lamenting that "many persons suffer needless anxiety with regard to benefits from social security measures to which they are entitled."[51] Wisdom's understanding of entitlement continued to expand so that it included not only eligibility for specific programs but also levels of support even within the primitive provincial system. In 1950, she expressed satisfaction that municipal rates of support had increased, although she still considered them "inadequate."[52]

As the only social welfare agency with an office in Glace Bay, individuals in need of help approached Wisdom, although she was not technically responsible for Children's Aid, Mothers' Allowance, war veterans' complaints, or problems with provincial programs for the aged. Wisdom began attempting to create order (producing her own city directory, for example) and introduce systems of efficiency and standardization. Many people on the Town Poor Roll who were eligible were enrolled in public programs, such as old age pensions, mothers' allowance, and military allowances. During the first year, for example, Wisdom was able to move four people on the Town Poor Roll onto old age pensions, two onto mothers' allowance, and one onto a military dependents' allowance.[53] Enrolling eligible individuals into relatively stable income-support programs was becoming a vital aspect of public welfare work. Poor Roll recipients were categorized into distinct living situations, and set rates of payment were introduced, ending the existing discretionary variations. The new system was less arbitrary and less subjective, bringing more generous benefits to some and penalizing those who had been especially favoured in the past. Unemployed women who had received Poor Roll relief rather than work were removed from the list and placed on the same basis as men. Unemployment might garner temporary relief from the town but, according to provincial statutes, unemployment alone did not entitle individuals to the meagre Poor Roll payment.[54] A new emphasis was placed on record keeping and confidentiality. Names of those receiving relief and their particular circumstances were no longer published in the local newspaper as part of the Poor Committee reports, and the committee's minutes were less likely to record specific personal details.

Concerns about efficiency and standardization extended to ad hoc, charitable, door-to-door collections and the enormous municipal burden of hospital billing. The Social Service Department sought to regulate door-to-door solicitation by establishing standards that required accountability, transparency, and non-interference with the annual campaigns of the Red Cross and Children's Aid Society. Hospital billing was a larger issue as institutions outside Glace Bay found it easier to bill the town rather than pursue delinquent patients. Municipalities were compelled by legislation to pay these bills and try to recover costs from their residents. Jane Wisdom addressed this issue before the 1951 meeting of the Union of Municipalities of Nova Scotia. She complained that "municipalities have become the investigation and collection agency for the hospitals – as far as public ward patients are concerned."[55] Although the 1943 Report on Social Security for Canada, authored by former McGill social scientist Leonard Marsh, discussed the difficulties of financing health care, it was not until the 1960s that all Canadians would receive full assistance. In Glace Bay in the 1940s, medical issues were compounded by the difficulty of providing good care outside a major urban centre. Polio and cancer treatments required trips to Halifax, and there was a great deal of confusion as many people conflated the private charity work of organizations such as the Rotary Club, which provided free polio-clinic care in Glace Bay, and Halifax hospital care for which patients were charged unless classified as "indigent."[56]

The emphasis on efficiency was popular among most of the council, the mayor, and many ratepayers, but it certainly did not appeal to all recipients. In November 1942, the union-owned Glace Bay Gazette publicized the case of a woman who could not get by on the seven emergency dollars for food provided by the town. The woman had explained her problem "to Mrs. Wisdom of the town several times, but she says the town can't do any more for me."[57] The cause was taken up by the Gazette, which facilitated meetings between Wisdom and members of a union local, who were informed that, in addition to the cash from the town, she was receiving a quart of milk a day, Pablum and cod liver oil from the Imperial Order of the Daughters of the Empire, and clothing from the Red Cross, and the town was supplying her rent money and coal. Newspaper reports indicated that the town welfare worker did not think this was sufficient but that there was little more that could be done within the law. Sometimes, Wisdom bent the rules and worked outside the legal limits of the poor law. For example, the town sometimes paid rent in emergencies for individuals who qualified as "employable."[58]

There is much to suggest that Wisdom found this work satisfying, exhausting, and ultimately frustrating. Surely, there was a great deal to do. In 1944, she began hiring summer-student assistants and, in 1946, hired someone year-round.[59] A 1942 confidential report by a Canadian Welfare Council official concluded that "Miss Wisdom herself appears rejuvenated under this employment, has greater enthusiasm and physical strength, and looks 10 years younger than she did when managing the Women's Directory in Montreal." The report continued that she appeared to be exceptionally well suited for this position and was fully integrated into the town's administrative structure. After two years, her influence had already extended beyond the town's borders. The Ottawa social worker reported that "she shows no desire to relinquish it, and that she recommended work in a pioneer area to any social worker who was tired and disillusioned."[60] Four years later, another Ottawa visitor reported that Wisdom would like to move, if someone was willing to take over the work. He concluded that "while she was inevitably 'bottled up' by her isolation, her stability and warmth were impressive, especially set against a background that was drab and uninviting to the outsider." For her last four years in Glace Bay, Wisdom regularly expressed frustration that she had been unable to establish any kind of voluntary community organization and that all her efforts remained in the realm of the public sector. This opinion was shared by the Canadian Welfare Council, which came to believe that Glace Bay's experiment with municipal welfare exonerated community groups of local responsibility, allowing them to leave everything to Wisdom.[61] In fact, Wisdom's experience, similar to that in Halifax during the First World War, constantly revealed the permeability of public and private welfare streams.

The war and its rhetoric provided an environment for public welfare concerns to flourish. The 1941 Atlantic Charter signed by Britain and the United States included social security as one of its objects. The same year, President Franklin D. Roosevelt articulated "freedom from want" as one of the four freedoms essential for international security. Canadian welfare expert Harry Cassidy explained that the current world crisis was a result of ignoring this need, writing in 1943 that "it was the poverty and insecurity and lack of opportunity of the lower middle class, the working class, and the peasantry of Europe after the last war that threw their youth into the arms of the fascist leaders and thus made possible the growth of the fascist military machines."[62]

Following the 1943 Marsh Report, which recommended universal social insurance for all, the August 1945 Dominion–Provincial Conference on Reconstruction proposed that the federal government support a comprehensive program of social security in exchange for the provinces' continuing the wartime taxation arrangement that had centralized resources in Ottawa. This was soundly rejected by Ontario and Quebec. The return of Angus L. Macdonald to Nova Scotia politics at the end of the war provided the large central provinces with a third ally. The federal government's failure to assert power in the provincial jurisdiction of welfare in 1945 meant that change would be uneven and piecemeal. Rather than through uniform programs, the national welfare state was built through federal–provincial negotiations, tax sharing, and shared cost programs. The federal government offered a growing number of conditional grants, often involving local governments such as Glace Bay, which chipped away at provincial autonomy through the back door as citizens came to expect higher standards of care and social security.[63]

Nevertheless, the 1944 Veterans Charter and the introduction of family allowance payments in 1945 permanently changed the role of the federal government in the lives of ordinary Canadians.[64] This pattern would continue with the 1951 introduction of non-contributory Old Age Security. The development of the federal welfare state and a new financial arrangement between the federal government and the provinces had the enthusiastic support of District 26 UMW. At its October 1946 convention in Truro, it called for "the reconvening of the Dominion–Provincial Conference and [for] the provincial government [to] come to an immediate agreement with federal authorities in accordance with the last offer." It demanded that "a complete program of social security" be established and financed nationally. Scholars of the welfare state have argued that, following the war, creative initiatives for social policy shifted to the provinces. This is a difficult argument to make in the case of Nova Scotia. Premier Angus L. Macdonald continued to adhere to older values of the free market and individual enterprise as he became increasingly concerned that an interventionist state limited individual freedom.[65] In Nova Scotia, creative initiatives were left to local government.

The particular economic circumstances that urged the Glace Bay Town Council to explore better ways of delivering welfare services did not end with the Depression, war, or peace. A post-war downturn in coal prices and production led to further unemployment, the expiry of veterans' benefits, and family desertion, as some men left their families behind in search of work elsewhere. Wisdom and her Poor Committee looked to the province to assist in the enforcement of court orders for family support and to expand the mothers' allowance program to include women left with no support. Mechanization in the mines meant fewer men at work there. A new federal program paid transportation expenses to single men so they could take job offers elsewhere. In February 1947, 13,000 miners went on strike in the first district-wide labour action since 1925. Striking workers received no strike pay until March, and the union distributed relief on the basis of need. To Glace Bay Mayor Dan Willie Morrison, the backdrop of high unemployment meant that it was "utterly impossible for the town to assume the responsibility of paying unemployment relief."[66]

During the more than four-months-long strike, local people organized a campaign to provide soup, milk, and crackers for schoolchildren, and eggs for tuberculosis and prenatal patients. This coalition brought together almost every voluntary association, service organization, and church group. It worked with the school board and UMW Local, but not middle-class members of the Board of Trade or Rotary Club. It is significant that in a private voluntary campaign such as this, the Glace Bay town social worker acted as treasurer, accepting all cash donations, keeping financial accounts, and making recommendations to those individuals in particular need. The town absolved itself of responsibility for aiding striking miners but it clearly supported their children.[67] Public and private assistance were not distinct spheres.

Wisdom's sanctioned support of the strike also reminds us of how different Glace Bay was from other communities in Canada as the chill of the Cold War set in across the country. In 1947, a Hamilton, Ontario, social worker was fired for supporting striking workers organizing a soup kitchen. In Glace Bay, support for the strike was informally regarded as part of Wisdom's job. The social democrats who dominated the town council and the union executive fought pockets of local communism, but the debate took place on the left of the political spectrum.[68]

It is notable that political activism would be part of a municipal social worker's responsibility. Wisdom increasingly spent time advocating for changes in provincial law. In August 1948, she addressed the local Rotary Club, arguing the inappropriateness of trying to make a 1763 law work in modern Nova Scotia and pointing out that "where the need is greatest there is less money to deal with it." In a series of UMW-sponsored radio broadcasts entitled *Labour Leads the Way*, Wisdom denounced the province's outmoded poor law. She placed particular emphasis on the problem of housing the aged, and on the unfair burden on municipalities.[69] According to Wisdom, the Nova Scotia Poor Relief Act was too restrictive. Help from municipalities was technically forbidden unless the person was destitute and legally qualified as an "indigent" or "pauper." Wisdom argued:

> So many people who are classed as paupers by this act have been hard-working citizens and have contributed their best to the community and the nation ... The Public Relief Act should be repealed in its entirety and a modern act put in its place similar to what other provinces now have. Provision both of funds and public welfare standards for families and individuals who are in need should be standardized throughout the province: and then the province should provide at least 75 percent of the funds. In this way social welfare assistance can be made uniform across the province and adequate: and at the same time the municipality will not have further financial burdens imposed upon it.[70]

The tax base for a "Provincial Statute administered and financed entirely by municipal governments" was not large enough to adequately provide for those who needed help. It also left employables (those classified as able to work) who did not have unemployment insurance with no help at all. Wisdom's research and clipping file on practices in other provinces provided evidence that there were ways of dealing with this problem more efficiently and more generously. According to Wisdom's research, matters in Nova Scotia were getting worse. Municipalities faced increased legal obligations. Money paid to institutions, Children's Aid, and hospitals made it necessary to "curtail the disbursement of general relief in order to keep within the bounds of local tax appropriation." It is easy to see the impact of provincial policy on the Glace Bay budget. Throughout the 1940s, relief expenditures remained largely unchanged at around $13,000, notwithstanding inflation and a decline in population. On the other hand, the amounts billed by orphanages and the Children's Aid Society increased from $2,087 in 1942 to $11,050 in 1950. Hospital bills increased from $1,551 to $11,019 over the same period.[71]

In 1949, after indicating her desire to retire, Jane Wisdom submitted what she may have falsely assumed to be her final annual report. As a municipal employee, she had a liberty of speech not shared with her provincial counterparts, but she was uncharacteristically blunt in her criticism of the province. She denounced its lack of consultation ("and democracy!") before placing additional financial burdens on the municipalities, and censured it for initiating another inquiry into welfare when it had not acted on the 1944 report. She called for "more assistance to individuals and families in their own homes," a demand that was impossible "within the framework of an antiquated Poor Law and the limits of local tax funds." This battle with the province continued over her final three years in Glace Bay. She took on leadership roles in provincial social-worker lobbying efforts and the Union of Nova Scotia Municipalities.[72] In 1951, the chairman of the provincial old age pension board declared that "relief was not a pressing problem in Nova Scotia at the present time," to Wisdom's ire. It was obvious that he had ignored completely a 1950 presentation at the Union of Nova Scotia Municipalities by the province's leading social workers, and he especially had disregarded Wisdom's contribution. Even worse for Wisdom, Hiram Farquhar, the bureaucrat responsible for old age pensions and blind persons allowance, claimed that municipal welfare had "never been attempted anywhere in Nova Scotia except Halifax!" This led her to comment that "some of our Public Welfare Officials live in ivory castles in Halifax."[73]

At the 1952 meeting of the Union of Nova Scotia Municipalities, she went on the offensive and stressed the problem of seemingly unbounded need. Municipalities could not support everyone: the able-bodied unemployed who were ineligible for unemployment insurance, the elderly or prematurely aged, the physically disabled, the mentally ill, families of prisoners, deserted families, unmarried mothers, widows and mothers not eligible for mothers' allowance, and those whose allowance had been discontinued. She concluded her talk with a powerful statement: "If it is *total destitution* which is the test then *total* maintenance is the logical provision to be made." Incorporating the post-war language of entitlement, Wisdom concluded that the Poor Relief Act was inappropriate for, and incongruous with, current economic and social conditions; the "time has long passed when local land taxes and land values can be used as the measure of local responsibility for social assistance and services." The only solution was to abolish poor-district financing of poor relief. Her address spearheaded a motion where it was unanimously resolved that the provincial government "direct its attention to the need for the early revision of the Nova Scotia Poor Relief Act and its associated statutes."[74]

While poor relief was the most pressing of concerns, Wisdom's other preoccupations remind us how much was left to local government. Health care and hospitalization in general consumed a great deal of Wisdom's time. In August 1951, Wisdom was invited to be the sole speaker at the annual convention of the Union of Nova Scotia Municipalities. She discussed hospital administration, a subject she had been studying even as she prepared for retirement. Wisdom condemned the province for making municipalities "the investigation and collection agency for the hospitals – as far as public ward patients are concerned."[75] Her discussion led the union to propose amendments to the provincial Hospital Act. Care for the elderly was another issue that occupied Wisdom's time: old-age problems were exacerbated by poverty, poor housing stocks, and out-migration, which removed extended family support. Wisdom also found herself assisting various provincial and federal bureaucracies. For example, she was sworn in as a Justice of the Peace to accompany a juvenile female to a detention facility outside Moncton (this was also her first flight). One of her last duties was serving on the province's first tribunal to determine the age of a pension applicant after all normal means of proving age had failed.[76]

Before Jane Wisdom publicly criticized the province, Nova Scotia's first deputy minister of public welfare, Ernest Blois, had celebrated Glace Bay's entry into welfare as an example of municipal progress. Yet, the province's commitment to the project was mixed. It did not necessarily want a knowledgeable and experienced critic working on behalf of the municipalities. Even as he praised the Glace Bay welfare department in 1944, Blois was lobbying to appoint Wisdom to the first full-time salaried position at the Maritime School of Social Work. Wisdom was always skeptical of the province's support for a Glace Bay social worker, believing that Blois (and Fred MacKinnon, Blois's successor) wanted organization not at the municipal level but at the larger district level to parallel the Cape Breton Island Health Unit.[77] Wisdom came to agree with this position, concluding that municipalities had too many other duties to be continually responsible for a broad welfare program. She also believed that the consolidation of welfare into larger administrative units to parallel what was happening in health and education might be implemented as at least an interim measure, "without waiting for 'the far off divine event' of provincial administration" of welfare services.[78]

Other Nova Scotia municipalities regarded Glace Bay's entry into welfare as a success and considered adopting it as a model. The town took great satisfaction in its provincial leadership, and Ottawa visitors understood this civic pride as a testament to their profession's success. The practice of social work in Glace Bay combined both administrative duties and what Wisdom referred to as "doorstep social work – like [that of] an undertaker or milkman." In 1944, for example, she recorded 1,025 home visits, 1,120 office consultations, and 130 outgoing letters. Going to people's homes was a challenge, as she did not drive. She generally walked, after discovering that hitching a ride in a police car meant "no one would answer the door." At age sixty-three, she learned to drive after the town provided her with a car. Her responsibilities were community-oriented, and ranged from making costumes for a school concert and arranging medical treatment for a local boy to conducting radio broadcasts in late 1948 on welfare issues for a local Sydney radio station. At times, she continued using the pre-professional term "friend."[79] She was responsible for the trivial policing of both recipients and providers of welfare. She went after a local merchant who inflated billings and claimed "three tins stove polish for a small coal stove" on the account of a wartime "dependent" she was overseeing, and pursued municipal-aid recipients who tried to procure cigarettes with their relief vouchers. The challenges of providing "doorstep" social work and administrative leadership were often frustrating. Throughout her ten years in Glace Bay, she repeated the phrase that she was "very much in the pioneering stage of my undertaking here." She supported the co-op movement, was a member of the local credit union, and, as a civic employee, joined the Congress of Industrial Organizations' affiliated Union of Municipal Workers, making her among the first social workers in Canada to be unionized.[80]

The often ad hoc and heterogeneous nature of Wisdom's work was perhaps at odds with local attempts at professionalism. Her arrival in Glace Bay coincided with the wartime expansion of welfare services and employees. By 1944, local workers and board members in public and quasi-public agencies were holding conferences that attracted seventy participants. A 1947 visit by Joy Maines of the Canadian Association of Social Workers launched a Cape Breton branch of that organization. The following year, Wisdom was elected branch vice-president. The group met regularly and focused on particular professional or social issues. For example, in 1949, it studied the "social questions" position paper of the Nova Scotia Federation of Labour.[81]

Jane Wisdom appreciated visits from colleagues in Ottawa and most professional contact with others in her field. She felt a contrast between the isolation of Glace Bay and the busyness of Montreal. After a 1944 visit from an Ottawa social worker, Nora Lea, Wisdom wrote that social service workers "seem to be such scattered atoms down here even among ourselves, but when someone like you comes along, I think we are conscious that we do cohere, as it were. In other words, it is encouraging to find ourselves thinking and talking together in a professional atmosphere in an almost natural way(!)." One response she had was to be involved in the establishment of both the Nova Scotia and Cape Breton branches of the Canadian Association of Social Workers.[82]

Although the professionalization of social work in Cape Breton was new, and Wisdom felt professionally isolated, the concerns she faced locally reflected continental trends. At the first 1944 conference of local social workers, the call to expand psychiatric services reflected the increasing use of psychotherapeutic rhetoric within the profession. It also revealed a growing recognition of the connection between poor mental health and indigence.[83] Historian Laura Curran has pointed out that, although various interpretations of Freud had been present in social work since the 1920s, the war and post-war periods were marked by "an individualized, psychological perspective," which suited politically conservative times. This complemented a political climate where those in power were reluctant to examine structural inequality. Moreover, psychiatry allowed social workers to improve their professional status by linking their "caring profession" to medical prestige. Despite the rhetoric, psychiatric services were severely underdeveloped in Nova Scotia, especially outside the Halifax area. In 1946, Wisdom reported that there were only three qualified psychiatrists in the entire province. Drawing attention to "mental illness" as a major social problem and the need for psychiatric health resources was as close as Wisdom came to adopting psychotherapeutic rhetoric as she continued to privilege environment in explaining the origins of social and community problems.[84]

Another aspect of Jane Wisdom's professional involvement was social-work education. Her 1941 arrival in Glace Bay coincided with an announcement for a regional training centre, the Maritime School of Social Work. The expanding welfare system required more trained workers, and some Maritimers wanted a local school to prevent prospective social workers from leaving the region for education and finding permanent employment elsewhere. Various personal connections kept Wisdom abreast of news, and she was frequently consulted for advice. In fact, she worried to Charlotte Whitton that her name was being used perhaps too freely in association with the endeavour.[85]

Planning for the Maritime School of Social Work began with two of Wisdom's former colleagues: Reginald V. Harris, whom she knew from her time at the Halifax Bureau of Social Service, and Samuel Prince, doyen of the public welfare circle in Halifax and teacher of sociology at King's College. The need was identified in February 1941. Harris recalled that there was a shortage of trained workers, since it was impossible to persuade graduates from Montreal and the University of Toronto "to come to Nova Scotia on the salaries we were able to pay." When the fledgling school decided in spring 1944 that it needed full-time staff assistance, it was not surprising that board members initially turned to Wisdom as a "very suitable person." When she declined, MacKinnon and Prince continued to lobby her throughout the summer, hoping she would change her mind.[86]

Although Wisdom would be formally linked to the school only as a field placement supervisor after 1945, she was connected to it in other important ways. The school's first full-time instructor, Phyllis Burns, had been a caseworker for the Montreal Women's Directory under Wisdom's supervision.[87] When Burns left in 1947, Frances Montgomery, another protégé, replaced her as assistant director and coordinator of field instruction. A graduate of the Montreal and University of Pennsylvania schools of social work, Montgomery had had an impressive international career and always credited Wisdom for bringing her into the profession. Montgomery also worked with Wisdom at the Montreal Women's Directory, starting as a student placement.[88] Wisdom proved to be a talented mentor to young women. Just as she had done in Montreal, she inspired a new cohort to enter the profession and achieve high professional standards once in service.

Wisdom never completely abandoned her ideal of community-based action beyond the state and her appreciation of co-operation, individual initiative, and self-enterprise. One of her final acts in Glace Bay was to publicize and celebrate a group of sixty-three families who, as the Bridgeport Row Street Athletic Club, constructed their own clubhouse and playground and had plans for a softball field. The grassroots community organization epitomized settlement house ideals; in fostering democratic citizenship and permitting individuals to contribute their respective skills, the club captured Wisdom's imagination.[89]

Despite her enthusiasm, by 1950, at the age of sixty-six, Wisdom was hoping to retire. Her family needed her and her doctor recommended it. She had already notified the Glace Bay Town Council of her plans but she delayed them, becoming caught up in municipal poor-law reform campaigns, along with initiatives for old age pensions, mothers' allowances, and mental health services. A field visit by a representative of the Canadian Welfare Council in February 1950 reported Wisdom's frustration that the welfare committee remained reluctant to establish policy and left "too much to her." Her concern was that if she left before a replacement was found, "everything would go back to the way it was before her appointment." She explained the council's reluctance to make long-term commitments in terms of its economic vulnerability related to a dependence on coal. But, in June 1950, Wisdom's friend Dorothy King retired from the McGill School of Social Work, and, six months later, the first advertisement for Wisdom's replacement was posted in the *Social Worker*. The notice emphasized the opportunity for "community welfare and provincial–municipal relations development." Not a single person applied. So, in addition to her regular duties, Wisdom now added the solicitation of applicants to her responsibilities. The Ottawa office began to worry that the welfare department would close if no solution emerged.

In the end, when Wisdom retired in August 1952, there was no immediate replacement. Jessy R. Casey, a provincial Department of Welfare worker, was seconded to the Glace Bay office for several days a week until Denis Chaisson, who had had a work placement with Wisdom as a student, graduated from the Maritime School of Social Work the following year.[90] The Ottawa organization was unsure how a new officer would fare in Wisdom's shadow, but a 1953 field report concluded that Chaisson "seemed to be prepared to meet ... problems in a very realistic way." Chaisson continued to consult Wisdom after her retirement, and her local influence continued. A 1966 report noted that town welfare continued to be associated with Wisdom even though there had been two replacement workers since her retirement. When she died in 1975, an obituary in the *Cape Breton Post* noted her importance to Glace Bay. It boasted that the provincial government often called upon her for advice and emphasized the service she had offered in counselling.[91]

Glace Bay became the first municipality in Nova Scotia to experiment within the very restrictive confines of provincial poor law. The creation of a municipal welfare department resulted from a vacuum in the voluntary private sector and a labour-controlled town council, whose mandate it was to balance justice with the ability of ratepayers to pay. The inadequate provincial welfare system downloaded health and welfare expenses to the local level despite municipalities' minimal taxation revenue. "Canada's biggest town" was dependent on a fragile coal economy, and Glace Bay emerged from the Depression and Second World War with a heavy municipal debt and no prospect of post-war prosperity. Aiming to cut costs through efficiency while being just to residents in need, the Social Service Department was a creative response that constantly blurred normal distinctions between public welfare and private charity. During the war and post-war period, which introduced a number of new federal spending initiatives, Wisdom helped Glace Bay take advantage of new opportunities. Many of the town's indigent were enrolled in relief programs, for example, but the municipality could not deal with the constant downloading of other expenses by the province. Change finally happened in 1956 and 1958 when Nova Scotia adopted social assistance acts. The influx of federal dollars lessened the burden on municipal units.

There was unintended irony in Wisdom's success. Although she arrived in Glace Bay touting the importance of professionalism, her success in the community continued to be attributed to her character. A short biography published in the 1970s by the Nova Scotia Department of Welfare attested to Wisdom's "unfailing tact and good humour," which "enabled her to get things done without giving offence – in fact, some of those who opposed her initially became her firm friends and enthusiastic supporters." When Wisdom supervised social-work students, she always emphasized that the "the relationships to Town Councilors and members of Poor Committee were paramount." She insisted there was "not room for set ideas"; rather, "blue prints" had to be used with "flexibility and imagination." To her one-time supervisee, Frances Montgomery, she conveyed "the feeling of adventure in the possibility ahead in the municipal approach to welfare matters."[92] Feelings, imagination, and relationships remained at the core of her professional practice.

Glace Bay was also swept up in a broader national trend – the ongoing centralization of authority – as provinces took over what had once been municipal responsibilities, such as roads, health, justice, and care for the poor. In turn, the federal government entered into what were previously provincial domains, such as pensions, family allowances, unemployment insurance, and health grants. According to one minister of municipal affairs, a "Canadian standard for certain social services" was emerging.[93] Politicians and bureaucrats were not the only ones to articulate a Canadian standard; those working at the community level also recognized it. Jane Wisdom regularly insisted that the federal government's assumption of social relief proved that local poor districts were no longer solely responsible for destitution. At the same time, she argued that local communities continued to carry all the hidden welfare costs in joint expenditures and that serious gaps in assistance also continued. There were still no provisions for a vast number of vulnerable Nova Scotians. Many among the unemployed, the ill, the disabled, the aged, and those without male breadwinners were dependent on local governments, who did not always have sufficient resources.

In May 1957, the Nova Scotia Social Assistance Act finally replaced the Poor Relief Act after the federal government began sharing the costs of unemployment assistance. The act established minimum standards and gave the province the authority to enforce them. The new act also contained what one critic characterized as modern euphemisms, larger administrative units, and funding from three levels of government. Even though "paupers" and "relief" became "persons in need" and "assistance," the critic continued that "wherever, regardless of legislation, the old stereotypes of thinking about the needy exist and wherever help is given so as to undermine human dignity, morale, or health, the spirit of the Poor Law is very much alive." Jane Wisdom would have agreed. Even as she helped construct the post-war welfare state, almost daily she encountered its limitations. In her 1949 annual report, she declared: "As far as humanly possible, services have been extended by the Welfare Department to meet a wide variety of social needs."[94]

Sutherland's River, 1952–1975

In August 1952, Jane Wisdom noted with ironic emphasis that she had "officially" retired, well aware that certain aspects of her professional life would continue, although she was no longer being paid. In retirement, she returned "home" to Sutherland's River, a place where she had never permanently resided, to live the remainder of her life among family. According to one of her great-nephews, Jane and her sisters Katherine and Bess played "musical houses," living in various combinations in various family households. Bess and her husband Dwight Burns had a farm about half a kilometre up the road. Katherine had retired earlier to Sutherland's River, but, to contribute to Canada's war effort, had worked temporarily at the Trenton Car Works. After the war, Katherine bought a surplus, prefabricated, wartime house and had it moved onto the homestead property when her daughter Relief and family had moved into the old McQueen home. Katherine spent one or two winters in what became known as the "Little House." With time, family members remember, it became more of a "summer cottage or bungalow" and eventually a "storage closet" for Katherine and Jane as they grew older.[1]

When Wisdom returned home in 1952, both Katherine and Bess were facing significant challenges. Although Bess continued to teach Sunday school and be active in community affairs, her health was failing, and she was widowed the following year. Katherine was also facing serious medical issues. In December 1951, she was diagnosed with high blood pressure and given "strict orders to avoid outside work requiring mental and physical effort."[2] Nevertheless, she continued to assist her daughter's family as much as she could and remained active in the New Glasgow Credit Union, the Co-operative movement, and the Pictou County Co-operative Commonwealth Federation.

Wisdom's own health remained remarkably good. Indeed, for someone who was a sickly child and had serious health problems in her thirties and forties, her health seemed to have greatly improved in her late fifties, right around the time she arrived in Glace Bay. It may have been the move away from Montreal and its particular institutional stresses, or the benefits of increased physical exercise through the amount of walking that her new job required. Perhaps it was menopause, suggesting that her adult health issues had been related to endometriosis. Whatever the cause, Wisdom seems to have enjoyed the best health later in life. She remained healthy and independent until her late eighties, when old age gradually caught up with her, with failing eyesight posing a challenge to her reading, newspaper clipping, and active correspondence.

Notwithstanding a career that rarely attracted any attention, Wisdom retired with some professional recognition. Upon her departure from Glace Bay, the Town Council wryly decreed "that the benefit the Town has derived from your services in Glace Bay has been repaid to some extent in that during the past eleven years you have acquired some of the better qualities of a Cape Bretoner." As a result, the town "would not be adverse to give you permission to calling yourself a Cape Bretoner when visiting other parts of Nova Scotia or the world." The council urged Wisdom to use her retirement to indulge in her "own interests rather than in the interests of others."[3] In 1953, she was one of 12,500 Canadians to be recommended by the federal government to receive the Queen Elizabeth II Coronation Medal. In 1964, she was named an honorary life member of the Nova Scotia Association of Social Workers, and a picture of her attending its 1967 meeting appeared in the *New Glasgow Evening News*. She remained an active member of her profession and continued to subscribe to the professional journal *Canadian Welfare* until her death. Her recognition at the end of her formal career reflected social work's new stability as a profession, which was now looking for "pioneers" as it continued to define itself. By 1961, the *Social Worker* was already arguing that today's social workers should "be aware of the early struggles of the profession and the community to establish professional education on a sound basis."[4]

When Wisdom first retired, she maintained a public presence. In 1953, she participated in St. Francis Xavier University's *People's School*, a radio broadcast on social service, along with Fred MacKinnon, now Nova Scotia's deputy minister of welfare, Don Coulter of the Cape Breton Children's Aid, and Don Macadam, a juvenile judge in Sydney.[5] In her radio address, she argued that legal and constitutional actions could not "guarantee" world peace and that the greatest problem facing society was the "moral and spiritual problems of creating community." Here, in the midst of the Cold War, we hear echoes of Victorian Christian socialist John Ruskin's insistence on the interconnection of cultural, social, and moral issues, and observe links taking us back to Wisdom's interest in the settlement house movement. Wisdom also published at least one book review – appropriately, on a guide to retirement living – and remained a source of professional advice throughout 1958 and 1959 for the Unmarried Parents Committee of the Nova Scotia Mainland Branch of the Canadian Association of Social Workers.[6] Frances Montgomery, who in 1961 went to work for the federal Emergency Welfare Services Division, received all Wisdom's notes from the Halifax explosion.

While Wisdom's profession helped build the welfare state, she personally benefited from its expansion. On 1 May 1954, she received her first Old Age Security cheque. An amendment to the British North America Act permitted the federal government to pass the Old Age Security Act. As of January 1952, all men and women, with the exception of Status Indians, who had lived in Canada for twenty years and were seventy years of age and older, received a federally funded universal pension without undergoing a means test. Wisdom received $40 a month – certainly not enough to live on, but a generous supplement to her private pension as a Glace Bay civic employee. Wisdom was atypical of her generation of social workers in having a pension, the result of her membership in the municipal workers union. Indeed, many never-married female social workers faced poverty in their old age. The files of the Canadian Association of Social Workers reveal the sad cases of Wisdom's contemporaries, Clare Gass and Gwen Lantz, who could no longer afford even the luxury of association membership in retirement.[7] Wisdom, on the other hand, had enough to buy a new car in July 1956, when she replaced her Ford Coupe with a new Volkswagen Beetle. I wish I had a photo of her and this car; it suggests to me a contemporary flare and openness that challenges my image of her in her early seventies. While the Beetle was available in Canada starting in 1952, I doubt there were many on the road in rural Pictou County just four years later. A great-nephew remembers that Wisdom was very proud of her car, and loved showing it off.

Wisdom was a busy woman. She was interested in family history, organizing papers and letters for placement in public archives, maintained correspondences with friends and former colleagues, and kept her eye out for coins for one of her great-nephews. Colleague Frances Montgomery described her as the family "factotum" – with Katherine's frail health, Jane took Bess to doctor appointments and coordinated nurses during her final illness in 1958. She continued to practise social work unofficially and discreetly, helping neighbours and socially marginal members of the community with legal problems and facilitating their access to expanding government benefits. A.A. Mackenzie recalled that she was "Aunt Jen" to many in the community and was confidante to many a local teenage girl. While the generational distance between a never-married woman in her late seventies and early eighties and rural Nova Scotian teenagers in the 1950s and 1960s was considerable, as a caseworker particularly committed to the lives of young women, Wisdom certainly would have had a broader experience with the world than many of her neighbours. Wisdom would not have approved of changing sexual mores, but it probably would have been more difficult to shock her than most. Meanwhile, her own family protected her from the more controversial details of their own private lives.

Wisdom's old age was rich and full with family, friends, pets, visits, and seasonal moves to the "little house" until her late eighties, when she moved permanently into the back bedroom behind the kitchen in the old McQueen homestead. She may have feared being a burden to her niece, whose own children had left home and who was left caring for two old women, her mother and aunt. At some point in the late 1960s, Wisdom temporarily moved for one winter to the Digby area, sharing a room in a seniors' home with a recently widowed, long-time friend, Agnes Dodds Lawley. This arrangement did not last, and she returned to Sutherland's River, where Relief cared for Katherine and Jane until their deaths. Both women died after strokes, Katherine in 1970 and Jane on 9 June 1975. Jane Wisdom's mind and sense of humour were sharp until the end, although the remnants of an interview recorded just weeks before she died suggest she was tiring easily.[8]

Wisdom's final years were spent in the house where her mother grew up. This physical continuity seems appropriate for a woman who herself spanned so many worlds. She linked a nineteenth-century world based on values of obligation and duty regarding religion, family, and community to a post-war welfare state based on rights and entitlements. Within the development of Canadian social welfare and the national profession of social work, she brought together the British influence of individuals such as Hilda Oakeley, Richard Lane, J. Howard Falk, Dorothy King, and Leonard Marsh, as well as important American practitioners such as Mary Richmond and Margaret Byington.[9] As social work became professionalized, she worked as an untrained amateur, in both the casework and settlement house sides of the profession. She moved from a predominantly women's world of private charity to a public system that usually privileged men in a shared, but hierarchical, workplace. The transitions over the course of Wisdom's life were rarely sequential; rather, they tended to be concurrent streams that mixed and joined together. Social work, considered through Wisdom's career, should not be thought of as a profession evolving strictly linearly, but rather as the culmination of ongoing influences and impact of individual practitioners.

Outside the profession, Wisdom's death in 1975 coincided with almost the very moment when the welfare state in Canada outside Quebec began its slow decline. That October, to cope with the combination of rapidly accelerating inflation and high unemployment, the Bank of Canada moved away from Keynesian practices of expanding money supply to deal with high unemployment and embraced a policy of monetary gradualism that lowered the rate of money growth. As the Anti-Inflation Board introduced wage and price controls, the Liberal majority government adopted a policy of budget restraint, casting all subsequent social policy discussion within the framework of fiscal capacity.[10]

When I first came across Wisdom's 1975 obituary, I was surprised by what I considered the marginalization of her significant professional career. It noted her membership in the local Presbyterian Women's Missionary Society before mentioning that she had been secretary of the Women's Directory of Montreal, a McGill graduate, and a social worker. Her identity as daughter, aunt, great-aunt, and sister was given pride of place. With time, her obituary has come to make sense.[11] The primacy given to her church-group membership reminds us that Jane Wisdom remained deeply religious all her life. This moral stance cannot be separated from her idea of service. She worked in a secular world, but her motivations and world view, while informed by social science, were also shaped by her understanding of justice and charity emanating from her faith. This was never a contradiction. She understood her religious beliefs as having an intellectual rather than emotional basis, and characterized them by a "quiet continuing testimony of a rightly ordered life governed by the spirit of Jesus." Throughout her life, she preferred translations of the New Testament that translated *agape* as 'charity' rather than 'love,' and that understood charity as loving kindness towards others.[12] I would not want to suggest that she always lived up to this ideal, but it was the standard that she set for herself.

It was also a moral stance that offered her considerable personal comfort and meaning. After researching Wisdom, I remain uncertain if she was ever involved with anyone in her life. Her great-niece vaguely recalled a family rumour that someone may have been lost in the First World War. This is distinctly possible, given that so many in Wisdom's cohort lost brothers, lovers, and future husbands. Whether this is true or not, I have come to believe she was rarely lonely, convinced that she shared novelist Nadine Gordimer's belief that "the real definition of loneliness [is] to live without social responsibility."[13] For Wisdom, social responsibility was reinforced through family, religion, and education. Being useful mattered to her and gave her life meaning and purpose.

Politically, Wisdom was very much a liberal with social democratic leanings. Influenced by John Dewey, the social gospel, and community-based democracy, she often reverted to the old word for 'client' as 'friend.' She seems to have gotten along well with conservatives such as Charlotte Whitton, and with older, American, social work pioneer Mary Richmond. But she was also one of the first residents of the McGill settlement house in the 1920s, and, in the1940s, she had a warm relationship with the left-leaning United Mine Workers (although not its Communist locals). She publicly identified herself with Canadian social work's progressive wing through her involvement in the Progressive Programme Committee.

Writing about Wisdom's public welfare work in Glace Bay, Jean Mac-Fadgen claimed in 1979 that "interwoven in the professional life of Jane Wisdom is much of the grassroots history of social work in Canada."[14] I clearly agree. Wisdom's uncanny knack for being in important places at pivotal moments meant that she witnessed and participated in the creation of the social work profession in Canada and the Canadian welfare state. Her career ties together the state intervention that followed the Halifax explosion, provincial governments' introduction of laws regarding minimum wages for women, and social programs such as Mothers' Allowance. She testified before Quebec's Montpetit Commission and the federal Rowell–Sirois Commission, and actively fought to dismantle the Nova Scotia poor law in the post-war period. Her career took her to New York City, the centre of North American social work, to Halifax as the First World War transformed Canadian society, to Montreal, one of the hardest-hit cities in Canada during the worst of the Depression, and, finally, to Glace Bay, where technical and market transformations marked the beginning of the end of a 300-year history of coal mining in Cape Breton and foreshadowed the deindustrialization of late-twentieth-century North America. Wisdom's professional life integrated things often considered distinct.

The "whats" and "whos" of Jane Wisdom's life do not tell the entire story. In an obituary in the *Social Worker*, Wisdom's protégé Frances Montgomery acknowledged her "substantial and qualitative contribution to our profession." "But," she concluded, "for those who knew and loved her, the important thing is not only what she did but how. Her professional performance exemplified our first code of ethics 1938 'a professional person ... motivated by an interest in the well-being of humanity rather than personal gain or advancement ... knowledge and competence ... integrity and open-mindedness.'"[15]

Social work and the Canadian welfare state took the forms they did as a consequence of how they were put into practice at the local community level through individual lives. Jane Wisdom inspired many of her professional contemporaries, and the affection and respect directed towards her were sincere and profound. Clearly, there were thousands of others who did not engender the same kind of admiration and esteem. The "how" of the welfare state and welfare bureaucracies at the local level mattered – for the policies were not simply produced by bureaucrats. Instead, they were implemented by individuals who were, in turn, shaped by particular cultural values and circumstances. Not all of them were gifted with Wisdom's "educated heart."

The liberal welfare state that Jane Wisdom helped construct reached its height in the final years of her life. It was never free of moral and gender assumptions linked to its charitable origins, and, as Richard Titmuss observed in 1951, it always conceived need and behaviour in terms of the individual, reflecting the time in which it emerged.[16] Its ad hoc and fragmentary nature was not able to serve simultaneously the diverse needs of those who required total maintenance or partial income support, and of a wider public who benefited from enriching programs and services. Professionalization and bureaucratization consumed resources, which were diverted from those in need, and, yet, those employed in the system faced daily frustration, stress, and sometimes burnout. But for all their limitations, the aspirations that no Canadian should be in need and that all Canadians, through an activist nation state, were responsible for assisting one another reflected the parallel traditions of charity and justice. Wisdom's professional life bridged charity and justice, much like the system that it helped to create.

Notes

Introduction

1 For examples, think of Christine Stansell, *City of Women: Sex and Class in New York, 1789–1860* (Urbana: University of Illinois Press, 1987); Judith Fingard's *Dark Side of Life in Victorian Halifax* (Porter's Lake, NS: Pottersfield Press, 1989); or Suzanne Morton, *Ideal Surroundings: Domestic Life in a Working-Class Suburb in the 1920s* (Toronto: University of Toronto Press, 1995). Two recent examples are Bettina Bradbury, *Wife to Widow: Lives, Laws, and Politics in Nineteenth-Century Montreal* (Vancouver: University of British Columbia Press, 2011); and Sherry Olson and Patricia A. Thornton, *Peopling the North American City: Montreal 1840–1900* (Montreal: McGill-Queen's University Press, 2011). See also Suzanne Morton, "Faire le saut: la biographie peut-elle être de l'histoire sociale?," *Revue d'histoire de l'Amérique française* 54, no.1 (Summer 2000): 103–9.

2 P.T. Rooke and R.L. Schnell, *No Bleeding Heart: Charlotte Whitton: A Feminist on the Right* (Vancouver: University of British Columbia Press, 1987), 38.

3 Steven King, *Women, Welfare and Local Politics, 1880–1920: 'We Might be Trusted'* (Brighton, UK: University of Sussex Academic Press, 2006), 4; S.J. Kleinberg, *Widows and Orphans First: The Family Economy and Social Welfare Policy, 1880–1939* (Urbana: University of Illinois Press, 2006).

4 Memo on a School for Social Workers, Montreal, Jan 1933, CCSD, CASW 1932, MG 28 I 10, vol. 30, 150, LAC. See Nancy Christie, *Engendering the State: Family, Work and Welfare in Canada* (Toronto: University of Toronto Press, 2000); and Therese Jennissen and Colleen Lundy, *One Hundred Years of Social Work: A History of the Profession in English Canada, 1900–2000* (Waterloo: Wilfrid Laurier University Press, 2011).

5 James Struthers, *The Limits of Affluence: Welfare in Ontario, 1920–1970* (Toronto: University of Toronto Press, 1994).

6 Shirley Tillotson, "Review of Christina Burr, *Spreading the Light: Work and Labour Reform in Late-Nineteenth-Century Toronto*; Gillian Creese, *Contracting Masculinity: Gender, Class, and Race in a White-Collar Union, 1944–1994*; Morton, *Ideal Surroundings*; Ruth Roach Pierson and Nupur Chaudhuri, eds., *Nation, Empire, Colony: Historicizing Gender and Race*," in *Atlantis* 25, no. 2 (Spring/Summer 2001): 113–17.

7 Diary, 3 May 1906, JBW Papers.

8 Joy Maines to Helen Gougeon, 13 Apr 1951, CASW, Board of Directors, General Corr (2) 1950–53, MG 28 I 441, vol. 6, 4, LAC.

9 "A Salutation To JBW FROM FLM," *Social Worker* (Dec 1952): 3.

10 Corr, Individuals and Organizations Recommended for Honours, 1935, King George V's Silver Jubilee Medal, Charlotte Whitton Fonds, MG 30 E 256, vol. 18, LAC.

11 David Cannadine, *Aspects of Aristocracy: Grandeur and Decline in Modern Britain* (New Haven: Yale University Press, 1994), 3.

12 Alice Kessler-Harris, "Why Biography?," *American Historical Review* 114, no. 3 (Jun 2009): 625–30; Andrée Lévesque, *Red Travellers: Jeanne Corbin & Her Comrades* (Montreal: McGill-Queen's University Press, 2006); Andrée Lévesque, *Eva Circé-Côté: femme de lettres* (Montreal: Les Éditions du remue-ménage, 2010); Linda Gordon, *Dorothea Lange: A Life Beyond Limits* (New York: WW Norton, 2009); Nick Salvatore, "Biography and Social History: An Intimate Relationship," *Labour History* 87 (Nov 2004): 187–92; Nick Salvatore, *Eugene V. Debs: Citizen and Socialist* (Urbana, IL: University of Illinois Press, 1982), xi; David Frank, *J.B. McLachlan: A Biography* (Toronto: Lorimer, 1999); Brian Young, *George-Étienne Cartier: Montreal Bourgeois* (Montreal: McGill-Queen's University Press, 1981); Barbara Roberts, *A Reconstructed World: A Feminist Biography of Gertrude Richardson* (Montreal & Kingston: McGill-Queen's University Press, 1996).

13 Mark Hearn and Harry Knowles, "Struggling for Recognition: Reading the Individual in Labour History," *Labour History* 87 (Nov 2004): 1–11. See also "Critical Feminist Biography II," *Journal of Women's History* 21, no. 4, (Winter 2009). See Peter Campbell's study of *Rose Henderson: A Woman of the People* (Montreal: McGill-Queen's University Press, 2010), and Jill Lepore, "Historians Who Love Too Much: Reflections on Microhistory and Biography," *Journal of American History* 88, no. 1 (Jun 2001): 129–44.

14 See Shirley Tillotson, "Dollars, Democracy and the Children's Aid Society: The Eclipse of Gwendolen Lantz," in *Mothers of the Municipality: Women, Work, and Social Policy in Post-1945 Halifax*, ed. Judith Fingard

and Janet Guildford (Toronto: University of Toronto Press, 2005), 76–109. A good example of a professional memoir is Monique Meloche, *Profession: Travailleuse sociale. Quarante-cinq ans de service social hospitalier, 1950–1995* (Montreal: Liber, 2011).

15 Gerda Lerner, "US Women's History: Past, Present and Future," *Journal of Women's History* 16, no. 4 (Winter 2004): 15.

16 David Nasaw, "AHR Roundtable: Historians and Biography," *American Historical Review* 114, no. 3 (Jun 2009): 576.

17 Barbara Caine, "Feminist Biography and Feminist History," *Women's History Review* 3, no. 2 (Jun 1994): 247–61.

18 Lois Banner, "AHR Roundtable: Biography as History," *American Historical Review* 114, no. 3 (Jun 2009): 582, referring to Jo Burr Margadent, ed., *New Biography: Performing Femininity in Nineteenth-Century France* (Berkeley: University of California Press, 2000), 7.

19 See McQueen Family Letters, http://atlanticportal.hil.unb.ca/acva/en/mcqueen/, accessed 27 Oct 2013, and Jean Barman, *Sojourning Sisters: The Lives and Letters of Jessie and Annie McQueen* (Toronto: University of Toronto Press, 2003).

20 Frances Louise Montgomery, *Gazette*, 15 Jan 2005, B 17.

21 Veronica Strong-Boag, "No Longer Dull: Women, Gender and the Renewal of Canadian History," *Canadian Social Studies* 32, no. 2 (Winter 1998): 55.

Chapter One

1 Phillip A. Buckner, "The 1870s: Political Integration," in *The Atlantic Provinces in Confederation*, ed. E.R. Forbes and D.A. Muise (Toronto: University of Toronto Press, 1993), 63.

2 T.W. Acheson, "The National Policy and the Industrialization of the Maritimes, 1880–1910," *Acadiensis* 1, no. 2 (Spring 1972): 3–28; E.R. Forbes, *The Maritime Rights Movement, 1919–1927* (Montreal: McGill-Queen's University Press, 1979); T.W. Acheson, *Saint John: The Making of a Colonial Urban Community* (Toronto: University of Toronto Press, 1984); Robert Babcock, "Economic Development in Portland (ME) and Saint John (NB) during the Age of Iron and Steam, 1850–1914," *American Review of Canadian Studies* 9, no. 1 (Spring 1979): 3–37; John Alexander Watt, "Uneven Regional Development in Canada: A Study of Saint John, NB, 1880–1910" (PhD diss., University of Waterloo, 1981); Elizabeth W. McGahan, *The Port of Saint John: Volume One: From Confederation to Nationalization, 1867–1927* (Saint John: National Harbours Board, 1982); Don Nerbas, "Adapting to Decline:

The Changing Business World of the Bourgeoisie in Saint John, NB, in the 1920s," *Canadian Historical Review* 89, no. 2 (Jun 2008): 151–87.

3 *Globe* (Saint John), 26 Jun 1883.

4 Alan A. Brookes, "Out-migration from the Maritime Provinces, 1860–1900: Some Preliminary Considerations," *Acadiensis* 5, no. 2 (Spring 1976): 26–55.

5 Judith Fingard, "The 1880s: Paradoxes of Progress," in *Atlantic Provinces*, ed. Forbes and Muise, 96.

6 *Lovell's Directory of Nova Scotia*, 1871; Relief Williams Mackay, *Simple Annals: The Story of the McQueens of Sutherland's River* (Pictou, NS: Advocate Publishing, 1986), 13.

7 Barman, *Sojourning Sisters*, 15.

8 Death: Pictou County, 1928, Nova Scotia Vital Statistics: Book 128, 61, NSA.

9 Mackay, *Simple Annals*, 84.

10 *Hutchison Directory Saint John*, 1865–66, 1867–68; *McAlpine's Saint John Directory*, 1874–75, 176, 314; 1875–76, 176; 1876–77; 1877–78.

11 Ibid., 1881–82.

12 *Globe*, 28 Dec 1883; *Eastern Chronicle* (New Glasgow, NS), 26 May 1925; *Halifax Herald*, 27 May 1925. These claims from his obituary are contradicted by William Franklin Bunting, *A History of St John's Lodge F & AM of St John, NB together with sketches of all Masonic Bodies in New Brunswick from AD 1784 to AD 1894* (Saint John, 1895); *Globe*, 1 Nov 1880; 22 Feb 1883; 25 Sept 1883. Justices of the Peace Appointment Register, 9 Sept 1881, Appointment in Saint John, register, RS 581, 716. PANB. *Canadian Journal of Commerce* (25 Aug 1893): 363; Canada, *Debates of the House of Commons*, 30 Mar 1893, 3110.

13 Canada, *Sessional Papers*, vol. 14, 4, 1880/81, 6–xiv; vol. 18, 4, 1885, 5–141; vol. 19, 3, 1886, 3–251, 3–252; vol. 20, 3, 1887, 3–230; vol. 20, 9, 1887, 11–xxvi.

14 Fingard, "Paradoxes of Progress," 97.

15 *Globe*, 8 Mar 1887.

16 Ibid., 14 Feb; 21 Aug; 7 Nov 1883; 4 Jan; 16 Mar; 28 May 1886. Elizabeth Cunningham to COM, 13 Nov 1885, MLFP, MG 1, vol. 3346.12, NSA; *Globe*, 22 Mar 1887. For nineteenth-century entrepreneurial literature on Saint John, see Acheson, *Saint John*; T. W. Acheson, "The Great Merchant and Economic Development in St. John, 1820–1850," *Acadiensis* VIII, no. 2 (Spring 1979), 3–27. Paula Chegwidden Felt and Lawrence F. Felt, "Capital Accumulation and Industrial Development in Nineteenth Century New Brunswick: Some Preliminary Comments," in *The Enterprising Canadians: Entrepreneurs and Economic Development in Eastern Canada, 1820–1914*, ed. Lewis Fischer and Eric Sager (St. John's: Memorial University, 1979), 62–63; McGahan, *The Port of Saint John*; C.M. Wallace, "Saint John, New

Brunswick (1800–1900)," *Urban History Review* 1 (1975): 14; Babcock, "Economic Development," 29.

17 *Globe*, 20 Jul 1892; 25 Jul 1893; 5 Aug 1896.

18 *Canadian Journal of Commerce*, 25 Aug 1893, 363; Elizabeth Cunningham to COM, 18 Aug 1893, MLFP, MG 1, vol. 3348.3, NSA.

19 Dove McQueen to Jessie McQueen, 11 Dec 1880, MLFP, MG 1, vol. 3345.19, NSA; Dove McQueen to COM, 14 Feb 1881; Elizabeth Cunningham to Jessie McQueen, 25 Oct 1882, MLFP, MG 1, vol. 3346.1, 3346.6, NSA.

20 Elizabeth Cunningham to COM, 4 Mar 1887, MLFP, MG 1, vol. 3347.4, NSA.

21 Elizabeth Cunningham to Sister, 29 Mar 1889, MBW to COM, 3 Sept 1888, MLFP, MG 1, vol. 3347.5, 3347.3, NSA; Madeline Maureen Boulanger, "The Nature of Park Creation: The Development of Rockwood Park, 1893–1907" (master's research essay, Concordia University, 2001).

22 COM to Jessie McQueen, 30 Jan 1890, McQueen Collection, 1887–1893, MS 0860, BCARS; MBW to COM, 20 Oct 1890; Elizabeth Cunningham to COM, 20 Nov 1891, MLFP, MG 1, vol. 3347.7, 3348.1, NSA.

23 Resumé c. 1939, JBW Papers.

24 MBW to COM, 26 May 1892, MLFP, MG 1, vol. 3348.2, NSA; *McAlpine's Saint John Directory*, 1883–4, 304; 1886–87, 290.

25 Elizabeth Cunningham to COM, 6 Apr 1894, MLFP, MG 1, vol. 3348.4, NSA.

26 MBW to COM, 22 Mar 1894, Elizabeth Cunningham to COM, 6 Jun 1894, MLFP, MG 1, vol. 3348.4, NSA.

27 MBW to COM, 4 Sept 1893, Elizabeth Cunningham to COM, 15 Sept 1893, MBW to COM, 29 Nov 1893, MLFP, MG 1, vol. 3348.3, NSA.

28 Mrs. Wisdom's name appears in the 1895 directory and remains listed through 1898, but she must have left shortly thereafter, as she did not appear in the 1901 census, and died in Wolfville in Sept 1903. MBW to COM, 12 Oct 1888, COM to Jessie McQueen, 21 Nov 1889, MLFP, MG 1, vol. 3347.5, 3347.6, NSA; *Presbyterian Witness*, 5 Sept 1903; Elizabeth Cunningham to COM, 12 Oct 1894, MBW to COM, 14 Feb 1895 MLFP, MG 1, vol. 3348.4, 3348.5, NSA; Daniel McQueen's obituary, *Presbyterian Witness*, 13 Oct. 1894, 321.

29 MBW to COM, 10 May 1898, MLFP, MG 1, vol. 3348.8, NSA.

30 Canada, Manuscript Census, 1901, New Brunswick, Saint John, Dufferin Ward, i-2: 34.

31 *St John Daily Sun*, 26 Apr 1906.

32 Allen F. Davis, *Spearheads of Reform: The Social Settlements and the Progressive Movement, 1890–1914* (New York: Oxford University Press, 1967), 33–37;

Roy Lubove, *Professional Altruism: The Emergence of Social Work as a Career, 1880–1930* (Cambridge: Harvard University Press, 1965).

33 Elizabeth Cunningham to COM, 1 Jun 1898, MLFP, MG 1, vol. 3348.8, NSA.

34 Mackay, *Simple Annals*, 37.

35 Elizabeth Cunningham to COM, 14 Mar 1881, MLFP, MG 1, vol. 3346.1, NSA.

36 Mackay, *Simple Annals*, 148.

37 Dove McQueen to COM, 19 Jan 1882, Jessie McQueen to Jane McQueen, 10 Mar 1882, MLFP, MG 1, vol. 3346.4, NSA.

38 MBW to COM, 22 Mar 1881, MBW to COM, 15 Apr 1881, Elizabeth Cunningham to COM., 2 Oct 1882, MBW to COM, 11 Dec 1882, MLFP, MG 1, vol. 3346.1, 3346.2, 3346.6, NSA.

39 Elizabeth Cunningham to COM, 31 Jan 1881, Elizabeth Cunningham to Jessie McQueen, 14 Oct 1881, MBW to COM, 5 Jan 1886, MLFP, MG 1, vol. 3346.1, 3346.3, 3347.1, NSA.

40 Freeman Wisdom to COM, 15 Feb 1886; COM to Jane McQueen, 5 Apr 1887, MBW to COM, 3 Sept 1888, MLFP, MG 1, vol. 3347.1, 3347.4, 3347.5, 3, NSA.

41 Barman, *Sojourning Sisters*, 17.

42 Ibid., 18.

43 Interview Esther Kerry by Jean MacFadgen, Aug 1979, St. Lambert, QC; interview Relief Williams Mackay by Jean MacFadgen, summer 1979, Sutherland's River, NS; tapes in Jean MacFadgen Papers, Beaton Institute, interview Jock Mackay by Suzanne Morton, 16 Feb 2006, Montreal, QC.

44 *Globe*, 2 Jun 1887, 7 Jun 1888, 6 Jun 1889 6 Jun 1890; *Halifax Herald*, 27 May 1925.

45 *75th Acts and Proceedings of the General Assembly of the Presbyterian Church in Canada* 1949, 333; *Presbyterian Record*, Dec 1948, 340; KFW to JBW, 3 Mar 1900 and n.d. c. 1900, Wisdom Papers, MG 2015, MUA; Daniel J. Fraser, St. Stephen's Christmas 1902, "The Sacrament of Comfort," n,p., n.d.; N. Keith Clifford, *The Resistance to Church Union in Canada, 1904–1939* (Vancouver: University of British Columbia Press, 1985), 112. See also Daniel J. Fraser, "Recent Church Union Movements in Canada," *Harvard Theological Review* 8 (Jul 1915): 363–78.

46 *Globe*, 12, 17 Mar; 26 Jun 1883; 21 Jan 1886; 17 Feb, 7 Apr 1887; *St John Daily Sun*, 18 Mar 1902.

47 *Globe*, 31 May; 2, 3 Jun 1887.

48 MBW to COM, 21 Jun 1894, MLFP, MG 1, vol. 3348.4, NSA.

49 *Globe*, 8, 11 Feb 1889; 2 Apr 1889.

50 Ibid., 9, 10 Sept 1891.

51 *Globe,* 16 Jul 1892; 15 Oct 1902; 27th *Acts and Proceedings of the General Assembly of the Presbyterian Church in Canada* 1900–01, 324.

52 *Globe,* 13, 14, 20 Jun 1894.

53 Barman, *Sojourning Sisters,* 15.

54 Dove McQueen to Jessie McQueen, 11 Dec 1880, MLFP, MG 1, vol. 3345.19, NSA. Both periodicals were forwarded to Bell's sister Jessie in British Columbia. Jessie McQueen to COM, 4 Jun 1888, Jessie McQueen to COM, 16 Mar 1891, McQueen Collection.

55 Jessie McQueen to COM, 21 Apr 1892, *Ibid.;* Mackay, *Simple Annals,* 35–36, 149; *Globe,* 3 Jun 1898, 27 Jan 1903; MBW to COM, 20 Dec 1892, MLFP, MG 1, vol. 3348.2, NSA.

56 *Report of the Board of School Trustees,* City of Saint John 1899, 39–40.

57 *Globe,* 16, 17 Dec 1897.

58 Ibid., 28 Sept 1895.

59 Saint John High School Alumnae, *A History of the Saint John Grammar School, 1805–1914* (Saint John, 1914), 41–42; *Globe,* 28 Dec 1898.

60 *History of the Saint John Grammar School,* 35.

61 *Globe,* 29 Aug 1898.

62 Ibid., 25 Jun 1902; 24 Jun 1898; 26 Jun 1900; 26 Aug 1902.

63 Janine Stingel, *Social Discredit: Antisemitism, Social Credit and the Jewish Response* (Montreal: McGill-Queen's University Press, 2000), 206.

64 Janice Cook, "Emma Skinner Fiske," *Dictionary of Canadian Biography,* online; Canada, Manuscript Census, 1901, New Brunswick, Saint John, Dufferin Ward, i-2; 32: 136; Janice Mary Cook, "Child Labour in Saint John, New Brunswick and the Campaign for Factory Legislation, 1880–1905" (master's thesis, University of New Brunswick, 1993). Hatheway also published under the name R. Belmont. See W. Stewart Wallace, *The Dictionary of Canadian Biography,* second edition revised and enlarged (Toronto: Macmillan, 1945). Mary Eileen Clarke, "The Saint John Women's Enfranchisement Association, 1894–1919" (master's thesis, University of New Brunswick, 1979), 78.

65 Notes, 11 Jul 1964, Recollections, JBW Papers.

66 Clarke, "Women's Enfranchisement Association," 26–27; Fingard, "Paradoxes of Progress," 168. Personal communication, Lorett Treese, College Archivist, Bryn Mawr, 27 Oct 2004. *Saint John Evening Transcript,* 22 Jun 1936, p. 12.

67 See Richard Allen's classic *The Social Passion, Religion and Social Reform in Canada, 1914–1928* (Toronto: University of Toronto Press, 1971); Michael Gauvreau and Nancy Christie, *A Full-Orbed Christianity: The Protestant Churches and Social Welfare in Canada, 1900–1940* (Montreal: McGill-Queen's

University Press, 1996); Brian J. Fraser, *The Social Uplifters: Presbyterian Progressives and the Social Gospel in Canada, 1875–1915* (Waterloo: Wilfrid Laurier Press, 1988).

68 *Globe,* 17 Mar 1899.

69 Ibid., 19 Feb 1897.

70 Clarke, "Women's Enfranchisement Association," 10.

71 *Globe,* 2 Dec 1898.

72 Brereton Greenhous, "Paupers and Poorhouses: The Development of Poor Relief in Early New Brunswick," *Histoire social/Social History* 1 (Apr 1968): 103. See Gerald Boychuk, *Patchwork of Purpose: The Development of Provincial Social Assistance Regimes in Canada* (Montreal: McGill-Queen's University Press, 1998).

73 Ibid., 106; Grace Aĭton, "The Selling of Paupers by Public Auction in Sussex Parish," *Collections of the New Brunswick Historical Society* 16 (1961): 93–110. In the nineteenth century, the poor law was not completely insensitive to local conditions. In 1837, an amendment was introduced so that Justices of the Peace in certain counties could exempt Acadians from the assessment, since they were "in the habit of supporting their own poor." Greenhous, "Paupers," 124; James A. Whalen, "Social Welfare in New Brunswick, 1784–1900," *Acadiensis* 2, no. 1 (Autumn 1972): 54; Judith Fingard, "The Relief of the Unemployed Poor in Saint John, Halifax and St John's, 1814–1860," *Acadiensis* 5, no. 1 (Autumn 1975): 32–55.

74 James Whalen, "Last Resort for the Poor: The Almshouse 1843–1900," *New Brunswick Reader,* 14 Sept 2002; Greenhous, "Paupers," 125; James M. Whalen, "The Nineteenth-Century Almshouse System in Saint John County," *Histoire sociale* 7 (Apr 1971): 5–27.

75 *27th National Conference of Charities and Correction, 1900,* 372. Report from New Brunswick; Whalen, "Almshouse System," 14.

76 Wendy Austin and Mary Ann Boyd, *Psychiatric & Mental Health Nursing for Canadian Practice* (Philadelphia: Lippincott Williams & Wilkins, 2010), 5–6.

77 William Bayard, *History of the General Public Hospital in the City of Saint John, N.B.* (Saint John, N. B.?: s.n, 1896).

78 Patricia Rooke and R.L. Schnell, "Guttersnipes and Charity Children: Nineteenth Century Child Rescue in the Atlantic Provinces," in *Studies in Childhood History: A Canadian Perspective,* ed. Rooke and Schnell (Calgary: Detselig, 1982). *Globe,* 15 Sept 1891; 4 Sept 1900. Fingard, "Paradoxes of Progress," 101–2. *Globe,* 18 Mar, 28 May 1887; 15 Jun 1897; 18 Aug 1893.

79 *Globe,* 1 Feb 1896; Greenhous, "Paupers," 108.

80 Whalen, "Social Welfare," 63; *Saint John Telegraph,* 2 Feb 1901, p. 5; *Globe,* 4 Mar 1899, "Editorial."

81 Cook, "Child Labour," 111. See also Eleanor J. Stebner, "More than Ma-
ternal Feminists and Good Samaritans: Women and the Social Gospel in
Canada," in *Women and the Social Gospel*, ed. Wendy J. Deichmann Edwards
and Carolyn De Swarte Gifford (Urbana: University of Illinois Press, 2003),
51–72; Anne B. Boylan, *The Origins of Women's Activism: New York and
Boston, 1797–1840* (Chapel Hill: The University of North Carolina Press,
2002); Lori Ginzberg, *Women and the Work of Benevolence: Morality, Politics
and Class in Nineteenth Century United States* (New Haven: Yale University Press, 1990); Nancy Hewitt, *Southern Discomfort: Women's Activism in
Tampa, Florida 1880s–1920s* (Urbana and Chicago: University of Illinois
Press, 2001); *Globe*, 11 Jan 1883, 3 Dec 1897, 3 Oct 1902.
82 Cook, "Child Labour," 100; *Globe*, 8 Aug 1894; Carol Lee Bacchi, *Liberation
Deferred? The Ideas of the English-Canadian Suffragists, 1877–1918* (Toronto:
University of Toronto Press, 1981).
83 Mrs (Julia) Drummond, "Co-operation as Shown in Associated Charities,"
*Women Workers of Canada. Being a report of the Proceedings of the First Annual
Meeting and Conference of the National Council of Women of Canada*, 1894, 57.
84 Mariana Valverde, *The Age of Light, Soap, and Water: Moral Reform in English
Canada, 1885–1925* (Toronto: University of Toronto Press, 2008), 19; Michael
J. D. Roberts, "Head versus Heart? Voluntary Associations and Charity
Organization in England c 1700–1850," in *Charity, Philanthropy and Reform
from the 1690s to 1850*, ed. Hugh Cunningham and Joanna Innes (London:
Macmillan Press, 1998).
85 Bernard Bosanquet, "The Duties of Citizenship," in *Aspects of the Social
Problem*, ed. Bernard Bosanquet (London: Macmillan, 1895), 10.
86 Helen R.Y. Reid, "The Problem of the Unemployed," Appendix, *Annual
Meeting and Conference of the National Council of Women of Canada*, 1898, 16,
18.
87 James Pitsula, "The Relief of Poverty in Toronto, 1880–1930" (PhD diss.,
York University, 1979), 125, 128, 208–9. Janice Harvey, "The Protestant Or-
phan Asylum and the Montreal Ladies' Benevolent Society: A Case Study
in Protestant Child Charity in Montreal" (PhD diss., McGill University,
2001), 302. Carrie M. Derick, "COS of Montreal (1919)," MLCW, P653 S2
SS3 D4, ANQM.
88 *National Bulletin of Charities and Correction*, Aug 1904, 101. This was one of
two Canadian reports.
89 *Globe*, 28 Oct 1902.
90 Ibid., 4, 11 Mar 1899.
91 Ibid., 16 Mar 1899. *National Bulletin of Charities and Correction*, Portland,
Oregon, 1905, 86. *Ibid.*, Minneapolis, MN, 1907, 576.

92 Ibid., Richmond, VA, 1908, 424.
93 *Globe*, 17 Jun 1899; *National Bulletin of Charities and Correction*, Aug 1904, 101.
94 *Globe*, 31 Dec 1900. During 1900–01, Associated Charities had a total of 487 applications, of whom 237 were provided with employment and 250 with relief. A total of forty-five were deemed to be fraudulent requests for assistance, with this number being broken down to twelve tramps and thirty-five already receiving aid from other sources. The numbers were virtually identical the following year. *Globe*, 30 Oct. 1901, 29 Oct 1902.
95 Frances L. Montgomery, "One of Our Pioneers: Jane B. Wisdom, 1884–1975," *Social Worker* (Fall 1975): 130; *Daily Telegraph*, 30 Dec 1908; *Educational Review* (Oct 1934): 7; *Saint John Sun*, 28 Nov 1906; Clarke, "Women's Enfranchisement Association," 78. There appears to have been an earlier day nursery at the Haven; *Globe*, 1 Nov 1893.
96 Clarke, "Women's Enfranchisement Association," 48, 94–95. Ian McKay, "The Truth about Freddy Goodspeed," Kingston Cultural Studies Working Group, 2003; *Globe*, 5 Sept 1902. Letter to editor from Clara B. Arthur, 9 Sept 1903; 8 Oct 1902.
97 *Globe*, 12 Apr 1899. *Globe*, 28 Jan 1903, 27 Apr 1903. Olding was also a prominent member of the Women's Christian Temperance Union and the Women's Enfranchisement Association until she left the city for marriage in 1903. Enid Johnson MacLeod, *Petticoat Doctors: The First Forty Years of Women in Medicine at Dalhousie University* (Lawrencetown Beach, NS, 1990), 16; Clarke, "Women's Enfranchisement Association.

Chapter Two

1 The bursary must have been partial, as there is a receipt for $55 dated 6 Oct 1899, paid by Katie Wisdom, Wisdom Papers; Annie McQueen Gordon to MBW, 8 Nov 1899, McQueen Collection.
2 Margaret Gillett, *We Walked Very Warily: A History of Women at McGill* (Montreal: Eden Press, 1981), 168.
3 Ibid., 164.
4 *McGill Outlook*, 13 Oct 1903.
5 Hilda D. Oakeley, *My Adventures in Education* (London: Williams and Norgate, 1939), 76, 115–17. In 1920, when Wisdom travelled to England, she saw Eleanor Rathborne speak in Oxford on "National Family Endowment." Flyleaf, 8 Sept 1920, JBW Papers. See also Susan Pedersen, *Eleanor Rathbone and the Politics of Conscience* (New Haven: Yale, 2004). Oakeley to JBW, Dec 1931; 23 Oct 1939, Wisdom Papers.

6 Gillett, *We Walked Very Warily*, 174. The *McGill University Calendar* for 1903–04 estimated that a room with board cost around $16 to $25 a month. In addition, arts students paid $61 per year with an additional $4 library fee. *McGill University Annual Calendar*, 1903–04, 7–8, 28.

7 Clipping, Oakeley, "Higher Education for Women," *Canadian Magazine*, 6, Wisdom Papers.

8 *McGill Outlook*, 10 Feb 1903, p. 342; 24 Feb 1903, p. 421; *Old McGill* 1904; *St John Daily Sun*, 11 Jan 1901; *McGill Outlook*, 11 Jan 1902.

9 "Prof C H McLeod McGill University Has Passed Away," *Montreal Daily Star*, 27 Dec 1917, p. 2; *McGill Outlook* Convocation Number, 1903.

10 KFW to JBW, 3 Mar 1900, KFW to JBW, 20 Oct 1900, KFW to JBW, 24 Jan 1902, KFW to JBW, 19 Sept 1901, KFW to JBW, 20 Nov 1902, Wisdom Papers. Oakeley, *My Adventures in Education*, 80.

11 KFW to JBW, 15 Oct 1902; KFW to JBW, c. 1900; KFW to JBW, 18 Sept 1901, Wisdom Papers.

12 KFW to JBW, 26 Feb 1902, ibid.

13 KFW to JBW, 15 Mar 1902, ibid.; Ian Ross Robertson notes a similar phenomenon in his *Sir Andrew Macphail: The Life and Legacy of a Canadian Man of Letters* (Montreal: McGill-Queen's University Press, 2008).

14 KFW to JBW, 4 Nov 1902, Wisdom Papers.

15 Oakeley to MBW, 14 Sept 1903, ibid.

16 *McGill University Annual Calendar*, 1903–04, 7–8.

17 JBW to "Folks," 20 Sept 1903, Wisdom Papers.

18 *Old McGill '07*.

19 Oct 1905 notes, RVC Daybook, SCVF, MG 4014, c 1, f 2457, MUA; Marjory Lang, *Women Who Made the News: Female Journalists in Canada 1880–1945* (Montreal: McGill-Queen's University Press, 1999), 87. "McGill- Donaldas 1907," http://www.rootsweb.ancestry.com/~qcmtl-w/McGillDonaldas 1907.html, accessed 8 Nov 2013.

20 JBW to Mother and Father and Bessie, 11 Oct 1906, Wisdom Papers. There was at least one Chinese Canadian man enrolled at McGill during this period. In 1906, Peter Hing arrived from British Columbia to begin a double course in law and economics. "McGill Has Yellow Peril – Boy Says He's 'All White,'" *Herald*, 3 Mar 1908, p. 1.

21 JBW diary 12 Oct 1906, JBW Papers.

22 *Old McGill '07*; *McGill Outlook*, 8 Mar 1906, p. 391; 22 Mar 1906, p. 443; Diana Pederson, "'Keeping Our Good Girls Good:' The YWCA and the 'Girl Problem' 1870–1939," *Canadian Women's Studies* 7, no. 4 (1986): 20–24; JBW Diary, 10 Oct 1906, JBW Papers.

23 *McGill Outlook*, 19 Jan 1904, p. 269; 25 Feb 1904, p. 382; 1 Dec 1904, p. 196.

24 Jennie Barnes Wisdom McGill University transcript, MUA.
25 JBW to Charlotte Whitton, 18 Apr 1931. CCSD, MG 28 I 10, vol. 30, 150 Recruitment & Training CASW 1929–31, LAC.
26 Stephen Leacock to JBW, n.d., Wisdom Papers.
27 H. Carl Goldenberg, "Joseph Clarence Hemmeon, 1879–1963," *Canadian Journal of Economics and Political Science* 30, no. 4 (Nov 1964): 595–96; Frank Milligan, *Eugene Forsey: An Intellectual Biography* (Calgary: Calgary University Press, 2004), 45.
28 "Jane B. Wisdom," *Social Welfare Pioneers of Nova Scotia* (Halifax: Minister of Public Welfare, 1979), 10; Anna Hendsbee, "Miss Jane Wisdom One of Canada's Pioneers in Social Welfare Movement," *New Glasgow Evening News*, 10 Jun 1964, p. 11.
29 17 Feb 1906. RVC Daybook, SCVF; JBW to unknown, 23 Oct 1907, Wisdom Papers.
30 *McGill Outlook*, 24 Nov 1903, p. 175.
31 *St John Daily Sun*, 26 Apr 1906; *McGill Outlook*, Mar 1905.
32 JBW to Mother and Father and Bessie, 11 Oct 1906, Wisdom Papers; 28 Mar 1906; Apr 1906, RVC Daybook, 1905–07, SCVF. Harriet Archibald was the widow of Henry Archibald of the firm Frothingham and Workman.
33 Apr 1906, RVC Daybook, SCVF; Oakeley to JBW, 7 Sept 1907, Wisdom Papers.
34 *Charities*, 16 Jun 1900; Annie Marion MacLean, *Wage Earning Women*, intro. Grace H. Dodge (New York: MacMillan, 1910); Steven Diner, "Department and Discipline: The Department of Sociology at the University of Chicago, 1892–1920," *Minerva* 13 (Winter 1975): 514–51; Anne Marion MacLean, "Nova Scotia's Crusade Against Tuberculosis," *Charities*, 6 May 1905. Tiffany Loiselle and Suzanne Morton, "Annie Marion MacLean," *Dictionary of Canadian Biography*, forthcoming; Tim Hallett and Greg Jeffers, "A Long-Neglected Mother of Contemporary Ethnography: Annie Marion MacLean and the Memory of a Method," *Journal of Contemporary Ethnography* 37, no. 1 (Feb 2008): 3–37. Mary Jo Deegan, Michael R. Hill, and Susan L. Wortmann, "Annie Marion MacLean, Feminist Pragmatist and Methodologist," *Journal of Contemporary Ethnography* 38, no. 6 (Dec 2009): 655–65.
35 *Globe*, 29 Apr 1899; Gillette, *We Walked Very Warily*, 99, 176, 183.
36 Oakeley to MBW, 3 Jan 1904, Wisdom Papers.
37 Oct 1905 notes, RVC Daybook, SCVF.
38 RVC Daybook 1906–07, ibid.
39 Index to Saint John Burial Permits, 13 Nov 1906, RS315A, I vol. 15, 933, F20751, PANB; *Saint John Sun*, 15, 16, 19 Nov 1906.
40 *McGill Outlook*, 29 Nov 1906, 203; Xmas 1906.

41 A.B. McKillop, *A Disciplined Intelligence: Critical Inquiry and Canadian Thought in the Victorian Era* (Montreal: McGill-Queen's University Press, 1979); Sara Burke, *Seeking the Highest Good: Social Service and Gender at the University of Toronto, 1888–1937* (Toronto: University of Toronto Press, 1996); Christie and Gauvreau, *A Full Orbed Christianity*; Barry Ferguson, *Remaking Liberalism: The Intellectual Legacy of Adam Shortt, O. D. Skelton, W.C. Lark, and W. A. Mackintosh, 1890–1925* (Montreal: McGill-Queen's University Press, 1993); Ken Moffatt and Allan Irving, "'Living for the Brethren': Idealism, Social Work's Lost Enlightenment Strain," *British Journal of Social Work* 32, no. 4 (Jun 2002): 415–27.

42 Pedersen, *Rathbone*, 48.

43 Priscilla Murolo, *The Common Ground of Womanhood: Class, Gender, and Working Girls' Clubs, 1884–1928* (Urbana: University of Illinois Press, 1998).

44 *AR* 1895–96, *AR*s of the Alumnae Society, 1895–1903, Alumnae Society, RG 76, c 88, f 79, MUA.

45 Historical and Biographical Notes, Alumnae Society, RG 76, c 88, f 76, MUA.

46 17 Dec 1901, 30 Jan 1902, Minutes of Alumnae Society, 17 Jan 1901 to 4 May 1911, Alumnae Society, RG 76, c 88, f 81, MUA.

47 Patricia T. Rooke and R.L. Schnell, *Discarding the Asylum: From Child Rescue to the Welfare State in English-Canada (1800–1950)* (Lanham, MD: University Press of America, 1983), 59, 63, especially chapter three.

48 JBW Recollections, 11 Jul 1964, JBW Papers.

49 Jan 1905 annual meeting; Special Meeting 26 Jan 1905, Minutes of Alumnae Society, 17 Jan 1901 to 4 May 1911.

50 "University Settlement," *McGill News*, Dec 1919, p. 12.

51 26 Nov 1908, Minutes of Alumnae Society, 17 Jan 1901 to 4 May 1911, Annual Meeting.

52 25 Feb 1909. Ibid. Elizabeth Hall should not be confused with Isabella (Bella) Elizabeth Hall, who later took over as headworker. Bella Hall was associated with J.S. Woodsworth in Winnipeg and came to Montreal in 1914 with his recommendation after a course in social service at the University of Toronto. She left the settlement movement in the early 1920s to pursue radical politics. Catherine Vance, *Not by Gods but by People: The Story of Bella Hall Gauld* (Toronto: Progress Books, 1968).

53 12 Oct 1909, 11 Nov 1909, Minutes of Alumnae Society, 17 Jan 1901 to 4 May 1911.

54 3 Dec 1909, ibid. The first settlement house in Toronto, Evangelia House, was established in 1902 for girls but expanded to serve the community in 1904. There are important parallels between the McGill alumnae and the

alumnae of St. Hilda's College in Toronto. See Cathy James, "A Passion for Service: Edith Elwood and the Social Character of Reform," in *Women Teaching, Women Learning: Historical Perspectives*, ed. Elizabeth M. Smyth and Paula Bourne (Toronto: Inanna, 2006), 105–30. Also her "Reforming Reform: Toronto's Settlement Movement, 1900–1920," *Canadian Historical Review* 82, no. 1 (Mar 2001): 55–90.

55 "Miss Sadie American – NY Settlement Worker, Addressed a Large Audience at RVC," *Gazette*, 9 Feb 1910; RVC Daybook, 1908–1910, SCVF. Elisabeth Israels Perry, *Belle Moskowitz: Feminine Politics and the Exercise of Power in the Age of Alfred E. Smith* (New York: Oxford University Press, 1987), 28–34.

56 Clipping, *Gazette*, 16 Nov 1907. RVC Daybook, 1907, SCVF.

57 Lorna Hurl, "Building a Profession: The Origins of the Dept of Social Service in the University of Toronto, 1914–1928," *Toronto Working Papers on Social Welfare in Canada*, 11 (1983): 24; "Prof JA Dale Leaves McGill," *McGill News*, Sept 1920, p. 26; Alfred Gordon, "James Alfred Dale," *Canadian Bookman*, 1 Dec 1920; *Star Weekly*, 12 Jan 1921, p. 53; *Globe*, 18 Feb 1920; Sir Michael Sadler, "JA Dale – A Character Sketch," 4 Apr 1923, Staff clipping file, James Alfred Dale 1874–1951; Department of Graduate Records, box 77, f 24, UTA; Mary Jennison, "Canadian Settlement Movement" (unpublished paper, undated), 22; *McGill News*, Sept 1920, p. 26. "James Alfred Dale," in William H. Atherton, *Montreal from 1535 to 1914 Biographical*, Vol. III (Montreal: S. J. Clarke, 1914), 350–2.

58 Clipping, *Gazette* 15 Dec [1909?]. RVC Daybook, 1910, SCVF.

59 The Kathleen Club, named after Mrs. Wright, née Miss Kathleen Finley. *Alumnae News* Reports 1910; Alumnae Society, RG 76, c 88, f 81, MUA; JBW Diary, hand-corrected article, Hensbee, "Miss Jane Wisdom," JBW Papers.

60 *Alumnae News* 1916, Alumnae Society, RG 76, c 88, f 81, MUA; Elisabeth Williams Anthony, Radcliffe College Alumnae Information 1940, Radcliffe College Archives.

61 For example, Miss Latham of the Woman's University Settlement, Southwark London, England, spoke in May 1912, Rev. Gaylord White of the Union Settlement NYC spoke in May 1913, Norman J. Ware of the University of Toronto Settlement spoke in Dec 1913, and Dr. John L. Elliot of the Hudson Guild NYC spoke in Jan 1915. 29 May 1912; Card Annual Meeting of University Settlement Semi-Annual Meeting of University Settlement, 1 Dec 1913; Semi-Annual Meeting notice 15 Jan 1915. RVC Daybook, 1912, 1913, 1915, SCVF. The publication of Addams's *Twenty Years at Hull-House* (1910) had a local audience. Philanthropist Elsie Meighen Reford read the book in Jul–Aug 1911. Karine Hébert, "Elsie Reford, une bourgeoise montréalaise et métissienne. Un exemple de spatialisation des spheres privée

et publique," *Revue d'histoire de l'Amérique Française* 63, nos. 2–3 (Autumn 2010): 282, fn 23.

62 "University Settlement," *McGill News*, Dec 1919, p.13.

63 Notation on Card, Annual Meeting of the University Settlement, 29 May 1912, RVC Daybook 1910–12, SCVF.

64 "McGill Settlement Club Organized," *Herald*, 16 Apr 1910, p. 14.

65 Speakers included James A. Dale, Rufus D. Smith, Charles K. Calhouse, Margaret Tree, Elizabeth Helm, and Rev. C. S. Laidman. Jennison, *Canadian Settlement Movement*, 76. In addition, a group of young women volunteers associated with the settlement provided the impetus for the establishment of the Montreal Junior League. Elise Chenier, "Class, Gender, and the Social Standard: The Montreal Junior League, 1912–1939," *Canadian Historical Review* 90, no. 4 (Dec 2009): 671–710.

66 "Many Problems Are Settled Now by Settlements," *Star*, 1 Feb 1913; J.A. Dale, "University Settlement Gets Its Own Building," *Witness*, 1 Feb 1913; Housewarming Invitation, 8 Mar 1913. RVC Daybook 1913, SCVF; Minutes, 26 Nov 1908, 23 Feb 1910, Minutes of Alumnae Society, 17 Jan 1901 to 4 May 1911.

67 "University Settlement, Where Real Christian Work Is Done," *Herald*, 20 Sept 1912; *Alumnae News* Reports 1916, Alumnae Society, RG 76 c 88, f 81, MUA; "University Settlement," *McGill News*, Dec 1919, p. 13.

68 Note, 5, 15, 18, 25 Jan 1914, RVC Daybook, 1914, SCVF. Less than five months later, Elizabeth Helm, with no current position, appeared at social workers' meetings in New York City. *Fourth New York Conference of Charities and Correction Proceedings* (New York, 1914).

69 "The Helpful Spirit Is Dominant Note of Work at Iverley Settlement," *Standard*, 9 Nov 1912, p. 21.

70 *Handbook of Catholic Charitable and Social Works in Montreal* (Catholic Social Study Guild, 1911), 58. "Iverley" was the name of Mrs. Wotherspoon's family estate in Ireland. Jennison, *Canadian Settlement Movement*, 142.

71 "Presbyterians Will Establish New Settlement," *Montreal Daily Witness*, 11 Sept 1912, p. 5.

72 "Social Work for Students," *Montreal Daily Witness*, 12 Sept 1912, p. 7.

73 *AR* Chalmers House 1912–1913.

74 Ibid.; *Presbyterian Witness*, 1 Jul 1916, 1984 6001 box 7 f 7, PCCA.

75 *AR* Chalmers House 1923, 1984 6001 box 7 f 7, PCCA; Beatrice Brigden, "One Woman's Campaign for Social Purity and Social Reform," in *The Social Gospel in Canada: Papers of the Interdisciplinary Conference on the Social Gospel in Canada, Mar 21–24, 1973 at the University of Regina*, ed. Richard Allen (Ottawa: National Museum of Man Mercury Series, 9, 1975), 105.

76 In 1913, Sara Libby Carson was still listed as supervisor but the settlement had a constant turnover of staff. *AR* Chalmers House 1912–13, 1984 6001 box 7 f 7, PCCA; Brigden, "One Woman's Campaign," 103, 112; Rooke and Schnell, *No Bleeding Heart*, 30. Parker, "Origins and Early History," 42.

77 Jennison, *Canadian Settlement Movement*, 151.

78 Ruth Rosen, ed., *The Maimie Papers* (New York: Feminist Press, 1977), 316–74, 379–411.

79 Jennison, *Canadian Settlement Movement*, 192–95, 142–48.

80 "Social Work for Students," *Montreal Daily Witness*, 12 Sept 1912, p. 7.

Chapter Three

1   Atherton, *Montreal*, 667, 669.

2   Hugh Pedley, *Looking Forward: The Strange Experience of the Rev. Fergus Mc-Cheyne* (Toronto, 1913), 137–38.

3   Rosalyn Trigger, "God's Mobile Mansions: Protestant Church Relocation and Extension in Montreal, 1850–1914" (PhD diss., McGill University, 2004). See Valverde, *Age of Light, Soap and Water*, as an example where Toronto stands in for English Canada.

4   Muriel H. Douglas, "A History of the Society for the Protection of Women and Children in Montreal from 1882–1966" (master's research report, McGill University), 7.

5   Atherton, *Montreal*, 477.

6   BBW to JBW, 1 Mar 1908, Wisdom Papers; Margaret Gillett, *Traf: A History of Trafalgar School for Girls* (Montreal: Trafalgar, 2000).

7   Hendsbee, "Miss Jane Wisdom," 11.

8   "Jane B. Wisdom," *Social Welfare Pioneers*; "A Salutation To JBW FROM FLM," 3.

9   *Saint John Sun*, 24 Dec 1908, p. 7; *Alumnae News* 1910.

10 Oakeley, *My Adventures in Education*, 107.

11 Ralph Ormsby, *A Man of Vision: Francis H. McLean, 1869–1945* (New York: Family Service Association of America, 1969), 21; Francis H. McLean, "Effects upon Private Charity of the Absence of All Public Relief," *28th National Conference of Charities and Correction*, Washington, DC, 1901, 143.

12 Atherton, *Montreal*, 373; Denise Helly, *Les Chinois à Montréal, 1877–1951* (Quebec: Institut québécois de recherche sur la culture, 1987); Eric Vallaincourt, "La société de Saint-Vincent de Paul de Montréal: Reflect du dynamisme du laicat catholique en matiere d'assistance aux pauvre (1848–1933)" (PhD diss., Université du Québec à Montréal, 2005).

13 See, for example, "Charity Ball Great Social Event," *Herald*, 24 Jan 1908, p. 5.

14 Atherton, *Montreal*, 670.

15 Susan Traverso, *Welfare Politics in Boston, 1910–1949* (Amherst: University of Massachusetts Press, 2003), 4.

16 *Handbook of Catholic Charitable and Social Works in Montreal* (Montreal: n.d.), Catholic Social Study Guild, 12, 16.

17 *Catholic Charitable and Social Works*, 2–11, 17–19, 27, 57–58; Atherton, *Montreal*, 470, 523.

18 Hélène Pelletier-Baillargeon, *Marie-Gérin-Lajoie: De mère en fille, la cause des femmes* (Montreal: Boréal, 1985), 79; Fernand Hébert, "La philanthropie et la violence maritale: le cas de la Montreal Society for the Protection of Women and Children et de la Women's Christian Temperance Union" (master's thesis, Université du Québec à Montréal, 1999), 94; Atherton, *Montreal*, 470.

19 Tamara Myers, "On Probation: The Rise and Fall of Jewish Women's Antidelinquency Work in Interwar Montreal," in *Negotiating Identities in 19th- and 20th-Century Montreal*, ed. Bettina Bradbury and Tamara Myers (Vancouver: University of British Columbia Press, 2005), 180–81.

20 *Catholic Charitable and Social Works*, 6–66; Douglas, "History of the Society for the Protection," 27. See also "Youth and Crime," *Gazette*, 22 Oct 1907, p. 7; Atherton, *Montreal*, 483–84. See Tamara Myers, *Caught: Montreal's Modern Girls and the Law, 1869–1945* (Toronto: University of Toronto Press, 2006), 29.

21 Douglas, "History of the Society for the Protection," 28, 31.

22 15 Dec 1915, Ethel Bird's corr, BCA; Paul U. Kellogg, "A Canadian City in War Time; The Patriotic Fund and the Women of Montreal," *Survey* (17 Mar 1917): 683; Helen R.Y. Reid, *Social Service and Hospital Efficiency*, issued by the COS of Montreal, May 1913. She also had a national presence as a member on the Dominion Council of Health, the Repatriation Committee of Canadian Government, the Child Welfare Association of Canada, and Canadian Public Health Association. Awarded an honorary doctorate from both her alma mater and Queen's University, Reid was the first woman to serve on the McGill Board of Governors and was responsible for the establishment of both the social service department and the graduate nursing program. *Gazette*, 8 Jun 1921, Helen R.Y. Reid Papers, P141-A/1, McCord Museum Archives, *Who's Who in Canada* 1922, 1258; Desmond Morton, *Fight or Pay: Soldiers' Families in the Great War* (Vancouver: University of British Columbia Press, 2004), 66, 240.

23 *AR* 1900, 9, MLCW, *ARs* 1896–1902, P653, S3, SS1, D1 4-6a, ANQM; G.B. Clarke, text n.d., FWA, MG 4172, MUA; Derick, "COS." For Julia Drummond, see Elizabeth Kirkland, "Mothering Citizens: Elite Women in Montreal 1890–1914" (PhD diss., McGill University, 2011).

24 Derick, "COS," 2; Helen Reid as Recording Secretary submitted report, "Report of a Committee on Employment for the Poor." *AR* 1899, MLCW, *AR*s 1896–1902, P653, S3, SS1, D1, 4-6a, ANQM.

25 *AR* 1900, 9, ibid.; *Montreal Daily Star*, 13 Dec 1899, p. 3. The group included Marguerite Thibaudeau, George Hague of the Merchant's Bank (Royal Bank), Laurent-Olivier David, and a Dr. Reid; Clarke, text n.d., FWA.

26 "Death Removes Leading Citizen," *Montreal Gazette*, 2 Oct 1911, p. 5; Alan Hustak, *Sir William Hingston: Montreal Mayor, Surgeon and Banker* (Montreal: Price-Patterson, 2004); Atherton, *Montreal*, 374.

27 Clarke text n.d., FWA.

28 Mary Ellen Richmond, *Friendly Visiting among the Poor: A Handbook for Charity Workers* (New York: MacMillan, 1899), 7–8.

29 Lady Drummond, Foreword, COS *AR* 1919, quoted in W. Reginald Smith, "The FWA of Montreal" (term paper, Sir George Williams College, 1951), 8. J.W. Ross Papers, P217-C/5, McCord Museum Archives; Clarke text n.d., FWA.

30 *32nd National Conference of Charities and Correction*, 1905, 89.

31 Ormsby, *Man of Vision*, 21.

32 Case Logs 1901–32 FWA.

33 Marcela Aranguiz, *Vagabonds et Sans Abris à Montréal: Perception et Prise en Charge de L'errance, 1840–1925* (Montreal: Le Bulletin du Regroupement des chercheurs-chercheures en histoire des travailleurs et travailleuses, 2000); Montreal COS Card, FWA.

34 *27th National Conference of Charities and Correction*, 1900, 370; *29th National Conference of Charities and Correction*, 1902, 117; National Council of Women, *Women of Canada: Their Life and Work* (1900), 318; Quebec, *Sessional Papers*, 33, no. 1, "Estimates of the expenditures of Province of Quebec for year ending 30th Jun 1900," ii, 12.

35 William Shepherd, "Genesis of the MCSA" (master's thesis, McGill University, 1957), 37, 38–39; Montreal, *AR* of the Municipal Assistance Department 1911, 42; *Catholic Charitable and Social Works*, 13–14.

36 "Put $5 into Poor Box and Thought Taxes Were Paid," *Herald*, 20 Feb 1908, p. 1.

37 Shepherd, "Genesis," 44; Rufus Smith to William Van Horne, 18 Nov 1913, copy of letter dated 8 Nov 1913 to Sir Lomer Gouin, Premier, William Van Horne Papers, The COS of Montreal, 1910–1915, MG 29 A60, vol. 70, LAC.

38 *AR of Diet Dispensary*, 1890, 1894, 1897, 1898, and 1899. *AR of Old Brewery Mission* 1903, 17; 1906–07, 27.

39 Marshall to Grandma, 26 Dec 1911, MLFP, MG 1, vol. 3349.1, NSA; "Social and Personal," *Herald*, 14 Sept 1912, p. 22; Trigger, "God's Mobile Mansions."

40 Notes, 11 Jul 1964, JBW Papers; Canada Census, 1911 manuscript, Hochel-
    aga Westmount District 47, page 2, line 13.
41 Joyce P. Davis, "Francis H. McLean," in *Biographical Dictionary of Social
    Welfare in America*, ed. Walter I. Trattner (Westport, CT: Greenwood Press,
    1986), 534–37; Ormsby, *Man of Vision*, 15.
42 Ormsby, *Man of Vision*, 27.
43 Montreal COS *AR* 1914, 13; Smith, "The FWA of Montreal," 8; Ormsby,
    Man of Vision, 22.
44 Shepherd, "Genesis," 12. See also "Division of Work between Public and
    Private Charities," *Charities* (1 Jun 1901): 471.
45 Ormsby, *Man of Vision*, 24.
46 Richmond, *Friendly Visiting*, 180.
47 "Mr Richard H Lane Charities Officer Dies in Sanatorium," *Star*, 5 Dec
    1910, p. 4. "Members and Their Special Studies," *Charities* (6 Jul 1901): 11;
    J.J. Kelso, "The 7th Canadian Conference of Charities and Correction,"
    Charities (22 Oct 1904): 93.
48 Kelso, "The Canadian Conference of Charities," *Charities* (10 Oct 1903):
    327; "Poor Helped by Mr Lane Mourn at His Funeral," *Daily Star*, 7 Dec
    1910, p. 3.
49 "Work for Charity Organization," *Herald*, 27 Jan 1909, p. 7.
50 Rufus D. Smith, Cornell University Archives; "Rufus D Smith Finally in
    Montreal," *Survey* (20 May 1911): 320.
51 "Personals," *Survey* (3 Jan 1920): 374; Robert Cloutman Dexter, Brown
    University Archives. Before coming to Montreal, he was a district secretary
    in Providence, RI, and a special agent for the Massachusetts Society for the
    Prevention of Cruelty to Children. He subsequently taught sociology at
    Skidmore College and later took a prominent role in developing refugee
    and humanitarian programs with the Unitarian Service Committee.
52 The Appointment Bureau of Radcliffe College. Elisabeth Williams An-
    thony, 22 Jan 1931, Radcliffe College Archives.
53 Mary McDonald to Arthur Currie, 6 Feb 1922, OP, Social Service, RG 2 box
    677 f 1058, MUA.
54 "This Family at Last Finds Temporary Shelter after Month on Street," *Her-
    ald*, 4 Jun 1909, p. 1; Ruth Cameron, "'Scientific Charity' that Sometimes
    Misses Fire," *Herald*, 31 May 1909, p. 9.
55 "Family at Last Finds Temporary Shelter after Month on Street."
56 "Tuberculosis Show Should Interest," *Herald*, 29 Feb 1908, p. 2; Valerie
    Minnett, "Inside and Outside: Pathology, Architecture and the Domestic
    Environment at the Montreal Tuberculosis Exhibition, 1908" (master's the-
    sis, McGill University, 2004), 36. Valerie Minnett, "Disease and Domesticity

on Display: The Montreal Tuberculosis Exhibition, 1908," *Canadian Bulletin of Medical History* 23, no. 2 (2006): 381–400.

57 "Prof JA Dale Leaves McGill," p. 26; "Working towards a Cleaner City," *Herald*, 29 Mar 1909, p. 5; "Child Welfare Exhibition Open," *Gazette*, 9 Oct 1912, p. 5; "Welfare Exhibit Inaugural Draws Large Gathering," *Herald*, 10 Oct 1912, p. 5.

58 "Child Welfare Exhibition Is Planned for 1912," *Herald*, 26 Apr 1911, p. 4; "Child Welfare Exhibit," *Herald*, 22 Oct 1912, p. 3; "Le bien-être de enfance," *Le Devoir*, 4 Oct 1912, p. 6.

59 "Child Welfare Exhibit in French and English," *Survey* (22 Jul 1911): 595; "Charts to Show Where Deaths Hit City Babies Most," *Herald*, 4 Sept 1912, p. 5; "To Save the Little Lives," *Herald*, 7 Sept 1912, p. 15; Anna Louise Strong and Rufus D. Smith, "Beneath the Surface in Montreal," *Survey* (16 Nov 1912): 195–98; "Flashlight Photograph Taken at the Child Welfare Exhibition, Montreal, Showing the Enormous Crowds that Visited the Exhibition," *Standard*, 26 Oct 1912, illustrated supplement, p. 3.

60 "Woman Faints Seeing Squalid Home Shown at Welfare Exhibit," *Herald*, 9 Oct 1912, p. 2.

61 "The Gist of It," *Survey* (1 Feb 1924): 431; Tracy B. Strong and Helene Keysaar, *Right in Her Soul: The Life of Anna Louise Strong* (New York: Random, 1983), 52.

62 "Furnishing a Home for $100," *Herald*, 16 Oct 1912, p. 3; "Welfare Show Is Over but Screens Will Be Preserved," *Herald*, 22 Oct 1912, p. 5; "Child Welfare Exhibition Over," *Gazette*, 23 Oct 1912, p. 2; "Soothing Syrup Firm Threatens Welfare Exhibit," *Herald*, 8 Oct 1912, p. 1; "Hebrew Day Was big Success for the Exhibition," *Herald*, 14 Oct 1912, p. 7.

63 "Canadian Conference Marks New Advance," *Survey* (28 Oct 1911): 1079; *13th Canadian Conference of Charities and Correction*, Montreal, Wed, 19 Oct 1912; "Kier Hardie Visitor to CWE," *Herald*, 21 Oct 1912, p. 5.

64 Minutes, Regular Exec meeting, 17 Dec 1913, MLCW, MG 28 I 64, vol. 2, 424, ANQM; 1913–14 3rd *AR of American Association of Societies for Organizing Charity*; 1914–15 4th *AR of American Association of Societies for Organizing Charity*; 1915–16 5th *AR of American Association of Societies for Organizing Charity*; 1916–17 *AR of American Association of Societies for Organizing Charity*; 1917–18 *AR of American Association of Societies for Organizing Charity*.

65 *13th Canadian Conference of Charities and Correction*.

66 "Friend of Poor Gone," *Witness*, 6 Dec 1910, p. 3.

67 "The Charity Organization," *Star*, 28 Dec 1910, p. 10.

68 Marshall to Grandma, 26 Dec 1911, MLFP, MG 1, vol. 3349.1, NSA. The engagement of Katherine Wisdom and Harry Williams was announced in

the *Montreal Star* in 1904 but the paper was forced to retract it as incorrect. *St. John Daily Sun*, 4 Apr 1904.

69 JBW Diary, JBW Papers. For Dunham Ladies' College, see Marie-Ève Harbec, "The Ideal Education to Construct an Ideal World: The Dunham Ladies' College and the Anglican Elite of the Montreal Diocese, 1860–1913," in *Negotiating Identities*, 149–74.

70 JBW to MBW, 4 Jul 1910; notes 11 Jul 1964, JBW Papers.

71 JBW to F.W. Wisdom, Night Lettergram, 27 Nov 1912. JBW Papers.

Chapter Four

1 Linda Gordon, *Pitied But Not Entitled: Single Mothers and the History of Welfare 1890–1935* (New York: Free Press, 1994), 73.

2 Hendsbee, "Miss Jane Wisdom," 11; Jennissen and Lundy, *One Hundred Years of Social Work*, 22.

3 Betsy Beattie, in her study of Maritime women living in Boston, identified eight English-Canadian women working as social workers in that city in 1910. Betsy Beattie, *Obligation and Opportunity: Single Maritime Women in Boston, 1870–1930* (Montreal: McGill-Queen's University Press, 2000), 134; Alice Vincent Massey, *Occupations for Trained Women in Canada* (London & Toronto: J M Dent, 1920), 69.

4 Kathryn McPherson, *Bedside Matters: The Transformation of Canadian Nursing, 1900–1990* (Toronto: Oxford University Press, 1996), 31, 39; *Report of the Protestant School Commission* (1 Oct 1909 to 30 Sept 1910), 19–20; Minutes, 9 Dec 1909, 16, Protestant Board School Commission, S-0124, English Montreal School Board Archives.

5 Exec Minutes, 9 Dec 1912, BBC.

6 Daniel Walkowitz, *Working with Class: Social Workers and the Politics of Middle Class Identity* (Chapel Hill: University of North Carolina, 1997), 27, 28.

7 Ibid., 7.

8 Christie and Gauvreau, *A Full-Orbed Christianity*, 158.

9 Dawn Greeley, "Beyond Benevolence: Gender, Class and the Development of Scientific Charity in New York City, 1882–1935" (PhD diss., State University of New York at Stonybrook, 1995), 294, 317, 344–49.

10 Linda Shoemaker, "Charity and Justice: Gender and the Mission of Social Work: Social Work Education in Boston, New York and Chicago, 1898–1930" (PhD diss., State University of New York at Binghamton, 2001), 83.

11 Shelton Stromquist, *Re-inventing "The People": The Progressive Movement, the Class Problem, and the Origins of Modern Liberalism* (Urbana/Champagne: University of Illinois Press, 2006), viii, 3, 4; Perry, *Belle Moskowitz*, 45.

12 Walkowitz, *Working with Class*, 27; Elizabeth N. Agnew, "Charity, Friendly Visiting, and Social Work: Mary E. Richmond and the Shaping of an American Profession" (PhD diss., Indiana University, 1999), 210.

13 Abraham Flexner, "Is Social Work a Profession?" *Studies in Social Work* 4 (New York: New York School of Philanthropy, n.d.); Walkowitz, *Working with Class*, 28–29.

14 Regina Kunzel, *Fallen Women, Problem Girls: Unmarried Mothers and the Professionalization of Social Work, 1890–1945* (New Haven: Yale University Press, 1993), 6; Linda Gordon, *Heroes of Their Own Lives: The Politics and History of Family Violence* (New York: Penguin, 1998), 298.

15 Peter Novick, *The Noble Dream: The "Objectivity Question" and the American Historical Profession* (Cambridge: Cambridge University Press, 1988), 90.

16 Mary Richmond, *Social Diagnosis* (New York: Russell Sage Foundation, 1917), 49, 57, 53, 72–73; Charles V. Langlois and Charles Seignobos, *Introduction to the Study of History*, trans. G. G. Berry (London: Duckworth, 1898).

17 Bonnie G. Smith, *The Gender of History: Men, Women, and Historical Practice* (Cambridge, MA: Harvard University Press, 2000).

18 Alice O'Connor, *Poverty Knowledge: Social Science, Social Policy and the Pool in Twentieth-Century U.S. History* (Princeton: Princeton University Press, 2001), 40; *Survey* (12 Jul 1913): 506; "Miss M Byington, A Social Worker," *New York Times*, 19 Aug 1952, p. 23.

19 Jean Bethke Elshtain, *Jane Addams and the Dream of American Democracy: A Life* (New York: Basic Books, 2001).

20 Agnew, "Charity, Friendly Visiting, and Social Work," 226; Ormsby, *Man of Vision*, 73–74.

21 *Charity Organization Bulletin* 1, no. 10 (Sept 1910): 85–86; 1, no. 7 (Jun 1910): 91.

22 Robert L. Barker, ed., *The Social Work Dictionary*, 5th edition (Washington, DC: National Association of Social Workers Press, 2003), 52. See also Beverly Stadum, *Poor Women and Their Families: Hard Working Charity Cases, 1900–1930* (Albany: State University of New York Press, 1992), 15.

23 JBW to MBW, 18 Jun 1910, JBW Papers.

24 *Charity Organization Bulletin* 1, no. 10 (Sept 1910): 91.

25 Montgomery, "One of Our Pioneers," 130; "A Quarter Century of Activities of the College Settlement," *Survey* (14 Nov 1914): 170; Robert Woods and Albert J. Kennedy, *Handbook of Settlements* (New York: Russell Sage Foundation, 1911), 193; Daphane Spain, *How Women Saved the City* (Minneapolis, MN: University of Minnesota Press, 2001), 264. See also Perry, *Belle Moskowitz*.

26 Annelise Orleck, *Common Sense and a Little Fire: Women and Working-Class Politics in the United States, 1900–1965* (Chapel Hill: University of North Carolina Press, 1995), 38, 40–42.

27 Earl F. Mulderink III, "Elizabeth Sprague Williams," in *Biographical Dictionary of Social Welfare in America*, ed. Walter I. Trattner (Westport, CT: Greenwood Press, 1986), 769–71.

28 JBW to MBW, 4 Jul 1910, JBW Papers.

29 Hendsbee, "Miss Jane Wisdom," 11.

30 Danyèle Lacombe, "Marie Gérin-Lajoie's Hidden Crucifixes: Social Catholicism, Feminism and Québec Modernity, 1910–1930" (master's thesis, University of Alberta, 1999), 40.

31 JBW to MBW, 18 Jun 1910, JBW Papers; 18 Oct 1910, Minutes, University Settlement, New York City, Series 2 Headworkers' Reports, Series Three, Mar 1911, Wisconsin Historical Society; Harry P. Kraus, "The Settlement House Movement in New York City, 1886–1914" (PhD diss., New York University, 1970), 113, 136; Cathy Leigh James, "Gender, Class and Ethnicity in the Organization of Neighbourhood and Nation: The Role of Toronto's Settlement Houses in the Formation of the Canadian State, 1902 to 1914" (PhD diss., University of Toronto, 1997), 1.

32 "Slavery of Slums Worse than That of Fifty Years Ago," *Herald*, 10 Mar 1911, p. 5; Currie to Wesley Frost, Consul General, 27 Aug 1931, OP, Subject Files, RG 2, c 93, f 2641, Social Work, 1926–1947, MUA; Christie and Gauvreau, *Full-Orbed*, 140.

33 C.C. Carstens, "A Study of the Child Welfare Division of the MCSA," Mar 1924. Reports, Students, Briefs & Surveys, 1924, MCSA, MG 2076, c 1, f 873, MUA. See also Tamara Hareven, "An Ambiguous Alliance: Some Aspects of American Influences on Canadian Social Welfare," *Histoire sociale* 1, no. 3 (Apr 1969): 82–98.

34 JBW to Aunt Jess, 5 Oct 1915, MLFP, MG 1, vol. 3349, NSA. It is strange that this settlement was in a well-to-do neighbourhood; generally, the purpose was to live among the poor where they actually resided. Its location related to the location of the church.

35 *New York Charities Directory* 1915, 193; *Brooklyn City Directory*, 1912.

36 David Von Drehle, *Triangle: The Fire that Changed America* (New York: Grove Press, 2003), 68–69; *4th NYC Conference of Charities and Correction Proceedings 1914*, 19 May United Charities Building (Brooklyn).

37 Robert Woods and Albert J. Kennedy, *Handbook of Settlements* (New York: Russell Sage Foundation, 1911), 186; Roscoe Brown, *Church of the Holy Trinity, Brooklyn Heights in the City of New York, 1847–1922* (New York: 1922), 34.

38 JBW to Aunt Jess, 5 Oct 1915; Bernard Scheiner, "Survey of the Bedford Branch of the Brooklyn Public Library with Particular Emphasis on its Youth Library," Columbia University, 1951.

39 *4th NYC Conference of Charities and Correction Proceedings*, 19 May 1914, United Charities Building (Brooklyn); JBW Diary. JBW Papers. Margaret Wherry, who had grown up next door to Wisdom's brother-in-law in Knowlton, moved to Montreal, where she took on the leadership to establish a Protestant home for working women in the city. During the interwar period, Wherry continued a public role as an active member of the MLCW and the suffrage movement. Wisdom met Wherry in September 1912 through Harry Stevens, and she saw her in New York in January 1913. Elizabeth Kirkland, "A Home Away from Home: Defining, Regulating, and Challenging Femininity at the Julia Drummond Residence in Montreal, 1920–1971," *Urban History Review* 34, no. 2 (Mar 2006): 1–17.

40 Minutes, 30 Oct 1912, Board of Directors and Exec Committee, BBC; Ellen J. Smith to JBW, 19 Nov 1912, JBW Papers.

41 Francis H. McLean, "What Will New York Do About Brooklyn?" *Survey* (23 Nov 1912): 247–48; "Our Brooklyn," http://www.bklynpubliclibrary. org/ourbrooklyn/williamsburg/, accessed 8 Nov 2013.

42 Betty Smith, *A Tree Grows in Brooklyn* (New York: Harpers, 1943).

43 Greeley, "Beyond Benevolence," 198; Olive and Ari Hoogenboom, "Alfred T. White: Settlement Worker and Housing Reformer," *Hayes Historical Journal* 9, no. 1 (Fall 1989): 5; New York, Commission on Relief for Widowed Mothers, *Report* (Albany: J.B. Lyon Co., 1914, reprinted Arno Press, 1974), 81–82, 139.

44 Alfred T. White (President BBC) to F. P. Hill, Librarian, 16 Feb 1909, 8 Feb 1909, Minutes, Board of Directors and Exec Committee, BBC.

45 *BBC, Year Ending 30 Apr 1910*, 2. At least one of the thirty-two district nurses who appeared in a 1915 photo was African-American. *BBC, Year Ending 30 Apr 1915*, 24.

46 *Charities and the Commons* (18 Jul 1908): 500. For a discussion of taking in laundry at home, see Stadum, *Poor Women*, 57–58.

47 Francis H. McLean, "William I. Nichols," *Survey* (23 Mar 1912): 1978–79; BBC, *AR 1912*, 6, 37–38.

48 New York, *Report*, 492–93.

49 *Charities and the Commons* (8 Jun 1912): 426; (7 Dec 1912): 273; (12 Jul 1913): 506.

50 Margaret F. Byington, paper before the American Academy of Political and Social Science, quoted in New York, *Report*, 124–25.

51 BBC, *AR 1913*, 7; Exec Committee, 25 Sept 1912, Minutes, BBC.

52 Board of Directors, 9 Nov 1914, Minutes, BBC.

53 Board of Directors and Exec Committee, 6 May 1909, 9 Nov 1914, Minutes, BBC; Margaret Byington to JBW, n.d., JBW Papers.

54 BBC, *AR 1914*, 32; Board of Directors, 8 Nov 1909, Minutes, BBC.

55 Board of Directors, 15 Mar 1912, 10 Mar 1913, 20 Oct 1913; 8 Feb 1915, Minutes, BBC.

56 Exec Committee, 9 Dec 1912, Minutes, BBC; 3rd NYC Conference of Charities and Correction *Proceedings* 1913; 4th NYC Conference of Charities and Correction *Proceedings* 1914; 5th NYC Conference of Charities and Correction *Proceedings* 1915; 6th NYC Conference of Charities and Correction *Proceedings* 1916.

57 Board of Directors, 8 Feb 1915, 18 Oct 1915, Minutes, BBC.

58 Exec Committee, 27 Dec 1912, Minutes, BBC.

59 BBC, *AR 1915*, 10, 13.

60 Exec Committee, 25 Nov 1914, 10 Dec 1914, 23 Dec 1914, Minutes, BBC; Board of Directors, 11 Jan 1915, Minutes, BBC.

61 BBC, *AR 1915*, 21–22.

62 JBW to Aunt Jess, 5 Oct 1915.

63 Karen Tice, *Tales of Wayward Girls and Immoral Women: Case Records and the Professionalization of Social Work* (Urbana: University of Illinois Press, 1998), 4; BBC, *AR 1914*, 80; *1915*, 68.

64 Mark Jackson, "Images of Deviance: Visual Representations of Mental Defectives in Early Twentieth-Century Medical Texts," *British Journal for the History of Science* 28, no. 3 (Sept 1995): 319–37; Beverly M. Bethune, "Things that Speak to the Eye: The Photographs of *Charities, 1897–1909*," *American Journalism* 11, no. 3 (Summer 1994): 204–18; James Opp, "Re-imaging the Moral Order of Urban Space: Religion and Photography in Winnipeg, 1900–1914," *Journal of the Canadian Historical Association* 13 (2002): 73–93. Maren Stange, "Jacob Riis and Urban Visual Culture: The Lantern Slide Exhibition as Entertainment and Ideology," *Journal of Urban History* 15, no. 3 (May 1989): 274–303.

65 Seth Koven, *Slumming: Sexual and Social Politics in Victorian London* (Princeton: Princeton University Press, 2004), 135–36.

66 BBC, *AR 1914*, 37; JBW to Aunt Jess, 5 Oct 1915; Board of Directors, 9 Nov 1914, Minutes, BBC.

67 New York, *Report*, 489–500.

68 Mary E. Shenstone, "The Neighborhood Idea and Brooklyn's Volunteer Service," *Charity Organization Bulletin* 2, no. 3 (Jan–Feb 1916): 27–32.

69 BBC, *AR 1914*, 38, 80; *1915*, 58.

70 Alan Gordon, "Ward Heelers and Honest Men: Urban Québécois Political Culture and the Montreal Reform of 1909," *Urban History Review* 23, no. 2 (Mar 1995): 20–32.

71 Gordon, *Pitied But Not Entitled*, 51; Greeley, "Beyond Benevolence," 58, 65.

72 Exec Committee, 10 Mar 1913, Minutes, BBC.

73 Board of Directors, 20 Oct 1913, Minutes, BBC; notes c. 1939, JBW Papers; Hendsbee, "Miss Jane Wisdom," 11.

74 Gordon, *Pitied But Not Entitled*, 61.

75 Traverso, *Welfare Politics in Boston*, 6, 14. This is debatable. In Smith's *A Tree Grows in Brooklyn*, the mother states she would kill herself and her children before accepting relief from the Catholic Charities (p. 273).

76 Gordon, *Pitied But Not Entitled*, 28.

77 Hendsbee, "Miss Jane Wisdom," 11; Memo Glace Bay, no name, 7 Apr 1948, Canadian Council on Social Development, Glace Bay Municipal Welfare Dept 1935–53, MG 28 I 10, vol. 237, 12, LAC.

78 Hendsbee, "Miss Jane Wisdom," 11.

79 Annual Meeting, 8 May 1916, Board of Directors, 9 Oct 1916, Minutes, BBC.

80 Interview Dr Patricia Tanabe with JBW, Sutherland's River, 14 May 1975, JBW Papers.

Chapter Five

1 Janet Guildford, "The End of the Poor Law: Public Welfare Reform in Nova Scotia before the Canada Assistance Plan," in *Mothers of the Municipality*, ed. Fingard and Guildford, 54.

2 Fred R. MacKinnon, "The Life and Times of Ernest H. Blois" (Halifax: Senior Citizens' Secretariat, 1992) http://www15.pair.com/buchanan/genes/docs/ernblois.htm, accessed 8 Nov 2013.

3 Ethel Bird corr, postmark 10 Jan 1916, BCA.

4 Report and Recommendation re: establishing a Children's Dept or Bureau, at Ottawa, 31 Jan 1914, 3. See also Reneé Lafferty, "'Modernity and the Denominational Imperative' The Children's Aid Society of Halifax, 1905–1925," *Journal of the Canadian Historical Association* (Toronto 2002): 95–118; Renée N. Lafferty, *The Guardianship of Best Interests. Institutional Care for the Children of the Poor in Halifax, 1850–1960* (Montreal & Kingston: McGill-Queen's University Press, 2013).

5 "Public Health in Halifax," *Survey* (25 Dec 1920): 446. Jane B. Wisdom, "Halifax and Public Health," *Social Welfare* (Jun 1920): 228–30; Fingard, *Dark Side of Life*, 119, 129, 130; Douglas, "History of the Society for the Protection," 7.

6 Hareven, "An Ambiguous Alliance."

7 Christina Simmons, "'Helping the Poorer Sisters'; Women of the Jost Mission, Halifax, 1905–1945," *Acadiensis* 14, no. 1 (Autumn 1984): 13.

8 Minutes, 23 Feb 1911, HLCW MG 20, vol. 535, 5, mfm 9596, NSA. For an overview of Halifax feminism, see E.R. Forbes, "Battles in Another War: Edith Archibald and the Halifax Feminist Movement," in *Challenging the Regional Stereotype: Essays on the 20th Century Maritimes* (Fredericton: Acadiensis Press, 1989), 67–89.

9 *National Bulletin of Charities and Correction*, Feb 1904; Aug 1910; Jul 1911, Registrar Student Enrollment. Chicago School of Civics and Philanthropy 1903–20, box 1 folder 11, University of Chicago Archives. His intimate exposure to professional social work makes his harsh criticism of the social work bureaucracy following the 1917 explosion all the more significant. Johnstone criticized the very objective of scientific charity when he wrote that efficiency, "embodied in expert investigations, card catalogues, involved indexes, multifarious office equipment, and what not, is often treated as a fetish. ... Sediment, the salt that preserves the humanness in social work, is squeezed out between the pages of the card catalogue; and the work often degenerates into a cold professionalism." Joseph Scanlon and Gillian Osborne, "More Source than Influence: Johnstone's Contribution to Prince's Dissertation," in *Ground Zero: A Reassessment of the 1917 Explosion in Halifax Harbour,* ed. Alan Ruffman and Colin D. Howell (Halifax: Nimbus, 1994), 79.

10 Andrew Nicholson, "Dreaming of 'the Perfect City': The Halifax Civic Improvement League 1905–1949" (master's thesis, Saint Mary's University, 2000), 25; Bird corr, 15 Dec 1915, BCA; Minutes, 23 Feb 1911, HLCW.

11 Nicholson, "Dreaming of 'the Perfect City,'" 2, 50. *Echo*, 17 Feb 1911; 9 Mar 1911. *Mail*, 17 Feb 1911. *Echo*, 24 Feb 1911. Civic Revival 1911, scrapbook, Harris Collection, MG 1 378, 5, NSA. Bureau of Social Service *AR* 1916–17, 9, Harris Collection MG 1 V 379, vol. 3, NSA.

12 Minutes, Feb 1912, 20 Jul 1911, HLCW; *Survey* (28 Oct 1911): 993.

13 Bureau of Social Service, *AR* 1916–17, 9, Harris Collection; City Council Minutes, 25 Sept 1914; clipping, *Chronicle*, 26 Sept 1914, Harris Papers, MG 1 358, vol. 1, NSA; E. Mackay, Greater Halifax Conference to D. Macgillivray 17 Oct 1914, North British Society, Accounts, Corr etc, 1913–16, MG 20, vol. 242, 71, NSA; 1915/16 *Fifth AR American Association of Societies for Organizing Charity*.

14 Minutes, 19 Aug 1915, HLCW, MG 20, vol. 353.6 mfm 9597, NSA; "Trained Social Worker Due in Halifax Tonight," *Echo*, 15 Dec 1915, p. 12; "Social Service Worker Now in Halifax," *Echo*, 16 Dec 1915, p. 2; Bureau of Social Service *AR* 1916–17, 9, Harris Collection.

15 Forbes, "Battles in Another War," 76.
16 Kellogg, "Canadian City in War Time," 677; Bird corr, 12 Dec 1915, BCA.
    See Morton, *Fight or Pay*; Desmond Morton, "Entente cordiale? La sec-
    tion montréalaise du fonds patriotique canadien, 1914–1923: la bénévolat
    de guerre à Montréal," *Revue d'histoire de l'Amérique française* 53, no. 2
    (Autumn 1999): 207–46.
17 Bureau of Social Service *AR* 1916–17, 9, Harris Collection.
18 Bird corr, 15 Dec 1915, 7 Feb 1916, BCA. She also commented on Miss
    A.T. Chisholm and Harriet Schon. Miss Chisholm was English and Catho-
    lic and "very old-fashioned" (Bird corr, 19 Dec 1915), while Schon was
    described as a New Yorker married to William Schon, proprietor of a large
    laundry, who was "supposed to be Austrian," with the clear undercurrent
    that she supposed them to be Jewish. They "certainly look Jewish despite
    the fact they attend the Church of England. Notwithstanding on initial
    meeting they were said to be charming people, very progressive and very
    broad minded" (Bird corr, 17 Dec 1915, postmark 7 Jan 1916, BCA). Sexton
    was a significant opponent to take on, as she was secure in status, both
    by her marriage to the principal of the Nova Scotia Technical College and
    by her leadership in the local reform community. She was another kind of
    outsider: a New Brunswicker with an American education. Her patriotic
    record with regard to fundraising and organizing for both the Red Cross
    and CPF raised her profile. After the outbreak of war, Sexton became one
    of the most visible local women in Halifax war work and, later, explosion
    relief. Lois K. Yorke, "Edna May Williston Best," *Dictionary of Canadian Bi-
    ography V. 15, 1921–1930*, ed. Ramsay Cook (Toronto: University of Toronto
    Press, 2006), 104–06.
19 Bird corr, 1 Jan 1916; 20 Jan 1916; postmark 10 Jan 1916, 10 Feb 1916; Min-
    utes, 17 Feb 1916, HLCW. With Sexton's absence from Halifax, the only ob-
    stacle to organization, according to Bird, was Ernest Blois. Blois continued
    to be unconvinced by the merits of organized charity, and proposed that
    the registration bureau be turned over to the Society for the Prevention of
    Cruelty and be incorporated as a Children's Aid Society. Bird corr, 10 Feb
    1916, BCA.
20 Bird corr, 22 Feb 1916, BCA; "Noted Social Worker Here for Series of Lec-
    tures," *Echo*, 22 Feb 1916, p. 5; "Miss Byington Opens Lectures," *Echo*, 24 Feb
    1916, p. 7; "Three Addresses Yesterday from Miss Byington," *Echo*, 26 Feb
    1918, p. 12; Bureau of Social Service *AR* 1916–17, 10, 11, Harris Collection;
    "Permanent Board for Service," *Echo*, 20 Mar 1916, p. 12.
21 "HR Silver Heads Bureau of Social Service," *Echo*, 29 Mar 1916, p. 3;
    Bureau of Social Service *AR* 1916–17, 12, Harris Collection.

22 *Halifax Herald*, 17 May 1916, p. 6; "Nova Scotian to Carry on Work of Social
Bureau," *Echo*, 16 May 1916, p. 1; "Miss Wisdom Here for Social Service
Work," *Echo*, 13 Jun 1916, p. 2.

23 Bird corr, 29 Dec 1915, BCA; Clipping, "Ethel Bird Dies: Name a Household Word in Halifax 47 Years Ago," *Mail Star*, 31 Jan 1962; "The Excellent
Work of Miss Bird," *Mail*, 10 Jan 1918, JBW Papers.

24 H.R. Silver to JBW, 3 May 1916; Harris to JBW, 11 May 1916, JBW Papers;
"Has Demonstrated the Need of Charities Bureau," *Echo*, 23 Jun 1916, p. 2.

25 Leonard F. Hatfield, *Sammy the Prince: The Story of Samuel Henry Prince: One
of Canada's Pioneering Sociologists* (Hantsport: Lancelot Press, 1990); "Miss
Wisdom Here for Social Service Work," *Echo*, 13 Jun 1916, p. 2.

26 See, for example, *St Matthew's Presbyterian Church Bulletin*, 8 Apr 1917, JBW
Papers.

27 Bureau of Social Service *AR* 1916–17, 12, Harris Collection; Observer,
"Social Workers and Their Part in the Rehabilitation of Halifax," *Morning
Chronicle*, 30 Mar 1918, p. 13, JBW Papers; Minutes, 4 Jul 1916, HLCW.

28 Bureau of Social Service, *AR* 1916–17, 16, Harris Collection. See also clipping,
"Is There Much Poverty in the City of Halifax?" n.d. Oct 1917, 8, JBW Papers.

29 Halifax Welfare Bureau (formerly Bureau of Social Service), *Third AR*,
1918–1919, 10.

30 Robert Wiebe, *The Search for Order* (New York: Hill and Wang, 1967), 166.

31 Minutes, 18 Oct 1917, HLCW.

32 Clippings, "Canada Should Have Uniform Health Laws," *Echo*, 5 Oct 1917,
JBW Papers; Jane B. Wisdom, "Some Reflections on the Recent Conference
in Ottawa on Canadian Social Work," *Alumnae News* (Dec 1917): 18–20.

33 Clippings, "Lieut. Governor Grant Presided at Annual Meeting of the
Halifax Welfare Bureau," 30 Oct 1919, JBW Papers.

34 Telephone conversation with Jean MacFadgen, Nanaimo, British Columbia, Dec 2005.

35 Russell R. Dynes and E.L. Quarantelli, "The Place of the Explosion in the
History of Disaster Research: The Work of Samuel H. Prince," in *Ground
Zero*, 55–67. See Michelle Hébert Boyd, *'Enriched by Catastrophe': Social Work
and Social Conflict after the Halifax Explosion* (Halifax: Fernwood, 2007).

36 30 Dec 1917, HRC, Massachusetts-Halifax Relief Commission, 1917–1918,
MG 36, Series C, vol. 113, NSA. See, for example, Rehabilitation Exec,
HRC, MG 36, Series C, 162.1, and 162.1bcd, NSA. There was also an overlap in personnel between these organizations. For example, John F. Moors,
president of Associated Charities of Boston, was officially in Halifax as
head of the American Red Cross unit. See "The Relief of Halifax," *Survey*
(15 Dec 1917): 305–7.

37 Chief of Staff to Charles Holt, 14 Jan 1918, Rehabilitation Exec, MG 36, Series C, 123.4b, NSA.

38 A Report of the Proceedings of the 1st Meeting of the Rehabilitation Committee, Thurs 13 Dec 1917, 5 p.m. in the Halifax Hotel, HRC, MG 36, Series C, 157.2, NSA; Samuel Prince, *Catastrophe and Social Change, Based on a Sociological Study of the Halifax Disaster* (New York: Columbia University Press, 1920), 83, 86, 94, 96, 97.

39 For an excellent account of the initial response, see Jacob Aaron Carliner Remes, "Cities of Comrades: Urban Disasters and the Formation of the North American Progressive State" (PhD diss., Duke University, 2010).

40 Interview with Archibald MacMechan, 7 Dec, 11 a.m., Halifax Disaster Relief Record Office, MG 1 2124, 3i, NSA.

41 Interview with MacMechan, Halifax Disaster Record Office, MG 1 2124, 337, NSA.

42 Report of the Dept of Material Relief and Applications, cited in Laura M. MacDonald, *Curse of the Narrows: The Halifax Explosion 1917* (Toronto: Harper Collins, 2005), 153. Interview with MacMechan, Halifax Disaster Record Office, MG 1 2124, 22, NSA; Mackay, *Simple Annals*, 189–90; Clipping, *Mail*, 30 Sept 1921, JBW Papers. Interview Kerry by MacFadgen, 1979.

43 Scrapbook, 20 Dec 1917, Commercial Club of Halifax, MG 20 71, NSA.

44 Prince, *Catastrophe*, 81.

45 C.C. Carstens, "From the Ashes of Halifax: The Relief Work for the Blinded, the Maimed and the Orphans," *Survey* (29 Dec 1917): 360–61; MacDonald, *Curse of the Narrows*, 222, 228.

46 General Supervisor, District Work HRC, MG 36, Series C, 125.6, NSA.

47 J.H. Falk to J.H. Winfield, 12 Feb 1918, HRC, MG 36, Series C, 158.102, NSA; Marlene Shore, *The Science of Social Redemption: McGill, the Chicago School, and the Origins of Social Research in Canada* (Toronto: University of Toronto Press, 1987), 53; Observer, "Social Workers"; Minutes, 22 Aug 1918, Dr. Cutten, JBW and T.S. Rogers, HRC, MG 36, HRC, Series C, 158.228, NSA.

48 Falk, "History of Rehabilitation Work Since January 9, 1918," HRC, MG 36, Series C, 162.5, NSA.

49 Falk, "The Future of the Work from Mar 1st. Some Suggestions," HRC, MG 36, Series C, 162.11, NSA.

50 Sister John Baptist to JBW, 27 May 1918 (37.13), Sister M. Stephanie to JBW, 19 Jun 1918 (37.14), HRC, MG 36, Series C, NSA.

51 G. Fred Pearson to JBW, 1 Aug 1918, JBW to Pearson, 31 Jul 1918, HRC, MG 36, Series C, 113.102, 113.102a, NSA.

52 31 Jul 1918, HRC, MG 36, Series C ,157.3d, NSA; Falk, 14 Jan 1918, HRC, MG 36, Series C, 162.1bcd; 123.b, NSA; 1 Mar 1918, Case Workers &

Records Dept. of the Rehabilitation Dept. HRC, MG 36, Series C, 162.2a, NSA.

53 Falk, "The Future of the Work from Mar 1st."

54 Personal testimony, Miss Constance Bell, Interview with MacMechan, Halifax Disaster Record Office, MG 2124 224, 117, NSA.

55 Tillotson, "Dollars, Democracy, and the Children's Aid Society," 76–109.

56 Fingard, "'Justice Tempered with Mercy': Policing as a Woman's Vocation," Paper presented at the Workshop on Women and the Canadian Criminal Justice System, Trent University, 15 May 1999, 3; Employees of Halifax Relief Commission, Case Workers and Records Department Staff, HRC, MG 36, Series C, 162.2; 162.1, NSA.

57 Prince, *Catastrophe*, 94, 96, 97.

58 A Report of the Proceedings of the 1st Meeting of the Rehabilitation Committee, Thurs 13 Dec 1917 5 p.m. in the Halifax Hotel, HRC, MG 36, Series C, 157.2 1, NSA.

59 HRC, MG 36, Series P, file 646, NSA.

60 HRC, MG 36, Series P, file 503, NSA.

61 JBW to Pearson, Mass Relief Committee, 1 Apr 1919, HRC, MG 36, Series P, file 286, NSA.

62 HRC, MG 36, Series P, file 412, NSA.

63 History of Rehabilitation Work Since Jan 9 1918, HRC, MG 36, Series C, 162.5, NSA; HRC, MG 36, Series P, file 3, NSA.

64 MacDonald, *Curse of the Narrows*, 236.

65 A Report of the Proceedings of the 1st Meeting of the Rehabilitation Committee, Thurs 13 Dec 1917 5 p.m. in the Halifax Hotel, HRC, MG 36, Series C, 157.2 1, NSA.

66 Second Registration, HRC Pension Files, MG 36, Series P, NSA; *Chronicle*, 29 Dec 1917; 31 Dec 1917.

67 Settler, HRC Pension Files, MG.36, Series P 23038, NSA. Interview. I use Settler's real name, as she published widely complaints under her own name.

68 A Report of the Proceedings of the 1st Meeting of the Rehabilitation Committee, Thurs 13 Dec 1917 5 p.m. in the Halifax Hotel, HRC, MG 36, Series C, 157.2 1, NSA.

69 Pearson to JBW, 1 Aug 1918, JBW to Pearson, 1 Aug 1918, HRC, MG 36, Series C, 113, NSA.

70 HRC, MG 36, Series P, file 1253, NSA.

71 Observer, "Social Workers." 'Observer' is the pen name Wisdom adopted in Cape Breton.

72 G.B. Cutten to JBW, 27 Sept 1918, HRC, MG 36, Series C, 44.20, NSA; Minutes, Dec 1911. HLCW notes an article by Marshall Saunders in the *Evening*

Mail, advocating a City Settlement House in new Market Hall; John
Shearer to Thomas Moore, 4 Apr 1918, Dept of Social Service and Evan-
gelism, Methodist Church Dept of Temperance, Prohibition and Moral
Reform, Fond 17 Series 0; box 5 Halifax, f 88, United Church Archives; Cut-
ten to JBW, 27 Sept 1918, HRC, MG 36, Series C, 44.29; 41.41 Community
House, NSA.

73 Minutes of the Meeting re Bureau of Social Service, 27 Aug 1918, HRC,
MG 36, Series C, 182, NSA; Clipping, "Has Stimulated Interest in Social
Service," n.d., JBW Papers; History of the HRC, 31 Dec 1918, HRC, MG 36,
Series C, 89.33, NSA; *Christian Science War Time Activities* (Boston, 1922), 61,
Scrapbook, 20 Dec 1917, Commercial Club, MG 20 71, NSA; Cutten to JBW,
27 Sept 1918, HRC, MG 36, Series C, 44.29, NSA; Cutten to T.S. Rogers, 27
Aug 1918, HRC, MG 36, Series C, 162.26, NSA.

74 Hareven, "An Ambiguous Alliance," 84, 91–92; Cynthia R. Comacchio,
Nations Are Built of Babies: Saving Ontario's Mothers and Children, 1900–1940
(Montreal: McGill-Queen's University Press, 1993). In 1935, the CCCW was
renamed the Canadian Welfare Council to reflect its interest in broader
welfare issues.

75 31 Dec 1918, HRC, History of the HRC, MG 36, Series C, 89.33, NSA.

76 JBW to Katherine Wisdom Williams, 17 Mar 1919, JBW Papers.

77 Clipping, "Has Stimulated Interest in Social Service," n.d.; Clipping,
"Dr Eben Mackay Died Last Night," *Chronicle*, 7 Jan 1920, JBW Papers;
Minutes 20 May 1920, HLCW; McAlpine's Halifax City Directory, 1920.

78 Peter Lambly, "'Towards a Living Wage': The Minimum Wage Campaign
for Women in Nova Scotia, 1920–1935" (honours thesis, Dalhousie University, 1977).

79 Ibid., 20.

80 Hendsbee, "Miss Jane Wisdom," 11.

81 See E. Frances O'Neill, *Survey of the Protestant and Non-Sectarian Relief-
Giving Organizations of Montreal* (Financial Federation of the MCSA, 1924).

82 Patricia Tanabe interview, JBW Papers; Minutes, 15 Apr 1916, HLCW.

83 Minutes, 20 May 1920, HLCW, MG 20, vol. 353.6 mfm 9597, NSA.

84 Jane B. Wisdom, "Notes on Halifax and Public Health," *Social Welfare*
(Jun 1920): 228–30; "Halifax Now Has Its Own Children's Aid Society,"
Social Welfare (Sept 1920): 330; "A New Feature of the Halifax Public
Playground," *Social Welfare* (Sept 1920): 331. Their brother Alex, a major
with the Salvation Army in Halifax, played a key role in the days following the explosion; the co-operative relationship between the Salvation Army and the bureau may be explained, in part, by this personal
relationship.

85 *McGill News*, Sept 1920, p. 12; JBW Diary, JBW Papers. For the importance of the European trip, see Cecilia Morgan, *'A Happy Holiday': English-Canadians and Transatlantic Tourism, 1870–1930* (Toronto: University of Toronto Press, 2008).

86 Clipping, "The Halifax Welfare Bureau Makes Appeal for Your Support," *Echo*, 14 May 1921, JBW Papers; Form letter from A.H Whitman, C.W. Ackhurst, Halifax Welfare Bureau, 25 Nov 1922, Various items, 1920–23, North British Society, MG 20, vol. 244, NSA.

87 Cutten to JBW, 5 Jul 1921; A.H. Whitman to JBW, 27 Jun 1921; clipping, "Tribute to Miss Wisdom," *Chronicle*, 29 Jun 1921, JBW Papers.

88 Clipping, "Miss Wisdom Honoured. A Notable Function," *Mail*, 30 Sept 1921, JBW Papers.

Chapter Six

1 Esther Wilson Kerry, "The Role and Function of the Volunteer in Social Work" (master's thesis, McGill University, 1939).

2 Morton, "Entente Cordiale?," 224; Kellogg, "Canadian City in War Time," 677–84, 705; Ethel Bird, corr, 15 Dec 1915, BCA. See also Morton, *Fight or Pay*; Shepherd, "Genesis," 56.

3 Latimer, "Social Action Behaviour of the Canadian Association of Social Workers," 84; Mary Jennison, "Coming of Age," *Social Worker* (Jul 1948): 3; James Struthers, "A Profession in Crisis: Charlotte Whitton and Canadian Social Work in the 1930s," *Canadian Historical Review* 62, no. 2 (Jun 1981): 169. See Shirley Tillotson, *Contributing Citizens: Modern Charitable Fundraising and the Making of the Welfare State, 1920–66* (Vancouver: University of British Columbia Press, 2009).

4 Christie, *Engendering the State*; Shore, *Science of Social Redemption*. See also Burke, *Seeking the Highest Good*; Ken Moffatt, *A Poetics of Social Work: Personal Agency and Social Transformation in Canada, 1920–1939* (Toronto: University of Toronto Press, 2001); Gale Willis, *A Marriage of Convenience: Business and Social Work in Toronto, 1918–1957* (Toronto: University of Toronto Press, 1995); Allan Irving, "The Scientific Imperative in Canadian Social Work: Social Work and Social Welfare Research in Canada, 1897–1945," *Canadian Social Work Review* 9, no. 1 (Winter 1992): 9–25; Hurl, "Building a Profession."

5 Application of Graduate Student, 10 Oct 1921, JBW Papers; "A Salutation To JBW FROM FLM," 3. Her mature age was not unusual; see Margrit Eichler, "Women Pioneers in Canadian Sociology: The Effects of a Politics of Gender and a Politics of Knowledge," *Canadian Journal of Sociology*

26, no. 3 (Summer 2001): 375–403. Newspaperwoman Lily Barry of the Montreal Catholic Social Service Bureau graduated from the Université de Montréal at the age of fifty-three. Amélie Bourbeau, "La réorganisation de l'assistance chez les catholiques montréalais: la Fédération des Œuvres de charité canadiennes-françaises et la Federation of Catholic Charities, 1930–1972" (PhD diss., Université du Québec à Montréal, 2009), 99.

6 Eugene Forsey, *A Life on the Fringe: The Memoirs of Eugene Forsey* (Toronto: Oxford University Press, 1990), 23.

7 Milligan, *Forsey*, 6, 45–46; Shore, *Science of Social Redemption*, 212–13; Michiel Horn, *The League for Social Reconstruction: Intellectual Origins of the Democratic* (Toronto: University of Toronto Press, 1980), 124; H. Carl Goldenberg, "Joseph Clarence Hemmeon, 1879–1963," *Canadian Journal of Economics and Political Science* 30, no. 4 (Nov 1964): 595–96.

8 Shore, *Science of Social Redemption*, 27; Katherine Relief Williams, "Social Conditions in Nova Scotia, 1749–1783" (master's thesis, McGill University, 1937). See also Alison Prentice, "Laying Siege to the History Professoriate," in *Creating Historical Memory: English-Canadian Women and the Work of History*, ed. Beverly Boutilier and Alison Prentice (Vancouver: University of British Columbia, 1997), 206, 215.

9 Ian McKay and Suzanne Morton, "The Maritimes," in *The Workers' Revolt in Canada, 1917–1925*, ed. Craig Heron (Toronto: University of Toronto Press, 1999), 43–86; Frank, *J.B. McLachlan*; David Frank, "Class Conflict in the Coal Industry: Cape Breton 1922," in *Essays in Canadian Working Class History*, ed. G. S. Kealey and Peter Warrian (Toronto: McClelland and Stewart, 1976), 161–84, 226–31; David Frank, "Coal Masters and Coal Miners: The 1922 Strike and the Roots of Class Conflict in the Cape Breton Coal Industry" (master's thesis, Dalhousie University, 1974); and Donald Macgillivray, "Industrial Unrest in Cape Breton, 1919–1925" (master's thesis, University of New Brunswick, 1971).

10 Stephen Kimber, *Sailors, Slackers and Blind Pigs: Halifax at War* (Toronto: Anchor Books, 2003), 33.

11 Richmond, *Social Diagnosis*, 52; "'Observer' at Glace Bay and Vicinity," *Post* (Sydney), 10 Aug 1922, p. 1.

12 Bruce Curtis, "Surveying the Social: Techniques, Practices, Power," *Histoire sociale* 35, no. 69 (May 2002): 83–108; Margaret Byington, *Homestead: The Households of a Mill Town* (New York: Russell Sage Foundation, 1910); Maurine Greenwauld and Margo Anderson, eds., *Pittsburgh Surveyed: Social Science and Social Reform in the Early Twentieth Century* (Pittsburgh: Pittsburgh University Press, 1996); Martin Bulmer, Kevin Bales, and Kathryn K. Sklar, eds., *The Social Survey in Historical Perspective, 1880–1940*

(Cambridge: Cambridge University Press, 1991). See also Mélanie Méthot, "Herbert Brown Ames: Political Reformers and Enforcer," *Urban History Review* 31, no. 2 (Spring 2003): 18–31; Terry Copp, *Anatomy of Poverty: The Condition of the Working Class in Montreal 1897–1929* (Toronto: McClelland and Stewart, 1974); Valverde, *Age of Light, Soap and Water*.

13 Alan Hunt, "Measuring Morals: The Beginnings of the Social Survey Movement in Canada, 1913–1917," *Histoire sociale* 35, no. 69 (May 2002): 172, 173, 176, 186. See also O'Connor, *Poverty Knowledge*.

14 Tice, *Tales of Wayward Girls*, 4, 7, 67.

15 Observer, "'Observer' at Office of Maritime Labor Herald," *Post*, 11 Aug 1922; Walkowitz, *Working With Class*, 58.

16 Hendsbee, "Miss Jane Wisdom," 11; Ellen Ross, *Love and Toil: Motherhood in Outcast London, 1870–1918* (New York: Oxford University Press, 1993); Hunt, "Measuring Morals," 180–81; Tice, *Tales of Wayward Girls*, 11.

17 "'Observer' at Glace Bay and Vicinity," *Post*, 10 Aug 1922.

18 Observer, "'Observer' at Office of Maritime Labor Herald," *Post*, 11 Aug 1922, p. 1.

19 Observer, "The Law of the Land," *Post*, 17 Aug 1922.

20 Observer, "The Soldiers of the King," *Post*, 18 Aug 1922.

21 Observer, "Observations on Authority," *Post*, 19 Aug 1922; Observer, "Hunger," *Post*, 21 Aug 1922.

22 Ibid.

23 Observer, "Sixteen Years of Co-operation," *Post*, 23 Aug 1922.

24 Observer, "A Man's a Man for a' that," *Post*, 24 Aug 1922.

25 Observer, "When One Stops to Think," *Post*, 25 Aug 1922.

26 Observer, "Our Daily Bread – and Milk," *Post*, 26 Aug 1922; Observer, "The Ounce of Prevention," *Post*, 3 Sept 1922.

27 Observer, "The Ounce of Prevention," *Post*, 3 Sept 1922.

28 Observer, "The Irreducible Minimum," *Post*, 1 Sept 1922.

29 Eugene Forsey, "The Economic and Social Aspects of the Nova Scotia Coal Industry" (master's thesis, McGill University, 1926). The thesis was published by MacMillan as a book the same year. See also Forsey, *A Life on the Fringe,* and Milligan, *Forsey*, 44–45.

30 Hendsbee, "Miss Jane Wisdom," 11.

31 Novick, *That Noble Dream*, 69; C. A. Dawson to JBW, 30 Apr 1924, JBW Papers.

32 Reid, *Social Service and Hospital Efficiency*, 2–4.

33 *University of Toronto Calendar*, 1915–16; Hurl, "Building a Profession," 4.

34 Hurl, "Building a Profession," 5, 7, 8, 11, 38. For more on Dale, see Barbara M. Finalyson, "Professor Dale," *Social Welfare* (Dec 1926): 324–25; Burke, *Seeking the Highest Good*.

35 W. W. Lee, in *Globe 1913*, quoted in Pitsula, "Relief of Poverty in Toronto," 268; Mary D. McDonald to Currie, 6 Feb 1922, OP, Social Service.

36 J.A. Dale to William Peterson, 16 Apr 1917, OP, Staff Appointments and Governors, 1913–1919, RG 2 c 29, f 117, MUA. At the same time, the Theological Colleges also established a Department of Religious Education. D.J. Fraser, "The Theological College and the University," Address Given at the Reunion of Alumni of the Co-operating Theological Colleges, Montreal, 1921; David Leigh, "The McGill School of Social Work, 1918–1959," Social Work, RG 66 box 79, f 1, MUA; *AR* 1917–18, 13.

37 Judy Slinn, "Falk, Oswald Toynbee (1879–1972)," *Oxford Dictionary of National Biography* (Oxford: Oxford University Press, 2004), http://www.oxforddnb.com/index/50/101050269/, accessed 29 Jan 2012.

38 Shepherd, "Genesis," 50. The statements were probably from Kathleen Moore and Clarke, general secretary of the Montreal FWA, who followed Falk from Winnipeg in 1924. Shepherd also spoke with Falk's oldest daughter. The comment about a public/private divide may refer to a scandal that followed after Falk left his wife Olive Meredith Nicholls. *Canadian Welfare* (15 Apr 1950): 17–18; *Montreal Star*, 17 Apr 1950. "John H. Falk Dies; Social Worker, 69," *New York Times*, 17 Apr 1950, p. 23. In the obituary, no mention is made of his three daughters and son, and his widow is named as Hazel M. Falk. Falk has all but disappeared from Canadian social work history and his absence from Francis Joseph Turner, ed., *Canadian Encyclopedia of Social Work* (Waterloo: Wilfrid Laurier University Press, 2005), is especially striking in light of his contemporary importance.

39 Blois to Whitton, 24 Jul 1930, CCSD, Sub-Committee on Delinquency 1928, MG 28 I 10, vol. 31, 151, LAC; Whitton to R.E. Mills, 7 Sept 1938, Whitton Fonds, Corr & Memo 1939, MG 30 E 256, LAC.

40 Falk to Peterson, 29 Apr 1918, OP, Social Service, Department Files, RG 2 box 29, f 116, MUA; Christie and Gauvreau, *A Full-Orbed Christianity*, 132.

41 Leacock to Falk, 16 Nov 1918, OP, Department Files; Falk to Currie, 17 Nov 1921, OP, Social Service; Minutes, Advisory Committee Meeting, 9 Oct 1918, S.D. Clark Papers, McGill Department of Social Service 1918–1931, B 1990-0029 box 18, UTA.

42 Minutes, 15 Aug 1918, meeting Dale and Falk, OP, Department Files; McGill University, *Annual Calendar* 1919, 164; Chalmers House, *AR* 1917–18.

43 This is quite a different interpretation from the argument put forward by Nancy Christie and Michael Gauvreau that concerns about feminization came from the Theological Colleges. Christie and Gauvreau, *Full-Orbed Christianity*, 133. At the same time that the Theological Colleges were co-operating with the Department of Social Service, they were also

co-operating with the Department of Physical Education in instituting
their own Department of Religious Education. Fraser, "Theological College
and the University"; Clarke, n.d., FWA.

44 McGill University, *Calendar* 1919–1920; *Calendar* 1920–21, 176–77. On John
B. Dawson, see "A Welfare Leader," *New York Times*, 10 May 1956, p. 31;
"John Dawson Is COS Secretary," *Montreal Star*, 11 Jan 1919, p. 1; "Social
Agency Leader Leaving," *Montreal Herald*, 15 Jun 1921.

45 Mar 1922, OP, Social Service.

46 "Treatment of Poverty," Miss J.B. Wisdom, ibid.

47 Lacombe, "Marie Gérin-Lajoie's Hidden Crucifixes," 40, 67, 107; Bourbeau,
"La réorganisation de l'assistance," 99–101; *Montreal Gazette*, 4 Sept 1918,
p. 3; 3 Jun 1929, p. 9. On 15 Jun 1937, p. 10, there was a notice in the *Gazette*
that the Loyola School of Sociology and Social Service, described as the
English section of the Department of Social Service, University of Montreal, would reopen in September.

48 Christie and Gauvreau, *Full-Orbed Christianity*, 133–34; Advisory Committee Minutes, 20 Feb 1922, S.D. Clark Papers.

49 Falk to Currie, 2 Feb 1922, OP, Social Service; "R C Dexter to Leave Montreal," *Montreal Daily Star*, 29 Oct 1918, p. 20; "Sees Big Progress in Social
Service," *Montreal Daily Star*, 5 Nov 1918, p. 7.

50 Dawson even rehired Falk as a part-time lecturer from 1925 to 1930; Index
to McGill Staff Members by Department, MUA.

51 Stanley B. Frost, *McGill University: For the Advancement of Learning, Volume
II 1895–1971* (Montreal: McGill-Queen's University Press, 1984), 149.

52 Allan Irving, "Leonard Marsh and the McGill Social Science Project,"
Journal of Canadian Studies 21, no. 2 (Summer 1986): 6–48. The second hire
in sociology was Warner Gettys, who left for the University of Texas in
1926 to found its sociology department. In 1928, the University of Texas
received a large Rockefeller grant to create a Bureau of Research in Social
Sciences, and these two projects should be linked. "In Memoriam Warner
Ensign Gettys 1891–1973," www.utexas.edu/faculty/council/2000-2001/
memorials/SCANNED/gettys.pdf, accessed 11 Nov 2013.

53 E.M. Best, E. Forsey, C. Kellogg, Esther Kerry, May Reid, and C.A. Dawson,
"McGill School of Social Work Report," 1931, OP, Social Work 1926–1947;
MCSA, "McGill School of Social Work," *Welfare Work in Montreal* (Montreal,
1925), 39.

54 Catherine Braithwaite, "'Let the Women Organize the Bazaar': Medical
Philanthropy, Religion and Montreal Hospitals, 1840–1940" (PhD diss.,
McGill University, in progress); Minutes, Committee of Management of the
School of Social Workers, 22 May 1928, OP, Social Work 1926–1947; 21 Oct

1928, 22 May 1928, McGill Department of Social Service Advisory Committee, S.D. Clark Papers.

55 "News and Notes," *Social Worker* (Jun 1947): 38; "Halifax Woman Welfare Council Child Secretary," *Ottawa Citizen*, 17 Apr 1947, "Jane Wisdom," http://users.eastlink.ca/~haroldbeals/leaders.html, accessed 11 Nov 2013. No Jewish students appear to have been placed at the Women's Directory and I never found any direct discussion of this issue. The Women's Directory, however, employed at least one Catholic caseworker, Mary Sweetland, who entered religious life at Chicoutimi, November 1930. JBW Diary, JBW Papers. Dr. Alton Goldbloom, prominent Jewish Montreal paediatrician, served on the WDM Advisory Medical Committee.

56 Wm. Birks to Currie, 18 Jan 1930, OP, Records Relating to Academic Matters, MSSW, RG 2 box 205, f 19280, MUA; McGill University *AR of the Corporation*, 1931–32, 11; "Chancellor Hebb Describes Psychological Research at McGill," in *The McGill You Knew: An Anthology of Memories, 1920–1960*, ed. Edgar Andrew Collard (Don Mills: Longman Canada, 1975), 167.

57 Social work also came under public criticism at public forums, such as the 1930 Conference of the Canadian National Committee for Mental Hygiene in Toronto. Whitton to Ethel Dodds Parker (confidential), 2 Dec 1930, CCSD, CASW 1930, MG 28 I 10, vol. 30, 150, LAC; Reid to Currie, 20 Jun 1930, Currie to Reid, 12 Jun 1930, 25 Jun 1930, OP, Records Relating to Academic Matters, MSSW. Whitton also held Dawson responsible; see Whitton to Archdeacon Henry Cody, 23 Nov 1931, CCSD, CASW 1931, MG 28 I 10, vol. 30, 150, LAC.

58 Barry Cahill, "Dismissal of a President: The Ordeal of Carleton Stanley at Dalhousie University, 1943–1945," *Acadiensis* 31, no. 1 (Autumn 2001): 77; Paul Axelrod and John Reid, "Introduction," in *Youth, University and Canadian Society: Essays in the Social History of Higher Education* (Montreal: McGill-Queen's University Press, 1989), xxii; "1931 Report," OP, Social Work 1926–1947.

59 "1931 Report"; Currie to Muriel B. McCall, 27 Nov 1931, ibid.

60 Sir Arthur Currie's remarks at BOG meeting 17 May 1932, "The Attitude of McGill University Regarding the School for Social Workers," Press release, 4 Aug 1931, OP, Records Relating to Academic Matters, MSSW; Clarke, n.d., FWA; Currie to McCall, 27 Nov 1931, OP, Social Work 1926–1947.

61 James Struthers, "'Lord Give Us Men': Women and Social Work in English Canada, 1918 to 1953," *Historical Papers* (1983): 96–112.

62 "Preliminary Report of the Sub-Committee on a Scheme of Training for Social Work in Montreal," 10 Mar 1932, 2, JBW Papers; Currie to Wesley

Frost Consul General, 2 Aug 1931; Currie to Reid, 2 Nov 1931, OP, Social Work 1926–1947.

63 Frank G. Pedley to Currie, 11 Mar 1932, OP, Records Relating to Academic Matters, MSSW; Temporary Committee on Social Work Training in Montreal, Report on the Work of the Sub-Committee on Arrangements and on Finance 15 Jun 1932, Submitted by Jane B. Wisdom; Whitton to Parker, 27 May 1932, CCSD, CASW 1932. The businessmen included Philip Fisher of Southam, Allan Bronfman, and Catholic lawyer and sportsman Henry Trihey; Reginald Whitaker, "The Liberal Corporatist Ideas of Mackenzie King," *Labour/Le Travailleur* 2 (1977): 137–39; Willis, *A Marriage of Convenience*.

64 B.B. Stevenson to Currie, 14 Aug 1933, OP, Records Relating to Academic Matters, MSSW. Parker to Whitton, 18 Aug 1931, CCSD, CASW 1931; "Dorothy King OBE Socwk '32," *McGill News* (Spring 1963): 38; "Dorothy King, 1882–1963," *McGill News* (Spring 1963): 38; Eva R Younge, "Dorothy King OBE, MA: Pioneer Social Work Educator," *Social Worker* 31, no. 2 (Apr–May 1963): 33–35; Dorothy Aikin, "Dorothy King: An Appreciation," *Canadian Welfare* 26 (Jun 1950): 17–19.

65 Rooke and Schnell, *No Bleeding Heart*, 38, 100. In October 1931, Whitton wanted King to move to Vancouver, and when King had her own agenda, Whitton wrote to Falk that "rather disturbing development that DK is beginning to take herself much more seriously than a person of her sense and sound judgment generally does, that upsets me somewhat." Whitton to Falk, 6 Oct 1931, Whitton Fonds, Corr & Memo 1930–31, MG 30 E 256, vol. 18, LAC.

66 Memo on School for Social Workers, Jan 1933; Preliminary Report of the Sub-Committee on a Scheme of Training for Social Work in Montreal, 10 Mar 1932, CCSD, CASW 1932(a); Esther S. Kerry, "Early Professional Development in Montreal," *Social Worker* 29, no.3 (Jun 1961): 40; Stevenson to Currie, 14 Aug 1933, Fisher to Currie, 1 Aug 1933, OP, Records Relating to Academic Matters, MSSW.

67 Day Book 1934–35, SCVF; Memo re school, "A Request for Affiliation with McGill University from the MSSW," 25 Mar 1944, OP, Social Work, 1926–1947; Leigh, "The McGill School of Social Work, 1918–1959"; Currie to Stevenson, 11 Sept 1935, School of Social Work 1937–51 RG 4, box 97, f 10738, MUA; MSSW, 27 Apr 1936, CASW, CASW National Organization 1936–37, MG 28 I, vol. 441, 155, LAC; Ira H. McKay Dean to Currie, 8 Aug 1933, OP, Social Work, 1926–1947. Whitton, in fact, held a MA from Queen's.

68 Struthers, "Lord Give Us Men."

69 Walkowitz, *Working with Class*, 147.
70 Clarke, "The Canadian Association of Social Workers," *Compass* (Nov 1927): 1–4.
71 Clarke, "The Canadian Association"; George Corbett to R. W. Hopper, 19 May 1927, CASW, Montreal Branch 1927, MG 28 I 441, vol. 28, 27, LAC; Minutes, 23 Apr 1930, CASW, Montreal Branch 1928–30, MG 28 I 441, vol. 28, 28, LAC; Clarke, "One of the 'Originals' Looks Back," *Social Worker* (Jul 1948): 1–2; 19 Dec 1936, CASW, National Organization 1936–37, MG 28 · I 10, vol. 155, LAC; Montgomery, "One of Our Pioneers," 130.
72 Nominations for Council 1930, CASW, MG 28 I 441, vol. 8, 10, LAC; *Conference Bulletin* (National Conference of Social Welfare), Nov 1930, 36; "Social Workers Look Toward Montreal," *Survey* (May 1935): 136; "Social Workers View their World," *Survey* (Jul 1935): 195–96. The National Conference of Jewish Social Service did not meet in Montreal at the request of the Montreal Jewish community, who feared "that a frank discussion of social problems at a large Jewish gathering might feed the flames of Canadian anti-Semitism." "Practitioners at Lake Placid," *Social Work Today* (Jul 1935): 9; Phyllis Lowell, "The Montreal Conference," *Social Work Today* (Jul 1935): 5–7. John Earl Haynes, "'The Rank and File Movement' in Private Social Work," *Labor History* 16, no. 1 (Winter 1975): 78–98; Patrick Selmi and Richard Hunter, "Beyond the Rank and File Movement: Mary van Kleeck and Social Work Radicalism in the Great Depression, 1931–1942," *Journal of Sociology and Social Welfare* 28, no. 2 (Jun 2001): 75–100.
73 C.M. Hincks, "The Canadian Conference on Social Work and the Future," *Social Welfare* (May 1928): 176–77; Canadian Conference on Social Work, *Proceedings*, 1928, 82; "Report on Quebec Conference," *Child & Family Welfare* (Mar 1931): 5–7; "Preliminary Draft 23 – 5 Feb 1931," Report, CCSD, National Bilingual Conference 1931, MG 28 I 10, vol. 11, 53A, LAC. A French translation of the 1931 paper exists. JBW, "L'enfant né hors du marriage," Société d'adoption et de protection de l'enfance, Fonds, Règlements, historique et correspondances 1937–1962, C041-205, Montréal, Centre Jeunesse de Montréal. My thanks to Chantale Quesney for locating this document.
74 Professional Training for Social Work, Report of a Joint National Committee CASW and CCCFW, 1. CCSD, CASW 1932; Interim Report re Recruiting and Training, n.d., CCSD, CASW 1931.
75 I.e., Whitton to Parker, 1 Dec 1931, CCSD, CASW 1931; Whitton to Parker, 16 Apr 1932, CCSD, CASW 1932; King to Whitton, 2 Apr 1931, JBW to Whitton, 18 Apr 1931; Whitton to JBW, 25 Apr 1931, CCSD, Recruitment & Training CASW 1929–31; CCSD.

76 Memorandum on the Education & Training of Social Workers, Commit-
tee on Community Surveys and Social Organization of the Community
Welfare Council of Ontario, E. D. MacPhee, Chairman, D. B. Harkness,
Sec., 19 Dec 1931, 1, 5; "Tentative Plans for Committee and Procedure on
Recruiting and Training," 18 Feb 1931, Report of Interview with Mr. Hark-
ness re: Training for Social Work, 3 Dec 1931, Reid to Whitton, 10 Jan 1931,
CCSD, CASW 1932; "Minutes of Exec Meeting of CASW," 27 Jan 1932; 10
Feb 1932; 16 Mar 1932; CASW 1931; C.W. Topping, "The Selection, Training
and Nurture of Social Workers in Canada," *Social Welfare* (Mar 1932): 116;
Rick Helmes-Hayes and Neil McLaughlin, "Public Sociology in Canada:
Debates, Research and Historical Context," *Canadian Journal of Sociology*
34, no. 3 (2009): 585; JBW to Whitton, 18 Apr 1931, CCSD, Recruitment &
Training CASW 1929–31; Jennifer Lyn Cote, "'Nobody Ever Paid Me for
Anything:' Crafting a Professional Work Identity in Progressive-Era Boston" (PhD diss., Boston College, 2007).
77 Memorandum on the Education and Training of Social Workers, Whitton
to Parker, 26 Aug 1932, CCSD, CASW 1932.
78 "Professional Training for Social Work," 5, 6, 8, 9, 10.
79 "Volunteer Worker and Social Records," *Social Worker* (Aug 1927): 501–2;
Dorothy King, "The Ethics of the Case Record," *Social Worker* (Jul 1929):
236–37; Report for biennial meeting 30 May 1934 [Capitals in original],
JBW to Parker, 15 May 1934, CASW, Ethics Committee 1934, MG 28 I 441,
vol. 13, 20, LAC.
80 King to Jean Walker, 31 Dec 1932, Minutes of the National Committee on
Ethics, 12 May 1938.
81 Patricia T. Rooke and R.L. Schnell, "Imperial Philanthropy and Colonial
Response: British Juvenile Emigration to Canada, 1896–1930," *The Historian*
46, no. 1 (Nov 1983): 56–77; B.L. Vigod, "The Quebec Government and Social Legislation During the 1930s: A Study in Political Self-Destruction," in
Social Welfare Policy in Canada: Historical Readings, ed. Raymond Blake and
Jeff Keshen (Toronto: Copp Clark 1995), 153–66; "Income Tax Topic at Row-
ell Inquiry," *Montreal Gazette*, 16 May 1938, p. 7; "Brief of Montreal Branch
Rowell Sirois," *Social Worker* (Jul/Jul 1938): 16–17; "Children's Bureau of
Montreal," *Welfare Work 1931*, 62.
82 Laurel Lee Lewey, "Nothing to Fear but Fear. Social Work in Cold War
Canada, 1945–1960" (PhD diss., University of Calgary, 2006); Minutes of a
Meeting of the Special Committee, CASW, on "Progressive Programme,"
13 Jan 1939, Progressive Programme Committee, CASW, MG 28 I 441,
vol. 20, 12, LAC; "Progressive Programme," *Social Worker* (May 1939).

83 Reid to Whitton, 30 Apr 1925, Whitton Fonds, Reid corr, 1924–25, MG 28 I
10, vol. 16, 26, LAC. "News of Social Workers and Agencies," *Social Welfare*
(Mar 1928): 142; Whitton to Parker, 26 Aug 1932, CCSD, CASW 1932.

84 JBW to Parker, 15 May 1934, CASW, Ethics Committee 1934; Notice, n.d.,
Day Book 1934–35, SCVF.

85 Modern Literature Group, 1933–34, Alumnae Society, Alumnae Society
Cash Books, RG 76, book 2, MUA; Maritime Women's Club of Montreal,
AR 1930–31; JBW Diary, JBW Papers; Kirkland, "A Home Away from
Home"; Kate Boyer, "The Feminization of Clerical Work in Early Twentieth-
Century Montreal" (PhD diss., McGill University, 2001), 160–68; K. Jane
Watt, "Passing Out of Memory: Georgina Sime and the Practice of Liter-
ary Recuperation" (PhD diss., University of Alberta 1997), 201; JBW Diary,
JBW papers.

86 Wisdom's graduate school correspondence was addressed to Helen
Grant's home, and the city directory lists Wisdom as accompanying them
on their move to a west-end English suburb. During the 1930s, she is listed
as living at the Women's University Club and boarding with individuals
who had a direct connection to English Montreal social services, including
Helen Reid: *Lovell Montreal City Directory*. In 1938–39, Wisdom is recorded
as sharing an apartment with her second cousin Catherine Hebb. Catherine's brother, prominent scientist and future McGill chancellor Donald
O. Hebb, was also close to Wisdom, naming his second daughter in her
honour.

87 Catherine Holland Joyce, *The First Forty Years of the University Women's Club
of Montreal, 1927–1967* (Montreal, 1962), 7, 9; *Alumnae News* (Mar 1927): xv.

88 Day Book 1935–6, SCVF; Minutes, 26 Nov 1934, University Women's Club
of Montreal (with organization); Clarke to Whitton, 29 Jan 1931; Whitton to
Parker, n.d., CCSD, CASW 1931.

89 Gordon, *Heroes of Their Own Lives*, 298; Kunzel, *Fallen Women, Problem Girls*,
42, 137. Struthers, "Lord Give Us Men," 104.

90 "A Salutation to JBW FROM FLM," 4.

91 Reprinted, Porter Lee, "Is Social Work Inspiration Declining?" *Social
Welfare* (Oct 1928): 19; Jane B. Wisdom, "Are Social Workers Themselves
Tapping the Sources of Life's Inspiration?" *Social Worker* (Nov 1928): 43.

Chapter Seven

1 Danielle Gauvreau, "Destins de femmes, destins de mères: images et
réalités historiques de la maternité au Québec," *Recherches sociographiques*
32, no. 3 (Sept–Dec 1991): 321–46. For example, see Andrée Lévesque, *La*

norme et les déviantes. Des femmes au Québec pendant l'entre-deux-guerres
(Montreal: Éditions du remue-ménage, 1989), 121–36; Lévesque, "La santé
des femmes pendant les années trente: les mères célibataires de l'Hôpital
de la Miséricorde à Montréal," *Bulletin du Regroupement des Chercheurs-
Chercheuses en Histoire des Travailleurs et des Travailleuses du Québec* (1991):
7–17; Lévesque, "Deviant Anonymous: Single Mothers at the Hôpital de la
Miséricorde in Montreal, 1929–1939," in *Rethinking Canada*, ed. V. Strong-
Boag and A. Clair Fellman, 3rd edition (Toronto: Oxford, 1997), 322–36;
Marie-Aimée Cliche, "Morale chrétienne et 'double standard sexuel'. Les
filles-mères à l'hôpital de la Miséricorde à Québec, 1874–1972," *Histoire
Sociale* 24, no. 47 (May 1991): 85–125; Denyse Baillargeon, *Québec en mal
d'enfants: la médicalisation de la maternité, 1910–1970* (Montreal: Éditions du
remue-ménage, 2004); Magda Fahrni, *Household Politics: Montreal Families
and Postwar Reconstruction* (Toronto: University of Toronto Press, 2005);
Marie-Aimée Cliche, "L'infanticide dans le région de Québec, 1660–1969,"
Revue d'histoire de l'Amérique française 44, no. 1 (Summer 1990): 39–40;
Marie-Paule Malouin, et al. (sous la direction de), *L'Univers Des Enfants
en Difficulté au Québec entre 1940 et 1960* (Montreal: Éditions Bellœarmin,
1996). See also the recent Marie-Hélène Brunet, "Doctrine catholique,
ambivalences et pragmatisme. L'œuvre des premères travailleuses sociales
à la Miséricorde de Montréal, 1945–1970," *Revue d'histoire de l'Amérique
française* 65, no. 1 (Summer 2011): 29–58.

2 Quebec, *Quebec Social Insurance Commission* (Quebec, 1933); WDM, *AR*
1927.

3 Morton, "Entente Cordiale?," 207–46; S. M. Jamieson, "French and English
in the Institutional Structure of Montreal" (master's thesis, McGill University, 1938); Everett C. Hughes and Margaret L. McDonald, "French
and English in the Economic Structure of Montreal," *Canadian Journal of
Economics and Political Science* 7 (1941): 493–505.

4 Chantale Quesney, "De la Charité au Bonheur Familial: Une histoire de la
Société d'Adoption et Protection de l'Enfance à Montréal, 1937–1972"
(PhD diss., Université du Québec à Montréal, 2010); Speech by Helen
R.Y. Reid, MCSA 1930, MCSA, Annual Meetings and *AR*s, 1931–1937, MG 2076
c 27, 998, MUA. The percentage of people who were neither English nor
French on the Island of Montreal increased from 12 per cent to 13.2 per cent.
Andrew Sancton, *Governing the Island of Montreal: Language Differences and
Metropolitan Politics* (Berkeley: University of California Press, 1985), 15.

5 Although this was fifteen years after Newfoundland granted the franchise
to women in 1925 (and only at the age of twenty-five, compared to men,
who could vote at twenty-one), Quebec's 1940 decision was made only six

years after a change in the law that permitted women to stand for provincial office in New Brunswick. In certain jurisdictions outside Quebec, married women who jointly owned property with their husband were excluded from certain municipal franchises until the 1960s. While not to diminish the late date of the franchise for women in Quebec, these other examples also need to be kept in mind so as not to exaggerate Quebec's exceptionalness. Jennifer Stoddart, "Quebec's Legal Elite Looks at Women's Rights: The Dorion Commission 1929–31," in *Essays in the History of Canadian Law: Volume I*, ed. David H. Flaherty (Toronto: University of Toronto Press, 1982), 323–57; Walter Shanks (Lawyer) to Lucy Phinney, General Secretary, 25 Apr 1918, Historical Children's Services Centre, WDM Papers, BYFC.

6 Margaret Kirkpatrick Strong, *Public Welfare Administration in Canada* (Chicago: University of Chicago Press, 1930), 220; John Kerry to JBW, 14 May 1928, CCSD, Unmarried Parenthood Act 1926–1934, MG 28 I 10, vol. 23, 108, LAC; JBW to Kathleen Snowdon, 6 Jun 1928, CASW 1932.

7 B.L. Vigod, "Ideology and Institutions in Quebec: The Public Charities Controversy, 1921–1926," *Histoire sociale* XI, no. 1 (May 1978): 167–82; Bernard L. Vigod, *Quebec before Duplessis: The Political Career of Louis-Alexandre Taschereau* (Montreal: McGill-Queen's University Press, 1986): 83–85; Strong, *Public Welfare Administration in Canada*, 147. See also the recent and important Martin Petitclerc, "L'indigent et l'assistance publique au Québec dans la première moitée du XXe siècle," *Revue d'histoire de l'Amérique française* 65, no.1 (Summer 2011): 29–58.

8 Paul-André Linteau, Paul Lindeau, René Durocher, Jean-Claude Robert, and François Ricard, *Quebec Since 1930* (Toronto: Lorimer, 1991); Dorothy Aikin, "The Role of the MCSA in the Establishment of Public Assistance" (master's thesis: University of Chicago, 1950); B.L. Vigod, "The Quebec Government and Social Legislation During the 1930s: A Study in Political Self-Destruction," *Journal of Canadian Studies* 14, no. 1 (Spring 1979): 59–69. Veronica Strong-Boag's recent *Fostering Nation? Canada Confronts Its History of Childhood Disadvantage* (Waterloo: Wilfrid Laurier University Press, 2011) provides the first comprehensive study of foster care in English-speaking Canada.

9 G.B. Clarke, "Quebec," *Compass* (Feb 1935): 3.

10 Gilles Piédalue, "Les groupes financiers au Canada 1900–1930 – étude préliminaire," *Revue d'histoire de l'Amérique française* 30, no. 1 (Jun 1976): 3–34; Paul-André Linteau, *Histoire de Montréal depuis la Confédération* (Montreal: Boréal, 1991); Copp, *Anatomy of Poverty*; Tarah Brookfield, "Divided by the Ballot Box: The Montreal Council of Women and the 1917 Election,"

Canadian Historical Review 89, no. 4 (Dec 2008): 473–501; Donald McKay, *The Square Mile: Merchant Princes of Montreal* (Vancouver: Douglas and McIntyre, 1987); Ronald Rudin, *The Forgotten Quebecers: A History of English-Speaking Quebec, 1759–1980* (Quebec: Institute Québéois de recherche sur la culture, 1985); Morton, "Entente Cordiale?," 212; MCSA, *Welfare Work 1930*.

11 Shepherd, "Genesis," 70–71. Falk's part-time appointment as secretary probably did not help cross-confessional co-operation, as his alleged prejudice against Catholics may have been especially inappropriate in light of Montreal's French Catholic majority population. His leadership coincided with the exodus of anglophone Catholics from the organization, although at least one Catholic individual, lawyer John Hackett, remained with the group and attempted to bridge the sectarian dissolution. Whitton to R.E. Mills, 7 Sept 1938; Whitton Fonds, Corr and Memo 1939, MG 30 E 256, vol. 18, LAC.

12 Shepherd, "Genesis," 46.

13 Tillotson, *Contributing Citizen*; Shepherd, "Genesis," 82, 84; Aileen Ross, "Philanthropy in an Urban Community," *Canadian Journal of Economics and Political Science* (Nov 1952): 474–86; *Child and Family Welfare* (Jan 1931): 1, 6; Bourbeau, "La réorganisation de l'assistance chez les catholiques montréalais."

14 Shepherd, "Genesis," 49, 64; "Family Welfare in Montreal," *Social Welfare* 4, no. 10 (Jul 1922): 219; Clarke, n.d., FWA; "Tributes Honour Service of Family Welfare Leader," *Gazette*, 15 Mar 1956, p. 2; Obituary, 14 Jun 1958. In 1922, Minneapolis COS also renamed itself the FWA; Stadum, *Poor Women*, xxii.

15 Betty (Kobayashi) Isserman, "The Casework Relationship in Work with Unmarried Mothers," *Social Worker* 17, no. 1 (Oct 1948): 12; Betty Kobayashi Isserman interview with author, Montreal, Oct 2004; photographs, JBW Papers.

16 WDM, *AR* 1927; JBW, "L'Enfant né hors du marriage."

17 "A Salutation To JBW FROM FLM," 3.

18 This progressive tradition in Montreal is the antecedent to later "experiments" such as the Open Door Society. See Karen Dubinsky, *Babies Without Borders: Adoption and Migration across the Americas* (Toronto: University of Toronto Press, 2010); Stromquist, *Re-inventing 'The People,'* 191.

19 See Suzanne Morton, "Managing the Unmarried Mother 'Problem': Halifax Maternity Homes," in *Mothers of the Municipality*, 110–40; Suzanne Morton, "Nova Scotia and Its Unmarried Mothers, 1945–1975," in *Mapping the Margins: The Family and Social Discipline in Canada, 1700–1975*, ed. Nancy Christie and Michael Gauvreau (Montreal: McGill-Queen's University Press, 2004), 327–48.

20 "Dr. Rebecca J. Cole," https://www.nlm.nih.gov/changingthefaceofmedicine/physicians/biography_66.html, accessed 11 Nov 2013.

21 Sherri Broder, *Tramps, Unfit Mothers, and Neglected Children: Negotiating the Family in Late Nineteenth-Century Philadelphia* (Philadelphia: University of Pennsylvania Press, 2002), 160, 173–74.

22 WDM, *AR* 1930. According to church registers, of the 998 children born out of wedlock in Montreal in 1929, about half died and the rest were left to the care of the community.

23 WDM, *AR* 1917.

24 "WDM AR," in MCSA, *Welfare 1924*, 84.

25 Constitution and Bylaws 1921, WDM, BYFC.

26 *AR of the WDM 1915*, 6.

27 The directory and the FWA were the only two charitable agencies engaged in the foundation of social work practice, although casework was also being conducted by probation officers at the juvenile court and for follow-up outpatient care at the Western Hospital. Falk to Currie, 17 Nov 1921, OP, Social Service. On Lucy Phinney, see "Lucy Phinney," Radcliffe Class of 1913 50th Reunion Report, 1963, 44–45; Class of 1913 Yearbook, Lucy Corliss Phinney; "Lucy Phinney Gregg," *The Althea Woodland Echoes* 14, no. 1 (Summer 1985): 1; Obituary, "Lucy Phinney Gregg, Religious Counselor," *Washington Post*, 26 Feb 1988, p. C4. For the Committee of Sixteen, see Lévesque, *La norme*; Karen Herland, "Organized Righteousness against Organized Viciousness: Constructing Prostitution in Post World War I Montreal" (master's thesis, McGill University, 2005). For Flora McNeill, see James, "A Passion for Service," 122; "Sincere Tribute Paid Miss McNeill," *Ottawa Citizen*, 2 Dec 1946, p. 11.

28 "WDM AR," in MCSA, *Welfare Work 1922;* WDM, *AR* 1938.

29 *Report of a Committee of the MCSA* (Montreal, 1919), 18.

30 WDM, *AR* 1919, 14.

31 *AR of the WDM*, 1920–1921, 7, 25; "Leacock Regaled Large Audience," *Montreal Gazette*, 7 Apr 1920, p. 5; "WDM AR," in MCSA, *Welfare Work 1925*, 93.

32 *Report of a Committee of the MCSA*, 19; Student Lucy C Phinney, Radcliffe Archives, Cambridge, Massachusetts.

33 "WDM AR," in MCSA, *Welfare Work 1922*, 102.

34 Margaret Westley, *Remembrance of Grandeur: The Anglo-Protestant Elite of Montreal, 1900–1950* (Montreal: Libre Expression, 1990); McDonald to Currie, 6 Feb 1922, OP, Social Service.

35 "WDM AR," in MCSA, *Welfare Work 1923*, 110; "WDM AR," in MCSA, *Welfare Work 1924*, 84; *AR of the WDM*, 1918, 8.

36 McDonald to Currie, 6 Feb 1922, OP, Social Service.

37 "WDM AR," in MCSA, *Welfare Work 1924*, 91–96; "WDM AR," in MCSA, *Welfare Work 1922*, 102; Kerry, "Early Professional Development," 39–40; "WDM AR," in MCSA, *Welfare Work 1923*, 92.

38 "WDM AR," in MCSA, *Welfare Work 1928*, 83–100.

39 "Unmarried Mother in Modern Light," *Montreal Gazette*, 7 Feb 1924, p. 5.

40 Finding Aid, Dorothy Heneker and Family Fonds, LAC.

41 Quesney, "De la Charité au Bonheur Familial," 47; quotes Mathilde Eon, "Les filles-meres a l'hôpital de la Miséricorde de Montréal, 1889–1921" (master's thesis, Université d'Angers, 2000), 55.

42 Sandra Djwa, "F. R. Scott," *Canadian Poetry* 4 (Spring/Summer 1979): 4–5.

43 Anne MacLennan, "Charity and Change: The MCSA's Attempts to Deal with the Depression" (master's thesis, McGill University, 1984), 75.

44 *Alumnae News*, 1916; "Thoughtless Rich Need Social Work as Well as Poor," *Gazette*, 25 Apr 1928, p. 10; "McDonald Voices Demand for Unity," *Gazette*, 29 Sept 1938, p. 13; "Done in Granite," *Gazette*, 2 Oct 1937, p. 10.

45 JBW, "The Illegitimate Family in New York City Treated by Social Agencies," *Child Welfare News* (Sept 1925): 13; "Quebec," *Child Welfare* (Jan–Mar 1925): 33; Whitton to Reid, 4 Oct 1924, CCSD, Reid Corr 1924–25, MG 28 I 10, vol. 6, 6, LAC; O'Neill, *Survey of the Protestant and Non-Sectarian*, 8; JBW to Eric Smith, 10 Nov 1945, Background History of Some Other Child Welfare, CSC Historical, BYFC; "Five Annual Meetings on One Day," *Child Welfare News* (Mar 1931): vi, 7; "Child Protection Problems Stated," *Gazette*, 4 Feb 1932, p. 4.

46 Douglas, "History of the Society for the Protection," 28.

47 Isabel Lillian Hicks, "A Study of Fifty Cases of the Unmarried Mothers' Division of the Catholic Welfare Bureau between the Years 1931 and 1945" (master's thesis, Université de Montréal, 1949), 13; JBW to Whitton, 19 Dec 1930, Whitton to JBW, 11 Dec 1930, CCSD, Montreal – Social and Welfare Agencies, 1928–41, MG 28 I 10, vol. 350, 12, LAC; John Kerry, *The Legal Status of the Unmarried Mother and Her Child in the Province of Quebec* (Ottawa: Canadian Council on Child Welfare, 1926); JBW, "Le Problème tel que nous le voyons," Preliminary Draft, CCSD, National Bilingual Conference, 1931; Muriel Tucker to Whitton, 22 Oct 1938, CCSD, Montreal, CAS, Protestant Foster Home, Women's Directory, 1930–51, MG 28 I 10, vol. 234, 16, LAC refers to translated 1931 paper.

48 E. Wayne Carp, *Family Matters: Secrecy and Disclosure in the History of Adoption* (Cambridge: Harvard University Press, 1998), 259. Carp makes the important point here that the extent of this shift would not be exaggerated or accelerated, as, with some important exceptions, psychoanalysis was not completely dominant until the early 1950s.

49 "WDM AR," in MCSA, *Welfare Work 1931*, 103–10; "WDM AR," in MCSA, *Welfare Work 1924*, 85.

50 "WDM AR," in MCSA, *Welfare Work 1933*, 91–96; "The Problem of Mental Defectives," *Canadian Medical Association Journal* 6, no. 3 (Mar 1916): 239; AR of Mental Hygiene Committee of Montreal 1922, found in MCSA, *Welfare Work 1922*, 63; W. T. B. Mitchell, (Mental Hygiene Committee) to JBW, 8 Feb 1926, WDM Papers, BYFC.

51 "WDM AR," in MCSA, *Welfare Work 1923*, 112.

52 WDM, *AR 1938*, WDM, *AR 1934*, BYFC; "WDM AR," in MCSA, *Welfare Work 1925*, 94; "WDM AR," in MCSA, *Welfare Work 1932*, 96.

53 "WDM AR," in MCSA, *Welfare Work in 1923*, 116; "WDM AR," in MCSA, *Welfare Work 1924*, 90; "WDM AR," in MCSA, *Welfare Work 1923*, 116.

54 "WDM AR," in MCSA, *Welfare Work 1926*, 89.

55 "WDM AR," in MCSA, *Welfare Work 1930*, 95; "WDM AR," in MCSA, *Welfare Work 1924*, 86; "WDM AR," in MCSA, *Welfare Work 1922*, 104.

56 Paper present by Frances Montgomery, n. d., WDM Papers, BYFC; Interview, Jean MacFadgen with Frances Montgomery, 20 Aug 1979, MacFadgen Papers, BI; Notes Halifax Feb 1950, CCSD, Nova Scotia: Department of Public Welfare 1936–1954, MG 28 I 10, vol. 216, 13, LAC; Martha M. Dore, "Functional Theory: Its History and Influence on Contemporary Social Work Practice," *The Social Service Review* 64, no. 3 (Sept 1990): 374, fn 75; Noel Timms, "Taking Social Work Seriously: The Contribution of the Functional School," *British Journal of Social Work* 27 (1997): 723–37.

57 Walkowitz, *Working with Class*, 146–47.

58 "WDM AR," in MCSA, *Welfare Work 1929*, 90; "WDM AR," in MCSA, *Welfare Work 1925*, 90; "WDM AR," in MCSA, *Welfare Work 1926*, 81; "WDM AR," in MCSA, *Welfare Work 1930*, 92. See also Dominique Marshall, "The Construction of Children as an Object of International Relations: The Declaration of Children's Rights and the Child Welfare Committee of the League of Nations, 1900–1924," *International Journal of Children's Rights* 7 (Apr 1999): 103–47.

59 "WDM AR," in MCSA, *Welfare Work 1926*, 83.

60 "WDM AR," in MCSA, *Welfare Work 1927*, 90.

61 Yolande Cohen, *Femmes Philanthropes: Catholiques, protestantes et juive dans les organisations caritative au Québec (1880–1945)* (Montreal: Les Presses de l'Université de Montréal, 2010), 13.

62 "WDM AR," in MCSA, *Welfare Work 1931*; National Bilingual Conference 1931, CCSD; Draft AR 1928 edited out, *AR 1929*, WDM Papers, BYFC; "WDM AR," in MCSA, *Welfare Work 1930*; "Seek Government Help in

Problem," *Gazette*, 14 Apr 1932, p. 9; "Protection Given Mother and Baby," *Gazette*, 3 Feb 1938, p. 7.

63 WDM, *AR* 1931, 103–10; JBW, "L'Enfant né hors du mariage." For example, see "Montreal's Child Welfare Work," *Child Welfare News* IV, no. 3 (15 Aug 1928): 56–57; WDM, *AR* 1938.

64 Minutes, 13 Jan 1939 and 30 Jan 1940 meeting, CASW, Progressive Program Committee, MG 28 1441, vol. 20, 12, LAC; Lewey, "Nothing to Fear but Fear," 52, 144.

65 Robert B. Westbrook, *John Dewey and American Democracy* (Ithaca, NY: Cornell University Press, 1991); WDM, Draft AR 1928, WDM Papers, BYFC; WDM, Draft AR 1934, WDM Papers, BYFC.

66 John Dewey, "The Ethics of Democracy," in *The Early Works, 1882–1898, Vol. 1*, ed. JoAnn Boydston (Carbondale: Southern Illinois University Press, 1969), 246.

67 John Dewey, *Individualism Old and New* (New York: G. P. Putnam and Sons, 1962), 121; Dewey, *Ethics, The Later Works, Vol. 7*, ed. JoAnn Boydston (Carbondale: Southern Illinois University Press, 1985), 285; Dewey, *Human Nature and Conduct* (New York: Henry Holt and Co., 1922), 210.

68 Spain, *How Women Saved the City*.

69 WDM, *AR* 1938.

70 Isserman interview; Howard Krager, *Social Workers and Labor Unions* (Westport, CT: Greenwood, 1988); Walkowitz, *Working with Class;* Jennissen and Lundy, *One Hundred Years of Social Work*, 152–55.

71 Section 3-1, "A Report on Certain Child Agencies," MCSA, Survey Committee (Montreal: s.n., 1935), 20, 22, 23; MacLennan, "Charity and Change."

72 Isserman, "Casework," 12, 13, 14, 16, 17.

73 "Membership Notes," *Social Worker* (Oct/Nov 1938): 14; "In Memoriam," *Social Welfare* (Dec 1934): 76; Clipping, *Gazette*, 20 Jul 1939; "Reported to the 'Social Worker,'" *Social Worker* (Oct 1939): 16; "Notes," *McGill News* 21, no. 1 (Autumn 1939): 53; JBW to Eric Smith, 10 Nov 1945, Background History of Some Other Child Welfare Agencies, BYFC.

74 "WDM AR," in MCSA, *Welfare Work 1928*, 86.

75 "WDM AR," in MCSA, *Welfare Work 1935*, 95.

Chapter Eight

1 Franca Iacovetta, *Gatekeepers: Reshaping Immigrant Lives in Cold War* (Toronto: Between the Lines Press, 2006).

2 Tillotson, "Dollars, Democracy, and the Children's Aid Society," 76–109.

3 Canada, *Survey of Welfare Positions Report* (Ottawa: Department of National Health and Welfare, 1954), 38.
4 Memorandum, n.d. (Home address Egerton, NS; temporary address University Women's Club of Montreal), JBW Papers.
5 JBW to Whitton, 9 Oct 1940, CCSD, Glace Bay Survey, MG 28 I 10, vol. 134, 600, LAC.
6 Lothar Richter, *Unemployment and Unemployment Relief in Nova Scotia*, Dalhousie University Bulletin on Public Affairs (Halifax: The Imperial Publishing Company, Limited, 1937), 5.
7 Kirkpatrick, *Strong Public Welfare*, 189–90; Morton, *Ideal Surroundings*, 65, 107.
8 Rusty Neal, *Brotherhood Economics: Women and Co-operatives in Nova Scotia* (Sydney, NS: University College of Cape Breton, 1998).
9 Jean MacFadgen, "A Study of a Social Worker Organization and Administration of a Municipal Welfare Department" (Research paper, MSW, Wilfrid Laurier University, 1980), 13–14, MacFadgen Papers, BI; E.R. Forbes, "Cutting the Pie into Smaller Pieces: Matching Grants and Relief in the Maritimes during the 1930s," in *Challenging the Regional Stereotype: Essays on the 20th Century Maritimes* (Fredericton: Acadiensis Press, 1989), 148–71.
10 Jane Wisdom, "From Poor Law to Child Protection," *Canadian Welfare* (Aug–Sept 1940): 28–31.
11 JBW, "Poor Relief in Nova Scotia," *Municipal Affairs* 1, no. 3 (Mar 1945): 1, 4.
12 Book 11, pp. 10, 86, quoted by H.A. Innis, "The Rowell–Sirois Report," *The Canadian Journal of Economics and Political Science* 6, no. 4 (Nov 1940): 568; D.V. Smiley, "The Rowell–Sirois Report, Provincial Autonomy, and Post-War Canadian Federalism," *The Canadian Journal of Economics and Political Science* 28, no. 1 (Feb 1962): 54–69; Alvin Finkel, "Paradise Postponed: A Re-Examination of the Green Book Proposals of 1945," *Journal of the Canadian Historical Association* (Ottawa 1993).
13 King to JBW, 27 Jul 1940; D.J. Macdonald to Whitton, Jul 1940, CCSD, GB Survey.
14 "Photographers for Montreal Papers Do Not Have to Leave that City to Find All the Squalor," *Post-Record*, 20 Sept 1941, p 12.
15 Michael Earle, "The 'People's Daily Paper': *The Glace Bay Gazette* under UMWA Ownership," *Journal of the Royal Nova Scotia Historical Society* 7 (2004): 63–81. On the Jewish community of Glace Bay, see Samantha Cherney, "The Jews of Glace Bay" (research paper, McGill University, 2008, in author's possession); JBW, "Social Work in a Maritime Outpost," *Social Worker* 12, no. 2 (Nov 1943): 9. See Peter McInnis, *Harnessing Labour*

Confrontation: Shaping the Postwar Settlement in Canada, 1943–1950 (Toronto: University of Toronto Press, 2002).

16 Burchell Papers, MG 14, vol. 216, F, BI; Dorothy Rose Bennett, "From Miners' Hospitals and Company Doctors to a Public Health Care System in Industrial Cape Breton, 1900–1969" (master's thesis, University of New Brunswick, 2003); Chryssa McAlister and Peter Twohig, "The Check-Off: A Precursor of Medicare in Canada?" *Canadian Medical Association Journal* 6 (Dec 2005): 173 (12).

17 JBW, "Maritime Outpost," 11.

18 "Glace Bay Looks Ahead," first draft, JBW Papers. See also Peter L. Twohig, "Public Health in Industrial Cape Breton, 1900–1930s," *Journal of the Royal Nova Scotia Historical Society* 4 (2001): 108–31.

19 Might Directories Sydney & District *City Directory*, 1948, p. 200; Clipping, "Extension of Catholic Charities," *Post-Record* (Sydney), 29 Nov 1938, Cape Breton Public Health, MG 14, vol. 223, K.2, BI; "New United Church House Is Dedicated at Passchendaele," *Post-Record*, 3 Jan 1940, p. 10.

20 Neal, *Brotherhood Economics.* Town Council Minutes, GB, 29 Oct 1940, mfm12315, NSA; *Sydney Post*, 31 Jan 1940, p. 6.

21 "Glace Bay Looks Ahead," first draft. Wisdom had excellent personal relations with the Sisters; when she left GB, Sister John Hugh and Sisters at Catholic Charities gave her a teacup as a parting gift (JBW Papers). "Community Chest for Glace Bay Advocated by Board of Trade," *Post-Record*, 1 Jan 1940, p. 13; Town of GB, *AR* 1942, 69; "Donations Sought for Needy Family," *Post-Record*, 10 Jan 1941, p. 17.

22 Memo, GB, 7 Apr 1948, CCSD, GBMWD 1935–53, MG 28 I 10, vol. 237, 12, LAC; JBW, "Maritime Outpost," 11.

23 Jessie Guthrie to Miss MacDonald, 14 Jun 1957, Cape Breton Public Health, MG 14, vol. 223, A, BI.

24 *Sydney Post*, 27 Mar 1940, p. 6; Gerry Harrop, *Clarie: A Political Memoir from the Coal Mines of Cape Breton to the Floor of the House of Commons* (Hantsport, NS: Lancelot Press, 1987); MacFadgen, "Study of a Social Worker Organization," 22.

25 For example, see "Council Notes," *Post-Record*, 6 Jan 1940, p. 12; "Poor Committee," *Post-Record*, 15 Mar 1940, p. 14; "Town Seeks Extension of Relief Agreement," *Post-Record*, 4 Apr 1940, p. 14; MacFadgen, "Study of a Social Worker Organization," 17.

26 Town of GB, *AR* 1940, 30.

27 "Social Service Worker Proposed for Glace Bay," *Post-Record*, 30 Mar 1940, p. 13; Clipping, no title, 2 Apr 1940, M. E. McKenzie to Hazel Macdonald, 16 Mar 1942, Cape Breton Public Health, K.2, MG 14, vol. 223, BI.

28 McPherson, *Bedside Matters*; "Town May Appoint Social Service Worker," *Post-Record*, 2 Apr 1940, p. 6.

29 Clippings, "The Social Service Proposal," 29 Apr 1940; "School Board Asked to Reconsider Decision on Social Welfare Project," *Post-Record*, 15 Apr 1940, "Motion that Miss Guthrie Work for Town Jul and Aug to Organize a Social Service Department Defeated," *Post-Record*, 11 May 1940, Cape Breton Public Health, MG 14, vol. 223, K.2, BI; D.J. Macdonald to Whitton, Jul 1940; Macdonald to King, 9 Sept 1940, CCSD, GB Survey.

30 King to JBW, 27 Jul 1940; Macdonald to King, 30 Jul 1940, CCSD, GB Survey.

31 Whitton to Macdonald, 14 Sept 1940, CCSD, GB Survey.

32 To JBW, 9 Aug 1940, Whitton to JBW, 14 Sept 1940, CCSD, GB Survey.

33 JBW to King, 6 Aug 1940; Macdonald to Whitton, 21 Oct 1940; JBW to Whitton, 30 Oct 1940; JBW to Whitton, 2 Nov 1940; CCSD, GB Survey; Clipping, "Social Worker to Conduct Survey in Glace Bay," 30 Oct 1940, JBW Papers; "Survey to Be Conducted by Social Worker," *Post-Record*, 30 Oct 1940. See Town Council Minutes, GB, 29 Oct 1940.

34 JBW to Whitton, 28 Feb 1941; JBW to Whitton, 13 Nov 1940, CCSD, GB Survey.

35 JBW to Whitton, 13 Nov 1940, CCSD, GB Survey.

36 Whitton to JBW, 18 Nov 1940, CCSD, GB Survey.

37 Fred R. MacKinnon, *Reflections: 55 Years in Public Service in Nova Scotia* (Halifax: Fernwood, 2004), 29. Their worlds overlapped further in 1944 when MacKinnon married a woman from Glace Bay. Joy Maines to Bessie Touzel, 24 Jun 1947, CASW, Placement Committee 1946–48, MG 28 I 441, vol. 441, vol. 18, LAC; JBW to Whitton, 24 Nov 1940, CCSD, GB Survey.

38 JBW to Whitton, telegram, 17 Feb 1941; Whitton to Macdonald, 14 Mar 1941, CCSD, GB Survey.

39 JBW to Whitton, 7 Jan 1941, CCSD, GB Survey.

40 JBW to Whitton, 13 Nov 1940; JBW to Whitton, 7 Jan 1941; Blois to Whitton, 20 Mar 1941; Whitton to Blois, 22 Mar 1941; Macdonald to Whitton, 2 May 1941, CCSD, GB Survey. See, for example, Ruth Shields to Joy Maines, 27 Oct 1948, CASW, Placement Committee Agencies' Requirement 1948–50, MG 28 I 441, vol. 18, 14, LAC; "Poor Committee," *Post-Record*, 13 Feb 1941, p. 12.

41 "Schools and Town Hall Closed Out of Respect for D J Macdonald," *Post-Record*, 23 May 1941, p. 17; "Lost in Swamp," *Post-Record*, 26 May 1941, p. 12; Clipping, "Find Town Clerk DJ Macdonald Dead Near S&L Track – Body Is Picked Up by Passing Train," *Gazette*, 22 May 1941, CCSD, GB

Survey; Clipping, "The Social Service Proposal," 29 Apr 1940, Cape Breton Public Health, MG 14 223, K.2, BI; MacFadgen, "Study of a Social Worker Organization," 33.

42 Gertrude O'Brien Hilchie (McGill '32) to Frances Montgomery, 27 Feb 1966, JBW Papers.

43 JBW to Whitton, 27 Jun 1941, CCSD, GB Survey.

44 "Social Service Worker Arrives in Glace Bay," *Post-Record*, 17 Jun 1941, p. 12. In 1940, there was a part-time social worker in New Glasgow whose salary was shared with the town and the LCW, and a worker in Yarmouth not under the town. Minutes, Town Council, GB, 29 Oct 1940.

45 Michael Earle, "'Down with Hitler and Silby Barrett': The Cape Breton Miners' Slowdown Strike of 1941," *Acadiensis* 18, no. 1 (Autumn 1988): 56–90; JBW Diary, JBW Papers.

46 Nova Scotia, Journal of House of Assembly, 1942, Part II, Appendix 27, "Report of RCMP," 11–12; JBW Diary, JBW Papers.

47 Michael D. Stevenson, "Conscripting Coal: The Regulation of Coal Labour Force in Nova Scotia during the Second World War," *Acadiensis* 29, no. 2 (Spring 2000): 58–88. See Jeffrey Keshen, *Saints, Sinners and Soldiers: Canada's Second World War* (Vancouver: University of British Columbia Press, 2004); JBW, "Maritime Outpost," 9, 11; Lantz to Maines, 27 May 1946, CASW, Placement Committee Agencies' Requirement 1946–48.

48 George F. Davidson to JBW, 22 Apr 1944, p. 108, CCSD, GBMWD.

49 Guildford, "Public Welfare Reform before the Canada Assistance Plan," 51.

50 JBW to Marie Hamel, Executive Assistant French-Speaking Services, Canadian Welfare Council, 15 Sept 1942; JBW to Hamel, 15 Sept 1942, CCSD, GBMWD.

51 Town of GB, *AR* 1946, 70.

52 "Synopsis of the Open Forum: A Round Table Discussion of Municipal Problems," *Proceedings of Union of Nova Scotia Municipalities*, 7 Sept 1950, 77–80; Dominique Marshall, *The Social Origins of the Welfare State: Quebec Families, Compulsory Education, and Family Allowances, 1940–1955*, trans. Nicola Doone Danby (Waterloo: Wilfrid Laurier Press, 2006); Keshen, *Saints, Sinners, and Soldiers*; Christie, *Engendering the State*.

53 JBW to Whitton, 27 Jun 1941, CCSD, GB Survey; Town of GB, *AR* 1942, 78; Poor Committee Minutes, 14 Oct 1942.

54 "Poor Committee," *Post-Record*, 13 Nov 1941, p. 17; Poor Committee Minutes, Town Council GB, 1 Nov 1941, 22 Apr 1942.

55 Memo on Public Collections for Medical Care, by Dr. Khattar and JBW, 17 Mar 1952, Town Council Minutes, GB mfm 12315, NSA; Poor Committee Minutes, 5 Oct 1948, as cited in MacFadgen, "Study of a Social Worker's

Organization," 53; Jane Wisdom, "Discussion on Hospital Administration," Union of Municipalities of Nova Scotia, *Proceedings*, 1951, 78–87.

56 Memo, E.S.L. Govan Field Visit, 8 Feb 1950, CCSD, GBMWD.
57 "Editorial," *Glace Bay Gazette*, 24 Nov 1942, p. 1. Mrs Wisdom in original.
58 "Please Call a Meeting, Mr Mayor," *Glace Bay Gazette*, 1 Dec 1942, p 1; "Council Decides Gazette Unfair," *Glace Bay Gazette*, 1 Dec 1942, p. 1; Govan Field Visit, 8 Feb 1950, CCSD, GBMWD.
59 Poor Committee Minutes, Town Council GB, 9 May 1942, 9 Dec 1946.
60 Memo for File Nora Lea, 25 Feb 1944, CCSD, GBMWD.
61 Memo re Glace Bay, K. M. Jackson, 6 Mar 1946; Memo, GB, 7 Apr 1948, CCSD, GBMWD.
62 H.M. Cassidy, *Social Security and Reconstruction in Canada* (Toronto: Ryerson Press, 1943), 3.
63 Smiley, "Rowell–Sirois Report."
64 Raymond B. Blake, *From Rights to Needs: A History of Family Allowances in Canada, 1929–1992* (Vancouver: University of British Columbia Press, 2009).
65 "Social Security Being Advanced by District," *Glace Bay Gazette*, 25 Oct 1946, p. 3. Don Ives, "The Veterans Charter: The Compensation Principle and the Principle of Recognition for Service," in *Veterans' Charter and Post World War II Canada*, ed. Peter Neary and J. L. Granatstein (Montreal: McGill-Queen's University Press, 1998), 88–89; Robert T. Bothwell, Ian Drummond, and John English, *Canada Since 1945* (Toronto: University of Toronto Press, 1989), 146–50. Antonia Maioni, *Parting at the Crossroads: The Emergence of Health Insurance in the United States and Canada* (Princeton: Princeton University Press, 1998); Jennifer Smith, "The Stanfield Government and Social Policy in Nova Scotia: 1956–1967," *Journal of the Royal Nova Scotia Historical Society* 6 (2003): 3.
66 Poor Committee, Town Council GB, 26 Jan 1948, 1 Jun 1948, 5 Oct 1948; Iacovetta, *Gatekeepers*; "13,000 Miners on Strike," *Post-Record*, 1 Feb 1947, p. 1; "Provision for Relief of Unemployed Sought," *Post-Record*, 25 Feb 1947, p. 12; Courtney MacIsaac, "The Coal Miners on Strike: Cape Breton 1947" (master's thesis, University of New Brunswick, 2007).
67 "Move Made to Supply Children with Milk by SA Officers," *Post-Record*, 22 Apr 1947, p. 12; "Relief Project Planned to Aid Needy Families," *Post-Record*, 25 Apr 1947, p. 16; "Adjt Cuthbert Heads Relief Organization," *Post-Record*, 30 Apr 1947, p. 17; "Children's Milk Fund Operations Are Successful," *Post-Record*, 14 May 1947, p. 10; "Fine Reports on Milk Fund Are Heard at Meet," *Post-Record*, 20 May 1947, p. 14; "Fine Response Made to School Milk Fund," *Glace Bay Gazette*, 19 Jun 1947, p. 2; "NS Coal Strike

Ends," *Post-Record*, 11 Jun 1947, p. 1; "1234 Men Seeking Work and 130 Females," *Post-Record*, 11 Jul 1947, p. 18.

68 Lewey, "Nothing to Fear but Fear." See also Jennissen and Lundy, *One Hundred Years of Social Work*, 120–25.

69 "Rotary Meeting," *Post-Record*, 27 Aug 1948, p. 15; Memo, 25–28 Feb 1949, Bessie Touzel, CCSD, GBMWD.

70 "Proposal Required to Provide Adequate and Uniform Social Welfare Standards," *Post-Record*, 6 Dec 1948, p. 13.

71 Town of GB, *AR* 1947, 72; Town of GB, *AR* 1948, 69; Town of GB, *AR* 1942, 1950.

72 Town of GB, *AR* 1949, 84; JBW to Govan, 24 Apr 1951, CCSD, GBMWD. See also "The Nova Scotia Association of Social Workers Part 1 – A History 1963–2010," 26, www.nsasw.org/files/File/History%20Project/Master2. pdf, accessed 11 Nov 2013.

73 24 Apr 1951, CCSD, GBMWD.

74 "Synopsis of the Open Forum: A Round Table Discussion of Municipal Problems," Annual Meeting, 4 Jun 1952, 79–81, 86, CASW, NS Mainland Branch, 1948–50, MG 28 I 441, vol. 32, 17, LAC.

75 "A Round Table Discussion of Municipal Problems; What if Anything Is the Matter with the Poor Relief Laws of This Province?" *Proceedings of the Annual Meeting of the Union of Nova Scotia Municipalities*, 1950, 78–87, mfm 3882, NSA.

76 Mrs. Arthur Roberts to JBW, 21 Aug 1951; Mrs. Arthur Roberts to George Crosby, 10 May 1952, Union of Nova Scotia Municipalities, Annual Conference, MG 25, vol. 21, 2, NSA; "Branch News," *Social Worker* (Feb 1952): 30; "Family Desertion Stressed in Report," *Glace Bay Gazette*, 8 May 1947, p. 2; "Home for Aged Considered – Before Council Tonight," *Sydney Post*, 21 Aug 1952, p. 19; "Proposal to Have Home for Aged Constructed," *Chronicle Herald*, 20 Aug 1952; *Sydney Post*, 25 Jun 1952, p. 20.

77 "Public Welfare in NS Faces Encouraging Future," *Post-Record*, 29 Dec 1944, p. 9; Minutes, 27 Apr 1944, Maritime School of Social Work Minutes, 1, 1941–49, MG 20, vol. 330, NSA; Blois to Wisdom, 28 Apr 1944, JBW Papers; JBW to Whitton, 13 Nov 1940, CCSD, GB Survey.

78 JBW to Govan, 24 Apr 1951, CCSD, GBMWD.

79 Gwendolen Lantz to Joy Maines, 27 May 1946, CASW, Placement Committee 1946–1948; Memo 25–28 Feb 1949, Bessie Touzel, CCSD, GBMWD; "And I Am in the Line – A Mother of Miners," *Canadian Welfare* (Sept 1941): 36. Although this article was not signed, the JBW papers make clear that she was its author. MacFadgen, "Study of a Social Worker Organization," 37.

80 JBW to Hamel, 15 Sept 1942; Memo for File Nora Lea, 25 Feb 1944, CCSD, GBMWD.

81 "Cape Breton's Welfare Conference," *Canadian Welfare* (1 Dec 1944): 22–25. See also "2nd conference 13–14 Nov 1945," *Canadian Welfare* (15 Jan 1946): 28; *Canadian Welfare* (Dec 1947): 31; *Social Worker* (Dec 1947): 31; "Cape Breton Branch," *Social Worker* (Feb 1948): 12; *Social Worker* (Summer 1949): 30.

82 JBW to Nora Lea, 14 Apr 1944, CCSD, GB (NS) General, MG 28 I 10, vol. 237, 11, LAC; "The Nova Scotia Association of Social Workers Part 1 – A History 1963–2010," 22–25, www.nsasw.org/files/File/History%20Project/Master2.pdf, accessed 11 Nov 2013.

83 "Cape Breton's Welfare Conference," *Canadian Welfare* (1 Dec 1944): 23; Mona Gleason, "Psychology and the Construction of the Normal Family in Postwar Canada, 1945–60," *Canadian Historical Review* 78, no. 3 (Sept 1997): 442–77; Mona Gleason, *Normalizing the Ideal: Psychology, Schooling and the Family in Postwar Canada* (Toronto: University of Toronto Press, 1999); Town of GB, *AR* 1946, 71.

84 Laura Curran, "Social Work's Revised Maternalism: Mothers, Workers, and Welfare in Early Cold War America, 1946–1963," *Journal of Women's History* 17, no. 1 (Spring 2005): 119; Judith Fingard and John Rutherford, *Protect, Befriend, Respect: Nova Scotia's Mental Health Movement, 1908–2008* (Halifax: Fernwood, 2008); Judith Fingard and John Rutherford, "Social Disintegration, Problem Pregnancies, Civilian Disasters: Psychiatric Research in Nova Scotia in the 1950s," in *Mental Health and Canadian Society: Historical Perspectives*, ed. James E. Moran and David Wright (Montreal: McGill-Queen's University Press, 2006), 193–220; Town of GB, *AR* 1946, 70–71, and *AR* 1948, 70.

85 JBW to Whitton, 30 May 1941; JBW to Whitton, 27 Jun 1941, CCSD, GB Survey.

86 Speech by Harris, n.d., Harris Collection, Assorted clippings speech, MG 1, vol. 358, 7, NSA; Minutes, 27 Apr 1944, 22 Aug 1944, Maritime School of Social Work Minutes, 1.

87 "Halifax Woman Welfare Council Child Secretary," *Ottawa Citizen*, 17 Apr 1947, p. 14.

88 Lawrence T. Hancock, *The Story of the Maritime School of Social Work* (Halifax: Maritime School of Social Work, 1992), 142–43.

89 Jane B. Wisdom, "When Everybody Plays the Game," *Canadian Welfare* (1 Nov 1952): 36–38. Originally published *Cape Breton Mirror*, Apr 1952.

90 "Cape Breton Branch," *Social Worker* (Dec 1952): 25. Town Council Minutes, GB, 9 Jul, 10 Sept 1952; Memo 25–28 Feb 1949, Bessie Touzel; Memo Govan, Field Visit, 8 Feb 1950, J. R. Carey to W. T. McGrath, 4 Nov 1953; JBW to

Govan, 24 Apr 1951, CCSD, GBMWD; Govan, 28 Sept 1951, CCSD, Field
Reports, Maritimes, 1951–53, MG 28 I 10, vol. 381, 10, LAC; *Social Worker*
(Jun 1950): 1; "Municipal Welfare Worker Wanted for Early Spring," *Social
Worker* (Feb 1951): n.p.

91 Field report, n.d., re Denis Chiasson, CCSD, GBMWD; Chiasson to
R.E. G. Davis, Exec Director CWC, 16 Jun 1953, CCSD, GB (NS) General;
Douglas Campbell, "Cape Breton County Welfare Services Study,"
financed by the Department of National Health and Welfare under the
Research Division of the Welfare Grants Program, 1966, p. 56; "Jane
Wisdom," *Cape Breton Post*, 11 Jun 1975, p. 2.

92 Clipping, "Jane Wisdom, Pioneer Social Worker," JBW Papers; "A Salutation To JBW FROM FLM," 5.

93 Address by R. M. Fielding, Minister of Municipal Affairs, *Proceedings of
Union Nova Scotia Municipalities*, 7 Sept 1950, 72.

94 George Hart, "The Death of the Poor Law in Nova Scotia," *Canadian Welfare* (Dec 1958): 230; Town of GB, *AR* 1949, 85.

Conclusion

1 Memorandum, Resumé, n.d., with hand notations, JBW Papers.

2 Diary, JBW Papers.

3 Glace Bay Council Resolution, 1952, JBW Papers.

4 Clipping, "Six Honored for Service in Field of Social Work," *Halifax Herald*,
26 May 1964; Doreen Gillen to JBW, 21 Apr 1964, JBW Papers. A copy with
her mailing address for Mar–Apr 1976 is among her papers. Clippings,
New Glasgow Evening News, 31 May 1967, JBW Papers. Editorial note,
Kerry, "Early Professional Development in Montreal," 35.

5 Doris Boyle to JBW, 10 Mar 1953, JBW Papers.

6 Marie Beynon Ray, *The Best Years of Your Life* (Toronto: McClelland and
Stewart, 1952), in *Canadian Welfare* (15 Jun 1953): 44–45; JBW Papers.

7 L. Clare Gass to Tom Blue, 15 Nov 1954, CASW, NS Mainland Branch
Membership 1954–55, MG 28 I 441 3, 2, LAC; Lillian R. Romkey to Joy
Maines, 3 Jan 1958, CASW, NS Mainland Branch Membership 1956–58,
MG 28 I 441 33, 4, LAC.

8 Tanabe interview. JBW Papers.

9 JBW, "American Influences on Canadian Social Work & *Workers*," n.d., JBW
Papers.

10 Timothy Lewis, *In the Long Run We're All Dead: The Canadian Turn to Fiscal
Restraint* (Vancouver: University of British Columbia Press, 2003). See Jennissen and Lundy, *One Hundred Years of Social Work*, ch. 13.

11 "Jane B Wisdom," *Chronicle Herald*, 11 Jun 1975, p. 42.
12 Interview, MacFadgen and Relief Williams Mackay, 1979, JBW Papers.
13 Nadine Gordimer, *Berger's Daughter* (London: Penguin, 1979).
14 MacFadgen, "Study of a Social Worker Organization," 2.
15 Montgomery, "One of Our Pioneers," 130–31.
16 Richard M. Titmuss, "Social Administration in a Changing Society," [1951 lecture] in *Essays on "The Welfare State"* (London: George Allen & Unwin, 1958), 20.

Index

Studies in Gender and History

General editors: Franca Iacovetta and Karen Dubinsky